BOB DYLAN ALBUM AND COMPLETE DISCOGRAPHY

BOB DYLAN ALBUM FILE & COMPLETE DISCOGRAPHY

BRIAN HINTON

First published in Great Britain in 2006 by Cassell Illustrated
a division of Octopus Publishing Group Limited
2-4 Heron Quays, London E14 4JP

Text copyright © Brian Hinton 2006
Layout copyright © Cassell Illustrated 2006

The moral right of Brian Hinton to be identified as the author
of this Work has been asserted in accordance with the Copyright,
Designs and Patents Act of 1988

All rights reserved. No part of this publication may be reproduced,
stored in a retrieval system, or transmitted in any form or
by any means, electronic, mechanical, photocopying, recording,
or otherwise, without the prior permission of the publisher.

A CIP catalogue record for this book is available from the British Library.

ISBN-13: 978-1-844035-27-4
ISBN-10: 1-844035-27-1

10 9 8 7 6 5 4 3 2 1

Design: Design 23

Printed in China

CONTENTS

Bob Dylan on Record	7
The Albums	13
More Dylan	377
Discography	409
The Written Word	447
Index	451

Bob Dylan on Record

*'I don't adhere to rabbis, preachers, evangelists, all of that.
The songs are my lexicon, I believe in the songs'. Bob Dylan*

It seems barely conceivable that this is, so far as we can ascertain, the first commercially available annotated discography of Bob Dylan's official US and UK releases, plus important variants from other countries. The last significant attempt was by Stuart Hoggard and Jim Shields (Transmedia 1977, 2nd revised ed. 1978), based on three articles in *Sounds*. The acknowledged authority, though, is Michael Krogsgaard, whose pioneering *20 Years of Recording* – based on a series of articles in Dylan fanzine *The Telegraph* – was first published in 1981 by the Scandinavian Institute for Rock Research, updated in 1988 as *Master of the Tracks*, and most recently revised as *Positively Bob Dylan* (Ann Arbor, 1991) a 500-page hardback limited to 2000 copies, and now extremely hard to track down.

    A huge and justified amount of obsessive energy has gone into the sorting out and listing of Dylan's career, and in particular the huge bulk of (officially) unreleased recording sessions and live concert tapes. Three people in particular have laboured hard in the vineyard. Glen Dundas's *Tangled Up In Tapes* (5th edition, 2004, as *Tangled*) concentrates on Dylan's concerts, cross referencing every performance and printing complete set lists, though it also chronicles recording sessions and record release dates. The latest edition runs to a closely packed 470 A4 pages, and is available from Thunder Bay, Ontario. Olof Bjorner's 12-volume *Olof's Files: A Bob Dylan Performance Guide 1958-2000* (Hardinge-Simpole 2002 onwards) is basically a print-out of the most comprehensive Dylan website, www.bjorner.com/bob.htm, bound into sections. Another comprehensive and trustworthy website is www.searchingforagem.com, with literally thousands of pages and glowing scans of every official release. The official Dylan website, www.bobdylan.com – put together in New York by Dan Levy – is another vital port of call where every officially released Dylan track is listed and can be sampled, and where there are regular news updates. The accuracy of its dating of album releases, though, is somewhat open to question.

The most precise and combative scholar of all, however, remains Clinton Heylin, in particular for *A Life In Stolen Moments* (1996), a day-by-day chronology and, more germane here, his definitive study of Dylan's recording sessions, *Behind Closed Doors* (revised ed. Penguin 1996). This is based on pioneering research in the Sony archives in New York and was the first book to lay bare the tangled and secret histories of many of Dylan's albums.

So why is this far more modest tome the first commercially published discography for almost 30 years? One reason might be that anyone who dares to undertake any such task throws himself open to the most vociferous and splenetic of all music fans, Bobcats, who take their cue from the vitriolic, accusatory Dylan of *Positively 4th Street*, but are also more than ready to shout 'Judas'.

I welcome corrections and additions directed to my publishers, Cassell illustrated. At present, the information out there is extremely contradictory. My own background as an academic researcher made me start, as one always must, with primary sources, the records themselves. All album sleeves illustrated here come from my own extensive collections. I have always trusted information from original vinyl albums, where available, above any printed source. The back issues of key fanzines like *The Telegraph* and Isis, and in particular *Record Collector* magazine during its golden days under the editor Pete Doggett have been extremely illuminating.

Even so, authorities often differ, particularly over the provenance of early and rare material and even the release dates of Dylan's original US albums are a matter of continuing conjecture. For example, bobdylan.com firmly anchors the US release of *The Times They Are A-Changin'* on 10 February 1964, while Olaf Bjorner's website puts it back to 3 January. Clinton Heylin, with full access to Sony's archives in New York, dates it to 13 January 1964, as do Michael Krogsgaard, Greg Dundas and Paul Williams in the discography appended to his three-volume chronicle of Dylan concerts. The equally reliable John Bauldie and *Record Collector* magazine both date the album to January without specifying a day. I have followed the instincts – and perhaps the prejudice – of a man who once sat at the feet of Dame Helen Gardner in a dusty Oxford seminar room, and have chosen to trust the printed record. Even so, I expect this book to start a vigorous debate.

UK album release dates tended, for many years, to slightly lag behind US release dates, and display the CBS rather than the Columbia logo. I have taken *Record Collector* as my template, with no official listings to follow. More recently, there have not been specifically

UK releases as such, with discs being imported straight from Europe or the States. I have also listed the first CD transfers of each album, plus the new series of CD upgrades and the like, while ignoring reissues, or indeed cassette or 8-track cartridge editions, that have not tended to attract the attentions of collectors. I have broken my own self-imposed rules where necessary by timing each track from the latest available CD upgrade, even though this includes a second or two of dead air until the next track kicks in. This necessarily conflicts with some of the timings printed on LP sleeves but if there has been a different edit, I note it. It can even differ when the same disc is placed in a PC and timings read from the screen.

In the discography I have listed 45 rpm, 12-inch and CD single releases, although there is no single reliable source of information here. I have seen at least four different dates given for the original US release of Dylan's debut US single *Mixed Up Confusion*, a fine slice of rackety rockabilly variously assigned to nine months or so before it was recorded, and more credibly to November 1962, December 1962 and January 1963. As this was Dylan's first release to feature an electric backing and the original single is now impossibly rare and valuable, deciding which date to choose is more of an art than a science.

The first sighting many UK Dylan fans got of this item was a Dutch single in a picture sleeve, issued some years later. I have included this in the discography at the end but space and sanity have forced me to abjure any attempt at listing too many variant pressings of Dylan material from outside the two prime territories of the UK and the US, or a few key Japanese releases imported in large numbers. These aside, differences tend to be of packaging rather than of songs, apart from some highly dubious live material issued during a copyright glitch in the EEC.

The same applies to any attempt to fully list bootleg recordings here, especially as many collectors' guides already exist of this material, most published far outside the mainstream. I have restricted myself to annotating only those key concerts and recording sessions that provide variants to official releases, sampled on a plethora of illegal and semi-legal discs, as have Columbia since *Biograph* when they begun to dip their own bucket into this sea of music. Many of these key songs appear in Dylan's *Lyrics 1962-2002* (2004), sans tune or voice.

As with the first book in this series, *The Beatles Album File & Complete Discography*, by Jeff Russell, I first list and discuss individual Dylan albums in chronological order of release. This applies both to new recordings and vintage studio and live tracks, including versions of *The Basement Tapes* and key concerts from 1964, 1966 and 1975 that Columbia have issued as part of their invaluable *Bootleg Series*. I then go on to list Dylan's contributions to other people's albums. This brings yet more problems: is *The Last Waltz* or the *Travelling Wilburys* or the soundtrack to *Hearts of Fire,* part of the official canon or not? As other artists are involved, I have decided not in these cases, whereas his 30th-Anniversary concert, largely cover versions of his songs by others, is included. I have not attempted to list Dylan releases in the form of videos, laserdiscs and DVDs as these would fill another book.

The world being full of over-opinionated books on Dylan, I have tried to stick to facts and speculations about each song, quoting key words from their author wherever possible, rather than trying to interpret them for anyone else and so shovelling into the ditch a glimpse of what each one means. And perhaps my own grave in the process. My own recent work on Americana, ancient and modern, in *Country Roads* (2000) and *South by South West* (2003) has certainly fed into my comments here, trying to tie Dylan back to the songs and voices that influenced him, and that he writes about so movingly in *Chronicles*.

Being the co-biographer of Ashley Hutchings, that seminal English interpreter of Dylan from early Fairport onwards, also has been a huge advantage to the task in hand, as have the writings of many fine interpreters of Dylan's every move. Far too numerous to list, and ranging from the illuminating to the plain batty, one can simply highlight three essential guides. Paul Williams's *Performing Artist 1960-73* (1990), *1974-1986* (1992) and *1996 to 1990 and Beyond* (2004) is a magnificent three-volume guide to Dylan in live performance. Equally idiosyncratic are Christopher Ricks' bizarre attempt to corral his lyrics into sins, virtues and heavenly graces (Dylan's *Vision of Sin*, 2003), and Michael Gray's monumental *Song and Dance Man III* (1972, revised ed. 2000), whose every new edition grows heavier on the shelf.

Some of the best writing on specific aspects of Dylan's life and art is to be found in fanzines, and is conveniently collected in *All Across the Telegraph*, and *Isis, A Bob Dylan Anthology*, while Nigel Williamson's short and lively *Rough Guide* is a perfect companion to this volume, because it has the rare virtue among Dylan tomes of not taking itself too seriously.

Most essential of all is the pioneering work of Greil Marcus, from his early review in *Rolling Stone* of the *Great White Wonder* bootleg that made this young Dylan fanatic's mouth water without having heard a note of the music he was raving on about to his key book on *The Basement Tapes*, that opened up new vistas in Dylanology. As Tom Waits once commented to *Uncut*, 'you get this weird feeling there's a lot of the past in him. But there's a lot of the future there, too'.

Sideman Charlie Sexton told the same magazine, *Uncut*, that glancing across the stage 'at times it seems as if there (is) a circle of light surrounding him, regardless of what the lights in the show are doing'. When I go to see Dylan playing live, I feel that the ghosts of all kinds of mountain men and Delta blues revenants, alongside visionary poets and movie actors, hover above this frail genius as he shuffles about on stage, nightly re-interpreting his canon. The young man who could clown like Charlie Chaplin now has the grave and stern look of Ralph Stanley.

It is interesting to note how many of his current audience are young in years as well as in heart, and how Dylan's albums remain stubbornly in catalogue and on record store shelves. They are already influencing – both directly and through the strange world of acid folk that his work inspired in the late 60s and early 70s – a whole new generation of creative musicians. Much like the fresh-faced urban hillbilly back on his debut album, predating the Beatles' first LP, sounding as old and world weary as Methuselah, and yet also boundlessly, joyfully full of life.

> Brian Hinton,
> Dimbola Lodge, Freshwater Bay, Isle of Wight

'So if I started with album One, Side One, Band One, I could truthfully watch Bob Dylan grow?'
Bob Dylan: 'No you could watch Bob Dylan laugh to himself. Or you could see Bob Dylan going through changes'. Dylan, interviewed by Paul Jay Robbins, In-Beat Magazine, May 1965

THE ALBUMS

BOB DYLAN

US Release: 19 March 1962

UK Release: July 1962/1963
CD Release: Columbia CD32001
Mono version re-pressed on 180g vinyl
January 2002 as Columbia/Sundazed 5120
Producer: John Hammond

Columbia CL 1779/Columbia CS 8579 (mono/stereo)
CBS CL119/CBS BGP 62022 (mono/stereo)
CD Remaster: Columbia 5198912001
Running Time: 36.48

SIDE ONE: You're No Good; Talkin' New York; In My Time Of Dyin'; Man Of Constant Sorrow; Fixin' To Die; Pretty Peggy-O; Highway 51.

SIDE TWO: Gospel Plow; Baby Let Me Follow You Down; House Of The Risin' Sun; Freight Train Blues; Song to Woody; See That My Grave Is Kept Clean.

Bob Dylan: vocals, guitar, harmonica

After hearing the young Dylan playing harmonica at a recording session with Carolyn Hester, John Hammond signed the 20-year-old to Columbia, got him straight into the studio and captured a typical coffee-house set. It was recorded in two three-hour sessions at Columbia Studio A on 20 and 22 November 1961 at a cost of $402 using just two mikes – one on Dylan's guitar and the other recording his vocal and harmonica. Many hardcore fans will only listen to the record in mono: the stereo separation of this album is brutal, with vocal and guitar each occupying a virtual exclusion zone. The new CD remaster adds a whole extra sense of presence.

    The front cover is a reversed-image photograph by Don Hunstein of an extremely youthful and quizzical Dylan in sheepskin jacket and trademark cap, holding his acoustic guitar in both hands. The new CD issue adds photos of Dylan in the studio, taken at the same session. The US album has a small black and white photograph of Dylan on the back cover that was omitted from the UK version. The back cover text is identical. Stacey Williams is a pseudonym for Robert Shelton.

Some early US stereo copies have the very collectable 6-eyes logo on the label. Other early US copies have 'A New Star on Columbia' on a silver star sticker. Some early US pressings misprint the opening track, 'You're No Good' as 'She's No Good'.

Even before its release Dylan was expressing dissatisfaction, bemoaning to Robert Shelton that his liner notes were better than the album. Dylan had brought to the studio 'some stuff I've written, some stuff I've discovered, some stuff I stole'. By the time of its release, just four months later, Dylan had already moved on. The album sold less than 5,000 copies and the record company insiders began calling the young singer Hammond's Folly.

However, it has never been deleted and it could have been recorded yesterday. This is a young man obsessed with the past but riding the zeitgeist. As he later observed, 'I played all the folk songs with a rock'n'roll attitude. This is what made me different and allowed me to cut through all the mess and be heard'. John Hammond remembered how Dylan 'popped every p, hissed every s and habitually wandered off mike. I'd never worked with anyone so undisciplined before'. Bob later admitted that 'there was a violent, angry emotion running through me then.' He refused to sing the same song twice. 'I tried a bunch of stuff. I was only doing a few of my own songs back then, anyway.'

There are two separate sleeve notes. Stacey Williams points out how he spanned musical categories. Dylan's steel-string playing 'runs strongly in the blues vein, although he will vary it with country configurations'. His guitar work is compared with Nashville icon Merle Travis and his harmonica with bluesmen Sonny Terry and Walter Jacobs. The other sleeve note is a reprint of a review of a gig at Gerdes Folk City by Robert Shelton. 'Resembling a cross between a choir boy and a beatnik…He composes new songs faster than he can remember them.'

SIDE ONE

You're No Good (Jesse Fuller) 1.37
A wonderfully life-affirming performance, rough and energetic, full of humour and dealing with a theme that Dylan would make his own – the power and mystery of women. Bob captures the all-guns-blazing style of one-man-band, blues legend Jesse 'Lone Cat' Fuller who played 12-string guitar, kazoo and harmonica in a brace around his neck, bass with his right foot and a hi-hat cymbal with his left. Dylan saw him perform at Denver coffee-house *The Exodus* in 1960.

Talkin' New York (Dylan) 3.16
Dylan's own composition, quoting Woody Guthrie and copying his talking blues style, bitingly sarcastic and exuberant at the same time, with whooping harmonica. Bob has the timing of a master comic as he riffs on his experiences on the Greenwich Village folk scene – pronounced Green-wich. An early example of the way he can skewer pretence with a phrase: 'you sound like a hillbilly, we want folk singers here'.

In My Time Of Dyin' (Dylan) 2.37
Credited to Dylan, but the sleeve notes give the game away about the author not recalling where or when he first heard this traditional blues song. Led Zeppelin later did a heavy metal cover on *Physical Graffiti*. Rather than a traditional bottleneck, Dylan used girlfriend Suze Rotolo's lipstick holder.

Man Of Constant Sorrow (arr. Dylan) 3.05
A traditional mountain song, with Dylan's voice echoing the Appalachian high lonesome sound as sung by the likes of Dock Boggs straight off the seminal Harry Smith *Anthology of American Folk Music*. He invests 'God's golden shore' with a longing for the transcendent that will echo throughout his work. The passion Bob drags from this hoary standard was already setting him apart from everyone else on the coffee-house scene.

Fixin' To Die (Bukka White) 2.18
Another song, another voice. This is a driving version of a song by Bukka White who was an ex-boxer and hobo noted for his breakneck train imitations. He spent time in the notorious Parchman prison farm for assault, and it soured him. White's post-1940 recordings were obsessed with death, drink and prison. Backed by aggressive slide guitar, Dylan growls the lyric like a grizzled old timer while also sounding absurdly young.

Pretty Peggy-O (arr. Dylan) 3.22
Starts with a comic aside that sets the tone, Dylan accentuates his rustic accent on this jovial run-through of an American variant of a traditional Scottish song told by a foot soldier. Dylan whoops like a cowboy and plays blazing harmonica.

Highway 51 (C. Jones) 2.50
Dylan partly rewrote this road song – a prototype for 'Highway 61 Revisited' – and uses open tuning. 'Of a type sung by the Everly Brothers' states Stacey Williams' sleeve notes. The composer is presumably Curtis Jones, born in Texas in 1906, who was rediscovered in the 60s and moved to Germany. He died in poverty. His grave was sold off when no-one paid for its upkeep.

SIDE TWO
Gospel Plow (arr. Dylan) 1.43
An uptempo version of a gospel song, sung with irony – Dylan never followed a plough in his life and neither, it is safe to assume, did any of his bohemian audience in 'the village'.

Baby, Let Me Follow You Down (Ric Von Schmidt) 2.32
Bob Dylan commented in *Biograph*: 'that's the way Ric von Schmidt played the song. I think it's a Reverend Gary Davis song . He used to sing it "Baby, Let Me Lay It On You"'. Von Schmidt was one of the Boston folk crowd. One of his albums later appeared on the cover of *Bringing It All Back Home*. Dylan also writes about him fondly in *Chronicles*. Here, though, Dylan skewers the pretence of middle-class kids playing at being farmhands. 'Ric's a blues guitar player, I met him one day in the green pastures of Harvard University'. The song would become an electric howl of pain live in 1966.

House Of The Risin' Sun (Trad) 5.15
Dylan points out in *Biograph* that this prostitute's lament is 'actually from a woman's point of view' and that helped him put himself into someone else's character in his own songs. Newcastle band The Animals covered this song in a fully electric, gritty r&b style and deservedly got a UK hit single for their pains. Their organist Alan Price appears backstage with Dylan in *Don't Look Back*. The song was learnt from Dave Von Ronk who asked Bob not to record this song but was ignored, although Dylan says on the sleeve that he never really knew this song 'until I heard Dave sing it'. Here he inhabits, rather than sings it.

Freight Train Blues (Trad) 2.16
Adapted from an old disc by Roy Acuff, who brought old-timey themes to the heart of Nashville, and made a speciality of railway songs. Dylan holds the note beyond human endurance, just like a lonely train hoot, then laughs at his own tricksiness.

Song To Woody (Dylan) 2.39
Dylan had come to New York specifically to meet his hero Woody Guthrie, who was dying of Huntingdon's Chorea in Greystone Hospital. Woody's autobiography *Bound For Glory* had been a key text in Bob's search for a mode of life outside the mainstream. The tune is taken from Guthrie's '1913 Massacre' and the line about coming with the dust and going with the wind from his 'Pastures Of Plenty'. Bob sings with true gravity, and as a valediction, while a new world is 'hardly born'; a world that Dylan would help shape.

See That My Grave Is Kept Clean (Blind Lemon Jefferson) 2.43
Startling guitar work, and a vocal that means – and feels – every word. As Dylan later said, 'What's depressing today is that so many young singers are trying to get inside the blues, forgetting that those older singers used them to get outside their troubles'. Blind Lemon Jefferson (1897-1929), one of the first bluesmen to be recorded, was noted for his dense and driving guitar style, without regard to time signature. He froze to death in Chicago. His body was brought back to his native Texas for burial.

OUTTAKES
20 November 1961: 'Connection Cowboy', 'He Was A Friend Of Mine'
22 November 1961: 'Man On The Street' (2 takes), 'House Carpenter'
Recorded at Columbia's Studio A, New York

'He Was A Friend Of Mine', 'Man On The Street', 'House Carpenter'on *The Bootleg Series*: The electric version of 'House of the Risin Sun' appears on the *Highway 61* Interactive CD Rom (Columbia/Graphix Zone CDAC 085700, February 1995) was simply the album track with electric instruments overdubbed retrospectively some three years later.

THE FREEWHEELIN' BOB DYLAN

US Release: 27 May 1963
27 May 1963
UK Release: November 1963
CD Release: Columbia CD32390
CD Remaster/SACD Release: Columbia 512348-6
Mono version re-pressed on 180g vinyl
in November 2001 Columbia/Sundazed 5115
Producers: John Hammond, Tom Wilson

Columbia CL 1986 mono
Columbia CS 8786 stereo
CBS BGP/SPGP 62193 mono/stereo
Running Time: 50.09

SIDE ONE: Blowin' In The Wind; Girl From The North Country; Masters Of War; Down The Highway; Bob Dylan's Blues; A Hard Rain's A-Gonna Fall.

SIDE TWO: Don't Think Twice, It's All Right; Bob Dylan's Dream; Oxford Town; Talkin' World War III Blues; Corrina, Corrina; Honey, Just Allow Me One More Chance; I Shall Be Free.

Bob Dylan: vocals, guitar, harmonica

Dylan originally agreed to a different track listing but four songs subsequently were withdrawn – 'Talking John Birch Blues', 'Gamblin' Willie's Dead Man's Hand', 'Rocks and Gravel' and 'Let Me Die In My Footsteps'. This original track listing was printed on promo versions, marked 'radio station copy – not for resale' and reproduced in *Record Collector*, issue 180 (August 1994).
Side One: Blowin' In The Wind (2.46), Rocks And Gravel (2.21), Let Me Die In My Footsteps (4.05), Down The Highway (3.10), Bob Dylan's Blues (2.19), A Hard Rain's A-Gonna Fall (6.48)
Side Two: Don't Think Twice, It's All Right (3.37), Gamblin' Willie's Dead Man's Hand (4.11), Oxford Town (1.47), Corrina, Corrina (2.42), Talkin' John Birch Blues (3.45), Honey Just Allow Me One More Chance (1.47), I Shall Be Free (4.46)

Very few US mono and stereo copies contain these songs that are not listed on the sleeve; they are hugely valuable. A Canadian release, in print until the early 70s, lists the original track listing, retitling 'Rocks and Gravel' as 'Solid Road' but the vinyl plays the revised track listing.

The recording process for *Freewheelin'* – its original working title was *Bob Dylan's Blues* – was far more tortuous than the first album. After two sessions at Studio A in April 1962, he revisited the same studio in July, October, November and December, all with John Hammond, then one final time in April 1963 with new producer Tom Wilson. At the time Wilson didn't even particularly like folk music having recorded jazz pioneers like Sun Ra and John Coltrane.

The front cover is again a photograph by Don Hunstein, of Dylan in blue jeans and a James Dean pose, out in the middle of a snowy Jones Street, with 'buildings going up to the sky', in New York City. They're near the junction with (positively) 4th Street and the apartment he rented with Suze Rotolo, a few steps away at 161 West 4th. Bob's suede jacket, described by Joan Baez as 'that horrible little coat with throw up all over the front of it' though it looks the epitome of cool now, is buttoned up against the cold. Suze cuddles up to him in an image of youthful togetherness. The CD remaster adds a shot of Dylan pointing, as if to the future. The UK front cover has more sky above and less ground below the loving couple than the US original. One of the rarest of all Dylan albums is the German Democratic Republic's version in a different sleeve.

As Dylan later said, 'I felt real good about doing an album with my own material', and he is also proud of his finger-picking guitar style. 'It was a big Gibson. I felt real accomplished on that.'

There are continuing problems with the stereo balance. Harmonica and vocals were again recorded on the same mike, and the harp then had to be switched to the left channel, with guitar in the right and Dylan's voice in the middle. The CD remaster was a revelation – *Record Collector* waxed lyrical its sense of sonic space, 'you can hear Dylan moving in and out from the mike as he sings "Blowin' In The Wind"', and how 'the jazz combo accompaniment for "Corrina, Corrina" now sounds as if it has moved from a distant annexe into the same room as Dylan without doing anything to diminish the power of the vocal'.

SIDE ONE
Blowin' In The Wind (Dylan) 2.46
An anthem for a generation, though it was Peter Paul and Mary who first took it up the pop charts, in July 1963. As Dylan recalls in *Biograph*, 'I wrote it in a café across the road from the *Gaslight* (the *Commons*, in April 1962). I wrote it for the moment, ya know. I remember running into Peter in the street, "Man" he said, "you're going to make 5,000 dollars". It seemed like a million at the time. Money was never a motivation to write anything'. It had ramifications far beyond the folk ghetto. When Sam Cooke heard it, he said 'if a young white guy can write a song like that then I got to get my pen in hand' and went off and wrote 'A Change Is Gonna Come'.

Girl From The North Country (Dylan) 3.21
Written in Italy, after Dylan made a short trip there with Albert Grossman, during a break in the filming of the TV play *Madhouse on Castle Street* in London. Nat Hentoff quotes Dylan in his extensive sleeve notes: 'I carry a song in my head for a long time and then it comes bursting out'. The subject of this song is supposedly Echo Helstrom, or Bonnie Beecher, or more likely a composite of both, plus a dose of homesickness. The tune certainly was learnt directly from Martin Carthy, whose arrangement of 'Scarborough Fair' was drawn from a traditional songbook edited by Ewan McColl.

Masters Of War (Dylan) 4.31
A song as true today as when he wrote it – the arms industry goes from strength to strength. The ferocity of this song even startled its composer. 'I don't sing songs which hope people will die, but I couldn't help it'. And if Dylan became less overt, this passion continues under the surface: 'I'm still there in some way, not protest for protest sake but always in the struggle for people's freedom'. The tune comes from the riddling Mummers song 'Nottamun Town' via the version by Jean Ritchie. Loudon Wainwright III saw him play this at the time: 'there's no chorus and the guitar playing – its unrelenting. His guitar playing swings and rocks very hard'.

Down The Highway (Dylan) 3.23
In the sleeve note, Dylan states 'what made the real blues singers so great is that they were able to state all the problems they had, but at the same time, they were standing outside of them and could look at them. And in that way, they had them beat'. Here he personalizes things to deal with his own loneliness with Suze away in Europe and throws in an allusion to one of Woody Guthrie's finest lines.

Bob Dylan's Blues (Dylan) 2.20
Another talking blues, one of Dylan's 'really off-the-cuff songs. 'I start with an idea, and then I feel what follows. Best way I can describe this one is that it's like walking by a side street. You gaze in and walk on'. Instant surrealism that he would later develop into a whole writing style. The spoken intro is priceless, 'Tin Pan Alley – that's where most of the folk songs come from nowadays, this wasn't written up there, this was written somewhere down in the United States'.

A Hard Rain's A-Gonna Fall (Dylan) 6.51
Folk protest meets Rimbaud. The poetic imagery turns personal terror into apocalypse. As he said at the time, 'its not atomic rain…I mean some sort of end that's just got to happen'. Later, he remembered 'I wrote it at the time of the Cuban crisis. I was in Bleecker Street in New York. People sat around wondering if it was the end, and so did I. It was a song of desperation. Could we control men on the verge of wiping us out. The words came fast, very fast. It was a song of terror. Line after line after line, trying to capture the feeling of nothingness'.

The tune – and basic structure – is taken from the traditional song 'Lord Randall', a question-and-answer session between a young man and his mother, that reveals gradually that he is dying of poison. It was Dylan's genius to turn this into a contemporary parallel. Both Leonard Cohen and Joni Mitchell are on record that it was hearing this that made them want to become songwriters. Dylan points out that 'every line in it is actually the start of a whole song. But when I wrote it I thought I wouldn't have enough time alive to write all those songs so I put all I could into this one'.

SIDE TWO
Don't Think Twice, It's All Right (Dylan) 3.37
George Barnes: bass guitar, **Bruce Langhorne:** guitar, **Herb Lovelle:** drums
Gene Rainey: bass, **Dick Wellstead:** piano
Dylan reveals that 'I can sing it sometimes, but I ain't that good yet. A lot of people make it sort of a love song – slow and easy going. But it isn't a love song. It's a statement that maybe you can say to make yourself feel better. It's as if you were talking to yourself'. Charlie Gillett sums up perfectly the confident humour of this let's-fall-out-of-love song. It is based on the traditional song 'Scarlet Ribbons For Her Hair', though Paul Clayton had an amicable legal tiff over a supposed debt to Clayton's own version, 'Who's Goin' Buy You Ribbons When I'm Gone'.

Bob Dylan's Dream (Dylan) 5.00
Set off after an all-night conversation between Dylan and Oscar Brand. 'Oscar is a groovy guy and the idea of this came from what we were talking about'. When Dylan visited London in the winter of 1962 to film *Madhouse on Castle Street* and hang out in Soho folk clubs, he heard Martin Carthy sing the traditional 'Lord Franklin'. He fitted the aching tune, then attached the narrative of a ship lost amidst the ice to this effortlessly sad look back to student life in Dinkytown and what the sleeve note calls the easy camaraderie of the young. Ironically, Dylan looks back in *Chronicles* to a similar sense of adventure and shared purpose among the coffee-house set, which his growing fame was beginning to isolate him from just as he wrote this.

Oxford Town (Dylan) 1.48
Dylan: 'It's a banjo tune I play on guitar'. Rather than take on directly the ordeal of civil rights activist James Meredith's initially unsuccessful attempt to enter the segregated University of Mississippi as its first Afro-American student, Dylan comes at it obliquely, 'Glib yet mournful', as *Mojo* put it.

Talkin' World War III Blues (Dylan) 6.25
Dylan brought this talking blues to the studio half formed and then improvised the rest and gives the song a continuing freshness. The harmonica playing is as witty as the words and gives a comic take on the same cold war brinkmanship as 'Hard Rain'.

Corrina, Corrina (adapted and arr Dylan) 2.42
Howie Collins: guitar, **Leonard Gaskin:** bass, **Bruce Langhorne:** guitar, **Herb Lovelle:** drums, **Dick Wellstead:** piano

Dylan made extensive alterations to this American folk tune sung by the likes of Mississippi John Hurt. 'I'm not one of those guys who goes around changing songs just for the sake of changing them. But I'd never heard (this) exactly the way it first was, so that this version is the way it came out of me'. As Matthew Zuckerman puts it, Dylan transmutes both the melody line and the underlying mood 'from a happy-go-lucky jug band song it becomes a wistful evocation of the memory of a woman'. Dylan goes electric in 1963 shock, but this swings rather than rock'n'rolls. For the latter go to the briefly available single 'Mixed Up Confusion' that was released the previous December as a taster for the album with a different take of this song on the flipside.

Honey, Just Allow Me One More Chance (H.Thomas-Dylan) 1.58
Learnt off a record by Texan singer Henry Thomas who receives a co-credit, Thomas was one of the first bluesmen to be recorded. He died in 1930. 'What especially stayed with me was the plea in the title'. Dylan largely re-wrote the words.

I Shall Be Free (Dylan) 4.47
Based loosely on 'We Shall Be Free' as recorded by Guthrie and Leadbelly. Dylan chuckles at his own wit, but the reference to President Kennedy suggests that some of the exuberance here died with him. Dylan happily coins phrases like 'onion gook' – excised from *Lyrics* – and immortal asides like 'greasy kid stuff'. Some of the cultural references might now need footnotes but the spiritedness here continues to appeal. Dylan's next album would be a far grimmer affair.

OUTTAKES:
24 April 1962: 'Going (Down) To New Orleans', 'Sally Gal', 'Ramblin' Gamblin' Willie', 'Corrina Corrina', 'The Death Of Emmett Till', 'Talkin' John Birch Paranoid Blues', '(I Heard That) Lonesome Whistle'
25 April 1962: 'Rocks and Gravel', 'Let Me Die In My Footsteps', 'Talkin' Hava Negeilah', 'Sally Gal', 'Baby Please Don't Go', 'Milkcow's Calf Blues' (x2), 'Wichita (Going to Louisiana)' (x2), 'Talkin' Bear Mountain Picnic Massacre Blues'
9 July 1962: 'Babe I'm In The Mood' (x2), 'Quit Your Low Down Ways', 'Worried Blues'
26 October 1962: 'Mixed Up Confusion', 'That's Alright Mama'
1 November 1962: 'Mixed Up Confusion', 'That's Alright Mama', 'Rocks and Gravel'
14 November 1962: 'Corrina Corrina', 'Mixed Up Confusion' (x2), 'Ballad Of Hollis Brown', 'Kingsport Town', 'Whatcha Gonna Do?'
6 December 1962: 'Hero Blues', 'Whatcha Gonna Do?', 'I Shall Be Free' (x2), 'Hero Blues' (x2)
24 April 1963: 'Walls of Redwing'

'Mixed Up Confusion' backed with an alternative take of 'Corrina, Corrina' appeared as a rare US 45 rpm single. It was later re-released in various European countries in 1966 as CBS Benelux 2476 in a picture sleeve of Dylan at the piano.
'Babe I'm In The Mood For You' and an alternative take of 'Mixed Up Confusion' on *Biograph*
'Ramblin' Gamblin' Willie', 'Let Me Die In My Footsteps', 'Talkin' Hava Negeilah Blues', 'Talkin' Bear Mountain Picnic Massacre Blues', 'Quit Your Lowdown Ways', 'Worried Blues' and 'Walls of Redwing' are all on *The Bootleg Series*.

There is also a US promo single of 'Blowin' In The Wind'/'Don't Think Twice, It's All Right' with a press release headlined 'Rebel With A Cause'. 'Twenty-one-year-old Bob Dylan has become in one short year the most talked about folk music talent in more than a decade. It would be presumptuous to make any predictions as to the ultimate career destination of this brilliant young man....'

THE TIMES THEY ARE A-CHANGIN'

US Release: 13 January 1964
UK Release: May 1964
CD Release: Columbia 32021
Mono version re-pressed on 180g vinyl
August 2001 as Columbia/Sundazed LP 5108
Producer: Tom Wilson

Columbia CL 2105/CS 8905 mono/stereo
CBS BGP/SBGP 62251 mono/stereo
CD Remaster: Columbia COL 519892 2
Running Time: 45.35

SIDE ONE: The Times They Are A-Changin'; Ballad Of Hollis Brown; With God On Our Side; One Too Many Mornings; North Country Blues.

SIDE TWO: Only A Pawn In Their Game; Boots of Spanish Leather; When The Ship Comes In; The Lonesome Death Of Hattie Carroll; Restless Farewell.

Bob Dylan: vocals, guitar, harmonica, piano

By now Tom Wilson was firmly in the producer's chair at Studio A, and the stereo mix worked just fine even before the CD remaster. Two sessions back to back on 6 and 7 August 1963 saw Dylan lay down five of the songs for the new album but a third session that month was less productive. Two more sessions on 23 and 24 October provided the remaining tracks apart from one brief return a week later that produced the final song, 'Restless Farewell'. But the disc hangs together perfectly, and its mood is reflected perfectly in the stern monochrome of the cover that shows a glowering Dylan in workshirt and Guthrie chic. The photograph was taken by Barry Feinstein, the husband of Mary Travers from Peter, Paul and Mary.

Billy Bragg is one of many who credits his discovery of this album with a 'seismic sea-change in my appreciation of music'. It started with the cover shot. 'He's got his head on one side, not looking out. He's asking a question, saying "Look, all this is happening around the world. What are you going to do about it?"'

Talking during that same year, Dylan said, about his plans for this album, 'I'm going through changes. Need some more finger-pointin' songs in it, 'cause that's where my head's at right now'. And as befits the political content here, 'I don't think when I write. I just react and put it down on paper. What comes out in my music is a call to action'. He later explained that the album owed

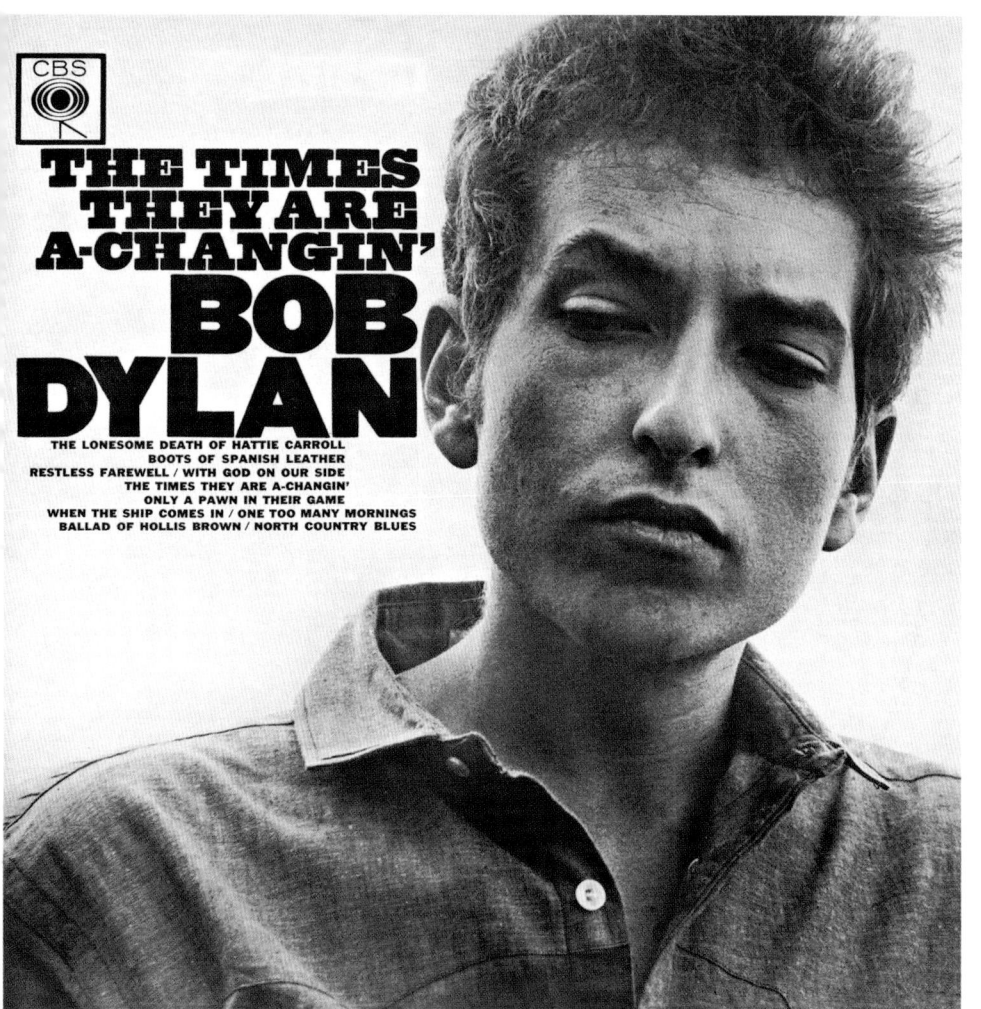

much to his 'listening to performers in the New York cafes and the talk in all the dingy parlours. I suppose there was some ambition in what I did. But I tried to make the songs genuine'.

There are no explanatory notes on the back sleeve this time around. Instead Dylan provides his prose poem *11 Outlined Epitaphs*, in a style much influenced by Beat writers like Allen Ginsberg. The UK got only four of them, although the latest CD version reprints the lot, albeit in a wobbly typescript. If you dig deep enough there are some fascinating autobiographical clues. There is a lament for the 'rainy mist' of Duluth and the 'dyin town' of Hibbing, a written counterpoint to 'North Country Blues'. There is a tribute to his 'last idol' Woody Guthrie, who taught him that one doesn't need idols, and a roll call of his heroes. Here are the 'hypnotic words' of folk singer and scholar A L Lloyd, the 'quiet fire' of Miles Davis, and Truffaut's 1960 movie *Tirez Sur Le Pianist*, with its last subtitled line, 'music, man, that's where it's at', all a long way from the grim world depicted in the songs here. It is a world without love, human, romantic or divine. Dylan was always more than just a one-dimensional protest singer even on this, the most intransigent of his albums.

The cover is a pastiche of a Woody Guthrie photograph. The South African issue censored 'With God On Our Side' and replaced it with two tracks, 'Motorpsycho Nitemare' and 'It Ain't Me Babe' but allowed in to the land of apartheid as revolutionary a song as 'Only A Pawn In Their Game'.

SIDE ONE
The Times They Are A-Changin' (Dylan) 3.12
Billy Bragg called this a clarion call. It was like a silent dog whistle for a generation, even if Dylan himself later said that 'maybe those were the only words I could find to separate aliveness from deadness. It had nothing to do with age'. In the notes to *Biograph*, he revealed: 'I was influenced by the Irish and Scottish ballads. I wanted to write a big song, some sort of theme song, with short concise verses that piled up on each other in a hypnotic way'. It was written at a time when the folk movement and political radicals were virtually one and the same

'I had to play this song the same night President Kennedy died. It sort of took over as the opening song and stayed that way for a long time'. In 1965, Dylan internalized his call to action. 'I didn't mean it as a statement, it's a feeling'. Thirty years on, he allowed Coopers & Lybrand to use the song in a TV advert.

Ballad Of Hollis Brown (Dylan) 5.03
One of the marks of this album is Dylan's compassion for poor whites as well as black victims. He might have learned this story from a newspaper article, but he matched it with the tune and the fatalism of the traditional 'Pretty Polly', as sung both by that hardest of all white bluesmen, Dock Boggs, who had recorded it back in 1927, and The Stanley Brothers. The repetition of each first line adds to the claustrophobia and the growing tension, while Dylan's guitar stabs like the dirty driving rain, as relentless as those shotgun blasts out in the badlands.

With God On Our Side (Dylan) 7.05
The tune is taken from Brendan Behan's *The Patriot Game*, as sung around Greenwich Village by the Clancy Brothers – hence the address to 'boys'. But this retelling of patriotic school history textbooks is pure Dylan, dazzlingly clever and with irrefutable logic. Linton Kwesi Johnson wrote of this song 'it goes to the heart of how little we value human life, how we kill for power, for greed and invoke the name of God while doing so'.

One Too Many Mornings (Dylan) 2.37
Dylan sings and plays this almost with a whisper, when compared to the howl of agony it had become by 1966. Suze Rotolo had just moved out of their New York apartment and even though Dylan was now seeing his folk singer Joan Baez, the hurt in this song is palpable though no-one is held to blame. It's just fate.

North Country Blues (Dylan) 4.31
The sadness from the previous song seeps into this narrative told by a miner's wife in Hibbing facing the consequences of free-market economics. He later addressed the same subject more angrily in 'Union Sundown'. Here no fingers are pointed and you feel that the diaspora of young people from this denuded pit town – Dylan among them – has real personal resonance.

SIDE TWO
Only A Pawn In Their Game (Dylan) 3.30
The air of depression continues with another song of entrapment, taking as its subject a victim of a political murder, not in this case Medger W Evers, Field Secretary of the National Association for the Advancement of Coloured People, slain in Jackson in June 1963, but the man who shot him. Years later this person made a death-bed confession and turned out to be a wealthy local businessman. This does not invalidate the song or Dylan's bravery in performing it at a voter registration rally in Greenwood, Mississippi, a month after the killing. To quote the *New York Times*, 'Three Northern folk singers led by Pete Seeger brought a folksong festival to the Deep South this evening. Joining Mr Seeger were Theodore Bikel and Bobby Dillon, who like Mr Seeger, are white. There was also a Negro trio, the Freedom Singers, from Albany, Ga. All paid their own expenses and sang without a fee'.

Boots of Spanish Leather (Dylan) 4.37
A song written to or about Suze when she was away in Europe. The gulf between them was far more than geographical, as this dialogue in song subtly indicates. The man admits defeat and asks her to bring back not a love token but a commodity.

When The Ship Comes In (Dylan) 3.15
Anyone startled by Dylan's later religious conversion had obviously forgotten songs like this, steeped in Old Testament imagery and the joys of salvation. What prompted it is almost farcical, Dylan being refused entrance to a hotel while on the road with Joan Baez: 'he looked so innocent and so shitty'. What this kicks off in his bruised soul is a vision of redemption, of Christ's second coming.

The Lonesome Death Of Hattie Carroll (Dylan) 5.44
Dylan recounts in *Biograph* that he wrote this song 'in a small notebook in a restaurant on 7th Avenue' doubtless having read the story in the *New York Times*. We used to go all the time and just sort of hang around. I felt I had a lot in common with this situation and was able to manifest my feelings. The set pattern to the song is based on Brecht, "The Ship, The Black Freighter"'. Hattie actually died of a brain haemorrhage, brought on by the stress of the situation: Zanzinger emerged to become a slum landlord and was later imprisoned for fraud.

As Grant-Lee Phillips later put it, ''Hattie Carroll' is like some dark American secret that refuses to subside. It's a ghost that beckons the truth to be known'.

Restless Farewell (Dylan) 5.33
Based on the traditional Irish song 'The Parting Glass', learnt from the Clancys. Frank Sinatra asked for Dylan to sing it at his 80th birthday celebration, so obviously it has more resonance than in its context here, a veiled farewell to one career as a politically charged protest singer. 'And not give a damn'.

OUTTAKES
6 August 1963: 'Seven Curses', 'Farewell'
7 August 1963: 'Eternal Circle'
12 August 1963: 'Paths of Victory', 'Bob Dylan's New Orleans Rag', 'Hero Blues', 'Moonshiner', 'Eternal Circle', 'Only A Hobo'
23 October 1963: 'Percy's Song', 'The Times They Are A-Changin'', 'East Laredo Blues', 'That's Alright Mama'
24 October 1963: 'Eternal Circle', ('Percy's Song '– included on *Biograph*), 'Lay Down Your Weary Tune', 'Suze', 'Bob Dylan's New Orleans Rag'

'Percy's Song' and 'Lay Down Your Weary Tune' on *Biograph*
'Seven Curses', 'Paths of Victory', 'Moonshiner Blues', 'Only A Hobo', 'Eternal Circle', and 'Suze (The Cough Song)' on *The Bootleg Series.*

Another side of Bob Dylan

All I Really Want To Do
Black Crow Blues
Spanish Harlem Incide
Chimes Of Freedom
I Shall Be Free No. 10
To Ramona
Motorpsycho Nitemare
My Back Pages
I Don't Believe You
Ballad In Plain D
It Ain't Me Babe

ANOTHER SIDE OF BOB DYLAN

US Release: 8 August 1964
UK Release: November 1964
CD Release: Columbia CD 32034
CD Remaster/SACD Release: Columbia 512354-6
Mono version re-pressed on 180g vinyl
August 2002 as Columbia/Sundazed LP 5121
Producer: Tom Wilson

Columbia CL 2193/CS8993 mono/stereo
CBS BGP/SBGP 62429 mono/stereo
Running Time: 50.52

SIDE ONE: All I Really Want To Do; Black Crow Blues; Spanish Harlem Incident; Chimes Of Freedom; I Shall Be Free No 10; To Ramona.

SIDE TWO: Motorpsycho Nitemare; My Back Pages; I Don't Believe You; Ballad in Plain D; It Ain't Me Babe.

Bob Dylan: vocal, guitar, harmonica, piano

The whole album was laid down in one evening recording session at Columbia Studio A on 7th Avenue on 9 June, 1964, starting at 7pm. Dylan arrived five minutes late with a couple of bottles of Beaujoulais and a small circle of friends including Rambling Jack Elliott and writer Nat Hentoff. Tom Wilson told Nat, 'it's all stuff he's written in the last couple of months'. Dylan said, 'we're going to make a good one tonight. There aren't any finger-pointing songs in here. Now a lot of people are doing finger-pointing songs. Me, I don't want to write for people anymore. You know, be a spokesman'. Instead the songs are laced with humour and poetry. If any fingers are pointed, they're pointed inwards. As the evening went on Dylan's voice became more acrid. The dynamics of his singing grew more pronounced, soft; intimate passages being abruptly followed by fierce surges in volume.

Dylan initially disagreed with Tom Wilson's choice of album title. 'I begged and pleaded with him not to do it. I thought it was overstating the obvious.' Later he thought that Wilson might have been right to do what he did. *Another Side Of Bob Dylan* indicates that this is a refocusing on the singer, away from the certainties of *The Times, They Are A-Changin'*. The front cover is another monochrome photograph by Sandy Speiser that shows Dylan again out on the New York streets in suede jacket and ubiquitous jeans, looking quizzical rather than fierce. The CD remaster adds some colour shots from the same session. Dylan's hair is a-growing as his consciousness expands.

Most of the album was written in Vermilya, Greece when Dylan stayed there in May 1964 after his first UK tour. Some rough drafts have survived, scrawled on paper appropriated from the Mayfair Hotel in London. The interview with Hentoff, printed in the *New Yorker* in October 1964, marks a sea change in Dylan's aesthetics. 'A song has to have some kind of form to fit into the music. You can bend the words and the meter, but it still has to fit somehow. That's why I write a lot of poetry, if that's the word. Poetry can make its own form'. Songs here like 'Chimes Of Freedom' would do the same for song. 'I once wrote about Emmett Till in the first person, pretending I was him. From now on, I want to write from inside me.... I'm going to have to get back writing like I used to when I was ten – having everything come out naturally. The way I like to write is for it to come out the way I walk or talk'. Nat Hentoff interview, 1964.

The densely written poems in style much like those on the previous album – are now titled 'Some Other Kinds of Songs'. Later Ben Carruthers and the Deep, followed by Fairport Convention on their first LP, turned 'Jack Of Diamonds' into a song in its own right. Less noticed at the time is the reference to 'needs some acid/in his lap'. Certainly it was around this time that Dylan began to experiment with LSD, a key influence on loosening up his writing style.

Presumably, the same sharpening up as *Record Collector* enthused over on the latest CD remaster programme, and this album in particular. 'The difference is staggering. The old release sounds like a one-dimensional plane of sound; the revamp moves the album into three-dimensional colour'. The album emerged in the UK on CD in 1988, previously having been available only as a double pack with *Blood on the Tracks*. The same could be said for the lyrics, after the stern monochrome of the previous album, here the words are in colour, sometimes risking pretension or straining beyond rational meaning but imbued with a new sense of verbal risk-taking.

SIDE ONE
All I Really Want To Do (Dylan) 4.05
Dylan performs acrobatics on the high wire of language, juggling his rhymes with the sly wit of Hank Williams and there is a touch of Jimmie Rodgers in here too, almost a yodel. He laughs at his own cleverness, and there was certainly no laughter inside 'The Times They Are A-Changin''. The energy in Bob's voice supports what one commentator later described as 'a rock album without electric guitars'.

Black Crow Blues (Dylan) 3.15
A gutbucket blues with Dylan showing off his storming style at the honky tonk and a new sneer in his voice, echoed by crowing harmonica. Maybe 'Sometimes I'm too high to fall' was his first drug song.

Spanish Harlem Incident (Dylan) 2.26
After laying this down that evening, Dylan asked a friend if he understood the song. He nodded. Bob replied 'Well, I didn't'. Rich with imagery and effortlessly lubricious, Howie Payne of the *Stands* reckons 'it's got the 4am feel of a sailor in New York, staggering up First Avenue while the dawn's rising over the East River, following a girl who's leading him into dangerous territory'.

Chimes Of Freedom (Dylan) 7.11
This could be set in a lightning storm, viewed from the shelter of a city doorway, but Bob wrote it in the back of a car down south while on a road trip with friends the day after visiting civil rights worker Bernice Johnson in Atlanta. Highly impressionistic and over-influenced by symbolist poets like Rimbaud, this takes the subject matter of, say, 'Oxford Town' into a psychedelic netherworld. It has been suggested that there is an echo here of Tom Glaser's 1948 song 'Because All Men Are Brothers', a model of enlightened patriotism: 'where chimes the bell of freedom, there is my native land'. A song of compassion and wonder.

I Shall Be Free No 10 (Dylan) 4.48
Another exuberant talking blues written when Muhammed Ali was still called Cassius Clay, but in the context of this album it already sounds as if it's from a previous era. Dylan expanded a couple of lines from the draft into a song in its own right, 'To Ramona'.

To Ramona (Dylan) 3.53
Dylan said in *Biograph*, : 'That's pretty literal. That was just somebody I knew. I think I'd played this for the first time at the *Gaslight*, probably after hours. There was a time when all the singers used to go there after their regular gigs and try out new songs'. For Lucinda Williams this is 'the ultimate love song. There's just something about it – the rhyming, the imagery' – though it is also a song about rejection.

SIDE TWO
Motorpsycho Nitemare (Dylan) 4.34
A parody of the Hitchcock shocker with a name check to Anthony Perkins and a side reference to Fellini. Perhaps this was inspired by various visits to the deep south, and its gun-crazy culture. A precursor to 'Maggie's Farm'.

My Back Pages (Dylan) 4.23
Dylan strains to the limits of his vocal range, singing almost in code, but the chorus provides the key, 'I was so much older then/I'm younger than that now'. This is as provocative as his speech to the Emergency Civil Rights Committee on 13 December 1963, when he collected the Tom Paine award; 'It's took me a long time to get young'.

I Don't Believe You (Dylan) 4.23
For his one-time session man John Sebastian with this song Dylan established an unprecedented relationship between man and woman in song. Tin Pan Alley could deal either with romance or heartbreak and nothing in between. 'What little shading there was usually came from the woman's point of view. Dylan turned the tables, offering romantic critiques of women, with a degree of emotional awareness and insight. He made it more real and opened up vast new territories for songs to explore'. This song opened up further territories within

itself when it was re-interpreted in the 1966 electric firestorm and re-addressed to some of his audience.

Ballad in Plain D (Dylan) 8.17
This is the one song that Dylan now seems to regret having let loose in public. As he said in *Biograph*, 'I don't write confessional songs. Well, actually I did write one once and it wasn't very good. It was a mistake to record it and I regret it'. It can be only this very personal hymn of hate to Suze Rotolo's 'parasite' sister Carla and mother Mary. He also told Bill Flanagan 'I must have been a real schmuck to write that'. But even this outlet of spleen is more crafted than it looks and echoes the traditional song 'Once I Had A Sweetheart': 'I once loved a fair maid both handsome and gay'. After increased bickering, the couple finally split up in spring 1964.

It Ain't Me Babe (Dylan) 3.35
Dylan recalls, 'I wrote that song in Italy. I went there after doing some shows in England. I'd gone there to get away for a while'. Forty or so years on, sideman Charlie Sexton noticed, 'often when it was played, there would be the same reaction from some of the fans, a sort of celebration – which is interesting when you listen to the words, it's shadow and light'.

OUTTAKES
9 June 1964: 'Denise', 'Mr Tambourine Man' (with Jack Elliott), 'I Shall Be Free #10', 'Mama You Been On My Mind'

'Mama, You Been On My Mind' on *The Bootleg Series*

The rough and ready 'Mr Tambourine Man' with Jack Elliott on what loosely could be called harmony vocals is a shorter version of the later, officially released track. It is from this tape that the Byrds took their hit single, hence the cut-down lyrics.

BRINGING IT ALL BACK HOME

US Release: 22 March 1965
UK Release: May 1965
CD Release: Columbia CD 32344
CD Remaster/SACD Release: Columbia 512353-6
Mono version was re-pressed on 180g vinyl
March 2001 as Columbia/Sundazed LP 5070
Producer: Tom Wilson

Columbia CL 2328/CS 9128 mono/stereo
CBS BGP/SBGP62515 mono/stereo
Running Time: 47.21

SIDE ONE: Subterranean Homesick Blues; She Belongs To Me; Maggie's Farm; Love Minus Zero/No Limit; Outlaw Blues; On The Road Again; Bob Dylan's 115th Dream.

SIDE TWO: Mr Tambourine Man; Gates Of Eden; It's Alright, Ma (I'm Only Bleeding); It's All Over Now, Baby Blue.

Bob Dylan: vocal, guitar, harmonica, piano, **Bobby Gregg**: drums, **Al Gorgoni**: guitar, **Paul Griffin**: piano, **John Hammond Jr**: guitar, **Bruce Langhorne**: guitar, **William E Lee**: bass, **Joseph Macho Jr**: bass, **Kenny Rankin**: guitar, **John Sebastian**: bass on various outtakes

In December 1964, Tom Wilson spent an afternoon trying to overdub electric instruments onto three pre-recorded Dylan songs including 'The House Of The Rising Sun', a trick he had pulled off with Simon and Garfunkel, but not here. When Dylan next entered Studio A on 13 January 1965 he was accompanied only by John Sebastian who was soon to form the *Lovin' Spoonful*, on electric bass. Six of the songs they laid down made the final album but not in this form. Dylan seems always to have envisioned his next album as part acoustic, part electic, and one song in particular encouraged him to repeat the experiment started on *Freewheelin'*, even down to calling again on guitarist Bruce Langhorne, a man well known around Greenwich Village. 'I had this thing called "Subterranean Homesick Blues" but it just didn't sound right by myself.' Tom Wilson had the task of finding the rest of the band who turned out to be mostly hard-bitten New York session men. Over the two days that followed, Dylan used the studio like an echo chamber for his thoughts, altering the tempo and improvising lyrics at will as the musicians responded to

Bob Dylan
Bringing It All Back Home

this spontaneity with a lovely, slightly ramshackle sound. He also found time to lay down the virtually acoustic songs that would be programmed onto side two of the vinyl release.

It was time to say farewell to work shirts. The Daniel Kramer front-cover photograph that took three hours to set up, features Albert Grossman's wife Sally as the epitome of cool, a colonial residence and Dylan cradling a Blue Persian cat called Rolling Stone, all through a psychedelic prism. The room is a treasure store of cultural references. There's *Time* magazine featuring Lyndon Johnson, a fallout-shelter sign, a Lord Buckley album on the mantelpiece, the rare Beat writing magazine *Gnaoua* and a slew of album covers by the Impressions, Lotte Lenya, Eric Von Schmidt, and Robert Johnson, the acetate of which Dylan writes about with such emotion in *Chronicles*. The back cover features monochrome shots of Barbara Rubin rubbing Dylan's head, Ginsberg in a white topper and Dylan with a Mad Hatter grin. The CD remaster adds some iconic shots of a *Reservoir Dogs* Dylan in the studio, in suit 'n' shades.

There are noticeable differences between the mono and stereo mixes of this album, the former of which is a far richer listen, particularly on side one. There the electric instruments are spread too thinly in the stereo mix that also runs slightly slower than the mono and correct version, other than 'Gates of Eden' that is mono anyway. To add to the confusion, the printed timings of both mono and stereo UK albums are identical and early UK CDs, imported from Holland, were retitled *Subterranean Homesick Blues*. Even so, neither mix does full justice to the electric tracks that have none of the fullness of sound of the two albums that follow, even on the hugely improved CD remaster whose timings I follow – it is six seconds shorter than the original CD. It can hardly be down to the producer, as Wilson also was responsible for 'Like A Rolling Stone' that is anything but thin or weedy, and went on to record seminal rock albums with the Mothers of Invention and the Velvet Underground.

Dylan's sleeve note this time around is a prose poem, about his songs now being written with 'a touch of anxious colour'. That same year, he said 'my old songs, they were what I call one-dimensional songs, but my new songs I'm trying to make more three dimensional, you know. There's more symbolism, they're written on more than one level'.

SIDE ONE
Subterranean Homesick Blues (Dylan) 2.21
This song was written in the apartment of John Court, an associate of Grossman, and provides a startling opening to the movie *Don't Look Back*, where a gum-chewing, impassive Dylan displays variants of the lyrics written out on cue cards and Ginsberg skulks in the background. 'Probably Chuck Berry's "Too Much Monkey Business" is in here somewhere. I don't even think we rehearsed it', he recounts on *Biograph*. Berry's song is a list of the daily task of a petrol attendant. Here it is extended to a whole urban lifestyle at the bottom of the pile. Guthrie's 'Takin' It Easy' is somewhere in there too, 'mom was in the kitchen, preparing to eat'. Singer-raconteur Gerard Langley nails this 'outpouring of rhyme' best: 'He's wired and in New York and not looking like anybody else…hipper than The Beatles'.

She Belongs To Me (Dylan) 2.50
A luminous performance. Dylan croons, with vitriol tempering the sweetness. Beach Boy Bruce Johnston was among those from the rock'n'roll community to be startled by this song in particular. 'Here's this Greenwich Village folkie who has turned the lyric-writing process upside down and suddenly he's making songs with a natural groove.' Autobiographical or not, Dylan had recently given Joan Baez an Egyptian ring.

Maggie's Farm (Dylan) 3.58
Vocally at the other extreme, with vocals like a bullwhip cracking and an alarm clock harmonica. Perhaps there is a nod here to 'Down on Penny's Farm' on the Harry Smith Anthology, a song based on Silas McGee's 'Negro work farm' in Greenwood, the same place where a younger Dylan had performed 'Only A Pawn In Their Game'. It gained a whole extra resonance in the UK during Maggie Thatcher's regime in the 80s, but this is essentially the American Civil War revisited, the north taking a slingshot at the south.

Love Minus Zero/No Limit (Dylan) 2.51
Rippling guitar, and Dylan goes all lyrical singing words like a poem. A happy and fulfilled love song for a change. It's a clever bit of writing, with each line almost a sentence in itself. This would be of no account were the images not so evocative and essentially mysterious: 'the bridge at midnight trembles'.

Outlaw Blues (Dylan) 3.06
Yet another change of pace and tone, with the musical equivalent of an argument. Everyone is vying for centre stage, but Dylan wins – you could almost cut yourself on his voice. The line 'nine below zero' was the title of a Sonny Boy Williamson song, and later a pub rock band in London.

On The Road Again (Dylan) 2.38
A song midway between the throwaway improv of 'I Shall Be Free' and the full-tilt surrealism of the next two albums, with chugging guitar and Dylan about as cuddly as Johnny Rotten.

Bob Dylan's 115th Dream (Dylan) 6.34
It is Tom Wilson who cracks up at the beginning, and forces a second take. He's probably laughing because the band has failed to appear on cue. This is an upside-down look at American history, essentially a shaggy dog story that alludes to the Pilgrim Fathers and Moby Dick.

SIDE TWO
Mr Tambourine Man (Dylan) 5.28
Having recorded this twice in June 1964, once as a Witmark demo and once during the session for *Another Side Of Bob Dylan*, Dylan was now fully ready to nail it down. Despite much speculation this song was inspired, not by LSD, which Dylan clearly states in the notes to *Biograph* he first took a couple of months after writing it, but literally by a giant Turkish tambourine, four inches deep with jingle bells around its circumference. Dylan remembers it as being 'as big as a wagonwheel. I wrote some of the song in New Orleans. Different things inspired me. That Fellini movie, *La Strada*. Drugs never played a part in that song, drugs were never that big a thing with me. I could take 'em or leave 'em'.

The song had been roughed out during a road trip across the south and the morning after a night in New Orleans following a close encounter with the Mardi Gras, then finished at the New Jersey home of Al Aronowitz. Maybe somewhere at the back of Dylan's mind was the opening song in Brendan Behan's play *The Quare Fellow*, sung by a prisoner – 'And the ould triangle, it went jingle jangle'– to wake the inmates, that gives the song a different spin. The Tambourine Man himself picks out a counter melody on electric guitar.

Gates Of Eden (Dylan)(5.44

Many fans, myself included, first encountered this mysterious song on the B-side of 'Like A Rolling Stone', and still haven't recovered from the double whammy. As Marc Carroll puts it, 'it's actually unsettling, almost frightening'. A vision of cold eternity set against a quick trip to 'Desolation Row'.

It's Alright, Ma (I'm Only Bleeding) (Dylan) 7.33

Dylan hardly seems to pause for breath between verse breaks. For former Byrd David Crosby, the opening line about darkness at noon – check out Arthur Koestler – is 'the apocalypse coming, nothing less'. No wonder Dennis Hopper and Peter Hopper chose this to accompany the credits of *Easy Rider*, over the aerial shots of a free spirit, shot full of holes.

It's All Over Now, Baby Blue (Dylan) 4.16

Bob Dylan says on *Biograph*: 'I had carried that song around in my head for a long time. When I was writing it, I remembered a Gene Vincent song, "Baby Blue". It was one of the songs I used to sing back in High School. Of course, I was singing about a different Baby Blue'. Many have speculated this was Paul Clayton who shared the trip across the deep South and was noted for his versions of sea shanties, hence all those seasick sailors sailing home. It also could be a farewell to Joan Baez even though they were about to set off on tour together. The break-up was chronicled on *Don't Look Back*.

    The most bizarre interpretation is from Richard Thompson. When *Mojo* asked him to discuss his favourite Dylan song, one of the few contemporary songwriters worthy of cleaning Dylan's boots went off on a staggering journey of erudition, or maybe a wind-up, 'Bob may have heard "Mary Queen Of Scots' Lament" on his visit to England in 1962. She was fond of blue stocking, indeed she was wearing sky-blue hose with an interwoven silver thread when she was beheaded in 1587. The orphan crying in the sun might be her son, and the empty-headed painter her secretary lover David Rizzio, also a fine musician'. That may be, but no-one can disagree with Richard's conclusion, 'a great song by someone who knows the tradition, innovates in it, and builds on it'.

OUTTAKES:
13 January 1965: 'Love Minus Zero'/'No Limit', 'I'll Keep It With Mine', 'Its All Over Now Baby Blue', 'She Belongs To Me', 'Subterranean Homesick Blues', 'California', 'Farewell Angelina', 'You Don't Have To Do That'
15 January 1965: 'If You Gotta Go, Go Now' (x2)

'If You Gotta Go, Go Now' as 45 rpm single
'I'll Keep It With Mine' on *Biograph*
Alternative version of 'Subterranean Homesick Blues', 'Farewell Angelina', alternative version of 'If You Gotta Go, Go Now' on *The Bootleg Series.*

HIGHWAY 61 REVISITED

US Release: 30 August 1965
UK Release: September 1965
CD Release: Columbia 460953-2
Mono version re-pressed on 180g vinyl
May 2001 as Columbia/Sundazed LP 5071
Producer: Bob Johnston, Tom Wilson on 'Like A Rolling Stone'

Columbia CL 2389/CS 9189 mono/stereo
CBS BGP/SBGP 62572 mono/stereo
CD Remaster/SACD Release: 512351-6
Running Time: 51.34 (SACD)

SIDE ONE: Like A Rolling Stone; Tombstone Blues; It Takes A Lot To Laugh, It Takes A Train To Cry; From A Buick 6; Ballad Of A Thin Man.

SIDE TWO: Queen Jane Approximately; Highway 61 Revisited; Just Like Tom Thumb's Blues; Desolation Row.

Bob Dylan: vocals, guitar, harmonica, piano, **Mike Bloomfield:** guitar, **Harvey Brooks:** bass
Bobby Gregg: drums, **Paul Griffin:** organ, piano, **Al Kooper:** organ, **Sam Lay:** drums, **Charlie McCoy:** guitar, vibes, **Frank Owen:** piano, maracas, **Ron Savakus:** bass

Dylan failed to spark with Eric Clapton, and the rest of John Mayall and the Bluesbreakers, in an abortive recording session in London in May 1965, during which Bobby Neuwirth complained 'you're playing too much blues man. He needs to be more country'. Dylan signed up Michael Bloomfield from the Butterfield Blues Band to play lead guitar on his next album. Bloomfield later recalled that 'Bob picked me up at the bus station and took me to this house where he lived. He was playing in weird keys, all on the black notes on the piano. Then we went to New York to cut the record'. Meanwhile, Al Kooper also turned up at that legendary first session, on 15 June 1965 and wandered over to the organ. Kooper described his keyboard style at the time as finding his 'way through the changes like a little kid fumbling in the dark for a light switch'. However, Dylan heard something he liked, asked Wilson to turn the organ up in the mix and found the musical alchemy he wanted.

    The next day they worked on repeated takes of the same song. The second complete version was rush released as a single on 20 July. Bloomfield reckoned, unfairly, that Tom Wilson was 'a non-producer. He didn't know what was happening, man. We did 20 alternate takes of

BOB DYLAN HIGHWAY 61 REVISITED

every song, and it got ridiculous because they were long songs'. When Dylan returned to Studio A after the Newport cataclysm on 29 July, the next day, and for two sessions in early August, Bob Johnston replaced Wilson in the control booth. The sessions flowed freely. The whole album and two stray singles all laid down safely. Only 'Desolation Row' proved to be elusive until Johnston suggested visiting Nashville session man Charlie McCoy to play a second guitar line.

The cover photo is another iconic shot by Daniel Kramer. Dylan is in a Triumph tee shirt bought in London, Bob Neuwirth stands behind him, his crotch lined up with Dylan's eyes. This does not look like a folk album. Dylan's enigmatic liner notes about a slow train coming, were revised for the UK back cover and the 'man from the newspaper' becomes 'the man from the hilltop' et al. The CD remaster reprints the US original. It is a fine example of the cut up style. The UK and the US back cover have different photographs of Dylan. On the US version he is seated at a piano rather than playing an electric guitar.

One reporter asked Dylan, who had just described himself as a trapeze artist, whether his new music had a carnival-type sound to match. 'That isn't a carnival sound, that's religious. That's very real, you can see that anywhere'. But whatever it was, he rejected the term folk-rock'. I call it the mathematical sound, sort of Indian music. I can't really explain it'. As to the new album, 'I'm not gonna be able to make a record better than that one. *Highway 61* is just too good. There's a lot of stuff on there that I would listen to'.

There are noticeable differences between mono and stereo mixes of this album. The original US stereo release contained an alternative take of 'From A Buick Six' and is now very collectable. It also appeared on the Japanese issue for many years. Bob Johnston's original mix pushed the drums well into the right-hand speaker. The stereo version boasted substantially longer tracks on everything except 'Desolation Row' because they were not faded too soon, as were the mono mixes. However, they also ran approximately one per cent slow and sounded lacklustre. The CD remaster is noticeably warmer than earlier digital transfers, and corrects the speed. *Record Collector* reckons 'the harsh sheet-metal effect of the original CDs has been replaced by richer, rounder and infinitely more accurate sound. Sample 'Like A Rolling Stone' with your eyes closed and you can picture the band spread around the studio with Dylan's voice perfectly positioned in the foreground'.

SIDE ONE
Like A Rolling Stone (Dylan) 6.11
One key scene in *Don't Look Back* has Dylan gazing lovingly at electric guitars in a London shop window. Having supposedly decided to jack in his musical career, he wrote 'just a rhythm thing on paper…directed at some point that was honest' and then turned it, by some alchemy, into his first US number one, though early promo copies chopped the song in half before Dylan intervened. 'My wife and I lived in a little cabin in Woodstock, which we rented from Peter Yarrow's mother. I wrote the song there. We had come up from New York and I had about three days off up there to get some stuff together. It just came, you know, it started with that "La Bamba" riff'. This was based on a traditional Mexican dance tune. The first take is in waltz time and is the palest of shadows of this stately-modern-day fairy tale 'once upon a time' – directed maybe to poor little rich girl Edie Sedgwick, or Bob Neuwirth, or Dylan himself, but was taken to the heart of a new, footloose generation.

Tombstone Blues (Dylan) 5.58
The original version was called 'Jet Pilot', resurrected on *Biograph*. A version with the Chambers Brothers on backing vocals was scrapped at the last moment.

Dylan noted in *Biograph*, 'there was this bar I used to play where cops would always come and hang out, mostly off duty. They'd always be talking stuff, saying stuff like "I don't know who killed him or why, but I'm sure glad he's gone". I think I wrote this either in that place or remembering some conversations'. Dylan sounds as unfeeling as the cops, the song has a rough, punky energy. Tombstone was part of the myth of the Wild West, a place beyond the reach of the law.

It Takes A Lot To Laugh, It Takes A Train To Cry (Dylan) 4.09
Originally titled 'Phantom Engineer', like some old-time country song, it borrows the line about the moon shining down through the trees from Charley Patton's 1934 song 'Poor Me'. This is a relaxed piano-led blues.

From A Buick 6 (Dylan) 3.19
A classic American car and a song to match. The tune comes from Sleepy John Estes' 'Milk Cow Blues' recorded in 1930 and covered by Elvis during his brief spell with Sun. A love song somehow.

Ballad Of A Thin Man (Dylan) 5.58
Dylan told Nora Ephron that Mr Jones is 'a real person. You know him, but not by that name'. He told another reporter in Austin that 'it's just about a fella who came into a truck-stop once'. Dylan laughs nervously near the start but this is pure character assassination. After laying it down, drummer Bobby Gregg turned to him and said 'That's a nasty song, Bob'. The piano bridge comes from Ray Charles. Phil Ochs reckoned that running into Dylan at this point was like walking into a threshing machine. Musically gorgeous with the double punch of organ and piano and Bloomfield riffing at the end.

SIDE TWO
Queen Jane Approximately (Dylan) 5.31
Ever helpful, Dylan told Nora Ephron that 'Queen Jane is a man'. It's as good an explanation as the obvious suspect, Joan Baez. Dylan sounds almost compassionate for a change, although his voice turns harsh at the end and his harmonica caws like a crow.

Highway 61 Revisited (Dylan) 3.31
The highway that runs due south from the frozen north to the land of the blues and race are just two of the issues dealt with through the mechanism of sarcasm. Plus electric piano and slide guitar and some kind of police siren.

Just Like Tom Thumb's Blues (Dylan) 5.31
Tom Thumb was a midget. The song takes place somewhere out on the road. Dylan introduced it at Melbourne 1966 – a famously stoned show – as being 'about this painter down in Mexico City…his name is Tom Thumb and right now he's about 125 years old but he's still going. Everybody likes him a lot down there, he's got a lot of friends and this is when he was going through his blue period'. As usual, a dream-like narrative where strange people do unfathomable things and Dylan chronicles it all, deadpan.

Desolation Row (Dylan) 11.21
Bob told Jann Wenner that he wrote the song in the back of a New York taxi cab.
T. S. Eliot's *The Waste Land* updated. Philip Larkin, a far lesser poet, couldn't quite decide about

the 'mysterious, possibly half-baked words'. But at the 1970 Isle of Wight Pop Festival, a makeshift hippy shanty town proudly called itself by the same name. And Dylan clone, '66 period, John Cooper Clark moved it to Manchester and updated it as 'Beasley Street'. But when asked at the December 1965 San Francisco press conference whether he was primarily a singer or a poet – he does both supremely here – Dylan replied 'Oh, I think of myself as a song and dance man'.

OUTTAKES
15 June 1965: 'Sitting On A Barbed Wire Fence', 'Phantom Engineer', 'Sitting On A Barbed Wire Fence', 'Like A Rolling Stone'
16 June 1965: 'Like A Rolling Stone', CO 86449
29 July 1965: 'Positively 4th Street', 'Desolation Row'
30 July 1965: 'From A Buick 6', 'Can You Please Crawl Out Your Window'

'Positively 4th Street' on *Biograph*
'Sitting On A Barbed Wire Fence', 'Phantom Engineer', early take of 'Like A Rolling Stone' on *The Bootleg Series.*

BLONDE ON BLONDE

US Release: 16 May 1966
UK Release: August 1966
CD Release: CBS 22130 (Dutch release)
CD Remaster/SACD Release: Columbia 512352-6
Mono version re-pressed on 180g vinyl
October 2002 as Columbia/Sundazed LP 5110
Producer: Bob Johnston

Columbia C2L 41/C2S 841 mono/stereo
CBS DDP/SDDP 66012 mono/stereo
Running Time: 39.59, 33.02 (SACD)

SIDE ONE: Rainy Day Women #12 & 35; Pledging My Time; Visions of Johanna; One Of Us Must Know (Sooner Or Later).

SIDE TWO: I Want You; Memphis Blues Again; Leopard-Skin Pill-Box Hat; Just Like A Woman.

SIDE THREE: Most Likely You Go Your Way And I'll Go Mine; Temporary Like Achilles; Absolutely Sweet Marie; 4th Time Around; Obviously 5 Believers.

SIDE FOUR: Sad Eyed Lady Of The Lowlands.

Bob Dylan: vocal, guitar, lead guitar on 'Leopard-Skin Pill-Box Hat', harmonica, piano, **Bill Aikens, Kenneth Buttrey:** drums, **Rick Danko:** bass, **Bobby Gregg:** drums, **Levon Helm:** drums, **Garth Hudson:** organ, **Jerry Kennedy:** guitar, **Al Kooper:** organ, **Richard Manuel:** piano, **Charlie McCoy:** guitar, harmonica on 'Obviously 5 Believers', **Wayne Moss:** guitar, **Robbie Jaime Robertson**: guitar, **Hargus 'Pig' Robbins:** piano, **Joe South:** bass, **Henry Strzelecki:** bass

Dylan re-entered New York's Studio A with his road band the Hawks on 5 October 1965, but even adding drummer Bobby Gregg and organist Al Kooper during five more sessions up to 27 January 1966 he laid down only the rogue single 'Can You Please Crawl Out Your Window' and one take – 'One of Us Must Know (Sooner Or Later) – that would make the final cut for the album. On 14 February, at Bob Johnston's suggestion, he moved down to Columbia's Music Row Studios in Nashville, taking Kooper and Robbie Robertson to join a crack crew of session men more used to working with the likes of Tammy Wynette and somehow it worked. Two

CBS 66012

featuring **I WANT YOU** and **RAINY DAY WOMEN Nos. 12 & 35**

more consecutive days, and three sessions between 8 and 10 March, and one of rock music's first double albums was in the can.

Kris Kristofferson was working as a janitor at the studios, and told *Uncut* 'those were the wildest sessions I ever saw in Nashville. Bob sat at the piano for hours while the musicians were out playing ping-pong and cards – and he's writing a song. It was the most bizarre behaviour anybody in Nashville had ever seen because he didn't record the damn thing until the sun came up'. Dylan would spend the daytime in his hotel room, running through song structures with Kooper, who would then high-tail it to the studio to teach the Nashville cats the chord changes. When it came to lay the song down, 'everyone would fall in with the drums'.

Johnston's masterstroke was to tear down the sound baffles between the players so that everyone was in the same room, establishing eye contact and playing in real time. Suddenly they were a gang, New York hipster and rednecks united – they started eating together, taking breaks together and having a good time. Dylan took care to credit them all individually on the album sleeve, leading to a rush to Nashville by every outsider from Buffy Sainte Marie to Skip Spence.

Dylan later reckoned 'You've got more space in Nashville than you do in New York. In Nashville, if they want to make good records, they just sit around and wait all night 'til you're ready. They don't do that in New York. I wrote out all the songs in the studio. The musicians played cards. I wrote out a song, we'd do it, they'd go back to their game and I'd write out another song'. He recalled, in 1978: 'the closest I ever got to the sound I hear in my mind was on the *Blonde on Blonde* album. It's that thin, that wild Mercury sound. It's metallic and bright gold, with whatever that conjures up. That's my particular sound. At the time of my *Blonde on Blonde* album, I was going at a tremendous speed'.

The original album cover conveys this perfectly, a fold-out and slightly blurred portrait that mirrors Dylan's inner landscape at this point taken close to the Chelsea Hotel by Jerrold Schatzberg. As to the montage of monochrome photos inside, one of Claudia Cardinale was excised from later pressings after she started court proceedings. There are no liner notes.

There are noticeable differences between the mono and stereo mixes, in particular on 'Visions of Johanna', 'One Of Us Must Know' and 'Pledging My Time'. That adds 30 seconds of fade-out and some wonderful harmonica. Stereo mixes mostly run slower than mono versions. The Japanese vinyl release featured longer mixes of some songs. Clinton Heylin describes the original CD transfer, crammed onto one disc, as 'the most publicized disaster' of CBS's entire back catalogue. Two minutes were chopped off, including a whole 36 seconds off 'Sad Eyed Lady Of The Lowlands'. This has since been replaced by the glowing CD-remaster treatment.

SIDE ONE
Rainy Day Women #12 & 35 (Dylan) 4.34
The album starts with a party and, as the raucous atmosphere suggests, this was recorded at four in the morning, with everyone suitably wasted. Dylan told everyone to 'play dumb', so they swopped instruments, hence the woozy feel. But this is far from a simple injunction to get wasted – the stoning here is also punitive. Maybe it's a response to those who threw verbal stones at Newport. Dylan once described this as a 'Portuguese folk song', and it is certainly a further twist on Ray Charles' 'Let's Go Get Stoned'.

Pledging My Time (Dylan) 3.50
This album is nothing less than a survey of American music, reflected in a fairground mirror, from ragtime to Chicago blues – like here – to country laments to torch song. Here at one end of the emotional scale is a love song from the gutter, couched in evangelical language. There are parallels both melodically and in an echo of the line 'some joker got lucky' with Robert Johnson's 'Come On In My Kitchen'. Dylan dedicated his first collection of *Writings and Drawings* jointly to the memory of Guthrie and Johnson.

Visions of Johanna (Dylan) 7.34)
Much of the album was written in the legendary Chelsea Hotel, notorious for its noisy plumbing that you would notice when you have been up all night thinking of a lost love and writing this verbal symphony. This was originally called 'Seems Like A Freeze Out' and remains supremely enigmatic, although these two rainy-day women, Louise, entwined with her lover, maybe in a drug den and the absent, sainted Johanna, obviously stand for something. Steve Harley remembers coming upon this poem in his teens: 'suddenly I wasn't a 15 year old listening to music anymore, I was hearing poetry'.

One Of Us Must Know (Sooner Or Later) (Dylan) 4.54
This was the breakthrough to locating that 'wild Mercury sound', when the chemistry in New York Studio A suddenly coalesced, releasing a gorgeousness absent from *Highway 61*. Music you can dance to, it's a kissing cousin of the supremely vitriolic 'She's Your Lover Now'.

SIDE TWO
I Want You (Dylan) 3.08
There is a lovely contrast between the ornate verses and the simple, aching three-word chorus (four, if you add 'honey'). Some have speculated that the muse here is Edie Sedgwick, and his rival, the 'dancing child in his Chinese suit', Brian Jones. Dylan squired him around New York in November 1965, he did indeed possess such a suit and 'Time was on his side' – even if Jagger sang that, not Brian. The guitar figure here was played by Wayne Moss who went on to form Area Code 615 with many of the musicians here, and then that great stoned redneck band, Barefoot Jerry. No-one has better described the sound here than BBC Radio 2's Jeremy Vine 'the melody is wrapped in tinsel, like turning on all the fairy lights, all bouncy and joyous'. One of the four US Hot Hundred singles to be drawn from the album.

Memphis Blues Again (Dylan) 7.06
Another song of the south. The line about railroad men drinking blood like wine comes straight from Bascom Lamar Lunsford's 1928 78 rpm 'I Wish I Was A Mole In The Ground', on the *Harry Smith Anthology*. Wilco's Jeff Tweedy identifies a musical structure that 'basically keeps rolling over itself over and over again. It's like a self-charging battery'. For Frank Black of the Pixies: 'it's a song with so much soul, but the more I listen, I always go back to those killer drums'.

Leopard-Skin Pill-Box Hat (Dylan) 3.59
Loosely based on Lightnin' Hopkins' 'Automobile Blues', another song of thwarted love and consumer envy. Dylan told Jann Wenner 'I think that's something I took out of a newspaper. Mighta seen a picture of one in a department store window. I know it can get blown up to some sort of illusion. In reality it's no more than that. Just a leopard-skin pill-box. That's all'.

Just Like A Woman (Dylan) 4.50
Bob Dylan says: 'I think I was on the road. I wrote it in Kansas City or something. I was invited out to somebody's home for Thanksgiving dinner, but I didn't go. I wasn't hungry. I stayed in my hotel room and wrote this'. Others attribute this to Andy Warhol acolyte, failed model and actress Edie Sedgwick – the song was later used in the movie about her brief life, *Ciao Manhattan*. They met at the Kettle of Fish in late 1964 and it came as a shock to her when Dylan married a very pregnant Sara Lownds in November 1965. No less than Jimmy Webb

enthuses 'what a fortuitous nexus of rhyme and purpose is the chorus. As songwriters we wait for the moment when words fall together like that. The way everything leads towards that last line is masterful'.

SIDE THREE
Most Likely You Go Your Way And I'll Go Mine (Dylan) 3.30
Dylan can only remember that this was 'probably written after some disappointing relationship where I was lucky to have escaped without a broken nose'.

Temporary Like Achilles (Dylan) 5.02
Achilles thought himself invincible, but was killed via his one weak spot, his heel, that had not been dipped in the waters of immortality. Not that this has much to do with the song.

Absolutely Sweet Marie (Dylan) 4.57
Paul Zollo and Dylan riff on the 'yellow railroad' line in their 'Song Talk' interview. Bob reckons this is a song that has matured like fine wine: 'that's as complete as you can be. Every single letter in that line. It's all true. On a literal and escapist level'.

4th Time Around (Dylan) 4.45
A biting parody of The Beatles' 'Norwegian Wood' on *Rubber Soul*, one of John Lennon's first attempts at Dylan-type obscurity and, supposedly, about a one-night stand he wanted to hide from his wife Cynthia. Lennon was said to be paranoid about whether the song was a jokey tribute or an insult, and whether the final line 'I never asked for your crutch, now don't ask for mine' was directed at him. It didn't stop him sharing a stoned ride with Dylan through the London streets, as captured in *Eat the Document*, Dylan's long lost 1966 tour film.

Obviously 5 Believers (Dylan) 3.36
Pure electric blues, like the Butterfield Band on a great night. Though simply an aside here, the black dog has long been a motif for death in English folklore as well as the blues. Nick Drake famously sung about one in one of his final, haunted songs.

SIDE FOUR
Sad Eyed Lady Of The Lowlands (Dylan) 11.20
Bob Dylan told *Rolling Stone* 'it started out as just a little thing, but I got carried away somewhere along the line. I just sat down at a table and started writing at the session itself. I just got carried away with the whole thing. After a period of time, I forgot what it was all about and I started trying to get back to the beginning'. A wedding present in advance for Sara Lownds on whom the title puns (just as the album spells out BOB) and a later account, in song, shifts the writing process to the Chelsea Hotel.

Nothing could follow this, taking up a whole side of vinyl where it really blossoms, so that every consonant rings out like a bell. Sung as if in a trance and recorded in the small hours of the morning in a single take with the session men kept in the dark by their enigmatic employer, constantly rising to a closing climax to find every time the singer had no intention of stopping. As Buttrey remembers, 'I was playing one-handed, looking at my watch. And it kept on and on. We'd never heard anything like this before'. It reminds Robert Wyatt of the finest jazz: 'this song has got that kind of momentum, it builds and grows, builds and grows. They keep…surging towards an end, which is Miles Davis-like in its wickedness. It's like very clever sex, really'. For Al Kooper, who was there, 'this is the definition of what 4am feels like'.

OUTTAKES
5 October 1965: 'Medicine Sunday', 'Can You Please Crawl Out Your Window', 'I Wanna Be Your Lover' (x3), 'Jet Pilot Eyes', 'Number One' (instrumental)
30 November 1965: 'Visions Of Johanna' (x2), 'Can You Please Crawl Out Your Window?' (x2)
21 January 1966: 'She's Your Lover Now' (x2)
27 January 1966: 'I'll Keep It With Mine'
At this point Dylan moved from Columbia's New York Studio A where all previous recording sessions were taped unless otherwise indicated, to their studios in Nashville, Tennessee.
15 February 1966: Instrumental

'Can You Please Crawl Out Your Window', 'I Wanna Be Your Lover' on *Biograph*.

'She's Your Lover Now', 'I'll Keep It With Mine' on *The Bootleg Series*.

GREATEST HITS

UK Version: March 1967
CD Release: 460907

CBS BGP/SBGP 62847 (mono/stereo)
Running Time: 48.23

SIDE ONE: Blowin' In The Wind; It Ain't Me Babe; The Times They Are A-Changin'; Mr Tambourine Man; She Belongs To Me; It's All Over Now, Baby Blue.

SIDE TWO: Subterranean Homesick Blues; One Of Us Must Know; Like A Rolling Stone; Just Like A Woman; Rainy Day Women Nos 12 & 35; I Want You.

After the release of *Blonde On Blonde*, and Dylan's final concert with the Hawks at London's Royal Albert Hall, on 27 May Dylan took to the hills eleven days later and did not re-emerge with a new album until the tail-end of 1967. What Dylan and the musicians, now about to rename themselves the Band, got up to at Big Pink in rural Woodstock in the summer and autumn of 1967 did not emerge officially until 1975, although the songs seeped out as cover versions and on bootleg albums. To fill the gap, two separate compilation albums were released, this one in the UK only, followed by a shorter ten-track effort in the US that included nine of the songs here in a different running order, plus 'Positively 4th Street'.

Some fans were upset by the very title, most of the songs had never been hits and Dylan was seen as more than a mere pop artist. Along with The Beatles, he had smashed the concept of an album as a unity in its own right, rather than a couple of A sides and lots of filler. But this had no sense of concept, no songs that had not previously appeared on a 12 inch, and the mono version was simply the two stereo channels combined, with a notably thinner sound than true mono. The only good thing was the sleeve in which a '65-era Dylan carries a huge book of Italian art with a Renaissance portrait of an extremely angry deity. The CD is no different. The cover photo is by Jerry Schatzberg.

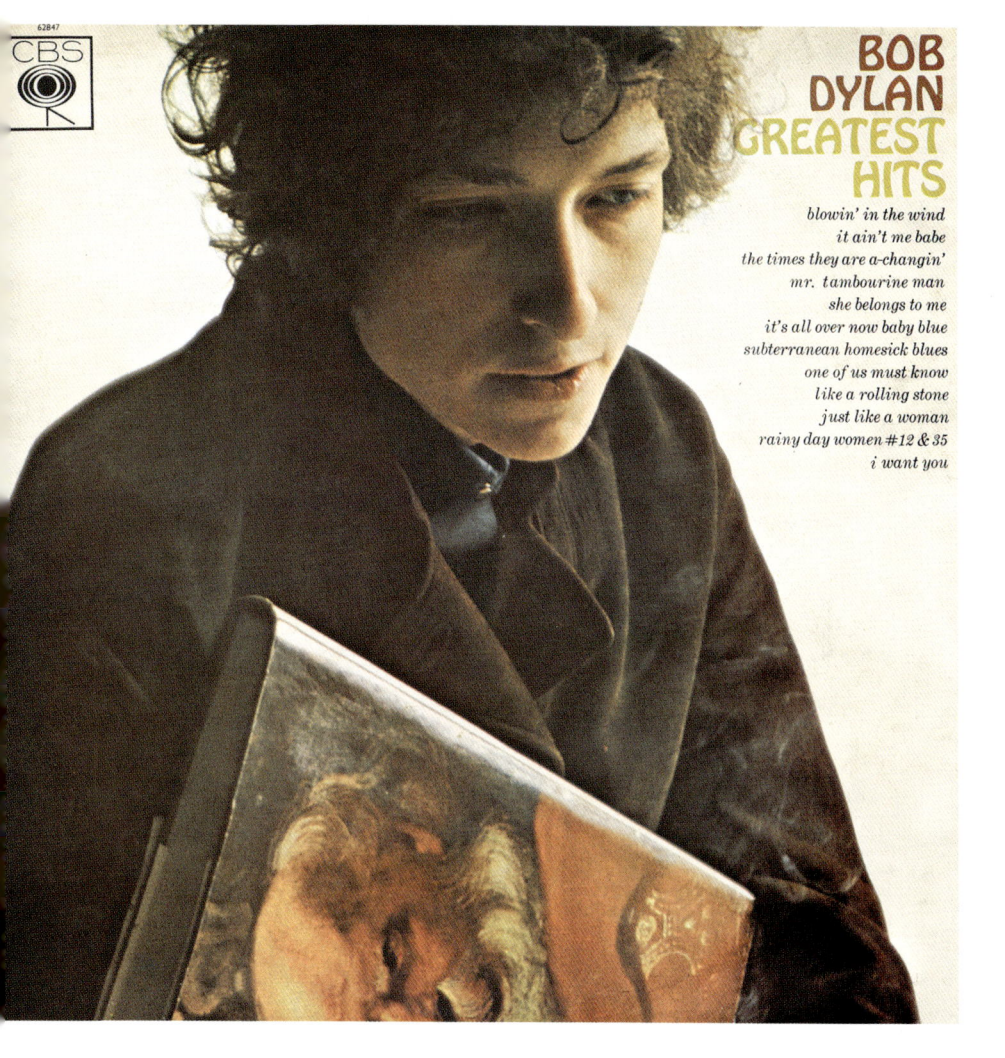

BOB DYLAN GREATEST HITS

blowin' in the wind
it ain't me babe
the times they are a-changin'
mr. tambourine man
she belongs to me
it's all over now baby blue
subterranean homesick blues
one of us must know
like a rolling stone
just like a woman
rainy day women #12 & 35
i want you

BOB DYLAN'S GREATEST HITS

US Release: 27 March 1967 **(mono/stereo)**
CD Release: CBS 450822-2
Mono version re-pressed on 180g vinyl
May 2003 as Columbia/Sundazed LP 5156

Columbia KCL 2263/KCS 9463
Running Time: 40.22

(The original 'Nice Price' UK CD followed not the UK but this shorter US version: this is no longer available and has been replaced with the UK predecessor)

SIDE ONE: Rainy Day Women #12 & 35; Blowin' In The Wind; The Times They Are A-Changin'; It Ain't Me Babe; Like A Rolling Stone.

SIDE TWO: Mr Tambourine Man; Subterranean Homesick Blues; I Want You; Positively 4th Street; Just Like A Woman.

The main difference from the UK version is to mess up the chronological order further, drop 'It's All Over Now, Baby Blue', 'She Belongs To Me' and 'One Of Us Must Know', add the single 'Positively 4th Street' but not 'Please Can You Crawl Out Your Window', let alone 'Mixed Up Confusion'. The sleeve is marvellous. A wild-haired Dylan (circa 1966) playing his harmonica, silhouetted in blue light, photographed by Roland Scherman with a matching shot in moody monochrome on the back cover.

'Positively 4th Street' was issued as a 45 on 7 September 1965 and drew the opprobrium of David Jacobs and the *Juke Box Jury* panel on the BBC who deemed it sick. Some of us rushed out and bought it the next day, this being a good sales pitch. Taking its title from Dylan's Greenwich Village haunts, it bears out David Blue's memory of the singer at this time as 'very hostile, a mean cat, very cruel to people'. Others see it as his farewell to the Factory crew, and indeed an influence on the early Velvet Underground. Over in LA, Johnny Echols of Love was not the only musician to take note – as he later told *Mojo*, 'it's a very New York song, but it made perfect sense out on the West Coast'. The release included a psychedelic poster of Dylan's head by Milton Glaser, and a new, stereo mix of 'Postively 4th Street'.

BOB DYLAN'S GREATEST HITS

Rainy Day Women #12 & 35
Blowin' in the Wind
The Times They Are A-Changin'
It Ain't Me Babe
Subterranean Homesick Blues
Mr. Tambourine Man
Like a Rolling Stone
I Want You
Positively 4th Street
Just Like a Woman

BOB DYLAN
JOHN WESLEY HARDING

JOHN WESLEY HARDING

US Release: January 1968
UK Release: 23 February 1968
CD Release: Columbia 463359-2
Mono version re-pressed on 180g vinyl
November 2003 as Columbia/Sundazed LP 5123
Producer: Bob Johnston

Columbia CL 2804/CS 9604 (mono/stereo)
CBS BGP/SBGP 63252 (mono/stereo)
CD Remaster/SACD Release: 512347-6
Running Time: 38.58

SIDE ONE: John Wesley Harding; As I Went Out One Morning; I Dreamed I Saw St Augustine; All Along The Watchtower; The Ballad of Frankie Lee and Judas Priest; Drifter's Escape.

SIDE TWO: Dear Landlord; I Am A Lonesome Hobo; I Pity The Poor Immigrant; The Wicked Messenger; Down Along The Cove; I'll Be Your Baby Tonight.

Bob Dylan: vocal, guitar, harmonica and piano, **Kenneth Buttrey**: drums, **Pete Drake:** steel guitar, **Charlie McCoy**: bass

Dylan re-entered Columbia Music Row Studios, Nashville on 17 October, the session stretched into the following morning, 6 November and 21 November 1967 with a new country-tinged vocal style and a rhythm section of Buttrey and McCoy, augmented by Drake on the final session. Gone were the swirling organ, the cutting lead guitar, the convoluted song structures. Dylan sounded sober and righteous, and to the amazement of Buttrey and McCoy, the epitome of professional cool. With his harmonica taking the lead between verses, this was the calm after the electric storm. Heylin has described it as a morning-after album, lacking the raucousness and dirty jokes of the Basement sessions. Guthrie had died two months before and Dylan had written the first three of what he described as 'an album of songs' – all newly minted – for the album on the two-day train journey from New York.

The front cover photograph, a polaroid by John Berg, features a grinning and lightly bearded Dylan alongside Purna and Lakhsman Das, two of the Bauls of Bengal, a travelling family of street musicians who were staying with Albert Grossman in Woodstock. Clinton Heylin quotes Levon Helm: 'they were real gypsies and real players, happy to get high and sing all night about rivers and goddesses and play their tablas, harmonium and fiddles'. They are joined by local carpenter Charlie Joy and a third Baul, visible only by his hat. It was so cold, they had to return to the house between photographs to thaw out. It is said – usually by the chemically altered – that if you reverse the image, you can see the faces of The Beatles in the tree trunk, plus Donovan, and even the hand of God. Hours of endless fun can be had imagining such things. Meanwhile the CD reissue boasts a wonderfully dramatic shot of Dylan strumming an acoustic guitar and looking like Moses just come down from the mountain.

The newly cleaned up Dylan had installed a lectern with an open bible in his Woodstock home and his sleeve notes are a knowing parody of a parable, featuring Frank (Dylan, perhaps), Terry Shute – Grossman, probably – and Vera, aka Sara. There are three kings too, who get healed (or rich) and 'the key is Frank', that seems a little inappropriate for Dylan's most enigmatic album.

As Dylan told Jann Wenner after the crash, 'I just took what came. That's how I made the changes. I took what came' And what came was a sense of restraint. As he said in 1968, 'What I'm trying to do now is not use too many words. There's no line that you can stick your finger through, there's no hole in any of those stanzas. There's no blank filler. Each line has something'. Indeed, Dylan has been extraordinarily forthcoming about his conscious change of style, without of course offering any real hints as to what any of these songs actually mean. He claimed to have been trying to emulate Canadian MOR singer-songwriter Gordon Lightfoot's easygoing sound, 'but we couldn't get it (laughs). We got a different sound…it's a muffled sound. Here I am not interested in taking up that much of anybody's time'. Economy is certainly the watchword here – there were no outtakes.

He talks over and over again about concentrating on craftsmanship, and concision. 'I took more care in the writing. I felt everyone expected me to be a poet, so that's what I tried to be'. All but two songs – presumably the final and throwaway ones – 'were written out on paper, and I found the tunes for them later. I didn't do it before, and I haven't done it since. That might account for the specialness of that album'. And, most revealing of all, 'John Wesley Harding was a fearful album…dealing with the devil in a fearful way, almost. All I wanted to do was get the words right'.

As to the sound, Buttrey later told a bemused George Harrison that the album mix was exactly what was laid down at the recording sessions: 'we just put it down and Columbia threw it out. Nobody ever went into the studio to mix a note'. The CD remaster is beautifully clear but commits serious damage to the soundscape of some of the tracks, in particular those that featured Dylan's piano in the original mix. This is a mere ghost of itself in the new dispensation. Just listen to 'Dear Landlord' – it's as if they've moved it to an adjacent room. This is a particular shame, as this is the first album where the stereo mix is unquestionably the better option, the mono mix being merely a conflation of the two channels.

The mono version was the first simply to combine left and right channels and not be specifically engineered, hence the collectable mono mixes on some earlier albums. This was the last US Dylan album to be released in mono. The German issue came with the Milton Glaser poster and so is hence highly collectable.

SIDE ONE
John Wesley Harding (Dylan) 3.00
Dylan chose the name to 'fit the tempo', adding a final g, and air-brushing the real outlaw's bloodthirsty nature. Here, he is a counterpart of Woody Guthrie's Pretty Boy Floyd, a genuine friend to the dispossessed. 'It started out to be a long ballad…but in the middle of the second verse I got tired. I had a tune, and it was a nice little melody, so I just wrote a quick third verse and recorded it'.

As I Went Out One Morning (Dylan) 2.52
Tom Paine, who wrote the *Rights of Man,* was one of the great fighters for freedom. He was a pamphleteer fired up by the French Revolution who fled from England to the United States for his life. Now safely dead for almost two centuries he is commemorated in Lewes, East Sussex, with a mural. This song, with its lovely bass pattern, starts like a traditional folk air, then our hero meets a temptress, but he gets rescued in the nick of time.

I Dreamed I Saw St Augustine (Dylan) 3.56
Augustine was a roustabout who repented, wrote confessions about his previous wicked life and became a leader of the early church. The song, with its slowed down military drumming, is based on a more recent text, the 1936 song that starts 'I dreamed I saw Joe Hill last night, alive as you or I'. Unlike St Augustine, who died in bed, Hill was a genuine martyr, a trades-union activist who was executed in Utah in 1915 on a trumped-up murder charge. Dylan sings with a newly acquired compassion and in tears, verbally anyway.

All Along The Watchtower (Dylan) 2.34
Dylan remembered, for *Biograph*, 'it probably came to me during a thunder and lightning storm, I'm sure it did'. See Isaiah 21, in which horsemen bring news of the fall of Babylon. Hendrix turned this into an apocalyptic freak-out that Dylan copied forever afterwards, so it is a shock to hear the bareness of the original – and its urgency.

The Ballad of Frankie Lee and Judas Priest (Dylan) 5.36
The longest song on the album and a tangled narrative in which the blasphemous shout barked out in Manchester's Free Trade Hall echoes in the name of this tempter-come-saviour. There is no instrumental break that adds to the implacable nature of the storytelling. 'Nothing is revealed', despite the moral helpfully tacked on at the end.

Drifter's Escape (Dylan) 2.49
The first song to be recorded. There is perhaps a side reference to Luke the Drifter, an alter ego adopted by Hank Williams. Joey Burns of Calexico enthuses over 'the looseness of delivery, the band's playing is just phenomenal. It's not overdone, it's not over-thought, it's just very organic and completely beautiful'.

SIDE TWO
Dear Landlord (Dylan) 3.18
Bob Dylan said in *Biograph*, '"Dear Landlord" was really just the first line. I woke up one morning with the words on my mind. Then I just figured, what else can I put to it?' It has been often speculated that this is Dylan's attempt to slough off the domineering nature of his manager who had pushed him to the limit with the 1966 world tour. Dylan had previously lodged at Albert Grossman's cottage on his Bearsville Estate and in an apartment in Gramercy Park. This is the last song recorded for the album. There is a hint of Ray Charles in the rolling piano style.

I Am A Lonesome Hobo (Dylan) 3.25
It is difficult not to read an autobiographical message here, especially given Dylan's previously reckless behaviour towards friends and lovers. Another song without a chorus where all the

(ostensible) emotion seems to have leeched into the lonesome harmonica that starts and ends the performance.

I Pity The Poor Immigrant (Dylan) 4.16
This song puts new words to the sonorous melody of Scottish ballad 'Tramps and Hawkers'. There are also multiple verbal parallels with the 26th chapter of Leviticus – 'I will make your heaven as iron and your earth as brass'. Dylan's voice is heartbreaking in its emotional nakedness, yet restrained. A deliberately quiet rendition.

The Wicked Messenger (Dylan) 2.05
Proverbs 13:16-17 has it that 'a wicked messenger falleth into mischief, but a faithful ambassador is health'. Dylan was seeking a biblical world view, beyond the temporal. 'Those melodies lack this traditional sense of time. As with the third verse of 'The Wicked Messenger' that opens it up, and then the time schedule takes a jump and soon the song becomes wider'. The Faces did a great, drunken version of this, that led to a sporadic working relationship with 'Honest' Ron Wood a few years down the line.

Down Along The Cove (Dylan) 2.26
The last song ended with the injunction 'if you can't bring good news, don't bring any' as this set the template for the next few years. A simple, piano-led blues that says nothing at all, but tunefully.

I'll Be Your Baby Tonight (Dylan) 2.39
This is Nashville, Jim Reeves style. Dylan later said, for *Biograph*, 'maybe it was tongue in cheek. It's just a simple song, a simple sentiment. I'd like to think this was written from a place where there's no struggle but I'm probably wrong. Sometimes you may be burning up inside but still do something that seems so cool and calm and collected. It could have been written from a baby's point of view, that's just occurred to me'. Nashville Skyline beckons. The language has got simple, no longer bare and resonant. Pete Drake's steel guitar lilts and Dylan even rhymes moon and spoon in a parody of tin pan alley songwriting. But the loving way in which Dylan sings is the final act of redemption on an album of spiritual renaissance.

NASHVILLE SKYLINE

US Release: 9 April 1969
UK Release:
CD Release: CBS CD 63601
Producer: Bob Johnston

Columbia KCS 9825 (stereo only)
CBS M/SPBG 63601 (mono/stereo)
CD Remaster/SACD Release: 512346 6
Running Time: 27.15

SIDE ONE: Girl From The North Country (with Johnny Cash); Nashville Skyline Rag; To Be Alone With You; I Threw It All Away; Peggy Day.

SIDE TWO: Lay Lady Lay; One More Night; Tell Me That It Isn't True; Country Pie; Tonight I'll Be Staying Here With You.

Bob Dylan: vocals, guitar, harmonica, **Norman Blake:** guitar, **Kenneth Buttrey**: drums, **Johnny Cash**: guitar, vocals, **Charlie Daniels:** guitar, **Pete Drake:** steel guitar, **Marshall Grant**: bass, **WS Holland**: drums, **Charlie McCoy**: bass, **Carl Perkins**: guitar, **Bob Wilson**: piano, **Bob Wootton**: guitar

It would be more than a year before Dylan travelled back to Tennessee and Columbia's Music Row Studios, to reconnect with the A-Team, and what they emerged with was an album that Owen Bradley would have been proud of, shockingly short and to the point, with lots of fine picking, Dylan crooning homilies, and none of that big city ambiguity. A masterpiece too, as it happens. 'Is it rolling, Bob?' Johnston asks, and yes indeed it was. Maybe even to Dylan's own surprise. 'The first time I went into the studio I had four songs. I pulled that instrumental one out. Then Johnny (Cash) came in and did a song with me. Then I wrote one in the motel. Pretty soon we had an album. I mean, we didn't go down with that in mind'. The working title was John Wesley Harding II, but that got changed. The two albums really could not be more different, in sound or tone, like conflating the pulpit and the bar-room.

Dylan the ventriloquist was singing in a higher register, less hillbilly or hellfire rock'n'roller, more sweet (indeed closer to home recordings back in Hibbing). 'When I stopped smoking, my voice changed. Speaking to *Mojo*, the great traditional singer Norma Waterson takes a professional view. 'When a singer has trouble with their voice, they try to sing from a different area. Here he is singing from his diaphragm for a change.

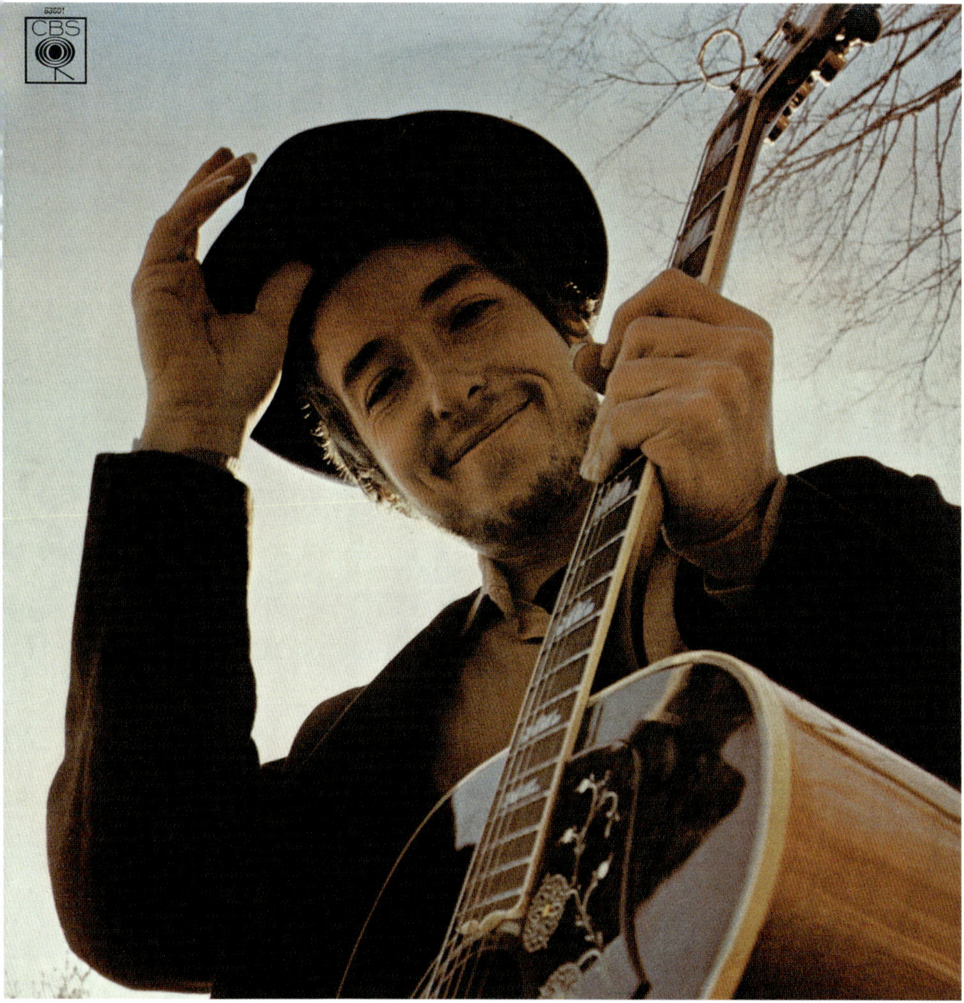
63601
CBS

As he later told *Rolling Stone*, the recording process was pain-free. 'We just take a song. I play it and everyone else just sort of fills in behind it. At the same time, there's someone in the control booth who's turning all those dials to where the proper sound is coming in. And then it's done.' All but one track was laid down – like the previous album – in three sessions, on 13, 14 and 17 February.

On the third day, Cash appeared in the studio and they spent the whole of 18 February duetting on all kinds of country standards, including Cash stalwart 'I Walk The Line'. Dylan's 'Girl From The North Country' was chosen to open the album. You can't get much more Nashville than a duet, let alone one with the Sun rocker turned national icon whose early support had kept Dylan on the label in the first place.

The front cover is a sly homage to Eric Von Schmidt on the album which forms part of the household clutter on *Bringing It All Back Home*. It is one of Elliott Landy's magnificent set of portraits of Dylan and his peers, later collected into a book (*Woodstock Vision*, 1994). Dylan is clutching one of George Harrison's guitars and wearing the jacket off *Blonde On Blonde* and the hat off *John Wesley Harding*.

The back cover is the Nashville skyline of the title. Dylan explains. 'Well, I always like to tie the name of the album in with some song. Or if not some song, some kind of general feeling. I think that just about fits because it was less in the way, and less specific than any of the other ones there. Certainly couldn't call the album Lay Lady Lay'. Overlaid is a poem by Cash entitled 'Of Bob Dylan', and comparing him implicitly to Walt Whitman – 'a source as leaves of grass, as stars' – as a poet who can rhyme the 'tick of time'.

Dylan later told Hubert Saal, 'these are the type of songs that I always felt like writing when I've been alone to do so. The songs reflect more of the inner me than the songs of the past. It's got a good spirit. Like a good door, a good house, a good car, a good road, a good girl. I feel like writing a lot more of them too'. Perhaps more revealingly, he also said that the new songs are 'easy to sing and there aren't too many words to remember'. Nine years later, on the cusp of a religious conversion, 'You had to read between the lines. I was trying to grasp something that would lead me on to where I thought I should be, and it didn't go nowhere – it just went down, down, down. I couldn't be anybody but myself, and at that point I didn't know it, or want to know it'. The album was released in mono (UK only), in stereo and in quadraphonic, slightly remixed, and includes an unfaded 'Country Pie', that is therefore some 15 seconds longer. It was the last UK Dylan album to be pressed in mono.

SIDE ONE
Girl From The North Country (with Johnny Cash) (Dylan) 3.44
Taken at a funereal pace, this reprise of a song from *Freewheelin'* sounds like a duet between master (Cash) and pupil (Dylan), with the two acoustic guitars playing off each other, as the voices, with Bob doing the descant.

Nashville Skyline Rag (Dylan) 3.14
Dylan's guitar figure could be taken virtually note for note from the much bootlegged outtake 'The Cough Song', laid down around 1963. Here it has a bluegrassy arrangement with each instrument showing off in turn.

To Be Alone With You (Dylan) 2.11
It sure does roll, if not rock. This song has an urgency maybe lacking elsewhere, and could easily be a Basement tape with Robbie Robertson-style guitar phrasing embroidering Dylan's vocal.

I Threw It All Away (Dylan) 2.26
A change of pace, and the closest thing to self-revelation here – 'take a tip from one who's tried' – as Dylan's voice is subject to heavenly reverb. As Nick Cave, another penitent, told *Mojo*, 'The production is so clean, fluid and uncluttered, and there's an ease and innocence to Dylan's voice in its phrasing, in its tone, that is in no Dylan song before or since. It's Mozart up against the wracked Beethoven of his other work. I can put this song on first thing in the morning or in the middle of a dark night and the song will serve me as a song should, lift me up, make me better, make me want to carry on'. For Laura Cantrell: 'he was writing a real country ballad, à la Merle Haggard, real straight, not a lot of metaphor but just really heartbroken'

Peggy Day (Dylan) 2.04
Like so many formulaic c&w songs, this is based on some clever word play, day and night. Dylan has not sounded so happy since some of his early talking blues.

SIDE TWO
Lay Lady Lay (Dylan) 3.22
Dylan's voice deepens for one of the key songs of his whole career. This is not as simple an album as it might appear on the surface. Here he adapts Blind Willie McTell's 'Rough Alley Blues' recorded in 1931 that includes the line 'I'll take you to my room and lay you 'cross my big brass bed'. In the summer of 1968 Dylan had been asked to write a song for the movie *Midnight Cowboy*, but missed the deadline. This adds an extra resonance; the Jon Voight character is doing it for the money. He then offered the song to the Everly Brothers but Phil turned it down, so he recorded it himself and earned himself a top ten single in the US.
As he told *Biograph*, 'the song came out of those first four chords. I filled it up with the lyrics, then the la la la type thing, well that turned into "Lay Lady Lay". Pete Drake played the steel guitar and that's what made it different. Clive Davis heard the song and wanted to release it as a single. I begged and pleaded with him not to. I never felt too close to the song, or thought it was representative of anything I do. He thought it was a hit single and he was right'. Kathryn Williams first heard it on a college jukebox. 'It was strange and smoky and sexy and I felt like I'd been seduced. It made me feel I could re-invent myself'. As Norma Waterson points out, 'it's a real working-class song', about an artisan with dirty clothes but clean hands.

One More Night (Dylan) 2.25
As artlessly simple as Hank Williams, and as artful a picture of a man abandoned. This has the archetypal Johnny Cash shuffle, a lover becomes a 'pal' that is certainly a long way from 'Sad Eyed Lady Of The Lowlands' and in this context – 'I had no idea what a woman in love would do' – a lot more realistic.

Tell Me That It Isn't True (Dylan) 2.43
Dylan told *Rolling Stone* that the song emerged 'completely different than I'd written it. It came out real slow and mellow. I had it written as sort of a jerky, kind of polka-type thing. I wrote it in F. I wrote a lot of songs on this new album in F. That's what gives it kind of a new sound. I try to be a little different on every album'.

Country Pie (Dylan) 1.40
Dylan might have seemed to be at odds with the rest of the 'hip' world – Gram Parsons aside – by plunging into country music but the world would follow with everyone from the Grateful Dead to the Eagles taking a detour off the highway down an old dirt road. And even the irony – throwing the pie back in your face could be either a pratfall or something more unpleasant – is ingrained in the Nashville template.

Tonight I'll Be Staying Here With You (Dylan) 3.25
A song about the joys of homecoming. Not that these sentiments were to last, for within a few short years Dylan was restless again, with a marriage running inexorably onto the rocks. It's only 'tonight' that he promises, anyway. Out on the road, this song took on a whole new lyric so that a version performed live at Maple Leaf Gardens, Toronto in 1975, now runs 'the changes that we run upon each others' heads/you come on to me like rolling thunder/I left my dreams on the river bed', but this doesn't invalidate the original. As Beck has it, 'for somebody who writes those great cinematic songs…to just toss out a good little tune – that's an aspect of Dylan I always really appreciated'.

OUTTAKES:
17 February 1969: 'One Too Many Mornings' (duet with Johnny Cash)
18 February 1969: 'One Too Many Mornings', '(Good Old) Mountain Dew', 'I Still Miss Someone', 'Careless Love', 'Matchbox', 'That's Alright (Mama)', 'Big River', 'Girl From The North Country', 'I Walk The Line', 'You Are My Sunshine', 'Ring Of Fire', 'Guess Things Happen That Way', '(Just) A Closer Walk With Thee', 'Blue Yodel No1', 'Blue Yodel No 6' (all of these duets with Johnny Cash, of which only a second take of 'One Too Many Mornings' made the official album)
Recorded at Columbia's Nashville Studios

SELF PORTRAIT

US Release: 8 June 1970
UK Release: June 1970
CD Release: Columbia 460112-2
Producer: Bob Johnston

Columbia C2X 30050
CBS 66250
Running Time: 74.17

Side One: All The Tired Horses; Alberta #1; I Forgot More Than You'll Ever Know; Days of 49; Early Mornin' Rain; In Search Of Little Sadie.

Side Two: Let It Be Me; Little Sadie; Woogie Boogie; Belle Isle; Living The Blues; Like A Rolling Stone.

Side Three: Copper Kettle (The Pale Moonlight); Gotta Travel On; Blue Moon; The Boxer; The Mighty Quinn (Quinn The Eskimo); Take Me As I Am (Or Let Me Go).

Side Four: Take A Message To Mary; It Hurts Me Too; Minstrel Boy; She Belongs To Me; Wigwam; Alberta #2.

Bob Dylan: vocals, guitar, piano

Byron F Bach: cello, **Brenton Banks**: synthesizer, violin, **George Binkley**: violin, **Norman Blake**: guitar, **David Bromberg**: guitar, dobro, **Albert W Butler**: saxophone, **Kenneth Buttrey**: drums, **Fred Carter Jr**: guitar, **Marvin D Chantry**: viola, **Ron Cornelius**: guitar, dobro, **Charlie Daniels**: guitar, dobro, **Rick Danko**: bass, **Dottie Dillard**: vocals, **Pete Drake**: slide guitar, **Dolores Edgin**: vocals, **Solie J Fott**: violin, **Bubba Fowler**: trombone, **Dennis A Good**: trombone, **Emanuel Green**, **Hilda Harris**: vocals, **Levon Helm**: drums, **Frederick Hill**, **Karl Himmel**: drums, **Garth Hudson**: organ, **Lillian Hunt**: viola, **Martin Katahn**: violin, **Doug Kershaw**: fiddle, **Millie Kirkham**: vocals, **Al Kooper**: guitar, keyboards, **Sheldon Kurland**: violin, **Charlie McCoy**: bass, marimbas, **Martha McCrory**: cello, **Barry McDonald**, **Richard Manuel**: piano, **Oliver Mitchell**, **Carol Montgomery**: vocals, **Bob Moore**: bass, **Gene A Mullins**: trombone, **Gary Van Osdale**: viola, **June Page**: vocals, **Rex Eugene Peer**: trombone, **Bill Pursell**: piano, **Robbie Robertson**: guitar, **Albertine Robinson**: backing vocals, **Alvin Rogers**: drums, **Maeretha Stewart**: backing vocals, **Anthony Terron**, **Bob Wilson**, **Stu Woods**: bass
Barry McDonald: arranger

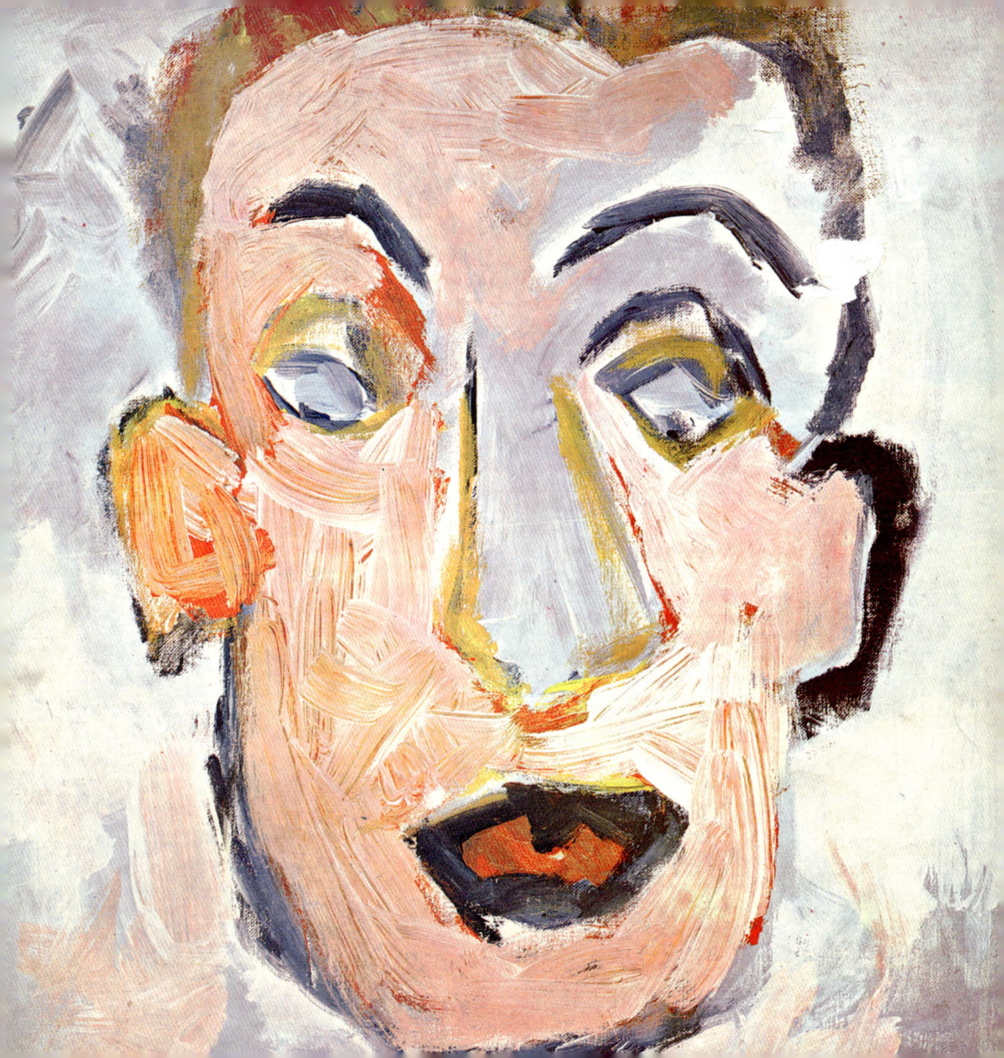

The second double album in Dylan's career is a patchwork drawn from three recording sessions in Nashville held in April and May 1969, and four more almost a year later in March 1970 home in New York. There were a further six sessions adding instrumental overdubs back in Music Row, hence the huge cast list above. The album was padded out with four songs taped with the Band, as they now were, live at the Isle of Wight Festival in August 1969. The public reaction to all this effort could be summed up by the opening to Greil Marcus's infamous *Rolling Stone* review, 'What is this sh*t?'

The album is currently subject to a spot of critical revision and seen as a precursor of a renewed interest in Americana led by post-punk bands rediscovering much the same musical heritage, such as Uncle Tupelo and Whiskeytown, whose one-time lead singer Ryan Adams described it as a '(expletive deleted) great album'. An encomium by Nigel Williamson appeared in *Uncut*'s 'Classic Albums Revisited' spot. The best tracks are 'modern Americana classics,' and as a personal scrapbook of the music that first turned Dylan on, 'it's a lot more audacious, witty and self-aware than David Bowie's *Pin-Ups* or John Lennon's nostalgic *Rock'n'Roll*'.

This is rather to gild the lily as the album certainly sounds far better than some described it at the time, but remains patchy. Heylin ties this down to a chronological context. Dylan at first sounds disinterested in the studio but gradually recovers his nasal whine and his appetite for music. Heylin thinks that the way the running order mixes up the syrupy early sessions and Dylan's tougher style, as it came back, plus the IOW tracks, half way between, is why the album works in patches, but not as a unified whole. Even so, when the material arrived back in Nashville for tidying up, McCoy is quoted in *Behind Closed Doors* to the effect that the tempos didn't really hold together real well and he wasn't real steady with the guitar. McCoy annotated the chord charts with arrows showing where Dylan speeded up or slowed down. Ken Buttrey's thought on first hearing the tapes was 'how weird', presumably that some of this stuff was to be given a commercial release.

Much the same applies to the enigmatic title that does not appear anywhere on the front or back cover, only on the record spine and on the discs. 'I did this portrait for the cover, I mean there was no title for that album, and I said "Well, I'm gonna call this album Self Portrait" and to me it was a joke'. But as Dylan adds, 'the way it turned out, the album became a concept record with a title that could be taken a ton of ways. Staring at the blank canvas for a while encouraged me to blindfoldingly make a picture that would paste all the songs together between the sleeves'. The result is a painting of his own face – clean shaven with jug ears –

created by Dylan in a faux naïve style (one hopes) much like the Chagall Jnr daub on the Band's *Music From Big Pink*. It is an image, like the album itself, that is deliberately blank, giving nothing away. The original vinyl pressing has some lovely photographs on the back and inside the double sleeve of Dylan in various pastoral settings, in a Nashville recording studio and live on the Isle of Wight singing to a battery of microphones. All this was lost in the minimal packaging of the single CD. There were lots of outtakes, including 'Universal Soldier' and an early 'Went To See The Gypsy', but none has yet slipped onto the bootleg market, perhaps thankfully.

Dylan has subjected the album to his own brand of revisionism. He said as early as 1974 'I didn't live with those songs for too long. They were just scraped together'. A decade on, he sounds even more cynical. '*Self Portrait* was a bunch of tracks we'd done all the time I'd gone to Nashville. We did that stuff to get a (studio) sound. So I just figured I'd put all this stuff together and put it out, my own bootleg record, so to speak. Also, I wasn't going to be anybody's puppet and I figured this record would put an end to that. I was just so fed up with all the people who thought I was nonsense.' Elsewhere, he was even more explicit. 'We released the album to get people off my back. That's the reason that album was put out, so people would just stop buying my records, and they did.'

He seems to have revised his views again, perhaps recognizing that the album was indeed an extremely good musical portrait as to where his mind and soul were at this point in time, not least the opening track.

SIDE ONE
All The Tired Horses (Dylan) 3.13
Dylan is too weary even to sing on his own opening track, leaving it to his perky female backing singers, augmented by Nashville strings at their most syrupy. Apt, as the one-line lyric is about a writing block. Never was the earlier line about a country music playing soft, with nothing to turn off, so dramatically embodied.

Alberta #1 (Dylan) 2.57
Heavily based on a traditional song: Greil Marcus damned this album as being 'characterized by borrowing, lifting and plagiarism', and still got the nod to write the sleeve notes to *The Basement Tapes* a few years later. Indeed, *Lyrics 1962-2001* prints only the words to 'Livin' The Blues' and 'Minstrel Boy'. The rest is silence.

I Forgot More Than You'll Ever Know (CA Null) 2.23
Could be Elvis with a head cold.

Days of 49 (Traditional) 5.27
Update of a song from the Gold Rush, like a Robert W Service poem put to music. A great performance, matched by some sparky piano and drums, both presumably added after the event, back in Nashville. 'Oh my goodness' Dylan exclaims half way through, and grunts at the end, almost orgasmically. The narrator – Tom Moore – is condemned to endlessly recycle his memories like the Ancient Mariner.

Early Mornin' Rain (Gordon Lightfoot) 3.34
A fine tribute to the man who supposedly influenced the sound of John Wesley Harding in what could be an outtake from that album, but isn't. Another New York track.

In Search Of Little Sadie (Dylan) 2.28
Delightful in its renewed urgency. It's based on the traditional song 'Badman's Blunder', and steps up a key each line, like an ever-rising staircase. It almost falls apart at the end – deliberately.

SIDE TWO
Let It Be Me (M Curtis/G Becaud/P Delano) 3.00
A re-run of the old standard, in his best Nashville Skyline voice. Unexpectedly touching, like a lullabye. Once again Dylan was ahead of the game: years later everyone from Rod Stewart to Linda Ronstadt would revisit classic songs from the 40s and 50s – Dylan did it first .

Little Sadie (Dylan) 2.00
Re-run of the song of much the same name, and at a quicker pace. In the great single album *Self Portrait* would have been, this would be an outtake of mild interest.

Woogie Boogie (Dylan) 2.07
An instrumental, taking Dylan back to his rock'n'roll roots. The squealing saxophone break takes it to another level.

Belle Isle (Dylan) 2.30
Sounds like a generic Irish love ballad. The orchestration is gorgeous, even if the language is deliberately antique and the vocal 'Oirish' and of uncertain pitch.

Living The Blues (Dylan) 2.43
Much more like it, tightly arranged and Dylan has a bounce in his voice completely at odds with the lyrics. Another quasi-Elvis pastiche.

Like A Rolling Stone (Dylan) 5.18
Live from Woodside Bay, on the Isle of Wight, a balmy evening in late August 1969, when you could have heard a pin drop during the hour Dylan was on stage. He might forget some of the words, miss a verse and add a somewhat inappropriate 'girl' every now and then to dilute the vitriol, but this newly compassionate version still kicks. Garth Hudson's swirling organ could be straight from May 1966, although the tempo is far more relaxed, and no-one is shouting out Judas anymore.

SIDE THREE
Copper Kettle (The Pale Moonlight) (Traditional) 3.35
This has much of the effortless sensuality and mystery that Van Morrison used to evoke at will. The background to all this is the illegal distilling of spirits, up in the Appalachians. Strangers not invited.

Gotta Travel On (Paul Clayton) 3.08
A reparation to an old friend from Greenwich Village who killed himself as the great Folk panic subsided.

Blue Moon (Richard Rodgers/Lorenz Hart) 2.30
Another super slow vocal as the sun sets over the Nashville skyline. Presley recorded this show tune. Doug Kershaw's fiddle steals the show here.

The Boxer (Paul Simon) (2.48)
Dylan duets with himself – his first known use of overdubbing his vocal – some say as a parody of Simon & Garfunkel, the mellifluous New York duo who first recorded and wrote this. Earlier, they had taken pleasure in taking the rise out of him when both were supposedly corralled by the same term, 'folk rock'. Game, set and match to Dylan after this deconstruction.

The Mighty Quinn (Quinn The Eskimo) (Bob Dylan) 2.49
Live from the Isle of Wight, this was the first official outing by their author of anything from *The Basement Tapes*. Manfred Mann had already hit the UK top 20 with their version. There is a real snap to Dylan's voice, the Band choruses lustily and Robbie Robertson lets fly on lead guitar through a haze of feedback. The exact mathematical genius – as Dylan once called him – at playing around the beat.

Take Me As I Am (Or Let Me Go) (B. Bryant) 3.06
Lonesome pedal steel and tinkling piano dominate this country weepie by a writer much favoured by the Everly Brothers. Dylan goes to the depth of his vocal range to squeeze out every ounce of emotion. It's the kind of performance that must have made his parents proud of him.

SIDE FOUR
Take A Message To Mary (B. and F. Bryant) 2.46
First a girly chorus announces the theme, a 'frontier man who lost his love when he turned bad', then Dylan takes on the Everly Brothers back catalogue and somehow pulls off this felon's lament. But could this cruise-ship crooner really be the man who wrote 'Gates Of Eden'?

It Hurts Me Too (Dylan) 3.16
This sounds extraordinarily similar to Big Bill Broonzy's 'When Things Go Wrong', and funnily enough Eric Burden and the New Animals covered this song well before Dylan wrote it.

Minstrel Boy (Dylan) (3.30
Again from the Isle of Wight with Dylan duetting with the massed voices of the Band – not to mention the sound of a coin being tossed. This could be *The Basement Tapes*, it's that loose and spontaneous, a hard trick to pull off with 150,000 people waiting on your every word.

She Belongs To Me (Dylan) 2.41
Once again from the Isle of Wight, a retread of the track from *Bringing It All Back Home*, and more urgent and driving even than the original. To those who had last seen him with the Hawks, he must have seemed that wolfish thin man's country cousin (or uncle). Nic Cohn captured the new Dylan perfectly.' He was a tubby little man. He wore a white suit, he had a curly beard and he didn't just walk, he ambled. Where once he'd been all angles and neuroses, he now seemed almost cosy.'

Wigwam (Dylan) 3.06
Dylan la-las over a brass arrangement straight out of James Last. Maybe this was something he hummed to his kids, and it certainly induces sleep. This is as provocative in its way in a world of progressive rock and meaningful lyrics as Dylan singing songs of freedom to white bigots, or playing wild rock'n'roll to members of the Young Communist League, but far less fun as a spectator sport. The biggest joke is that, as a 45, it almost made the US Top 50.

Alberta #2 (Dylan) 3.12
Reprise of Alberta #1 that concludes the album on a pleasant note without engaging the brain. Nice harmonica.

OUTTAKES
4 March 1969, Columbia Studio A, New York: 'Went To See The Gypsy'
3 May 1969: Music Row Studio, Nashville: 'Ring Of Fire', 'Folsom Prison Blues'

'Spanish Is The Loving Tongue', 'A Fool Such As I', on *Dylan*.

NEW MORNING

US Release: 21 October 1970
UK Release: October 1970
CD Release: Columbia 32267
Producer: Bob Johnston

Columbia KC 30290
CBS 69001
Running Time: 35.59

SIDE ONE: If Not For You; Day Of The Locusts; Time Passes Slowly; Went To See The Gypsy; Winterlude; If Dogs Run Free.

SIDE TWO: New Morning; Sign On The Window; One More Weekend; The Man In Me; Three Angels; Father Of Night.

Bob Dylan: vocals, acoustic guitar, electric guitar, organ, piano on 'Day Of The Locusts', 'Time Passes Slowly', 'Went To See The Gypsy', 'Winterlude', 'Sign On The Window', 'The Man In Me' and 'Father Of Night', **David Bromberg:** electric guitar, dobro, **Harvey Brooks:** electric bass **Ron Cornelius:** electric guitar, **Charlie Daniels:** electric bass, **Barry Feiten:** electric guitar, **Al Kooper:** organ, piano, electric guitar, French horn, **Russ Kunkel:** drums, **Billy Mundi:** drums, **Hilda Harris**, **Albertine Robinson** and **Maeretha Stewart:** background vocals

Self Portrait had been in the shops for only four months when another Dylan album hit the racks. The story behind its inception was full of twists and turns. In early 1970, Dylan was approached by the poet Archibald MacLeish to work on *Scratch*, a musical version of *The Devil and Daniel Webster*. He wrote three songs for this project – 'New Morning', 'Time Passes Slowly' and 'Father of Night' – before MacLeish pulled the plug and used older Dylan songs instead.

These became the fulcrum of the new album. To complete the project it took seven recording sessions at Columbia's studios B and E in New York, from 1 May to 4 June, plus a final unspecified session to produce an acceptable version of 'Day Of The Locusts'. The original plan was *Self Portrait II*, combining cover versions and new songs. An early track listing includes 'Mr Bojangles' and 'Ballad of Ira Hayes' – both resurrected on *Dylan* – and 'Tomorrow Is A Long Time', first recorded as a Witmark demo circa 1963. A studio session with George Harrison, consisting mainly of two old friends jamming on rock'n'roll classics was aborted.

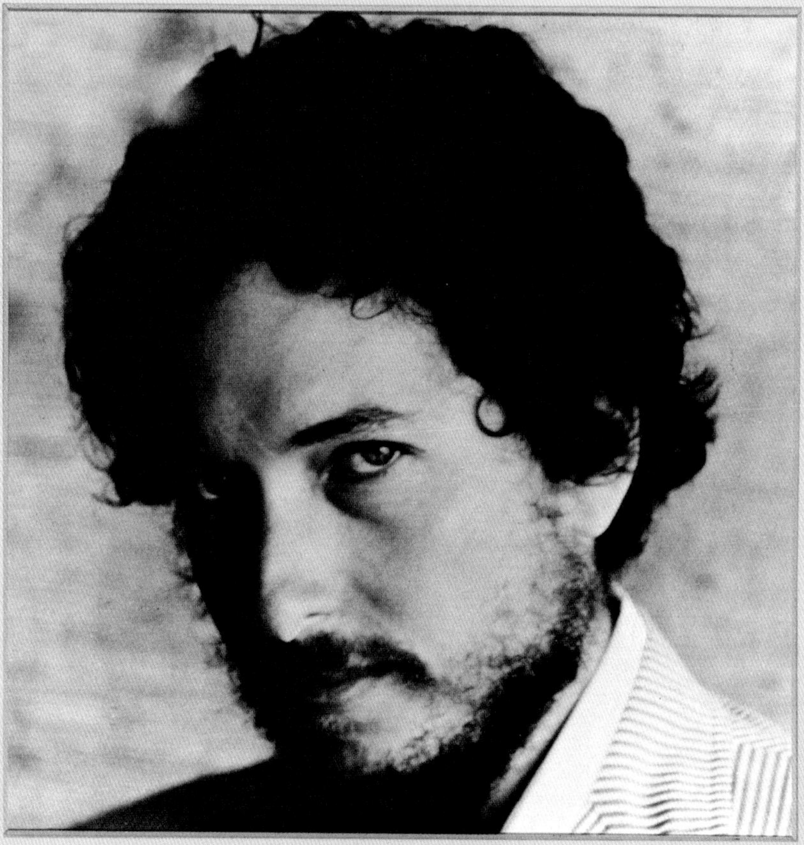

Dylan never worked with Bob Johnston again. Al Kooper complained that Bob changed his mind about every three minutes.

The album attracted ecstatic reviews, although the critical consensus now is that it is more of a holding operation, a far more genuine self portrait of a man happy in his domesticity, but with his creativity in limbo. The cover is all of a piece, a photograph by Len Seigler in which Bob glances up quizzically. The pose is mirrored on the back, a youthful Dylan standing with blues legend Victoria Spivey in the Cue Recording Studio New York, 2 March 1962. A mono version was issued in Brazil only.

SIDE ONE
If Not For You (Dylan) 2.39
Al Kooper's organ adds to the sense here of *Highway 61 Revisted* lite, with xylophone and pedal steel as sweetening. Billy Mundi from Rhinocerous plays drums. Dylan wrote this song 'thinking about my wife. It seemed simple enough, sort of Tex-Mex. It came off kind of folky'. He plays tricks with rhyme: 'blue', 'you', 'too' and this thank-you card to domestic romance sets the tone for the album. The song was later a hit single for Olivia Newton-John who responded to its essential perkiness, while George Harrison included a version on *All Things Must Pass*, even before *New Morning* got released.

Day Of The Locusts (Dylan) 3.57
Supposedly, ex-Byrd David Crosby was the man whose head was exploding, sitting next to Dylan as he waited to receive a Doctorate of Music at Princeton in June 1970. His feelings of unease are expanded in *Chronicles*. The title is a reference to the short novel by Nathaniel West, about the iniquities of Hollywood. Here it is academia that goes on trial.

Time Passes Slowly (Dylan) 2.33
A song of domestic harmony, or is it really about feeling trapped, as time slips away. Unusually, Sara visited the studios during recording. It is good to hear Dylan singing with such emotion again, the piano/guitar interplay is exhilarating with a simple drum pattern outlasting everything.

Went To See The Gypsy (Dylan) 2.49
A modern parable that could have fitted onto *John Wesley Harding*. Some say this is about meeting an ageing Elvis, but the Minnesota setting could suggest a memory from childhood.

Winterlude (Dylan) 2.21
Dylan waltzes, and sends up his new found faith in romance. A song about the delights of lazing around based on childhood memories from the frozen north.

If Dogs Run Free (Dylan) 3.37
Some fans react more violently to this than anything on *Self Portrait*. Maybe it's the female scatting like Les Swingles. Dylan's half-spoken rendition suggests a jazz club after hours, with tinkling piano and Django-style gypsy guitar. All very 50s.

SIDE TWO
New Morning (Dylan) 3.56
On early copies Bob Johnston is heard urging everyone 'Okay, here we go' at the start. This was excised on the CD, as was this title track on some early US copies that seems to rather lose the point. This is the theme song of the album as well as its title track with Dylan singing with joy in his voice – 'so happy just to be alive' – and great swirls of organ.

Sign On The Window (Dylan) 3.39
As one of the Black Crowes puts it, 'it's just Bob on the piano at first, then his band are trying to catch up. He's trying to figure out the world'. Others have read all kinds of things into this, like the 'dissolution of the counter-culture'. It certainly catches a mood of come-down at the end of the 60s dream that happened sometime in the early 70s. Dylan sings with passion; the pathos and uncertainty in his voice as he pictures the 'idyll' of a cabin in Utah speak volumes.

One More Weekend (Dylan) 3.09
A tough rock'n'roll song worthy of John Lennon's recreations at much the same time, and about seduction, not taking the kids fishing. The sexier side of a long- term relationship.

The Man In Me (Dylan) 3.07
Mojo described this song as 'all woozy organ and jake-leg drums, it's a stoned surrender to companionship but still cautious, like a junk yard dog offering a nervy paw'. Dylan la-las far more energetically than on 'Wigwam' and his voice is wonderfully expressive, ranging from macho pride to a sense of wonder, to vulnerability.

Three Angels (Dylan) 2.07
Inspired by a Christmas decoration outside a New York store, but whereas an early spoken rap like that on *Hezekiah Jones* was tongue in cheek, here Dylan seems to be serious. Whereas a song like 'Who's Your Lover Now' could tap effortlessly into surrealism with its picture of a strange hallucinatory world, here the details of street life seem truly without meaning. The organ sounds churchy and then a heavenly choir come in. Johnny Cash did lots of recitations like this but they have been airbrushed out of history.

Father Of Night (Dylan) 1.29
A hymn to God, no less, but with none of the genuine awe of, say, 'Dear Landlord', or of the real hellfire and damnation Dylan would release lyrically less than a decade on.

OUTTAKES:
1 May am 1970, Columbia Studio B, New York: 'Working On A Guru', 'If Not For You'
1 May pm 1970, Columbia Studio B, New York: 'Song To Woody', 'Mama You Been On My Mind', 'Don't Think Twice Its Alright', 'Yesterday', 'Just Like Tom Thumb's Blues', 'Da Doo Ron Ron', 'One Too Many Mornings', '(Ghost) Riders In The Sky', 'Cupid', 'All You Have To Do Is Dream', 'Gates Of Eden', 'I Threw It All Away', 'I Don't Believe You', 'Matchbox', 'Your True Love', 'Las Vegas Blues', 'Fishing Blues', 'Just Allow Me One More Chance', 'Rainy Day Women #12 & 35'
All of these are loose jams with George Harrison

'Lily Of The West (Flora)', 'Can't Help Falling In Love', 'Sara Jane', 'Ballad Of Ira Hayes', *Dylan*
'If Not For You', *Bootleg Series*.

MORE BOB DYLAN'S GREATEST HITS

US Release: 17 November 1971
UK Release: December 1971
CD Release: Columbia 467851 2

Double LP Col KG 31120
CBS 67239
Running Time: 36.12, 42.35

SIDE ONE: Watching The River Flow; Don't Think Twice It's All Right; Lay Lady Lay; Stuck Inside of Mobile With The Memphis Blues Again.

SIDE TWO: I'll Be Your Baby Tonight; All I Really Want To Do; My Back Pages; Maggie's Farm; Tonight I'll Be Staying Here With You.

SIDE THREE: She Belongs To Me; All Along The Watchtower; The Mighty Quinn (Quinn The Eskimo); Just Like Tom Thumb's Blues; A Hard Rain's A-Gonna Fall.

SIDE FOUR: If Not For You; It's All Over Now, Baby Blue; Tomorrow Is A Long Time; When I Paint My Masterpiece; I Shall Be Released; You Ain't Going Nowhere; Down in the Flood.

With his career in stasis, Dylan made three visits to the studio in 1971 on his own account, plus two days in November at the Record Plant laying down backing tracks for Allen Ginsberg. The earlier sessions seemed to be either to record a stand-alone single or to revive some of *The Basement Tapes* for this double-album retrospective. Programmed by Dylan himself and ignoring his first album completely, it flows to a logic of its own, ignoring chronology in favour of mood, with a few treats for committed fans. Many of these songs were anything but hits except in some celestial jukebox of the mind.

Three days in March spent at Blue Rock Studios in New York, produced by Leon Russell, resulted in 'Watching The River Flow', released as a single in June, and 'When I Paint My Masterpiece'. Then, after making a triumphant return to live performance at the Concert for Bangla Desh in August, Dylan and Happy Traum spent 24 September at Columbia Studio B, rehashing three of the *Basement* songs, plus an as yet unreleased 'Only A Hobo'. Finally that year, Dylan returned to Blue Rock in November with Ken Buttrey on drums and Ben Keith on steel guitar to record the urgent 'George Jackson', who was murdered by his prison guards, in both acoustic and big band form. This was rush released as a single that same month. Dylan

MORE
BOB
DYLAN
GREATEST
HITS

then took the next year off, working on his collected lyrics and generally chilling out.

So once again a *Greatest Hits* had to suffice. The photographs, taken by Barry Feinstein, are of Dylan in a blue denim jacket bathed in blue light at the Concert for Bangla Desh looking revived and refreshed. Clinton Heylin is surely right that the two new songs here 'have both stood the test of time better than anything on *New Morning*'. On the original vinyl UK edition 'Positively 4th Street and 'New Morning' replaced 'She Belongs To Me' and 'Its All Over Now Baby Blue'.

SIDE ONE
Watching The River Flow (Dylan) 3.37
Leon Russell: piano and bass, **Chuck Blackwell**: drums, **Joey Cooper**: guitar, **Don Preston**: guitar, **Carl Radle**: bass.
Previously a single produced by Leon Russell, Dylan confronts full-on his current state – 'What's the matter with me, I don't have a lot to say' – and places it provocatively as the opening track. The band is hot and he sings with spirit with some sizzling slide guitar, so it could be taken as a message that he was back on full power. No more 'Country Pie'. His wish to be 'back in the city' was soon to be fulfilled, but with the unexpected consequence of finding A J Weberman going through his dustbin.

Don't Think Twice, It's All Right (Dylan) 3.39
From *Freewheelin'*.

Lay Lady Lay (Dylan) 3.20
From *Nashville Skyline*.

Stuck Inside of Mobile With The Memphis Blues Again (Dylan) 7.09
From *Blonde On Blonde*.

SIDE TWO
I'll Be Your Baby Tonight (Dylan) 2.42
From *John Wesley Harding.*

All I Really Want To Do (Dylan) 4.04
From *Another Side Of Bob Dylan.*

My Back Pages (Dylan) 4.24
From *Another Side Of Bob Dylan.*

Maggie's Farm (Dylan) 3.54
From *Bringing It All Back Home.*

Tonight I'll Be Staying Here With You (Dylan) 3.21
From *Nashville Skyline.*

Positively 4th Street
Released as a single in 1965, this was omitted from the CD issue, although there was plenty of space for it – it appears on the US *Greatest Hits*. This means that UK fans wanting to find this on CD have to go to *The Best of Bob Dylan Vol 2*, *The Essential Bob Dylan*, or track down *Masterpieces*. Dylan placed it here for a purpose, between a song of simple domesticity and of sexual possession.

SIDE THREE
She Belongs To Me (Dylan) 2.50
From *Bringing It All Back Home.*

All Along The Watchtower (Dylan) 2.33
From *John Wesley Harding.*

The Mighty Quinn (Quinn The Eskimo) (Dylan) 2.48
Not the original *Basement Tape*, but the live version taped at the Isle of Wight. From *Self Portrait* and the only track from that album to make the cut here. When some of what went down in Big Pink in 1967 was finally given an official release in 1975, this song was omitted, although a giant Eskimo dominates the front cover. As to Dylan, 'I don't know what it was about, I guess it was some kind of a nursery rhyme' (*Biograph* notes).

Just Like Tom Thumb's Blues (Dylan) 5.29
Not the live B-side, for which fans would have to buy *Masterpieces*, but the studio version from *Highway 61 Revisited*.

A Hard Rain's A-Gonna Fall (Dylan) 6.51
From *Freewheelin'*.

SIDE FOUR
If Not For You (Dylan) 2.40
From *New Morning*.

It's All Over Now, Baby Blue (Dylan) 4.17
From *Bringing It All Back Home*, replaced by 'New Morning' on the UK vinyl edition.

Tomorrow Is A Long Time (Dylan) 3.02
Previously unreleased, this is live from New York Town Hall, 1963. Dylan reckoned Elvis's version of this to be the best ever cover of any of his songs, and laid down a take for the *New Morning sessions*, but nothing could beat the tense stillness of this early rendition. Samantha Parton of the Be Good Tanyas speaking to Mojo about this track said that she was inspired by what Dylan draws from a traditional song. 'All the disturbing, mysterious qualities, the sickness and danger. He's like a shaman, reaching outside this world into the nest, and bringing things back for us to wonder at.'

When I Paint My Masterpiece (Dylan) 3.23
Leon Russell: piano and bass, **Chuck Blackwell:** drums, **Joey Cooper:** guitar, **Don Preston:** guitar, **Carl Radle:** bass.
Previously unreleased, and produced by Leon Russell, the Band had already recorded this on Cahoots. It was probably being on the road with them that inspired this traveller's tale of being on the road. This is the Dylan of old, witty, showing off his brilliance by rhyming 'gondola' with 'coca cola', and looking forward to pulling off a great work of art that would turn out to be *Blood On The Tracks* – although it is a pipe dream that in this life 'everything's going to be smooth, like a rhapsody'.

I Shall Be Released (Dylan) 3.05
Happy Traum: bass, banjo, second guitar, vocal harmony.
Dylan's first official recording of one of his finest songs from *The Basement Tapes* or indeed anywhere. This was one of the tracks specially recorded in September 1971. It is more matter of fact than the original, less mysterious. It lacks Richard Manuel's keening harmonies. Sparkling instrumental interplay all the same. The Band had already recorded this for their debut album.

You Ain't Going Nowhere (Dylan) 2.46
Happy Traum: bass, banjo, second guitar, vocal harmony.
Another of the 'new' and refried *Basement Tapes*. This has been subtly rewritten to incorporate some friendly barbs against Roger McGuinn – 'pull up your tent' – who had recorded this with the country Byrds on *Sweetheart of the Rodeo*.

Down in the Flood (Dylan) 2.48
Happy Traum: bass, banjo, second guitar, vocal harmony.
Another *Basement Tape* retread, perhaps referring to the Great Flood that Noah survived, or the one that hit the South and is recreated jokily in the movie *O Brother Where Art Thou.*

PAT GARRETT AND BILLY THE KID: ORIGINAL SOUNDTRACK RECORDING

US Release: 13 July 1973
UK Release: November 1973
CD Release: Columbia 32098
Producer: Gordon Carroll

Columbia KC 32460
CBS 69042
Running Time: 35.25

SIDE ONE: Main Title Theme (Billy); Cantina Theme (Workin' For The Law); Billy 1; Bunkhouse Theme; River Theme.

SIDE TWO: Turkey Chase; Knockin' On Heaven's Door; Final Theme; Billy 4; Billy 7.

Bob Dylan: vocal, guitar, **Stephen Bruton:** electric guitar, **Byron Berline:** fiddle, vocals, **Fred Catz:** cello, **Sammy Creason:** drums, **Carl Fortina:** harmonium, **Gary Foster:** flute, **Carol Hunter:** guitar, backing vocals, **Priscilla Jones:** vocals, **Jim Keltner:** drums, **Russ Kunkel:** tambourine, vocals, **Bruce Langhorn:** guitar, **Roger McGuinn:** guitar, **Ted Michel:** cello, **Brenda Patterson:** vocals, **Terry Paul:** bass, vocals, **Booker T:** bass, **Mike Uttley:** organ, **Donna Weiss:** vocals

1973 saw Dylan writing his first film soundtrack. The first recording session took place on location at the CBS studio in Mexico City, through the night of 20 January. More productive were two sessions the next month at Burbank Studios in California. It was from these recordings in February that producer Gordon Carroll compiled the bulk of both the album and the movie soundtrack of which there are now three versions, the original movie, the director's cut and a new cut just issued in the US at the time of writing. As the *Hollow Horn* anthology puts it, 'this album would mark the start of a renewed urgency in Dylan's studio work. The circulating outtakes form a semi-continuous work tape, and detail a fascinating insight into Dylan's informal approach to studio recording'. Another review talks of the music as having a dusty, border town acoustic charm.

Dylan's input came almost by chance. 'I wasn't doing anything. Rudy sent me the script and I read it and I liked it and we got together and he needed a title song'. His first attempt was called 'Goodbye Holly', a raucous two-verse song about death. What was really needed, though, was a lament to counterpoint the movie action. Dylan thought it over-ambitious to expect one song to carry an entire picture but he came up with the goods, if for no other reason than to annoy Peckinpah's arranger. 'This guy Jerry Fielding's gonna go nuts when he hears this.'

The keynote of the album is restraint, as befits strong and silent men who let their guns do the talking. The front cover is to match, simple text on a white background. The back cover is a still from the movie, not Dylan playing 'Alias', but Kris Kristofferson with a shotgun pressed to his chest and praying for mercy. It is a situation that those unfortunate enough to encounter Kristofferson's set at the 1970 Isle of Wight Festival would still wish upon him. There is also a cast list in very small type.

SIDE ONE
Main Title Theme (Billy) (Dylan) 6.05
Booker T: bass, **Bruce Langhorne, Bob Dylan**: guitars, **Russ Kunkel**: tambourine.
Instrumental for 12 nylon strings. Dylan strums, Langhorne picks out a melody line while the tambourine is like a cicada in the grass.

Cantina Theme (Workin' For The Law) (Dylan) 2.57
Roger McGuinn, Bob Dylan, Bruce Langhorne: guitars, **Russ Kunkel**: bongos.
Lots of moody bongos and a stately, almost sinister guitar instrumental.

Billy 1 (Dylan) 3.55
Booker T: bass, **Bruce Langhorne**: guitar, **Dylan**; vocals, harmonica.
'There's guns across the river', Dylan sings urgently, warning the kid that the law is out to get him and they want to dispatch him to Boot Hill. His harmonica leads into the song and provides punctuation, grounded by solid electric bass.

Bob Dylan / Soundtrack

PAT GARRETT & BILLY THE KID

Bunkhouse Theme (Dylan) 2.16
Carol Hunter, Bob Dylan: guitars.
There seems to be three guitars rather than two here, duelling in a relaxed kind of way.

River Theme (Dylan) 1.29
Booker T: bass, Bruce Langhorn, **Bob Dylan:** guitars, **Donna Weiss, Priscilla Jones, Byron Berline:** vocals
Wordless vocals, like a lament.

SIDE TWO
Turkey Chase (Dylan) 3.34
Byron Berline: fiddle, **Roger McGuinn aka Jolly Roger:** banjo, **Bruce Langhorne:** acoustic guitar, **Bob Dylan:** rhythm guitar, **Booker T:** bass
A bluegrass strut with chuckling banjo and country fiddle courtesy of Byron Berline. Bruce Langhorne and Roger McGuinn are just two familiar names among the musical cast list here.

Knockin' On Heaven's Door (Dylan) 2.32
Terry Paul: bass, **Roger McGuinn:** guitar, **Jim Keltner:** drums, **Bob Dylan:** vocal, guitar, **Carol Hunter, Donna Weiss, Brenda Patterson:** vocals, **Carl Fortina:** harmonium
There is a lot of reverb on Bob's voice and a funereal feel to the song, spot on in this context, halfway between life and death. Kris Kristofferson remembers Dylan watching the rushes in Mexico, 'it was one of the reels that came back from the lab f*cked up. The picture was getting dark. But the result – the spirit soared. I know Sam never liked it. Jerry Fielding didn't like it either. Thought it was too literal'.

    This haunting song was written specifically for the charged scene in which the town sheriff lies dying in the arms of his wife.

    Out of this came Dylan's best and most resonant song – and performance – for years. 'I wrote it for Slim Pickens and Katy Jurardo. I just had to do it.' For his pains, Bob had a hit single on his hands, and Eric Clapton later memorably covered it. There are subtexts to both versions, Dylan's abdication as a prophet of the counter-culture and Clapton's immersion in hard drugs that he was battling at the time. Rachid Taha remembers being a teenager when the song came out, 'and I didn't speak a word of English, nor did any of my friends, but we could all sing "knock, knock, knocking", we didn't know what it meant, but we liked the sound of it'.

Final Theme (Dylan) 5.24
Roger McGuinn, Carol Hunter, Bob Dylan: guitars, **Donna Weiss, Brenda Patterson**: vocals, **Terry Paul**: bass, **Gary Foster**: recorder, flute, **Carl Fortina**: harmonium, **Fred Katz, Ted Michel**: cellos, **Terry Paul**: bass, **Jim Keltner**: drums
A very musically rich track, led by flute and mellifluous female voices and a low drone from the cellos. A sense of time trickling away that would have made it a perfect way to end the album, too. Instead, we have two more Dylan vocals.

Billy 4 (Dylan) 5.03
Bob Dylan: vocals and guitar, **Terry Paul**: bass
Dylan sings with real emotion. These are the lyrics that appear in the latest songbook with some variations, ie 'haunted' becomes 'shot down' and it is 'gypsy queens' not guitars that now play his finale, but the occasional chorus of 'Billy you're so far away from home' is retained – part celebration, part valediction. No lyric book could reproduce the melancholy of Dylan's rendition here.

This is the only track on the album drawn from the sessions taped down in Mexico City. The film soundtrack contains more, most notably 'Billy Surrenders', whose genesis Chet Flippo reported for *Rolling Stone*. Dylan 'loped into a chunky, accelerating rhythm, trading off his licks with Mike Uttley (on organ). Both were laughing and weaving and daring and challenging each other. Dylan and Terry Paul started a hypnotic "la la" lyric that grew more manic as they stood head to head and urged each other on'. On and off set male power games, so valued by the bloodthirsty Peckinpah, were not just confined to gun play.

Billy 7 (Dylan) 2.08
Jim Keltner: drums, **Roger McGuinn**: guitar, **Terry Paul**: bass, **Bob Dylan**: vocal, guitar
Much slower, like an echo, possibly from beyond the grave. Dylan's vocal plumbs the depths and the percussion echoes thunder, or maybe gunfire.

OUTTAKES:
20 January 1973, Mexico: 'Billy 1' (x2), 'Turkey', 'Tom Turkey', 'Billy Surrenders', 'And He's Killed Me Too', 'Goodbye Holly' (x2), 'Pecos Blues' (x2), 'Billy 4', 'Wild Track'
February 1973, Burbank Studios, California: 'Knockin' On Heaven's Door', 'Sweet Amarillo', 'Knockin' on Heaven's Door 2', 'Knockin' On Heaven's Door 3', 'Final Theme' (x2), 'Rock Me Mama' (x2), 'Billy version 7' (x2) 'Cold Turkey', 'Turkey Trot', 'Final Theme 3', 'Ride Billy Ride'

FILM SCORE:
Pat Garrett and Billy the Kid (original movie) released May 1973:
'Main Theme (Billy)', 'Cantina Theme', 'Billy', 'Billy Surrenders', 'River Theme', 'Billy 1, Bunkhouse Theme', 'Knockin' On Heaven's Door', 'Turkey Chase', 'Final Theme', 'Knockin' On Heaven's Door (instrumental)', 'Billy 4'

Pat Garrett and Billy the Kid (Director's Cut) released 1988:
'Main Theme (Billy)', 'Cantina Theme', 'Billy Surrenders', 'River Theme', 'Billy 1. Bunkhouse Theme', 'Billy', 'Knockin' On Heaven's Door (instrumental), 'Turkey Chase', 'Final Theme', 'Billy'

Video (MGM/UA UMV 10159) issued in 1982, deleted in favour of revised version with less incidental music (Warner PES 80159, 1991).

DVD 2-disc special edition with 2005 reconstruction of Director's Cut version (115 minutes) and 1988 Turner Preview version (122 minutes)
Released January 2006, Warner Home Video 65165
Region 1 format (US and Canada only).

DYLAN

US Release: 16 November 1973   **Columbia PC 32747**
UK Release: **CBS 69049**
CD Release: Columbia CD 32286 UK only,   **Running Time:** 32.49 (approx)
full title *Dylan (A Fool Such As I)*. Highly
sought after by collectors
CDs were issued in mainland Europe only in 1991, but not in the US
Producer: Bob Johnston

SIDE ONE: Lily Of The West; Can't Help Falling In Love; Sarah Jane; The Ballad Of Ira Hayes.

SIDE TWO: Mr Bojangles; Mary Ann; Big Yellow Taxi; A Fool Such As I; Spanish Is The Loving Tongue.

Bob Dylan: vocal, guitar, harmonica. Backing musicians, see *Self Portrait* and *New Morning*

Maybe this should be retitled *Bob Johnston's Revenge*. What is most astonishing about this album is that at one point Dylan seriously intended some of these tracks for release. They certainly provided Columbia with some blackmail material a few years down the tracks. Even so, Dylan seemed more amused than affronted. These were songs, 'not to be used. I thought it was well understood. They were just to warm up for a tune. I didn't think it was that bad really! (laughs)'

Rolling Stone's review was damning, an album 'guaranteed to net only horselaughs'. Giving it the title *Dylan*, as if it were his definitive statement, merely added insult to injury. When Dylan returned to Columbia he quietly demanded its deletion, the only album to suffer this treatment other than what many think is the equally wretched *Down In The Groove* although it did surface briefly as a UK-only CD.

However, as the more fair-minded have pointed out, Dylan alone is not to blame. Michael Gray's review for *Let It Rock* nailed it at the time, 'basically the album has been given an horrendous re-mix by some anonymous apeman who plainly has the hots for all the girls in the chorus'. On 'Lily Of The West', a harpsichord is reduced to 'an irritating little tinkle at the edge of one speaker'. And Gray does not exaggerate one iota when he describes the hatchet job on 'Sarah Jane'. The song 'has a very muggy, boomy, indistinct sound, yet the girls come in as clear as a bell. You can almost hear the click as they're switched on at the start of each chorus'.

As for the cover of this album – now far more rare and sought after on CD than on vinyl – both front and back are versions of the same photograph by Al Clayton, with Dylan bent forward in contemplation. Or maybe about to throw up having heard the record. On the front – a serigraph by Richard Kenerson – this seems to have had paint tipped down it, and on the back it is marbled like an old book, for which John Berg takes credit. Both have a certain mausoleum-like quality, as if Dylan has been embalmed. Given the circumstances in which this album was both issued and then deleted, that would seem extremely appropriate.

SIDE ONE

Lily Of The West (Davies/Peterson) 3.44
Jog trot rhythm with Dylan singing an ornate ballad of the old west. A girl chorus echo the chorus. Inconsequential.

Can't Help Falling In Love (Creatore/Peretti/Weiss) 4.17
Made famous by Elvis, Dylan might be singing this in his sleep. There is something stately in the way he croons these platitudes and actually imbues them with some meaning. The backing track is strictly painting by numbers.

Sarah Jane (Dylan) 2.43
The one Dylan original here, and absent from his book of collected lyrics. By any critical standard, this is woeful, like a witless parody. The backing singers are indeed louder than Bob, as suggested by Michael Gray.

The Ballad Of Ira Hayes (LaFarge) 5.08
Gather round and hear this tale about a 'brave young Indian' who raised Old Glory on a distant battlefield during World War II, then succumbed to whisky, and try not to fall asleep before the end of the song. Beyond parody.

DYLAN

Mr. Bojangles
The Ballad Of Ira Hayes
A Fool Such As I
Spanish Is The Loving Tongue
Mary Ann
Big Yellow Taxi
Sarah Jane
Lily Of The West
Can't Help Falling In Love

SIDE TWO
Mr Bojangles (Walker) 5.31
Jerry Jeff's classic is given a treatment much like those albums that used to be sold in bargain shops of unknown session men covering top 20 hits for a pittance. Again the backing singers outweigh Dylan, like a midget overwhelmed.

Mary Ann (Traditional) 2.40
'Oh fare thee well, my own true love' this starts, and it starts well, then the singing crones muscle in, Dylan sings as if on a see-saw – it makes one quite seasick to listen – and the whole thing drags out its allotted span.

Big Yellow Taxi (Joni Mitchell) 2.12
An emotionless run through a paeon to ecology, set to rinky-dink organ – 'Like A Rolling Stone' this is not, and if this is Al Kooper he should be ashamed. This is so bad, you really can't blame the mix, bad as it is. Joni would have the chorus girls here shot for less.

A Fool Such As I (Abner) 2.41
At least this shows signs of life – a Nashville Skyline outtake that certainly has all the hallmarks of a warm-up track, and the musicians sound interested for a change on this wretched album.

Spanish Is The Loving Tongue (Traditional) 4.13
Dylan's voice is properly up in the mix, he sings over finger-picked guitar stylings like the kind of waiter who serenades you over dinner hoping for a gratuity. Then the backing singers drown him out and the only response is hilarity.

PLANET WAVES

US Release: 17 January 1974

UK Release:
CD Release: Columbia 32154
There is also a quad remix.
Producer: Bob Dylan, Robbie Robertson and Rob Fraboni (all 3 uncredited), engineered by Rob Fraboni

Asylum 7E 1003
Later reissued by Columbia in 1982 as PC 37637
Island ISLP 9261
CD Remaster/SACD Release: Columbia 512356-6
Running Time: 42.12

SIDE ONE: On A Night Like This; Going, Going, Gone; Tough Mama; Hazel; Something There Is About You; Forever Young.

SIDE TWO: Forever Young; Dirge; You Angel You; Never Say Goodbye; Wedding Song.

Bob Dylan: vocals, guitar, harmonica, **Rick Danko:** bass, **Levon Helm:** drums, **Garth Hudson:** organ, accordion, **Richard Manuel:** piano, drums, **Robbie Robertson:** guitar

In June 1973, Dylan visited the office of his music publishers in New York to lay down a demo of a new song, 'Forever Young'. It was the first sign that Bob had rediscovered his inspiration and was working towards a new album for his new label, Asylum. Two more songs were copyrighted that month and he completed work on the lyrics of a new album in October. Dylan was in the process of moving west to Malibu and this seemed to jolt him into memories of his youth in Minnesota. When word leaked out that the Band were to record with him, the excitement level mounted, as indicated by the huge demand for tickets for a subsequent US tour.

Dylan and the Band, minus drummer Levon Helm, entered the Village Recorder in West LA on 2 November that same year, to 'get set up and get a feel for the studio'. According to *Hollow Horn*, three outtakes circulate of the first time they had got together as a unit since the Isle of Wight four years before a dishevelled 'House Of The Rising Sun', an instrumental 'Crosswind

PLANET WAVES

MOONGLOW

CAST-IRON SONGS & TORCH BALLADS

Jamboree' and a formative take of 'Nobody Cept You". In fact, a finished take of the last and of 'Never Say Goodbye' both made the final cut.

The working title of the forthcoming album was Ceremonies Of The Horsemen, a line from 'Love Minus Zero/No Limit': maybe this pawn still held a grudge against Columbia Records. According to the sleeve, the sessions stretched over 5, 6 and 9 November with many of the songs first takes. Of the Band, only Robertson turned up on 9 November, when a final take of 'Dirge' was laid down, Dylan arrived alone the following day to record 'Wedding Song'. There is no named producer but the sleeve thanks Robbie for special assistance, so in effect it was him. He is quoted on *Biograph*: 'we were rehearsing to go on tour and everything was very hectic. We went in and knocked off the album. We had played so much together that I don't think it occurred to any of us that this was the first time we'd actually recorded an album as Bob Dylan and the Band'.

The result is one of Dylan's most emotionally complex albums, one which Michael Gray had described as 'nostalgia soaked but genuinely beautiful, with an eerie, compelling quality which marks this as unique'. And one, like fine wine, that improves with ageing.

The front cover is a weird drawing of three figures, plus an anchor, a heart and the CND symbol, plus the captions 'Moonglow' and 'Cast-Iron Songs & Torch Ballads'. Nothing is explained, including the enigmatic title, in which waves could be either a noun or a verb. The back cover includes a roughly written account, in his own scrawly hand, of Bob's mythical life. Torn out of his tour journal, it populates the places of his childhood with literature and myth: 'Duluth – where Baudelaire lived and Goya cashed in his chips, where Joshua brought the house down'. By turns sexual, replete with circus imagery and allusive, it is like a dip into Dylan's subconscious, and is in tune with the album's theme of retrospection: 'yeah the ole days are gone forever and the new ones ain't far behind'. The vinyl album had as an insert, a copy of part of the back cover printed on gold. Richard Manuel is spelt Manual, doubtless some in-joke.

The album came out both in stereo and in quadraphonic, a short-lived craze that results in six tracks being issued in a significantly different mix. Of far more significance was the last-minute replacement with one song of love and desperation to Sara – 'Nobody 'Cept You' – with another, 'Wedding Song'. The supplanted track, that many think is by far the superior of the two, was resurrected on the *Bootleg Series*, and in *Lyrics 1962-2001* – as close to an official canon as exists.

.

SIDE ONE
On A Night Like This (Dylan) 2.56
Dylan told *Biograph* that 'I wrote this in New York. I think this comes off as like a drunk man who's temporarily sober. This is not my type of song. I just did it to do it'. It makes a perfect opening track, Bob's eager rendition of a meeting with an old girl friend, building sparks on a cold night, the Band entwining around him like a snake. This is a more muted collaboration than the days of '66, but that endearing roughness is still in place.

Going, Going, Gone (Dylan) 3.26
The tempo slows to a funeral march, stately and serious. A song about letting go, maybe even about suicide. Dylan sings with desperation, immersing himself in the negative emotion. Tim Riley describes perfectly how master technician Robertson 'makes his guitar entrance choke as if a noose had suddenly tightened around its neck; you get the feeling these guys could shadow Dylan in their sleep'.

Tough Mama (Dylan) 4.13
These songs share some of the unknowableness of the best of *The Basement Tapes*, that Dylan does nothing to dispel in his rare interviews. Jonathon Cott asked him about the line 'Sweet Goddess/Born of a blinding light and a changing wind', which probably is best left unexplained. The poetry suffices. Bob answered 'That's the mother and father, the yin and yang. That's the coming together of destiny and the fulfilment of destiny'. That's clear then! This is an extremely sexy song to a woman, or maybe many women, a sister under the skin with the 'furious girls with garters' of the sleeve note. Dylan takes up Robert Graves' injunction to all true poets to worship and surrender himself to the White Goddess, the matriarchal principle throughout history. And Garth Hudson blows up a storm.

Hazel (Dylan) 2.47
Another song to a soiled goddess. The Band sound celestial, and Dylan's harmonica adds to the aural richness. His voice implores and rages and seduces. 'Just Like A Woman' reborn.

Something There Is About You (Dylan) 4.41
Dylan was only six when he moved from Duluth to Hibbing, but those early years spent on the shoreline of the Great Lakes entered his soul. Here he exorcizes 'phantoms of my youth', sparked off – of course – by a woman. This is Wordsworth put to music, and the Band enter the sublime, spurred on by Dylan's voice and harmonica.

Forever Young (Dylan) 4.54
From the Lake Poets to William Blake in *Songs Of Innocence* mode (Bob does the lacerating prophet mode too, but not in this song). Manuel's peerless piano playing comes to the fore here.

Dylan reminisced for *Biograph*: 'I wrote (it) in Tucson. I wrote it thinking about one of my boys and not wanting to be too sentimental. The lines came to me, they were done in a minute. I certainly didn't intend to write it – I was going for something else, the song wrote itself'. The moment of creation came in early 1972 when the family were spending the winter on a ranch he had just bought near Phoenix. The subject was probably his son Jakob, born in December 1969, who later formed the Wallflowers.

SIDE TWO
Forever Young (Dylan) 2.47
Same song, different tone. If the first version was a prayer, then this is a hoedown.

Yet another version appears on Biograph, the original demo laid down solo by Dylan in New York and sung straight into an ageing reel-to-reel tape recorder.

Matthew Zuckerman makes an interesting comparison with the Talmudic blessing, that is read after a circumcision, with lines addressed to the boy child thus: 'May your heart be filled with intuition/and your words filled with insight'. Allen Ginsberg reckoned that this song should be sung every morning by every child in every school in every country: Roddy of Idlewild added that 'Forever Young' is Dylan's national anthem.

Dirge (Dylan) 5.34
Acoustic guitar picking and piano, just Robbie and Bobby, and an autopsy on living flesh. Riley reckons the sound is 'brittle, spooked', Heylin that Dylan has discovered 'his most biting post-accident vocal for this withering look at love and fame'. The only false note is the title, that is superfluous whether taken as death song or tuneless moan. This is a song full of horrid pain, and the human response is to look away, like from a car crash.

You Angel You (Dylan) 2.52
Bob Dylan is dismissive in *Biograph*. 'I might have written this at one of the sessions, probably on the spot, standing in front of the mike. It sounds to me like dummy lyrics'. One thing you certainly don't expect when Dylan and the Band get together is polish – the Eagles they are not. But they sure do rock 'n' roll, with an emphasis on the latter. Lyrically it is an antidote to the bitterness of the previous song. It would be all too human if the same woman inspired both.

Never Say Goodbye (Dylan) 2.50
This seems again a return to Duluth, in mood at least, moonlight on the frozen lake. And this enigmatic lyric might well refer to Dylan's daughter – or not.

Wedding Song (Dylan) 4.41
John Landau complained of hearing Dylan's shirt buttons rattle against his acoustic guitar but that is part of the charm. Suddenly naked, with the Band notable by their absence, this ends a mysterious album with a song that is perhaps a little too straightforward. Heylin accuses the words of 'slipshod sentimentality' then admits that Dylan's vocal intensity redeems them. Like the later 'Sara', this sounds like a man pleading for something he already knows that he has lost.

OUTTAKES:
June 1973, Ram's Horn Music, New York: 'Forever Young'
2 November 1973, Village Recorder Studios, California: 'House Of The Rising Sun', 'Crosswind Jubilee' (instrumental), 'Nobody Cept You', all with the Band

'Forever Young' alternative version, *Biograph*
'Nobody 'Cept You', *Bootleg Series*.

BEFORE THE FLOOD

US Release: 20 June 1974

UK Release: Island IDBD1
CD Release: Columbia 22137
Recording Engineers: Phil Ramone/Rob Fraboni, mixing engineers Rob Fraboni/Nat Jeffrey

Asylum AB 201
Later reissued by Columbia as KC 37661

Running Time: 45.53, 46.51

SIDE ONE: Most Likely You Go Your Way (And I'll Go Mine); Lay Lady Lay; Rainy Day Women #12 & 35; Knockin' On Heaven's Door; It Ain't Me Babe; Ballad Of A Thin Man.

SIDE TWO: Up On Cripple Creek*; I Shall Be Released*; Endless Highway*; The Night They Drove Old Dixie Down*; Stage Fright*.

SIDE THREE: Don't Think Twice, It's Alright; Just Like A Woman; It's Alright, Ma (I'm Only Bleeding); The Shape I'm In*; When You Awake*; The Weight*.

SIDE FOUR: All Along The Watchtower; Highway 61 Revisited; Like A Rolling Stone; Blowin' In The Wind.

Bob Dylan: vocals, guitar, harmonica, piano, **Rick Danko**: bass, **Levon Helm**: drums, vocals, **Garth Hudson**: organ, piano, clavinette, **Richard Manuel**: piano, electric piano, organ, drums, vocals, **Robbie Robertson**: guitar, vocals
*The Band only

Twelve million people applied for tickets for a forty-date tour, playing large arenas. Looking back, Dylan recalled that 'It wasn't a tour where a bunch of guys get together and say "let's go out and play". There was a great demand for that tour, and it had been building up, so we went out and did it. We were playin' three, four nights at Madison Square Garden, but what justified that? We hadn't made any records'. He actually played one afternoon and two evening shows at Madison Square – it just must have seemed that way. Dylan had not toured since 1966 and it was now a different world; what had been adventure was now big business – 'everybody had a piece of the action. The publicity people. The promoters. I had no control over what was going on'. *Planet Waves* was slipped out about a third of the way through the tour, delayed by Dylan's change in title. He rarely played songs from it on stage. This led to disappointing sales of just over half a million, and Dylan returning to Columbia. This double live album – one of the first – was owed as a contractual obligation.

It has been a subject of controversy among Dylan fans ever since. Rather than capture the ebb and flow of a live show, tracks were cherry-picked from four separate concerts. Songs excised included 'Just Like Tom Thumb's Blues', 'Ballad of Hollis Brown', 'Gates Of Eden' and 'Maggie's Farm'. Even so, the album was brilliantly programmed over four sides of vinyl, each with its own atmosphere, and it does convey the structure of each show – Dylan with the Band, the Band solo, Dylan solo, the Band again and back together till the end of the show.

On the front cover fans hold matches alight and aloft, while other shots by Barry Feinstein catch the six men onstage, intent and serious. A nightly highlight was Richard Manuel's hoarse, straining vocal on 'I Shall Be Released' that is captured here on the Band's set. The critical dispute centres over the quality of the tour as a whole that was much the same from stadium to stadium. Dylan himself makes a comparison with Elvis, the 'sensitivity and power' of the Sun sessions as compared to the 'full-out' power of his 1969 TV comeback.

There is an urgency and sense of rush here that makes this concert tour unmistakeable. For Michael Gray, 'there is an over-speedy, breakneck quality here that does little justice to the lyrics' with Dylan simply throwing his head back and yelling, like a hound. Subtlety and nuance, forget 'em. Real fans have never liked it.

David Cavanagh revaluates the album, 'it lacks the usual smugness shared by performer and audience of such affairs. This is feral, and Dylan is aggressive not cuddly. The verses are punched out…the four-man choruses are all but screamed. The next time people heard music this bilious, it was being made by The Clash'. He is backed up by Tim Riley: 'this is the nostalgia album that beat the oldies trap, a tour of 60s landmarks that made a glance backwards seem entirely contemporary. Paul Williams saw one of the concerts sampled here in real time and didn't enjoy watching a show from so far away – 'about a mile in back of the singer's head' – is amazed how good it now sounds, and so well recorded, especially Levon's drums. It captures the moment when a great artist 'saw daylight'.

BOB DYLAN/THE BAND

SIDE ONE
Most Likely You Go Your Way (And I'll Go Mine) (Dylan) 4.18
LA Forum, 14 February, evening show. Originally on *Blonde on Blonde*.
The album starts with an expectant audience who then catch on that Bob is among them and whistle and clap before a note is played. The recording is pin sharp, as compared, ironically, to the garage rock of the studio album. As Dylan gets stuck in, Cavanagh perceives through his headphones that 'something has definitely occurred in the room', a vast inhalation or exhalation, as everyone reacts to Dylan's bellow simultaneously. This is how he's going to re-work the old tunes? Jesus....'

Lay Lady Lay (Dylan) 3.15
LA Forum, 13 February. Originally on *Nashville Skyline*.
Good to hear this with a real rock band. The twin scimitars of Robertson's questioning guitar and Garth's fairground organ embroider Dylan who no longer croons this but sings with intensity. He must have hurt his throat singing like this day after day. Robert Christgau described his method here as 'mowing down his old songs like a truck'.

Rainy Day Women #12 & 35 (Dylan) 3.27
LA Forum, 13 February. Originally on *Blonde on Blonde*.
New lyrics, 'they'll stone you when you're trying to take a bath' et al. The Band make the music dance, it's carnival time.

Knockin' On Heaven's Door (Dylan) 3.52
Madison Square Gardens, 30 January 1974. Originally on *Pat Garrett and Billy the Kid*.
Riley describes this as 'a resentful eulogy of lost hopes', and the spectre of Vietnam – 'I'm sick and tired of the war' – overlays this rendition just as much as myths of the old West. Dylan sings as if with tears in his eyes, dancing around the beat, and the Band respond to every nuance. Maybe the badge he pleads to have taken 'off of me' is his own legend.

It Ain't Me Babe (Dylan) 3.40
LA Forum, 14 February, evening show. Originally on *Another Side Of Bob Dylan*.
Certainly a radical retake, now set to a Mexicali bounce. It lacks the sheer shock value of the song when it first appeared, dismissing the whole romantic song tradition in one line, but the audience reaction suggests that Dylan will be a lover for their lives too, and surely that is enough.

Ballad Of A Thin Man (Dylan) 3.42
LA Forum, 14 February, afternoon show. Originally on *Highway 61 Revisited*.
More laid back than the extraordinary razor blades on flesh, 1966 take, although Hudson is playing much the same organ fills. Dylan sounds almost convivial, the Band jog trots and the great Levon Helm uses not one beat too many. Mr Jones now should be made to wear 'telephones'. Some great rock'n'roll piano at the very end.

SIDE THREE
Don't Think Twice, It's Alright (Dylan) 4.37
LA Forum, 14 February, evening show. Originally on *Freewheelin'*.
Applause first, as Dylan hits the stage again after the Band's own mini-set. His acoustic section also has its own inbuilt electricity and his voice seems to have gone up half an octave since that boyish Huck Finn laid this down back in the early 60s, an aeon away. It has also picked up speed.

Just Like A Woman (Dylan) 4.06
LA Forum, 14 February, evening show. Originally on *Blonde on Blonde*.
There is a touch of Presley to this very artful rendition, and a laugh in his throat.

It's Alright, Ma (I'm Only Bleeding) (Dylan) 5.48
LA Forum, 14 February, evening show. Originally on *Bringing It All Back Home*.
The line about the president having to stand naked draws a huge cheer, as could be predicted shortly after Watergate. Bill Graham demanded red, white and blue stage lights at this point. The song took on a quite different resonance in the late days of Clinton, literally naked. This version is breathless, as if he is going for a land speed record. Dylan leaves out three verses, and as Paul Williams notes 'always with that edge of tension because he can't relax his guard'.

SIDE FOUR
All Along The Watchtower (Dylan) 3.08
LA Forum, 14 February, afternoon show. Originally on *John Wesley Harding*.
Dylan told *Biograph*, 'I liked Jimi Hendrix's record of this, and since he died I've been doing it this way. Strange how when I sing it I always feel it's a tribute to him in some way. First time I saw him he was playing with John Hammond. He was incredible then. The last time I saw him was a couple of months before he died. It was an eerie scene.' It starts gentle, like something south of the border, then the crowd catch on, and Dylan comes in roaring.
The space of the original has gone. This is a smash-and-grab raid.

Highway 61 Revisited (Dylan) 4.27
LA Forum, 14 February, evening show. Originally on *Highway 61 Revisited*.
Robertson makes a noise like a truck blowing off its horn on the highway. This is slower and more menacing than the original. Helm drives from the back seat.

Like A Rolling Stone (Dylan) 7.10
LA Forum, 13 February. Originally on *Highway 61 Revisited*.
Paul Williams enthuses over 'a lilting, roaring beautiful arrangement and performance'. It starts with the wonderful double keyboard punch of Hudson and Manuel that set Procol Harum going for a start – and the song has become more of a celebration than an accusation. At the end the crowd bay their approval and no-one shouts Judas.

Blowin' In The Wind (Dylan) 4.31
Part recorded at LA Forum, 13 February, part at LA Forum, 14 February, afternoon show. Originally on *The Freewheelin' Bob Dylan*.
For the encore the Band take a country ramble and Dylan addresses this old chestnut with new energy and that matchless male rugger-scrum choir join in on the chorus. The album leaves the massive crowd stamping and cheering.

Given the greater length accorded to CDs over a single album, Jeff Rosen should give this tour the full legacy treatment and give us a fuller version – including acoustic versions of the likes of 'Desolation Row', 'Nobody Cept You' and a one off 'hard, vicious' 'Visions of Johanna' and full band treatments of 'Forever Young', 'Tough Mama' and 'As I Went Out One Morning'. It is a tour that demands revaluation.

BLOOD ON THE TRACKS

US Release: 17 January 1975
UK Release:
CD Release: 467842-2
Producer: Engineered by Phil Ramone

Columbia PC 33235
CBS 69097
CD Remaster/SACD Release: Columbia 512350-6
Running Time: 51.41

SIDE ONE: Tangled Up In Blue; Simple Twist Of Fate; You're A Big Girl Now; Idiot Wind; You're Gonna Make Me Lonesome When You Go.

SIDE TWO: Meet Me In The Morning; Lily, Rosemary And The Jack Of Hearts; If You See Her, Say Hello; Shelter From The Storm; Buckets Of Rain.

Bob Dylan: vocals, guitar, harmonica, **Charles Brown III:** guitar, **Tony Brown:** bass, **Buddy Cage:** steel guitar, **Richard Crooks:** drums, **Paul Griffin:** Hammond B-3 organ, **Barry Kornfeld:** guitar, **Thomas McFall:** piano, **Eric Weissberg:** guitar, (Columbia A&R Studios, New York 16-25 September 1974)

Track listing of the original acetate drawn from these New York sessions, marked A&R, 799 Seventh Avenue, New York, dated 10.8.74 (American notation, 8 October 1974) and given the catalogue number Stereo S-19322. Timings as printed on the label.

SIDE A: *Tangled Up In Blue (6.48); Lonesome (3.53; Simple Twist Of Fate (4.18); *You're A Big Girl Now (4.22); *Idiot Wind (8.50).

SIDE B: Meet Me In The Morning (4.24); * Lillie (sic) Rosemary And The Jack Of Hearts (9.50); *If You See Her, Say Hello (3.23); Shelter From The Storm (4.49); Buckets Of Rain (3.21).

*Tracks substituted on final album, recorded with Bill Berg (drums), Greg Inhofer (organ), Kevin Odegard (guitar), Peter Ostroushko (mandolin), Bill Preston (bass), Chris Weber (guitar), Sound 80 Studios, Minneapolis Minnesota, 27 and 30 December 1974.

BOB
DYLAN
BLOOD
ON
THE
TRACKS

The genesis of this extraordinary album occurred when college drop-out Bob went back to school to relearn the skills of painting – and some would say, on the basis of *Self Portrait*, not a day too soon. The results impacted on his day job as a musician, just as did a later spell of biblical study. The charismatic teacher who unbeknowingly drew Dylan to him, just as Woody Guthrie had more than a decade before, was a 73-year-old artist called Norman Raeben who taught art classes at Carnegie Hall. Dylan 'dropped in to see him one day and I wound up staying there for two months'. One teaching method was for Dylan to look closely at a vase, then take it away, and tell him to draw it. His pupil reckoned Raeben was 'more powerful than any magician'. And the effects were devastating. 'I went home after that and my wife never understood me ever since that day'. No wonder that the subsequent album was so wracked with a sense of loss and despair.

Dylan began an affair with 24-year-old Ellen Bernstein who worked in A&R for Columbia, though still married to Sara with whom he would stumble on until February 1977. As to Raeben, 'he didn't teach you how to paint. He taught you about putting your head and your mind and your eye together. He taught me how to see in a way that allowed me to do consciously what I unconsciously felt. I wasn't sure it could be done in songs because I'd never written a song like that. When I started doing it, the first album I made was *Blood on the Tracks*'.

Hence the album's extraordinary sense of narrative, as if viewed from outside space and time. The stroke of genius on Dylan's part was to focus this technique – like 'a magnifying glass under the sun' – onto his songwriting. 'What I was trying to do had nothing to do with the characters or what was going on. I wanted to defy time. When you look at a painting you can see any part of it or see all of it together. I wanted it to be like a painting'. Dylan had recently bought a farm in Minnesota, with his younger brother David – a key player in what was to follow – and it was here that Ellen would visit him, and where he began to write the songs which became *Blood on the Tracks*.

The most reliable authority on this 'album of ghosts', to quote Heylin, is Kevin Odegard, who played on some of the later sessions and subsequently co-wrote *A Simple Twist Of Fate – Bob Dylan and the Making of Blood on the Tracks* (2004). The story starts with the tour captured on *Before The Flood*. Dylan went on the road without Sara who despised the rock'n'roll lifestyle, and was prey to all the usual temptations, before beginning frantically to write lyrics for the new album. 'Originally he wrote everything in the key of E. He would play much of it for various friends and he got mostly negative reactions'. Not that Dylan cared,

Ellen Bernstein told Heylin that 'as he wrote the songs and as he played them for people the sequencing decided itself. He knew what he was going to do and he knew how he was going to do it'.

Dylan visited old cohort Michael Bloomfield at his house in Marin County. According to Odegard, 'the whole thing went so poorly that Mike very nearly kicked him out of the house. Bob wouldn't slow down, wouldn't stop between songs, wouldn't give him keys'. Bloomfield wanted to play along, but found Dylan's guitar tuning hard to follow. 'He just played it top to bottom', the entire album in embryo.

He had already played about eight of the songs to Stephen Stills and Tim Drummond at the St Paul Hilton on 22 July 1974. Listening outside were Dave Crosby and Graham Nash, literally with his ear to the door. Bob sat on the floor, cross legged, and again played the whole suite, without pause, and obviously proud of what he had created. Stills, for one, was unimpressed, and to Nash's disbelief commented 'Well, he's an OK songwriter but he's not much of a musician'.

When he described the new material to John Hammond Sr, with whom Dylan had signed back to Columbia, it was as 'private songs'. They would soon become public. Dylan booked time at A&R Studios in New York – previously known as Columbia Studio A, and the scene of all his recordings up to *Highway 61* – and quickly laid down an album's worth of material, recording it between 16 and 19 September 1974, with 23rd to 25th of that month set aside for overdubs. For Ella, 'the theme of returning ran through the sessions. The sound of the album was such a return that it made a lot of sense to do it there'. Ironically, the place where Bob would really recapture a stripped-down *Highway 61* sound was up in Minneapolis in late December, but that is to get ahead of the story.

On the morning of 16 September, Eric Weissberg, who had found celebrity via the soundtrack of *Deliverance*, was up at A&R Studios recording an advertising jingle when Dylan's engineer Phil Ramone bumped into him and asked him to put together a session crew. As listed on an American Federation of Musicians' payment sheet, these were bassist Tony Brown, Thomas McFall on piano, Richard Crooks on drums and Charlie Brown III and Barry Kornfeld on guitars. Brown remembers that Dylan 'didn't want to do a lot of takes. We'd just watch his hands and pray we had the right changes'.

Dylan cut at least six songs solo and acoustic on the afternoon of the 16, none of them intended for release. The band then joined him for a session that ran through to midnight.

The songs typed up on the union agreement are 'Tangled Up In Blue', 'Simple Twist Of Fate', 'You're A Big Girl Now', 'Early In The Morning' aka 'Meet Me In The Morning', 'If You See Her Say Hello' and 'Jack Of Hearts'. The only one of these to make it to the finished album was 'Meet Me In The Morning'.

Only Tony Brown was retained the next day, and with organist Paul Griffin they joined Dylan for a seven-hour session, during which Dylan said not a word to them. 'Dylan was so focused. He just got on with it'. 'Shelter From The Storm' and 'You're Gonna Make Me Lonesome When You Go' made it all the way through onto the final album. At some point over the next few days, definitive versions of 'Simple Twist Of Fate' and 'Buckets Of Rain' also were laid down. Dylan asked Ellen Bernstein to bring in Buddy Cage from the New Riders Of The Purple Sage on pedal steel. He can be heard providing overdubs on 'Meet Me In The Morning'.

Phil Ramone cut an acetate at the end of the day for Dylan, and it was a copy of this that later reached a wider public via the *Blood On The Tracks* bootleg. The results are fascinating, but in all honesty sound one-dimensional, bare and sombre, like open heart surgery for a paying audience. Plans were in progress to release the album on Christmas Day and a handful of acetates were sent out to radio stations and the like. But then Dylan had a rethink and phoned Columbia on Christmas Eve, cancelling the release date. 'I had the acetate. I hadn't listened to it for a couple of months. The record still hadn't come out, and I put it on. I thought the songs could have sounded differently, better, so I went in and re-recorded them'.

Dylan turned up virtually unannounced at Sound 80 Studio in Minneapolis on 27 and 30 December with local musicians and replaced half of the original album, softening its angst, and making it perhaps more publically acceptable. The alchemy of the final result was a triumph in the short term and perhaps a disaster over time as Dylan began to make changing an album at the last minute a habit, without the exquisite judgements he made here.

When David Zimmerman heard the New York acetate he told him it was not radio friendly and 'it's just not going to sell'. David worked mainly at Sound 80 recording advertising jingles, so he quickly put together a band including Kevin Odegard and the 'house rhythm section' of Billy Peterson and Bill Berg. Both had just recorded with Leo Kottke. On keyboards was Gregg Inhofer, 'the new whiz kid in town', who had just completed a tour with Olivia Newton-John, and loved fusion jazz. 'It was specifically made clear to us', Odegard recalls. 'that Bob wanted to duplicate the sound he'd gotten on *Highway 61*'. Local music-store owner Chris Weber was asked to bring in a rare 1934 double-O size Martin – now known colloquially as the Joan Baez guitar – and found himself the intermediary between Dylan and the session men, just as Al Kooper had been back in Nashville – and playing on the record.

They worked late into the night of the 27 December and nailed 'Idiot Wind' after a few run throughs, and 'You're A Big Girl Now', over which Dylan himself dubbed flamenco-style guitar. Billy Peterson had had to leave the studio to play a gig down at a local nightclub, so the latter song is bass free. The same crew were then summoned back three days later to find Bob 'much more relaxed, much more upbeat and talkative' and they breezed through 'Tangled Up In Blue', 'Lily, Rosemary And The Jack Of Hearts' and 'If You See Her, Say Hello', all first takes. Dylan added mandolin 'like birds' wings flapping', after session player Peter Oustroushko refused to play so high up the neck. Dylan had brought his children with him, Jakob later said that the eventual record was 'my parents talking'.

On New Year's Day, Bob and his brother and studio engineer Paul Martinson came in to do final mixes, but other than 'Idiot Wind' needing some equalization, the four first takes were left alone. Dylan had suddenly declared 'I don't want it to sound all polished and clean and steely….I want it to sound exactly like this'. All four were left as recorded, except for a few discreet overdubs.

According to Heylin, Dylan then speeded up the whole album, both the New York and Minneapolis final takes, by roughly two per cent, and this is the version that hit the shops and has been in print ever since. Certainly 'Lily, Rosemary And The Jack Of Hearts' is almost unfeasibly fast, especially when compared to the abandoned New York take.

Of course, in interviews ever since, Dylan has made a point of denying that such personal songs have anything to do with their author. Suggesting instead that they were based on the writing of Chekhov. But he has been astonishingly open about opening up, if not himself, then the mechanics of creation. 'What's different about it is that there's a code in the lyrics and there's also no sense of time. There's no respect for it. You've got yesterday, today and tomorrow all in the same room, and there's very little you can't imagine not happening'. But maybe the debt is even more to Ibsen, whose Peer Gynt unravels himself like peeling an onion. *Blood on the Tracks* 'locked me into the present time more than anything else I ever did. I was constantly being intermingled with myself, and all the different selves that were in there until this one left, then that one left, and I finally go down to the one that I was familiar with'.

'A lot of people thought that album pertained to me'. He finds this 'hard for me to relate to that, I mean, people enjoying the type of pain, you know'. So why, asks Jonathon Cott, is it so extraordinarily intense. 'Because there's physical blood in the soul, and flesh and blood are portraying it to you. Will-power is what makes it an intense album'.

The front cover is to match, reproducing a photograph by Paul Till based on a photograph he took in Toronto in January 1974, with Dylan and his mop of hair looking blurred, as if a detail from a painting by Seurat. The colour chosen to edge it changed from light purple to what could be a blood stain. (The original CD took on the same hue with the remastered CD back to mauve.) The album originally boasted a surreal drawing by David Oppenheim and sleeve notes by Peter Hamill – the journalist husband of Shirley MacLaine. Hamill writes about the great hangover from the 60s' days of hope; 'in the end, the plague touched us all'. But Dylan is still 'bringing feeling back home', like William Blake, or W. B. Yeats, or Allen Ginsberg. As Hamill quotes lyrics from the original acetate, since rewritten, like 'If you're making love to her, kiss her for the kid', the sleeve notes were dropped, and another scratchy artwork by Oppenheim laid in. Then the original sleeve notes won a Grammy and they are restored to the latest CD reissue.

Dylan went to stay with Oppenheim in France for his 34th birthday, but Sara refused to accompany him. He would attempt to win her back, via a song on his next album, but as long as people can access music, this set of songs will continue to commemorate a marriage, and the seeds of its dissolution.

The official album's printed list of musicians appended to each track here is not taken from the album, that acknowledges only Eric Weissberg and Deliverance, Tony Brown, Buddy Cage and Paul Griffin, with no mention at all of the Minnesota contingent. Their first official acknowledgement was on *Greatest Hits Vol 3*. The list below is the result of the best possible guesswork by *Isis*.

SIDE ONE
Tangled Up In Blue (Dylan) 5.40
Recorded 30 December, 1974, Minneapolis.
Bob Dylan: vocal, guitar, harmonica, **Bill Preston**: electric bass, **Kevin Odegard**: guitar,
Chris Weber: Guild 512 12-string guitar, **Greg Inhofer**: keyboards, **Bill Berg**: drums

Dylan told Craig McGregor, 'Yeah, that's the first (song) I ever wrote that I felt free enough to change all the tenses around. The he and the she and the I and the you and the we and the us. I figured it was all the same anyway – I could throw them all in where they floated right – and it works on that level'. He introduced it on stage one night as a song that took ten years to live, and two more to write.

    The rejected and more relaxed New York version is one of the songs where you can hear the clack of his fingernails on the guitar. Dylan added a whole extra dynamic up north, with mandolin, drums and organ giving the song much more of a punch. He also changed many of the 'he's' to I, making things far more personal. The penultimate verse was almost completely rewritten, scrubbing lines like 'he was always in a hurry, too busy or too stoned/and everything that she had ever planned just had to be postponed'. But the Italian poet of the 13th century remains, presumably Dante (born 1265) and his visions of heaven and hell. Some live versions refer to an Italian poet of the 14th century, that would suggest Petrarch, who wrote love sonnets as opposed to Dante's 13th-century vision of hell, purgatory and heaven with an idealised love object in Beatrice. One reviewer described this song as being 'like a five-and-a-half-minute Proust', a poem that flows like a river. For Jackie Leven, 'it gave me a feeling of being healed'. Howe Gelb takes a professional view; 'some would wait all their lives to write a song like this, just to sell the movie rights' then joins in the chorus of amazement. 'How is it possible that so much ground gets covered with so much grace and off-handed delivery'. The album served as a 'flotational device' in an era of corporate rock, It kept a flame alive and fuelled a whole new breed of singer-songwriters who learnt from this masterpiece how to use personal material without being confessional. Songs of love and hatred.

Simple Twist Of Fate (Dylan) 4.17
Recorded 19 September 1974, New York City
Bob Dylan: vocal, guitar, harmonica, **Tony Brown:** bass
Another track that seems to loop around itself in endless recurrence. A movie you can watch in your mind each time you hear the song. The bare rendition suits the words, as does Dylan's extraordinarily sensitive reading, picking out every syllable and singing as if in a reverie.

You're A Big Girl Now (Dylan) 4.35
Recorded 27 December, 1974, Minneapolis
Bob Dylan: vocal, guitar, harmonica, Hammond B-3 organ and flamenco-style guitar, **Kevin Odegard:** guitar, **Chris Weber:** Martin 0042 guitar, **Greg Inhofer:** piano **Bill Berg:** drums
Interviewed for *Biograph*, Dylan poured scorn on those who would explain him. 'I read this was supposed to be about my wife. Fools, they limit you to their own unimaginable mentality. I don't constantly "re-invent" myself – I was there from the beginning'. The update adds a drummer and rolling piano, and a more up-front vocal, but loses the almost holy stillness of the original where Dylan seems lost in his own thoughts. The organ is sweet too, like a ghost in the wind, and the pedal steel sighs in the breeze. But the new version has its glories too, more musically upbeat. Dylan's howl of pain as he makes the vocal leap in each verse cuts through to the soul but there is tenderness and hope in his voice too. Anyone who says he cannot sing, direct them here.

Richard Hell told *Mojo* that 'this song is the most revealing of his bewildering powers because it's the one that has the greatest distance between its emotional impact and its actual words. No one line is much more than banal, but it's the way they follow from each other that makes "I can change, I swear" choke me up every time'.

Idiot Wind (Dylan) 7.47
Recorded 27 December, 1974, Minneapolis
Bob Dylan: vocal, guitar, harmonica, Hammond B-3 organ, **Bill Preston:** electric bass, **Kevin Odegard:** guitar, **Chris Weber:** Martin 0042 guitar, **Greg Inhofer:** keyboards, **Bill Berg:** drums
Paul Zollo points out the key lyric change, from New York's 'Idiot wind, blowing every time you move your jaw/from the Grand Coulee Dam to the Mardi Gras' to the words here, 'Idiot wind, blowing like a circle around my skull/from the Grand Coulee Dam to the Capitol'. And Dylan replies, 'if you've heard both versions, you realize, of course, there could be a myriad of verses

for the thing. It doesn't stop. Where do you end? You could still be writing it, really. It's something that could be a work continually in progress'. But no other version can ever quite match this one, with Dylan's voice crashing in a fraction before the backing that is richly textured with that piano-organ double punch and Bob at his most scarily judgemental. But what really grabs you by the guts is the way that Dylan will suddenly pause or shout for emphasis, and the way he literally acts out the lyrics, moving from spiteful to cold to impassioned.

Rather than tone things down, Dylan chose to be less specific but even more hurtful on the final version. In New York, you left your bags behind', in Minnesota 'your corrupt ways had finally made you blind'. A picture of a relationship with problems – 'In order to get a word in with you, I'd have to make up some excuse' – has been supplanted with a verse of near-apocalyptic pain: 'I kissed goodbye the howling beast on the borderline which separated you from me'. And new, seemingly effortless imagery, has been grafted on, like the priceless line about 'smoke pouring out of a boxcar door', which takes us straight back to *Bound For Glory*.

As Nick Hasted puts it, 'Dylan's voice and harrying Hammond playing brought out the raw nastiness he had flinched from in New York. This was where the blood was spilt'. Mojo reckons the 'relative fraility of his backing band make his singing so apocalyptic – the way he spits 'sweeeet lady' and 'iiiidiot wind' before ending with the unexpectedly inclusive 'we're idiots, babe'.

There are three separate versions of this extensive song, the version here and two, earlier takes laid down in New York. Heylin says of the version that made the acetate, it is only one to 'bridge the gap between bitterness and sorrow'. There is a 'wretchedness' here unmatched either on the Minneapolis retake or on an outtake that emerged on the *Bootleg Series* in 1991. And yet Zollo finds in this 'new' outtake 'a quiet, tender reading of the same lines that makes the inherit disquiet of the song even more disturbing', and the bareness of the arrangement – no organ overdubs – gives it a melancholy all its own.

All three versions are truly Shakespearean – you can just picture Bob as King Lear, railing on a blasted heath – and one reference point comes from mouth of another great tragic figure, Macbeth, life as 'a tale told by an idiot, full of sound and fury, signifying nothing'. Closer to home. Norman Raeben had a favourite phrase about the enemy of creativity, 'an idiot wind blowing and blinding all human existence'.

You're Gonna Make Me Lonesome When You Go (Dylan) 2.55
Recorded 17 September, 1974 New York City
Bob Dylan: vocal, guitar, harmonica, **Tony Brown**: bass, **Paul Griffin**: organ
Supposedly written for Ellen Bernstein, this is a song of fulfilled love, tied in with flowers and clouds and lazy rivers and French symbolist poets. But viewed from the framework of this album, one does need to 'realize the time'. This is a busy career woman with schedules and jets to catch, and he already dreads her leaving without too much feeling of pain in the way he sings about it.

SIDE TWO
Meet Me In The Morning (Dylan) 4.21
Recorded 16 September, 1974 New York City
Bob Dylan: vocal, guitar, harmonica, **Charles Brown III**: guitar, **Eric Weissberg**: guitar, **Barry Kornfeld**: guitar, **Thomas McFaul**: Hammond B-3 organ, **Tony Brown**: bass, **Richard Crooks**: drums, **Buddy Cage**: pedal steel guitar
The aftermath of the previous song, missing his lover, and dubbed directly onto the rhythm track of 'Call Letter Blues'. Vibrant imagery lifts this above the formulaic and the band add a punch that suggests Dylan should maybe have persevered with them. A distant cousin of the 1965 outtake 'Sitting On A Barbed Fire'.

Lily, Rosemary And The Jack Of Hearts (Dylan) 8.52
Recorded 30 December, 1974, Minneapolis
Bob Dylan: vocal, Martin 0042 guitar, harmonica **Bill Preston**; upright bass, **Kevin Odegard**: guitar, **Chris Weber**: Guild 512 12- string guitar, **Greg Inhofer**: keyboards, **Bill Berg**: drums
The original version lasts a minute longer and seems feature-film length, although there is a certain laconic tone to Dylan's voice that surrenders here to an urgent storyteller who hurries you through this complex tale, breathless. If the New York original sounds bare, then this sounds especially speedy with a fairground backing and a jog-trot rhythm as patented by Johnny Cash. Bob's narration is wonderfully sly with strongly defined characters – Lily, Big Jim, Rosemary, maybe the Jack of Hearts too – and no moral whatsoever. Except that the real criminals get away – the occasional drilling turns out to be a bank raid. This song dips into the same well as Dylan's early songs – an unworthy judge, card sharps, outlaws, and mysterious women.

Ron Wood reckoned this 'a strong mini-novel with twists and dark turns like something Ray Bradbury would have written. I love that it gathers momentum and the lyric makes you picture mysterious, mining town incidents, bank robbers and hookers'.

If You See Her, Say Hello (Dylan) 4.48
Recorded 30 December, 1974, Minneapolis
Bob Dylan: vocal, Martin 0042 guitar, mandolin, twelve string guitar, **Kevin Odegard**: guitar, **Chris Weber**: guitar and Guild 512 12-string guitar, **Greg Inhofer**: Hammond B-3 organ, **Bill Berg**: drums, **Peter Ostroushko**: second mandolin, very low in mix

The original take makes almost unbearable listening and does indeed pierce the listener to the heart. This version is sweeter musically, with Dylan's tender despair counterpointed by a mandolin. Maybe because his children were in the studio at time the third verse is rewritten, replacing 'If you're making love to her, kiss her for the Kid' with 'If you get close to her, kiss her once for me'. The song is certainly worthy of Chekhov in its picture of self delusion coming unstuck. As Robert Fisher of Willard Grant Conspiracy puts it, 'you've got this amazing transformation from the opening verse where he's looking at this love almost casually to the final verse where we see it's obviously a huge deal'. The arrangement, a lush melange of 12-strings and organ chords 'gives the lie to the gunslinger swagger he's affecting. In the beginning Dylan's songs were jammed with words. By now, he's allowing more to be filled in by the listener'.

Shelter From The Storm (Dylan) 5.01
Recorded 17 September, 1974 New York City
Bob Dylan: vocal, guitar, harmonica, **Tony Brown**: bass, **Paul Griffin**: organ

The 'one-eyed undertaker' could have come straight from *Highway 61*, but here surrealism is tied to self-loathing, a self-image of 'a creature void of form'. This is 'I Threw It All Away' with teeth. Only Dylan could gamble with such dangerous imagery – a crown of thorns, the locals gambling for his clothes – and make it personal. Sheryl Crow sees this as 'an example of how good he is at making a verse melody so circular it becomes the hook and he doesn't have to use a chorus. It's almost like a nursery rhyme. You never know who 'she' is. A spiritual figure? Is she a prostitute? There's just so little fat in (the) lyrics'. In the music too, with bass guitar playing a counter melody, Dylan's strummed acoustic and woe-begun harmonica at the end, and hushed vocals.

Buckets Of Rain (Dylan) 3.22
Recorded 19 September, 1974 New York City
Bob Dylan: vocal, guitar, **Tony Brown**: bass
Another skeletal New York take which really couldn't be bettered. The guitar part here is very reminiscent of Mississippi John Hurt. The sentiment is reminiscent of Shakespeare's final plays, tragedy shading into comedy. Laughing through the tears. The song leaves this emotionally wracked album on a note of humour in the face of a world where people 'disappear like smoke'. Even when he sings about a new love bringing him 'misery', here it is with an ironic grin in his voice. 'All that you can do is do what you must'.

OUTTAKES:
16 September 1974, A&R Recording Studio, New York: 'If You See Her Say Hello', 'Lily Rosemary and the Jack Of Hearts', 'Call Letter Blues', 'Idiot Wind', 'Tangled Up In Blue'
17 September 1974, A&R Recording Studio, New York: 'You're A Big Girl Now', 'Shelter From The Storm'
19 September 1974, A&R Recording Studio, New York: 'If You See Her Say Hello 2', 'Tangled Up In Blue 2', 'Up To Me', 'Idiot Wind 2'
Dates and tracks taken from the bootleg CD *Blood On The Tapes*, information that runs counter to all printed accounts

'Up To Me', 'You're A Big Girl Now' (NY version) on *Biograph*
'Call Letter Blues', 'Tangled Up In Blue' (NY version), 'Idiot Wind' (NY version), 'If You See Her Say Hello' (NY version) on *The Bootleg Series*
'Shelter From The Storm' (alternative version) on the original soundtrack to Jerry Maguire, and *The Best Of Bob Dylan*.

THE BASEMENT TAPES

US Release: 1 July 1975
UK Release: 1975
CD Release: Columbia 466137 2
Producer: Recorded in the basement of Big Pink, West Saugerties, NY June – October 1967, recording engineer Garth Hudson, mixed at Village Recorders and Shangri-La Studios, compiled by Robbie Robertson, produced by Bob Dylan and the Band

Columbia C2 33682
CBS 88147
Running Time: 38.27, 38.08

Recorded June-October 1967

SIDE ONE: Odds And Ends; Orange Juice Blues (Blues For Breakfast); Million Dollar Bash; Yazoo Street Scandal; Going To Acapulco; Katie's Been Gone.

SIDE TWO: Lo And Behold; Bessie Smith; Clothes Line Saga; Apple Sucking Tree; Please Mrs Henry; Tears Of Rage.

SIDE THREE: Too Much Of Nothing; Yea! Heavy And A Bottle Of Bread; Ain't No More Cane; Crash On The Levee (Down In The Flood); Ruben Remus; Tiny Montgomery.

SIDE FOUR: You Ain't Goin' Nowhere; Don't Ya Tell Henry; Nothing Was Delivered; Open The Door, Homer; Long Distance Operator; This Wheel's On Fire.

The UK pressing has sides 1 and 4 on disc 1, sides 2 and 3 on disc 2, for use in multichanger record players.

Bob Dylan: vocals, guitar, piano **Rick Danko:** bass, mandolin, vocals, **Levon Helm:** drums – in later sessions, only, **Garth Hudson:** organ, clavinette, accordion, piano, **Richard Manuel:** piano, drums, vocals, **Robbie Robertson:** guitar, drums

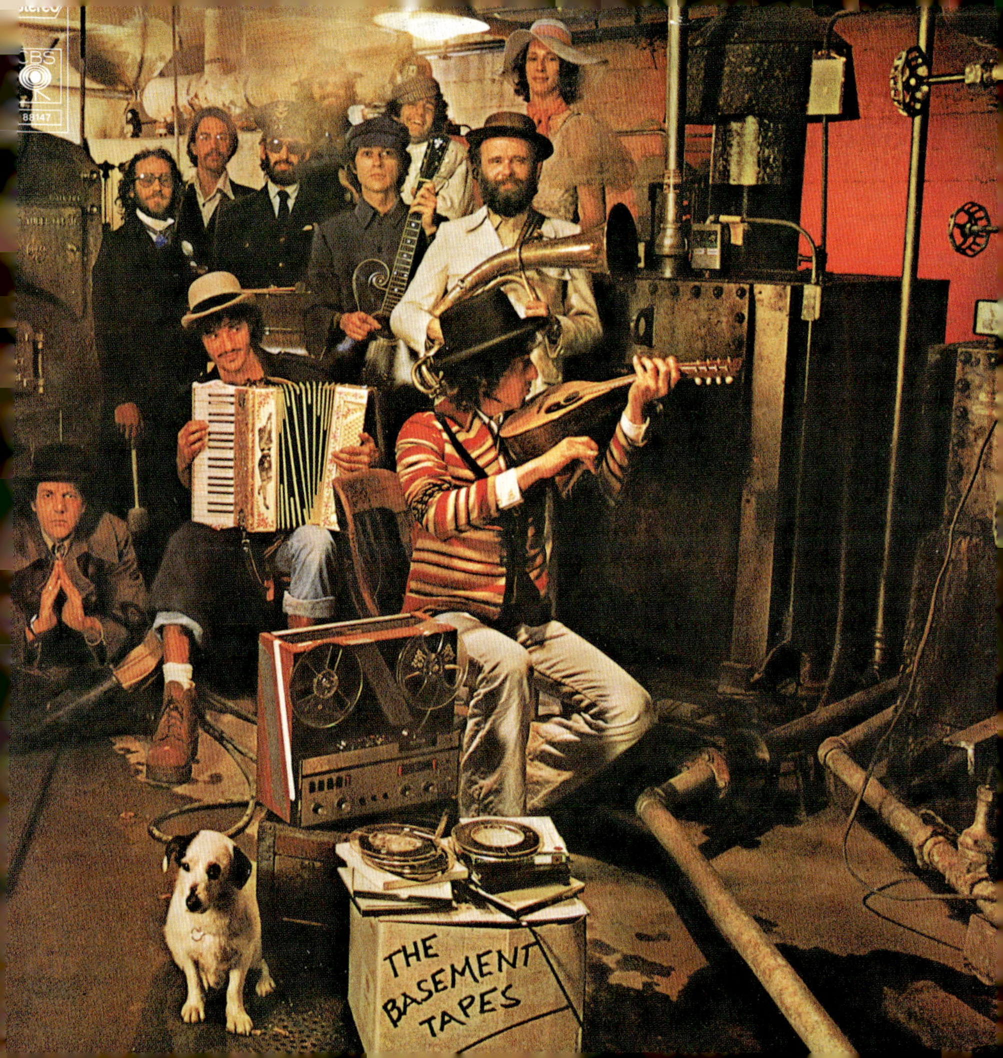
CBS
88147
THE BASEMENT TAPES

'The songs were mostly done in humour,' Robbie Robertson told *Biograph*. 'They were either outrageous or comical. It was a big songwriting period, and we all had lots of songs. The idea was to record some demos for other people. They were never intended to be a record. It was somewhat annoying that the songs were bootlegged. The album was finally released in the spirit of "well, if this is going to be documented, let's at least make it good quality"'.

'Highlights have been brought out, tones sharpened, tape hiss removed'. Cue a dispute which echoes to this day. Although first a double album, and now a double CD with lots of unused musical capacity, this dip into the *Basement Tape* bran tub is both too much, lacking the unity of the demo tape(s) hawked round in the late 60s, or too little, lacking the breadth and eccentricity of the five hours or so of the complete sessions. Both are described and listed in full in the bootleg section later in this book.

And it seems perverse to throw away the home-made stereo mix supervised by Garth Hudson, bent over equipment salvaged from the ruins of the '66 tour to which the *Basement* material serves as both delayed encore and antidote. Rough, but effective, with vocals bleeding across the tracks, much of the warmth of the tapes comes from this (then) state-of-the-art combination of Altech PA tube mixers and Neumann mikes, capturing musicians at play, and facing each other in a small room. And it is just this quality that gets lost in the shuffle here. Perversely, the remix now sounds more dated than the original tapes.

Criticism of the album centres on two issues, what has been added and what has been taken away. The additions are discreet overdubs on some of this material, and eight new tracks by the Band, supposedly also recorded at the same time. Clinton Heylin dissects them with forensic skill. Four are what they say on the tin, two songs recorded towards the end of the *Basement* recordings, when Levon Helm returned, and two piano demos laid down by Richard Manuel at Big Pink in summer 1967, but these have guitars and drums added in 1975. Two more are the right period, September 1967, but were demos cut in New York City. Two are brand new recordings. And yet three Richard Manuel songs which were laid down on the original reel-to-reels, including the wonderful 'Ferdinand The Imposter', are left in the bootleg ghetto at least until the CD reissue of *Music From Big Pink*.

These are not the only vital omissions. You will have to access a bootleg copy to hear the delights of the true original, or locate the likes of 'I Shall Be Released' or 'Quinn The Eskimo', though maybe such recondite delights as Tiny Tim taking the mike over from Dylan for some falsetto cover versions are best left in the dustbin. The loss of 'The Mighty Quinn' is particularly irksome as he is among the cast of characters acted out on the cover. The current package is surely crying out for the meticulous attentions of Mr Rosen. But, for all of that, this album was a first step in getting out into into the public arena some of the extraordinary music that emerged from that mysterious rehearsal room, down in the earth.

Dylan threw some light into the room when he talked to *Rolling Stone*, two years later. 'They were just fun to do. That's really the way to do a recording – in a peaceful, relaxed setting, in somebody's basement with the windows open. And a dog lying on the floor'. He was being pushed by management to come up with new songs, if not for himself then for others to cover. 'We must have recorded 50 songs at that place. At that time psychedelic rock was overtaking the universe and so we were singing those homespun ballads, or whatever they were'. A form of rehab. 'We were all up there sorta drying out, making music and watching time go by. So in the meantime we made this record. Actually it wasn't a record, just songs that we'd come to in this basement and recorded. Out in the woods'. In the Catskills in fact.

Greil Marcus' sleeve notes capture the music perfectly, 'a testing and discovery of roots memory more compelling today than when they were made'. Dylan's songs tap into 'a plain-talk mystery; it has nothing to do with mumbo-jumbo, charms or spells'. Talking about the book he wrote some 20 years later, he nailed down in words how 'over and over again you have an ordinary song that seems to be about nothing, and some apocalyptic element either in tone of voice or lyric just upends it'. And it came as no surprise that there were plans to turn Big Pink into a museum and rehearsal space (again), having been sold to Dylan fan Linda Mesch for the bargain price of $144,500. 'I'm not a rich person, but spiritually, mystically and magically, the value of this property is beyond what I can even say or add up'.

The jokey front cover is a photograph by Reid Miles, taken not at Big Pink but at the LA branch of the YMCA that seems somehow appropriate for these (Greenwich) village people. Here are characters from some of the songs within, fire-eaters and dwarves and a blowsy Mrs Henry, plus Quinn the Eskimo despite his song having been omitted for some fathomless reason, plus Dylan playing mandolin with an imaginery bow, the Band, Ringo Starr, Neil Young, David Blue and – star of the show – a reel-to-reel tape recorder.

SIDE ONE
Odds And Ends (Dylan) 1.46
'Lost time is not found again'. A raucous start, like a country cousin of the rougher parts of *Blonde on Blonde*, with Robertson blowing up a storm, and Manuel on drums. The juice here could be alcohol, or something worse. Dylan slurs his words, appropriately.

Orange Juice Blues (Blues For Breakfast) (Richard Manuel) 3.37
The Band alone.

Million Dollar Bash (Dylan) 2.31
Comically apocalyptic, with lots of weird characters doing unmentionable things. Dylan adopts his bemused persona, maybe he was Mr Jones all along. Spookily, a cover version of this was one of the last things Fairport Convention recorded before the road crash that decimated them. Hugely influenced by Dylan and Music From Big Pink, they made their own retreat, to a Hampshire rectory, and re-invented British roots music just as the crew here are doing with Americana.

Yazoo Street Scandal (JR Robertson) 3.28
The Band only

Going To Acapulco (Dylan) 5.26
Never bootlegged or even chronicled before 1975, this is weird and mysterious, with Dylan at the edge of his voice. One of his travelogues, with the Taj Mahal in there too, so you know this is an Acapulco of the mind, as well as on the map. The Band fit him like the proverbial glove and Manuel and Danko lend their all to the chorus. *Mojo* waxes lyrical: 'a soaring banshee wail embracing fear and joy and heartbreaking sadness'. They invest this outlaw tale with 'a patina of the divine'. The perfect funeral song.

Katie's Been Gone (JR Robertson) 2.44
The Band only

SIDE TWO
Lo And Behold (Dylan) 2.45
A road song, in the world of Fellini. The words read comically, but there is something in Dylan's voice that scares you too. The kind of man who picks you up in his truck, spins you some tall tales, then you notice the switchblade….

Bessie Smith (R Danko/J R Robertson) 4.16
The Band only

Clothes Line Saga (Dylan) 2.56
Robbie Robertson plays drums, and Dylan piano. A deadpan and laconic parody of Bobbie Gentry's 'Ode To Billy Joe', a 1967 smash hit. Like that song it presents the inconsequential as a mask for what is really going on. Here the vice president going mad is a distraction from getting his sheets dry on the line. For Jeff Tweedy, it is the 'fractured nature of the story' that intrigues. 'I think *The Basement Tapes* is a field recording. Masterpieces are created out of forgetting who you are and what you are…anything that sidesteps the awareness of the thing itself is what you try for when you write.'

Apple Sucking Tree (Dylan) 2.47
Little Sadie revisited. Paul Williams reckons this songs is 'simple proof that rock'n'roll and American folk music are one and the same'. As to the latter, this is based on the tune and shaggy dog tale narrative of 'Froggie Went A-Courtin'. The original song appeared on the Harry Smith Anthology sung by Chubby Parker and was also collected in the Appalachians by Cecil Sharp. As to the former, it is more country hoedown than the Blue Caps.
    Compare and contrast this with Nick Drake's 'Fruit Tree'. Both allude to death, but Bob has loving on his mind, while Nick is singing about posthumous fame.

Please Mrs Henry (Dylan) 2.31
Drink-fuelled friskiness from a 'sweet bourbon daddy'. Dylan creates a new vernacular. Or maybe he is just pissed. The Band go Nashville, with organ imitating pedal steel. The scene is a drunk man serenading a barmaid, with ribald humour, to get another drink. Dylan acts deadpan, but he almost cracks up in the last waltz, as the double entendres get to him.

Tears Of Rage (Dylan/Richard Manuel) 4.11
The other side of country music. Stately and patriotic and bitter. Toby Litt suggests a parallel with Shakespeare's *King Lear* – a play from which Dylan also drew his 'wheels of fire' image. If that text deals with two daughters' ingratitude, then this is about the 'terror of being a father'. Dylan wrote the lyric first, then gave them to Richard as he fooled around on the piano. The tune is pure melancholic Manuel and the high harmony singing here brings tears to the eye, especially the descant as Dylan growls about a heart 'filled with gold/as if it was a purse'.

SIDE THREE
Too Much Of Nothing (Dylan) 3.01
Taken at a funeral pace with an extraordinary girly chorus from the Band. The tune is based on a rising chord sequence that can make the listener feel queasy. By what is surely a huge coincidence, Vivien and Valerie were the two wives of T. S. Eliot, whose *The Waste Land* contains the lines 'Do you see nothing? Do you remember nothing?'

Yea! Heavy And A Bottle Of Bread (Dylan) 2.13
Starts with a comic book, and there is some cartoonish violence – 'slap that drummer with a pie that smells'. The drummer for many of *The Basement Tapes* is Richard Manuel, but here he is surely playing those brilliant piano licks. There is a great bit of deep bass singing at the end, probably from Hudson.

Ain't No More Cane (Trad, arr the Band) 3.54
The Band only, particularly dire, however bravely Greil Marcus talks it up.

Crash On The Levee (Down In The Flood) (Dylan) 2.03
Clearly influenced by Richard 'Rabbit' Brown's 'James Alley Blues', a song Dylan performed back on one of the Minnesota tapes: 'I been giving sugar for sugar, let you get salt for salt/And if you can't get along with me, well it's your own fault'. As to this, Dylan adds a millennial sense of upcoming catastrophe – New Orleans in 2005, perhaps – couched in humour. No Noah this time around, though.

Ruben Remus (J R Robertson/Richard Manuel) 3.13
The Band only, the most marginal of tracks. Why on earth did this take precious vinyl away from performances of the quality of 'The Mighty Quinn', or 'I Shall Be Released'?

Tiny Montgomery (Dylan) 2.44
The backing vocals pay homage to the Animals' 'I'm Crying', while the lyrics of the last verse – 'honk that stink' – are particularly nasty, like the folk tradition as recast in the very meanest Appalachian hollow. Dylan's voice is mean and sneering, like a Hollywood villain.

SIDE FOUR
You Ain't Goin' Nowhere (Dylan) 2.41
Robbie Robertson on drums. This was covered by the Byrds on their own back-to-the-country album *Sweetheart of the Rodeo*. It has a grace and danger which had gone missing on the affable retread (issued earlier) on *Greatest Hits Vol 2*, with its spoof lyric 'pack up your money, sell up your tent, McGuinn 'cos you ain't going nowhere'. The protagonist sits in his easy chair, waiting for his mail-order bride, with the simple injunction 'strap yourself to the tree with roots'. But there is also a sense, part of Dylan's unreadable vocal here, that the title refers to the void, the nothing everafter that makes the 'easy chair' something very sinister indeed.

Don't Ya Tell Henry (Dylan) 3.12
A Dylan song of course, and in its rightful place in the collected lyrics, but Levon Helm – who came back at the very end of the *Basement* sessions – is singing it in his patented Arkansas drawl. Maybe Dylan is playing spoons or something.

Nothing Was Delivered (Dylan) 4.22
A cynic would say this song applies perfectly to the *Self Portrait* album, or some of his efforts in the 80s. But the way Dylan sings this is as serious as your life.

Open The Door, Homer (Dylan) 2.48
There is a song called 'Open the Door Richard', as performed by Louis Jordan and Count Basie. This isn't it, but it is presumably an affectionate dig at Manuel whatever the title. It is Richard who is addressed here, not the notional Homer. A song full of rustic wisdom, or idiocy.

Long Distance Operator (Dylan) 3.38
Dylan wrote it, but leaves it to the Band to perform.

This Wheel's On Fire (Dylan/Rick Danko) 3.49
In his notes, Marcus describes Dylan's vocal here as 'as sly as Jerry Lee Lewis and as knowing as the old man of the mountains'. Dylan appeared one afternoon at Big Pink with the words but no music. Rick Danko added a major part of the melody. Robertson played drums on the original tape and for this release further drums and piano were overdubbed. The song obviously alludes to Dylan's feelings after the motorbike crash, but what 'explodes' is far more than the tyre on a Triumph 500.

The rhythm is that of a slow march, with Dylan singing in his highest register, and this song has been re-interpreted by some great female singers, among them Julie Driscoll and Siouxie Sue, who had thought the song was written by Driscoll (who should be so lucky). 'Then I found out it was f*cking Bob Dylan. I liked the song so it stayed on anyway. Have I heard his version? No, never. He wasn't someone who captured my imagination back in the mid 70s'. The kind of bolshy attitude that is right in line with the music cooked up in that rural basement.

OUTTAKES:
'The Mighty Quinn (Quinn The Eskimo)' on *Biograph*
'I Shall Be Released', 'Santa Fe' on *The Bootleg Series*

See Greil Marcus's ground-breaking book *Invisible Republic: Bob Dylan's Basement Tapes (1997)*.

DESIRE

US Release: 16 January 1976　　　　　　　　**Columbia PC 33893**
Quadrophonic Release:　　　　　　　　　　**Columbia Q – 86003**, different mixes
UK Release:　　　　　　　　　　　　　　　**CBS 86003**
CD Release:　　　　　　　　　　　　　　　**Columbia 32570**
CD Remaster/SACD Release:　　　　　　　　**Columbia 512345 6**
Producer: Don DeVito　　　　　　　　　　　**Running Time:** 56.17

SIDE ONE: Hurricane; Isis; Mozambique; One More Cup Of Coffee; Oh, Sister.

SIDE TWO: Joey; Romance In Durango; Black Diamond Bay; Sara.

Bob Dylan: vocals, guitar, harmonica, piano, **Vincent Bell:** (bellzouki), **Dom Cortese**: mandolin, **Emmylou Harris:** vocals, **Scarlet Rivera:** violin, **Rob Stoner:** bass, vocals, **Howard Werth:** drums, **Ronee Blakley:** vocals, **Luther:** congas, **Steve Soles:** vocals on 'Hurricane'

Rather than try to attempt to repeat *Blood on the Tracks*, Dylan pulled off his usual trick and developed both a new writing style and a new sound for his next album. Patti Smith remembers 'he was thinking about improvisation, about extending himself language-wise. In Greenwich Village he recruited electric violinist Scarlet Rivera and Jack Elliot's bassist Rob Stoner. Then at the Other End he ran into Jacques Levy who had directed *Oh! Calcutta!* and worked with Roger McGuinn on the musical *Gene Trypp*, from whose ashes emerged the hit single 'Chestnut Mare'. Dylan had often appropriated other people's tunes and twisted traditional lyrics to his own devices, but surrendering writing autonomy was something new.

Dylan later related 'I had bits and pieces of some songs I was working on and I played them for him on the piano. He took it someplace else, then I took it someplace else, and he went further and I went further and it wound up that we had ('Isis') which was out there'. They moved out to Dylan's beach house in Long Island to continue the experiment. As Bob later told Paul Zollo, the results were 'very panoramic songs, because after one of my lines, one of his would come out. It just didn't stop. Of course my melodies are very simple anyway, so they're very easy to remember' What Levy brought to Dylan's muse – apart from introducing it to a

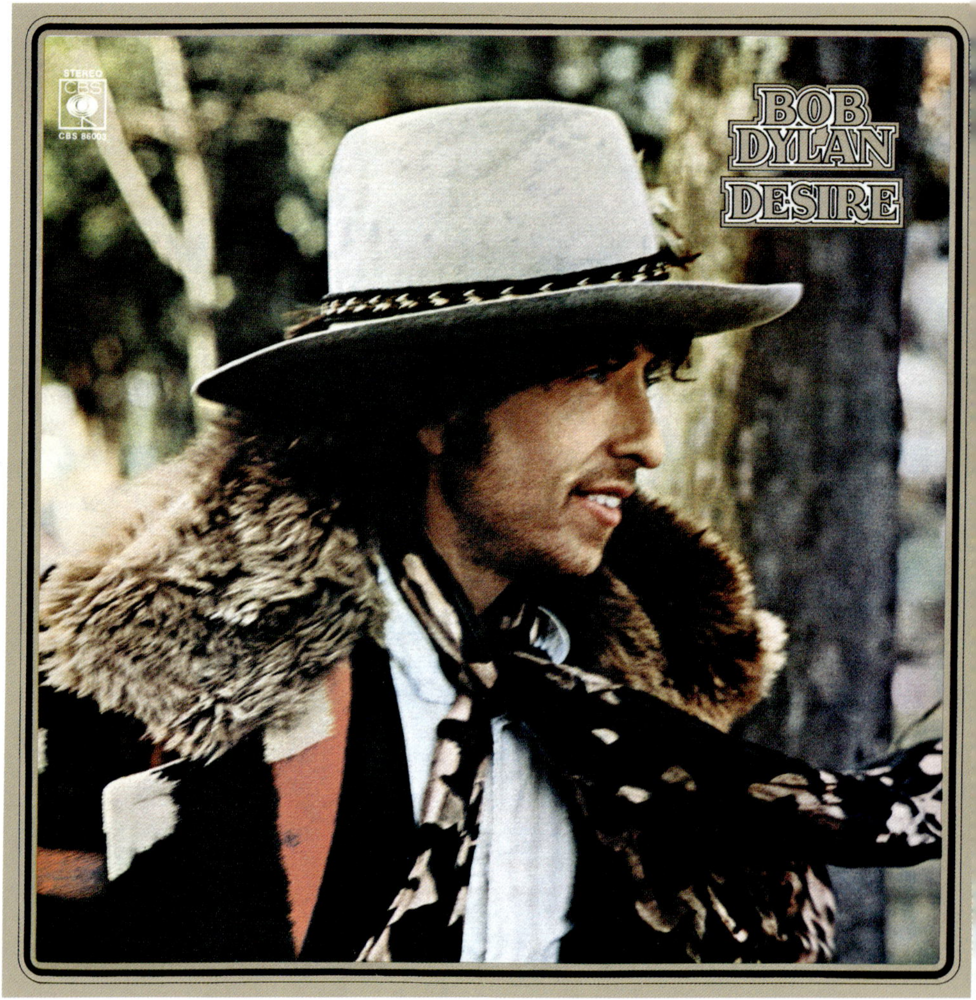
STEREO
CBS
CBS 86003
BOB
DYLAN
DESIRE

rhyming dictionary – was a sense of theatricality. As Levy later said, these new songs 'gave Dylan a chance to act', something fully unleashed on the *Rolling Thunder Revue*. The album now sounds like a rehearsal for that cataclysmic tour.

Dylan visited Columbia Studios on 52nd Street in New York on 14 July 1975 to run through some of these new songs with the Dave Mason band, and more importantly the gypsy violin of Scarlet Rivera. The glimmerings of a new sound can be heard in these outtakes, a combination of accordion, violin and female backing singers. Dylan returned for an intensive four days in the same studio, 28 to 31 July, 'I never slept when I made that album', and worked through a huge musical cast – including Eric Clapton and Kokomo – before abandoning his idea for a big band, to lay down virtually the whole album on 30 July with the nucleus of the Rolling Thunder band.

'We had tried it with a lot of different people in the studio, a lot of different types of sound, and I even had back-up singers on that album for two or three days, a lot of of percussion, a lot going on. But as it got down, I got more irritated with all that sound going on and eventually we just settled on bass, drums and violin'. Drummer Howie Wyeth locked into a loose groove with Stoner, Scarlett provided the musical colour, and Emmylou Harris came in to sing harmonies as only she can, but never in such an improvised way. Denied a lyric sheet, and unfamiliar with the songs, 'I just watched his mouth, and watched what he was saying. That's where all that humming on the record comes from'. Dylan scorned overdubs, and that was that, in the bare minimum of takes. 'That was new. I didn't take that one as far as I wanted to. I wanted to do more harmonica and violin together, but we never got a chance to do that'.

Except that following legal advice, Dylan and his road crew re-entered the studio on 24 October to re-record 'Hurricane', this time without the line suggesting that one of the villains of the piece had been seen 'robbing the bodies'. *The Rolling Thunder Revue* hit the road six days later.

By the time the album came out, these songs had been fully road tested and, as the recently issued Live 1975 album shows, leave many of these studio takes standing at the gate. But there is a cinematic quality to *Desire* that makes it unique in Dylan's album stack. The cover boasts a photograph of Bob in full *Rolling Thunder* costume by Ken Regan, a direct parody of Mamas and Papas mainman John Phillips' The Wolf King Of LA. The back cover is a collage that includes, for no apparent reason, a Tarot card, Joseph Conrad, a pensive Emmylou

Harris, a statue of the Buddha, and Sara. Reconciled since *Blood on the Tracks*, she accompanied Dylan for much of the tour, and appears in the subsequent 'on the road' movie *Renaldo and Clara*, that features some explosive live music, interspersed with impenetrable goings on, with a cast including Joan Baez, Allen Ginsberg and a wise-talking David Blue, back in the Village playing pinball and reminiscing.

The album was remixed for quadraphonic, including minor vocal errors on 'Romance in Durango' and 'Isis'. This was this mix used for the first CD release that included a full lyric booklet. This was missing from the CD upgrade, for no good reason. There are two sets of sleevenotes, one unsigned but probably by Dylan – it is copyrighted to his publishing company – running through the songs in an impressionistic way 'from a bathtub in Maine in ideal conditions'. The ghost of Rimbaud is invoked, 'moving like a dancing bullet thru the secret streets of a hot New Jersey night filled with venom and wonder'.

On the original album's inner sleeve was a prose piece on Dylan by Allen Ginsberg, writing as co-director of the Jack Kerouac School of Disembodied Poetics, Naropa Institute, York Harbour, Maine. One of the (few) non-musical highlights of *Renaldo and Clara* was Dylan and Ginsberg standing in contemplation by Kerouac's grave. Titling his piece 'Songs of Redemption', it is packed with information about the formation of the revue, and a song-by-song discussion that goes right off the meter as only a great poet can. Thus, for 'One More Cup Of Coffee', he gravely notes 'voice lifts in Hebraic cantillation never before heard in US song, ancient blood singing – a new age, a new Dylan again redeemed'.

The US Quad remix has two vocal mistakes, 'to this boss I say he said' in 'Joey', and 'in this face of God will appeal' in 'Romance In Durango', plus an out of tune trumpet part. The sound is very different to both LP and CD remaster.

SIDE ONE
Hurricane (Dylan/Jacques Levy) 8.32
Strummed guitar, then some gypsy violin, the rhythm section kicks in and Dylan is off and running. This song is relentless for eight minutes plus, like a series of punches to the solar plexus. Boxer Rubin 'Hurricane' Carter was convicted for murder in 1967 and imprisoned in a tiny metal pen in Trenton, New Jersey. After reading his autobiography *The Sixteenth Round* Dylan visited Rubin in jail. And we sat and talked for hours and hours. I realised that the man's philosophy and my philosophy were running on the same road, and you don't meet too many people like that. I took notes because I wasn't aware of all the facts. I thought that maybe sometime I could condense it all down and put it into a song'.

Levy confirms 'it was Bob's idea to write a song about Hurricane. I wanted to try to take the part of an attorney almost, and tell the story to the jury. Of course that needed a lot of detail'. And no jury would fail to bring in a verdict of not guilty after this forensic display. It was his first protest song since 'George Jackson', and a sign that Dylan had not abandoned his quest for obtaining justice through the power of popular song. The recording is to match, rough and ready and lo-fi, even on the CD remaster.

Mojo reckoned that Dylan's 'snarled quatrains predated the advent of poetry slams by decades. It's pure poetic passion delivered via the screaming headlines of a scandal sheet'. Jeff Tweedy agrees. 'It happens once every 10 years that somebody can perform a song like that. Maybe all of the first Sex Pistols record has that kind of intensity. There's the rawness to Scarlet Rivera's playing and then there's Dylan just spitting out the lyrics. He's angry, and Dylan's at his best when he's angry'.

Isis (Dylan/Jacques Levy) 6.59
Dylan played a rough draft to Levy, and the story grew in the telling as the two tossed it between each other like a beach ball. Dylan reckoned 'it just seemed to take on a life of its own, as another view of history (laughs). Ancient history but history nevertheless'. As to Levy, 'we are sitting at a piano together and we are writing these verses in an old Western ballad kind of style. "Isis" was just a funeral dirge when we first worked on it. It was so slow and rather stately and sad. It would have taken a whole side of an album'.

It starts with piano and drums, then Dylan comes in singing as if possessed, accentuating every word. But this version is nothing to the emotional heights it could reach on stage. In

Montreal, he announced it as 'here's a song about marriage'. Sara was backstage that night, wearing an Isis amulet around her neck of her own design. Suddenly this millennia-old tale of a man losing his bride, being misdirected, but finding a way back home is made contemporary.

Mozambique (Dylan/Jacques Levy) 3.02
Derek Barker: 'I take it that neither of you had visited Mozambique'. Jacques Levy: 'No, I was writing about a little idyllic spot where nothing but romance was going on. It was a little deceptive that song'. Especially as there was a Marxist insurgency going on at the time. Dylan finds, as did Gram Parsons before him, that Emmylou is the magic ingredient that can sprinkle any song with a little bit of gold dust. A jaunty rendition, and it certainly does act as a wonderful tourist advert, even if obviously a daydream.

One More Cup Of Coffee (Dylan) 3.47
Dylan asked Paul Zollo, 'was that for a coffee commercial? No, it's a gypsy song. That song was written during a gypsy festival in the south of France one summer'. Their holy days coincided with his birthday. 'Hanging around for a week probably influenced the writing of that song. But the 'valley below' probably came from someplace else. It became the fixture to hang it on. But the 'valley below' could mean anything'.

It starts quietly, with strummed guitar and melodic bass, then in comes Scarlet weaving her gypsy violin around Bob's mysterious words, and Emmylou soars in for the chorus. Robert Fisher rightly says that their duet is 'seemingly effortless and amazing. Sweet melancholy music that suggest salvation and hope are just within reach'. Dylan's vocal here has been compared to a second violin, 'with a really reedy edge'. Ronnie Sparks of the Handsome Family told *Mojo* 'it's a cliché festival of psychic knife-throwing gypsy outlaws and it sounds corny on paper but when you hear it, it works on this very natural dream-like level, like magic realism. There's no Bob Dylan in it anywhere as such. It's not a page from his diary'.

Oh, Sister (Dylan/Jacques Levy) 4.03
But this song could indeed be just that, a lovely and pensive duet about a love affair with religious connotations. The father here is not Abe Zimmerman.

SIDE TWO
Joey (Dylan/Jacques Levy) 11.06
Long and slow, and deliberately heroic. That year, Dylan said 'I remembered Joey. At that time I wasn't involved in anything that he was involved in, but he left a certain impression on me. I never considered him a gangster. I always thought of him as some kind of hero in some kind of way'.

Time for some facts. Joey Gallo was a New York mobster who Robert Kennedy once dubbed Public Enemy Number One. He beat his wife, abused his children, was a well-known racist, and took part in a brutal gang rape of a young boy in prison. After he connived in the killing of fellow hood Joe Columbo, there was a contract out on him. He was gunned down at Umberto's Clam House in Little Italy, in 1972 as he celebrated his 43rd birthday. A long way from the secular saint portrayed here. But a legend is not history. Dylan 'always grew up admiring those heroes, Robin Hood, Jesse James. It amazes me that I should write a song about Joey Gallo, (but) I feel that if I didn't, who would? I think I picked that up from the folk tradition. I used to sing a lot of those songs and it just kinda carried over'. And as a song, it has lasted.

Romance In Durango (Dylan/Jacques Levy) 5.44
'Knockin' On Heaven's Door' relocated to Mexico. The tinkling accompaniment sounds like something south of the border, and so do Dylan's gringo vocals. Jacques Levy sees this threnody on a dying gunman as a piece of cinema. 'That's just a kind of old western movie, with a little bit of politics thrown in. The desk clerk, well he's straight out of a Sidney Greenstreet movie. The men are dressed in crumpled white suits and it wouldn't be surprising to see Peter Lorre come round the corner at any moment.

The poet John Cooper-Clarke, for whom it is always May 1966, thinks just the same. 'It's a movie isn't it? The mariachi accompaniment (those trumpets!) and even the way he pitches his voice conjures the Mexican desert – 'hot chilli peppers in the blistering sun' – you're straight there'.

Black Diamond Bay (Dylan/Jacques Levy) 7.30
None of the songs on *Desire* hurry themselves, and this is another movie in verse. The verse form here is fiendishly complicated, and would leave many professional poets gasping. The

title is from that poet of the Islands, Joseph Conrad, but the narrative is new. Levy remembers that they started with one phrase, 'from the mountain high above', and developed it into this tangled tale of volcanoes erupting and sinking islands. 'Both I and Bob had read Conrad. The sting finally comes at the end when the listener realises that the whole thing is being seen through the eyes of someone watching TV in LA, someone who simply couldn't care less'. It is like the poem by W H Auden about Icarus falling to the sea while a ship sails unconcernedly by.

Sara (Dylan) 5.32
Sprightly harmonica, and then a devastating song about memories of playing with the wife and kids on the beach at Hampton, with Scarlet playing for her life. Dylan might have tried to sidestep the autobiographical elements here, but this is surely his most personal song since 'Ballad In Plain D'. 'When people say 'Sara' was written for 'his wife Sara', it doesn't necessarily have to be about her just because my wife's name happened to be Sara. Anyway, was it the real Sara, or the Sara in the dream? I still don't know'. Strange, then, that Jacques Levy recalls the 'real' Sara visiting the *Desire* sessions, and her husband singing this through the studio glass, begging forgiveness. She was apparently absolutely stunned.

OUTTAKES:
14 July 1975, Columbia Studio E, New York: 'Rita Mae'
28 July 1975, Columbia Studios, New York: 'Catfish', with Eric Clapton
30 July 1975, Columbia Studios, New York: 'Golden Loom', with Emmylou Harris, 'Rita Mae 2'
31 July 1975, Columbia Studios, New York: 'Abandoned Love'
24 October 1975, Columbia Studios, New York: 'Hurricane'

'Rita Mae' 45 rpm single
'Abandoned Love', Biograph
'Catfish', 'Golden Loom', *The Bootleg Series*.

A composite 2CD set drawn from the first leg of the *Rolling Thunder Review*, in late 1975, was released as volume 5 in the *Bootleg Series* in November 2002.

HARD RAIN

US Release: September 1976
UK Release:
CD Release: Columbia 32308
Producer: Don DeVito and Bob Dylan, recording and mixing engineer Don Meehan

Columbia PC 34349
CBS 86016

Running Time: 51.17

SIDE ONE: Maggie's Farm*; One Too Many Mornings*; Stuck Inside Of Mobile With The Memphis Blues Again**; Oh, Sister**; Lay, Lady, Lay**.

SIDE TWO: Shelter From The Storm*; You're A Big Girl Now*; I Threw It All Away**; Idiot Wind*.

* Recorded at Hughes Stadium, Fort Collins Colorado, 23 May 1976, 11 songs also appeared on the *Hard Rain* video, including the five soundtracked here.
** Recorded at Tarrant County Convention Centre, Fort Worth, Texas, 16 May 1976

Bob Dylan: vocal, guitar, harmonica, **T-Bone Burnette:** guitar, piano, **Gary Burke:** drums, **David Mansfield:** guitars, **Scarlet Rivera:** violin, **Stephen Soles:** guitar, vocals, **Rob Stoner:** bass, vocal, **Howard Wyeth:** piano, **Mick Ronson:** guitar on 'Maggie's Farm'

The second leg of the *Rolling Thunder Revue* got rolling on 18 April 1976 in Lakeland, Florida, but much of its spontaneity seemed to have disappeared during the winter break. What it was replaced with, when things were really sparking, was a kind of anger and desperation coming off Dylan like steam.

The plan was to tour America's Gulf Coast, well off the usual fashionable rock'n'roll shrines, but Dylan turned up for rehearsals grumpy beyond belief. Mick Ronson had been plucked from his lead guitar duties with the Spiders from Mars but, for some inscrutable reason lost in Bob's head, he found himself spending a great deal of time not on stage but backstage waiting for a call. The results, when he did get a chance, were spectacular.

NBC had filmed another gig in Florida for a TV in-concert but Dylan was dissatisfied and

Bob Dylan
Hard Rain

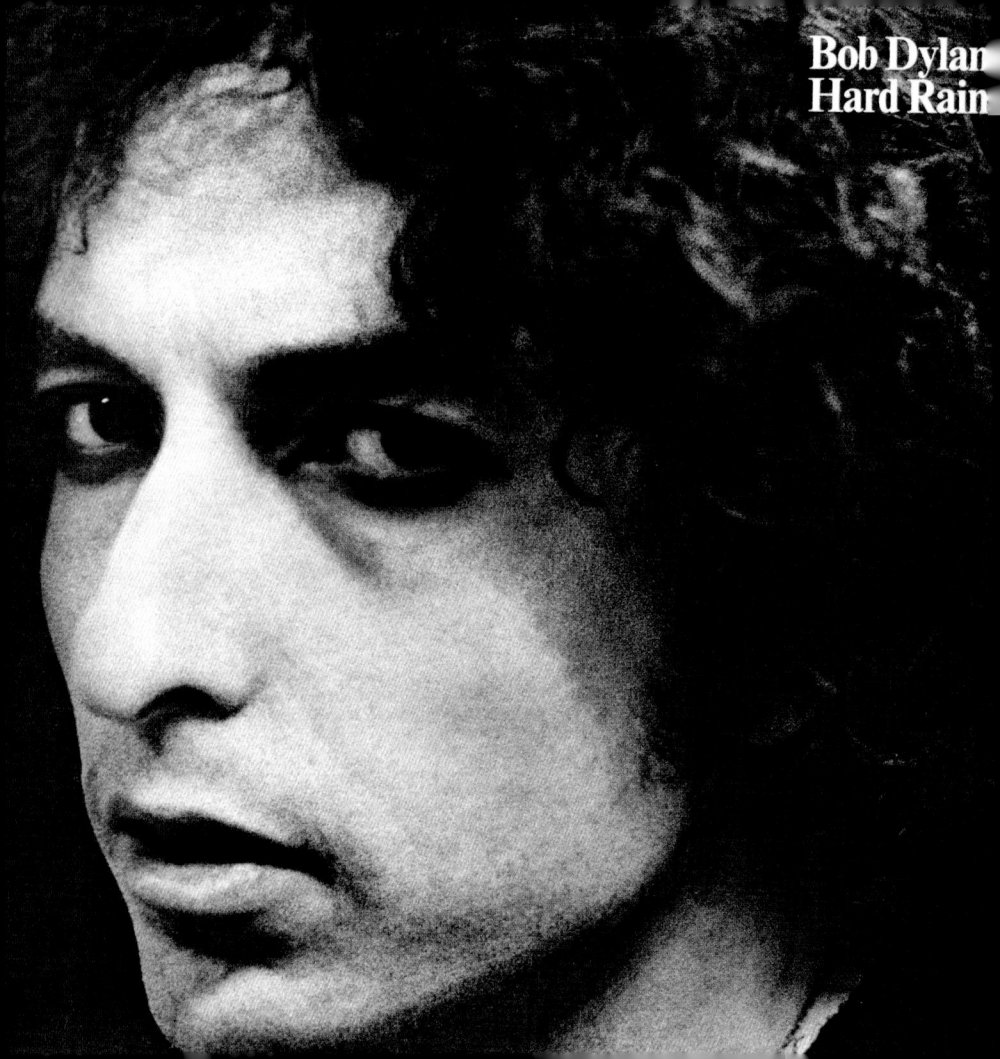

filmed the penultimate show of the whole tour, an open-air gig at Hughes Stadium in a mixture of sunshine and pouring rain to a drenched audience of 25,000, at his own expense. It was a day before his 35th birthday but he had the energy levels of a teenager that day. As *Village Voice* reported, 'not since the final frames of Queen Christina, when the camera enshrined Greta Garbo in silent spellbound reverence, has any face been so obsequiously honoured'. The non-sellout crowd and inclement weather seems to have pricked Dylan's ego. Sara had turned up unannounced for the gig, from which the bulk of the tracks here are taken, sparking a highly charged performance of startling intensity. 'It's like a punk record', Rob Stoner said later, 'it's got such energy and anger'. 'Bob was really hitting the bottle that weekend.'

Michael Gray sees this all-or-nothing performance as heralding 'the ragged, postmodern Bob Dylan right from the grungy instrumental ground-pawing ahead of the start of the first number. The running order now seems surprisingly well thought out'.

There are significant losses, though. When compared to the video release, the album omits all the duets with Joan Baez. This is a particular shame as these include electric (in both senses) versions of 'Blowin' In The Wind' and 'I Pity The Poor Immigrant' – gone Latino – plus a 'frantic retooling' of 'A Hard Rain's A Gonna Fall', from which both album and filmed concert take their title. Ditto a version of 'Knockin' On Heaven's Door' with Roger McGuinn. Harris splutters 'contractual Nazi-ism, the bane of so many 70s multi-artist enterprises. Either that or Dylan was still grumpy'.

The main critical differences are over the worth of Dylan's latest band. Tim Riley reckons Howard Wyeth is the wrong kind of drummer: 'whatever he is playing on 'Maggie's Farm' it isn't a two-four beat that the players can sit back on, he's pushing instead of cushioning. Robert Christgau complains that these folkies' 'idea of rock 'n' roll is rock 'n' roll cliché'. Others reckon, conversely, that this is a rewriting of the rock'n'roll rulebook, deconstructing the template. An added bonus is T-Bone Burnette on guitar and keyboards, years away from his respectability as a sonic magician for movies such as *O Brother*.

The cover is to match, a monochrome full-face photograph of Bob wearing eyeliner,by Ken Regan. Something far removed from the butch young folkie on those early albums. The back cover is an equally dramatic colour shot by Joel Bernstein of Dylan seen from the back, with a white headscarf, a crowd of faces in front of him, a sea of dark eyes. The CD booklet adds a lyric book and a significant upgrade in sound, beefing up the bass. It also runs together the applause to make this hybrid show like one continuous performance.

SIDE ONE
Maggie's Farm (Dylan) 5.23
A bit of tuning up, then Mick Ronson thunders in with a brand new riff. It is a new arrangement with melodramatic silences before each final line. The band clatter and Dylan attacks the lyrics like a prize fighter, and bellows wordlessly, like a bull. Paul Williams reckons the song is thus 'opened up musically and more energy gets through'.

One Too Many Mornings (Dylan) 3.47
Again a different arrangement, both to the acoustic original and the '66 edition. Dylan sounds resentful, and changes the final lines to 'I've no right to be here/and you've no right to stay'. The rhythm section fracture the beat and Rivera wails on her fiddle like a banshee.

Stuck Inside Of Mobile With The Memphis Blues Again (Dylan) 6.01
The band trash the *Blonde On Blonde* version, punks let loose in the museum with bouncy bass and a touch of reggae in there too. Dylan sings 'oooh' with relish. Paul Williams reckons this is born-again music, a new squalling baby with no chains on'. Certainly seeing the CBGB bands that year has energized Dylan.

Oh, Sister (Dylan/Levy) 4.08
Dylan emotes, the band match his mood with some lovely violin and lead guitar interplay, sweet and rough at the same time. This makes the album version the palest of shadows. The way he sings about being reborn makes his later conversion – in the wake of most of the band here – almost a foregone conclusion.

Lay, Lady, Lay (Dylan) 5.47
One reviewer criticised the new version's 'crude carnality'. But that is the whole point, a lullabye recast in the brothel: 'forget this dance, let's go upstairs'. And the band sing as lustily as the Band.

SIDE TWO
Shelter From The Storm (Dylan) 5.29
First of an extraordinary rebirth of three key songs from *Blood On The Tracks*, with a *Nashville Skyline* song thrown in the middle as a tease. Brilliant programming from two completely separate shows, here as one. Of this, John Harris opines 'it's The Clash-esque reading of this song – featuring Dylan playing hands of concrete slide guitar – that exercises the most addictive spell'. Mystery has been sacrificed for urgency and Dylan is like a madman ranting in the street.

You're A Big Girl Now (Dylan) 7.01
Seven minutes and not a second wasted. This one will tear your heart out, even slower and more ominous than the original, a man drowning as his love waits on dry land. Paul Williams is almost beyond speech, this version is 'messing with the fabric of time itself'. This band knows the value of silence, and Scarlet goes deep in the register over a post-modern string band.

I Threw It All Away (Dylan) 3.18
Another corkscrew to the heart. Dylan gets lost, singing the second verse ending too soon, so in the second he has to improvise and later he throws in a new closing couplet, 'one thing for sure/there ain't no cure'. But he sounds so wracked and the slide work is worthy of Brian Jones: they repeat the title line twice, for emphasis.

Idiot Wind (Dylan) 10.12
To conclude this brilliantly constructed concert that never was, ten minutes of bile, and Dylan is back to his most accusatory. Remarkably, this band top the crack crew in Minnesota, keeping it slow yet violent. Perhaps out of deference to McGuinn, the chestnut mare is here replaced with what sounds like a smoking tomb. Bass and drums interlock here, like a jigsaw puzzle, and steel guitar sweetens a very bitter pill. But Dylan is truly speaking in tongues – 'you left me standing in the middle of the air'.

STREET LEGAL

US Release: 15 June 1978　　　　　　　　**Columbia JC 35453**
UK Release: 1978　　　　　　　　　　　　**CBS 86067**
CD Release:　　　　　　　　　　　　　　**Columbia COL 494788 2**
CD Remaster/SACD Release:　　　　　　**Columbia 512355 6**
Producer: Don DeVito, reissue/remix produced　**Running Time:** 50.28
by Don DeVito and Steve Berkovitz,
engineer Biff Dawes

SIDE ONE: Changing Of The Guards; New Pony; No Time To Think; Baby Stop Crying.

SIDE TWO: Is Your Love In Vain?; Senor (Tales Of Yankee Power); True Love Tends To Forget; We Better Talk This Over; Where Are You Tonight (Journey Through Dark Heat).

Bob Dylan: vocals and electric rhythm guitar, **Billy Cross**: lead guitar, **Steve Douglas**: tenor and soprano sax, **Bobbye Hall**: percussion, **David Mansfield**: violin and mandolin, **Alan Pasqua**: keyboards, **Jerry Scheff**: bass, **Steven Soles**: rhythm guitar and vocals, **Ian Wallace**: drums, **Carolyn Dennis, Jo Ann Harris, Helena Springs**: vocals, **Steve Madaio**: trumpet on 'Is Your Love In Vain?'

In late 1977 Dylan bought a rehearsal space in Santa Monica that he renamed Rundown Studios, aptly as it proved, and installed a basic recording rig. It was a place where he and his showband could rehearse for their world tour. Disastrously as it turned out, he decided to record here too, so that a loose jam could be laid down there and used to build a new song or arrangement.

As *Biograph* puts it, the eight-piece band, and the three girl harmony singers that Dylan assembled here was 'larger and more varied than any he'd ever toured with. 'Senor' was typical of the richly textured new songs he began writing'. Rob Stoner had quit, so Presley's bass player Jerry Scheff took his place. Having road-tested the band in the far east and left behind tapes that would shortly afterwards be released as *At Budokan* – he spent a break from touring

BOB DYLAN
STREET-LEGAL

in April 1978 to lay down his next album. 'It took us a week to make *Street Legal*. We mixed it the following week and put it out the week after. If we hadn't done it so fast, we wouldn't have made an album at all because we were ready to go back on the road'.

And it sounds it, fluffed backing vocals, missed cues, Dylan sounding as if his voice had already having too much taken out of it by constant touring. Clinton Heylin gives the lowdown. Dylan had already demoed some of these new songs to Jerry Wexler in LA. However, the only new song that Dylan performed during the concerts in Japan and Australia was 'Is Your Love In Vain?', twice. He tried to book a professional studio, but none could accommodate so large a band, playing in real time, together. So they decided to keep things in-house and bring in a mobile truck, and producer Don DeVito. But the way the recording space was set up for rehearsal, with musicians hearing themselves naturally and not through headphones was great for live performance, but a disaster when it came to laying Dylan's vocals down. A '16 track morass', Clinton calls the results and no-one can disagree.

Except one. As a man who embraced chaos, Dylan announced that *Street Legal* is closest to where my music is going'. After the bike crash he had developed amnesia and had to learn how to do what before had come naturally. 'To write consciously is a trick,' and this was the culmination of that process. But what might well prove in the long run to be one of Dylan's most profound records drew a hail of criticism. Greil Marcus found it 'utterly fake' and 'sexist, mannered cr*p' to boot. 'I think the obvious reason for the poor couplets was that some unknown person had introduced Bob to a rhyming dictionary.'

Dylan attacked back. 'The critics treated this record spitefully – I saw one review that accused me of going to Vegas and copying Bruce Springsteen because I was using Steve Douglas, a saxophone player. I don't copy guys that are under 50 years old'. Announcing sniffily, 'I wasn't familiar with Bruce's work' though he can hardly have missed his 1975 breakthrough concerts in New York, or indeed Springsteen's role as pretender to Dylan's crown, Bob then pointed out testily that Douglas had played with Duane Eddy and 'on literally all of Phil Spector's records'. Michael Gray gives perhaps the fairest of the reactions: documenting as he does a crucial time in Dylan's life, between divorce and being born again, it is 'of astonishing complexity and confidence, delivered in Dylan's most authoritative voice and extremely badly produced'.

The front cover photograph was taken by Howard Alk outside the entrance to Rundown Studios. *Street Legal* describes a hot rod modified to run on public roads but could also refer to Dylan's newly divorced status, although he still wears his wedding ring. The back cover is an amazingly unflattering photo by Alk – the co-director of *Eat the Document* – with a paunchy and white-clad Dylan, his mascara running, looking like a member of the Gary Glitter band. Inside shots by Joel Bernstein are more flattering and the original vinyl issue had a separate lyric sheet that demonstrated the clever word play and rhyme schemes to these extremely crafted songs. The album is dedicated to the memory of counter-culture revolutionary Emmett Grogan.

The original vinyl recording of this album and CD transfers present a notoriously muddy sound. *Street Legal* was remixed in the early 90s, and the result was a huge upgrade in sound so that you could finally hear which instrument was which, with longer mixes of 'Changing Of The Guard' and 'New Pony' as an extra bonus. This also applies to the subsequent CD remaster. At last it sounds as good as these songs sounded with the punch of a big band at Earls Court and Blackbushe Aerodrome later that same year.

And what emerges from the aural murk is an enigma, an album of huge poetic range and lyrical ambition, played competently and sung with edge-of-the-seat determination, and as unreadable as the sphinx. Dylan seems to be singing to himself. It is as if you took the most extreme imagery from 'My Back Pages' or the wilder reaches of 1966 and then mixed them up at random with the help of a rhyming dictionary. Dylan seems to have lost (temporarily) his primal gift of creating lines that stick in the head, 'memorable speech' as poetry was once memorably defined.

These are stories with the narrative left out. Everything here seems to be an echo of something from the 16 years since he began recording. Take the opening lines 'Can you tell me where we are headin'/is it Lincoln County Road or Armageddon'. The guiding idea of 'The Times They Are A-Changin' is reversed from statement to question, then the two most famous lines from 'Idiot Wind' are recast, to a place without resonance and a concept with a capital letter. Every commentator has a view on this, the one point of consensus is that of Paul Williams: 'in retrospect what he's saying in this album – unconsciously for the most part – is "Help"'.

The two guiding reference points seem to be the Bible and demon-haunted bluesman Robert Johnston. Plus the Tarot and various occult and mystical practices.

And his divorce hangs heavy in the air here. The album is full of images of betrayal and loss. It shares the same post-cocaine burn out atmosphere as, say, the Eagles Hotel California, or Steely Dan's later output, bulletins from the palaces of excess. But as to what it all means, best go to the evangelists. Robin Witting's booklet *There's A New Day At Dawn* gives a relatively straightforward Christian interpretation. Michael Gray does much the same with footnotes in his chapter 'The Coming Of The Slow Train'. But who really knows?

SIDE ONE
Changing Of The Guards (Dylan) 7.04
Patti Smith says 'I would never presume to know what his songs are about, but it has such a mix of tarot card and Joan-of-Arc imagery. Joan of Arc was 16 when they shaved her head and burned her at the stake. No matter how bitter or melancholy his songs are, there's always so much resilience, a sense of him striking back'. Yet the *Rough Guide* comments that 'you are left wondering what it is he is trying to say'. The female chorus echo his every thought and get on some listener's nerves – they are hardly in the Emmylou Harris league. As to the sound, it's boogie with a saxophone.

New Pony (Dylan) 4.40
Supposedly inspired by Dylan's romance with Helena Springs, with whom he co-wrote some songs this same year that are the obverse of the material here: witty, easy to understand, full of memorable lines. It is certainly part inspired by Son House's 'Pony Blues' with a bit of satanism thrown in. The band sound much crisper, with muscular drumming pinning down the 12-bar structure, but this lacks the lightness of touch of the greatest heavy rock. Cue Led Zeppelin who understand all about dynamics and ripping off the rural blues.

No Time To Think (Dylan) 8.24
A catalogue song like 'All I Really Want To Do', technically brilliant, but Paul Williams considers that what is really being laid out here is the 'disintegration of a subjective, personal reality rather than any kind of prophetic vision of the world. Something is catching up with the person singing the song'. 'Too damn clever by half' opines Clinton Heylin.

Baby Stop Crying (Dylan) 5.21
The band catch fire on this one, a 'catchy rewrite' of Robert Johnson's 'Stop Breaking Down'. Suddenly there is compassion in Dylan's voice, but there is still something opaque here. Again performed at a snail's pace.

SIDE TWO
Is Your Love In Vain? (Dylan) 4.35
A virtual rewrite of Robert Johnson's 'Love In Vain', but where that was crisp and full of mysterious imagery, this is verbally blurred and feminists rightly took umbrage at the line about 'can you cook and sew, make flowers grow/do you understand my pain?' But look deeper, and here is a man whose self confidence is shot away. Just listen to the weariness in his voice. Musically, this is the *Blonde on Blonde* 'thin wild Mercury sound' through a xerox of a xerox.

Senor (Tales Of Yankee Power) (Dylan) 5.45
This is the key track of the album. Dylan told *Biograph* that '"Senor" was one of them border-type things, sort of lost yankee on gloomy Sunday-carnival-embassy-type of thing, the unforgettable wench, not a friend in the world, all messed up for something like a murder charge, having to pay for sins you didn't commit. I see this as the aftermath of when two people who were leaning on each other because neither of them has the guts to stand up alone, all of a sudden they break apart. I think I felt that way when I wrote it'. Well that's clear then.

Just like the Eagles, this is rife with Carlos Castenada, especially his book *Tales of Power*. Maybe he is the senor addressed here, a magus who takes Dylan up in the air to look down on US history from the Wild West to Jimmy Carter. In this picture of a United States still scarred by memories of Vietnam, the 'tail of the dragon' could be the coming power of the far east, or a retreat into oblivion, like Noodles in *Once Upon A Time In America*. As in Leones' last movie, this could be either reality or an opium dream. But this is the song where everything comes into focus, the imagery suddenly resonates, like the 'marching band still playing in that vacant lot', and the band show their chops. Even the singing girls blend into the soundscape, and Douglas winds around the tune like a serpent.

True Love Tends To Forget (Dylan) 4.17
A song about being half in love, with piano tinkles straight out of Highway 61.

We Better Talk This Over (Dylan) 4.05
More of the same. As Paul Williams puts it, 'he's having a hard time finding a woman to save him'. 'One Too Many Mornings' revisited, with bongos.

Where Are You Tonight (Journey Through Dark Heat) (Dylan) 6.15
This quotes directly from Robert Johnson's 'Travelling Riverside Blues' and is obviously a key song although what door it unlocks remains unclear. Given Dylan's habit of using the final song of every studio album to look forward to his next chameleon change, this is certainly a look forward to the *Slow Train* coming. Indeed it is already rolling down the tracks in the opening line. It also looks back, to a ten-year marriage; 'without you, it just doesn't seem right'. For Robin Witting, 'we are able to discern Dylan's move towards Christ'. Well maybe, but it is a very real woman on his mind all the same, as the cloaked memories here attest. The eversensible Derek Barker reckons what is important to this album is the mood it cascades down on the listener, 'deep, dark and mysterious'.

OUTTAKES:
1 May, Rundown Studios, Santa Monica: Coming From The Heart, Stop Now (2 takes)

AT BUDOKAN

Japanese Release: 21 August 1978

US Release: April 1979
UK Release:
All contain booklet, UK version also contains a fold-out poster
CD Release: Columbia 467850-2

CBS/Sony 40AP 1100/01 with lyric sheet
Columbia PC2 – 36067
CBS 96004

Producer: Don DeVito
Running Time: 51.59, 51.02

Side One: Mr Tambourine Man; Shelter From The Storm; Love Minus Zero/No Limit; Ballad Of A Thin Man; Don't Think Twice, It's All Right.

Side Two: Maggie's Farm; One More Cup Of Coffee (Valley Below); Like A Rolling Stone; I Shall Be Released; Is Your Love In Vain?; Going, Going, Gone.

Side Three: Blowin' In The Wind; Just Like A Woman; Oh Sister; Simple Twist Of Fate; All Along The Watchtower; I Want You.

Side Four: All I Really Want To Do; Knockin' On Heaven's Door; It's Alright, Ma (I'm Only Bleeding); Forever Young; The Times They Are A-Changin'.

Bob Dylan: vocal, guitar, harmonica, **Billy Cross:** lead guitar, **Steve Douglas:** saxophone, flute, recorder, **Bobbye Hall:** percussion, **David Mansfield:** pedal steel, violin, mandolin, guitar, dobro, **Alan Pasqua:** keyboards, **Steven Soles:** rhythm guitar and vocals, **Rob Stoner:** bass, vocals, **Ian Wallace:** drums, **Debi Dye, Jo Ann Harris** and **Helena Springs:** vocals

Recorded in Japan, 28 February and 1 March 1978, Nippon Budokan, Tokyo

Having recorded two live albums in the recent past, Dylan was not looking to issue a tour souvenir, let alone one before the band and the complex new arrangements really bedded down. With 115 dates booked in advance, there was no sense of hurry. But Dylan had not reckoned with the determination of Sony Japan who wanted something to lay before those who had politely attended his ten shows there, his first visit to the land of the rising sun. Dylan had a new manager too, Jerry Weintraub who also handled Neil Diamond and Frank Sinatra – both made of sterner commercial instincts even than Bob – and was unlikely to turn down so easy a pay day. But the album sold so well on import to the UK and US, particularly among those curious to hear in advance what they had booked up tickets for, that it was eventually issued in both the UK and the US, due to popular demand.

Dylan later complained, rightly, 'they asked me to do a live album for Japan. We had just started findin' our way into things on that tour when they recorded it'. Then the criticism continued. 'Writers complain the show's disco or Las Vegas. I don't know how they came up with those theories. We never heard them when we played Australia or Japan or Europe. I made an album called *New Morning* and we used singers on just about every track. I used the horn sound in Nashville on 'Rainy Day Women'. There isn't really anything new, just a bunch of pieces put together'.

Michael Gray takes the point: 'it is a pity it caught the band before they reached the magical, incandescent form they hit later that year in Europe and North America. The album is a pale souvenir of what went down'. But Nigel Williamson admits that these criticisms do apply to *At Budokan*. 'The band sounds like they haven't yet been broken in, and the doodlings of sax/flute player Steve Douglas are particularly irritating. Dylan's vocals lack his usual forceful presence and he sounds oddly detached – there's little sense of him feeding off the band who are waiting for their employer to energize the proceedings'. That would change, even if another tour critic reckoned that 'Dylan's mix'n'match arrangements seem as out of date as his sequins'.

But this is a sumptuous package all the same, with a clarity of sound to match. The front cover is a stunning colour photo by Joel Bernstein of Dylan onstage, intent and alert and in discreet eyeliner, and there are three more such portraits by Hirosuke Katsuyama on the original vinyl issue, one flanked by members of his band. They lose some of their impact in the smaller CD format that adds a lyric sheet in reparation. The original vinyl also has a lyric book, but it is written in Japanese! It also boasts some lovely monochrome shots of Dylan in Japan.

They suggest that his sleeve notes, a rarity by now, are more than just a case of 'loving to be over in your little country'. Dylan realises what he left behind when he jetted away, 'my soul, my music and that sweet girl in the geisha house – I wonder does she remember me?'. His heart is still beating 'in Kyoto at the Zen Rock Garden. Someday I will be back to reclaim it'.

BOB DYLAN AT BUDOKAN

SIDE ONE
Mr Tambourine Man (Dylan) 5.04
Playful electric guitar, then a glazed sounding Dylan comes in with that 'damned flute' as one critic described it. Certainly the arrangement here is more 'I Want You' than the magic and mystery of the bare original. The organist shows his chops early too, and you can all clap along.

Shelter From The Storm (Dylan) 4.39
If this were anyone other than Dylan daring to take this great song to Vegas via Tokyo, there really would be murder. Maybe the man shouted 'Judas' 12 years too soon. Pallid white reggae and the girls sing along in unison, with sax and guitar breaks, like painting by numbers.

Love Minus Zero/No Limit (Dylan) 3.57
As the initial shock wears off and you realize that this album is strictly showtime, this jaunty take has a charm of its own, although Dylan really could be singing anything.

Ballad Of A Thin Man (Dylan) 4.53
Polite applause and then the tempo slows with some nice Spanish-style guitar and sultry organ. Then the tempo speeds up again, the girls come in, and its Dylan a-go-go.

Don't Think Twice, It's All Right (Dylan) 5.02
Some consider that this reggae-style arrangement deflates the song and certainly Bob Marley – Dylan's only real artistic equal in real time – would never have released anything this twee. But it's fun, with the emphasis on 'babe' in the chorus. A toytown rendition.

SIDE TWO
Maggie's Farm (Dylan) 5.25)
The first truly interesting new arrangement, vaguely oriental, that is appropriate. Suddenly you can hear the potential of this band, as a well drilled outfit brilliant at musical pastiche – but with an underlying power. And there is no doubt as to who is boss. Madonna should have been taking notes.

One More Cup Of Coffee (Valley Below) (Dylan) 3.30
Dylan suddenly sounds engaged and this is almost Cuban in its joy and tightness of arrangement. Good percussion, too.

Like A Rolling Stone (Dylan) 6.36
Dylan sings as if without full stops. The band thunders and whatever Dylan might say to the contrary, bring a Springsteen-ish feel to proceedings.

I Shall Be Released (Dylan) 4.24
The drums thump and the guitar player gets lyrical as Dylan sings as if not really there. The saxophone emotes more than Bob's voice that is strictly professional. Whoever this lounge singer is, he is covering Dylan's songs well.

Is Your Love In Vain? (Dylan) 4.02
'Here's an unrecorded song – see if you can guess which one it is.' The one song from the forthcoming album and this road test goes well, if with funereal slowness. Dylan's voice still lacks its full richness but suddenly he is singing as if he means it.

Going, Going, Gone (Dylan) 4.23
Rough Guide reckons this is an 'underwhelming rewrite'. Lyrically, it is almost completely new, turned from a suicide note to a mild expression of dissatisfaction. 'Fix me one more drink and hold me one more time/but don't get too close to make me change my mind'. But Dylan sings sweetly, and sounds fully connected. The band manage the changes of time signature like the old pros they are.

SIDE THREE
Blowin' In The Wind (Dylan) 4.32
Then suddenly Bob pulls this one out of his back catalogue, tender and regretful and different enough from the original take to maybe outdo it. A lovely arrangement too, with tinkling piano and the girls singing wordlessly (which is better) plus some Duane Eddy-style bass.

Just Like A Woman (Dylan) 5.06
Apparently Dylan was handed a list of the most requested songs by the promoter, rather like a master chef being handed a menu to follow. This does the job, but without any frills. Or feeling.

Oh Sister (Dylan/Levy) 4.50
A touch of the Spencer Davis Group in the arrangement, and though no Stevie Winwood, Dylan picks up the urgency, and there is a voodoo undercurrent. Dylan's wordless interjections here say more than many of his complete vocals elsewhere on these discs. Spooky guitar too, and Steve Douglas cutting loose to good effect.

Simple Twist Of Fate (Dylan) 4.27
'Here's a simple love story, it happened to me,' Dylan deadpans to a largely uncomprehending foreign-language audience. Those who heard him sing this later in England will take the memory to the grave. This isn't quite that fine yet, but getting there. The band are suddenly playing with feeling, not just chord charts.

All Along The Watchtower (Dylan) 3.26
'From the Mojave desert', Bob explains. This is driven by tom tom drums with some driving guitar, more Clapton than Hendrix, then violin but without Rivera's lack of control. Cheerful rather than apocalyptic this time around.

I Want You (Dylan) 2.40
So having jazzed up a sombre original, Dylan now takes a singalong and slows it down to a lament. Nothing beats being perverse, and this justifies the purchase price alone.

SIDE FOUR
All I Really Want To Do (Dylan) 3.45
Strictly vaudeville, but no it's not 'Rainy Day Women' but another side of *Another Side*, even if the arrangement is straight out of 'Feeling Groovy'.

Knockin' On Heaven's Door (Dylan) 4.03
This takes far more from Clapton's reggae-ish cover than from Dylan's own original, and passes the time pleasantly.

It's Alright, Ma (I'm Only Bleeding) (Dylan) 6.08
The lengthy original in a nutshell, now gone heavy, and against all the odds it is a triumph with Dylan singing urgently and the girl singers on fire. But why no acoustic solo spot Bob?

Forever Young (Dylan) 5.38
'Once again its the time of the hour when we have to run', Dylan quips in his latest incarnation as a cheesy nightclub singer. Then sings his most tender vocal of the night and the band are now fully warmed up. They need just a bit more self-confidence to muscle Bob out of the spotlight occasionally.

The Times They Are A-Changin' (Dylan) 5.29
'I wrote this about 15 years ago. It still means a lot to me, and I know it means a lot to you too'. The reaction is hardly tumultuous and the urgency of the original has now turned into what sounds like a lament. There is a typhoon of backing voices, the band keeps it simple and Dylan sings with the conviction of the gospel singer he will shortly become.

Also originating from Japan, where it was released on 25 February 1978 by CBS Sony, was the 3-LP set *Masterpieces*. Sumptuously packaged with photos of Dylan from the *Rolling Thunder* era, this sampled various tracks previously available only on single, including an alternative take of 'Mixed Up Confusion' from 1962, the 1965 single 'Can You Please Crawl Out Your Window', the Liverpool 1966 live take of 'Just Like Tom Thumb's Blues' that had been on the B-side of 'I Want You', another B-side 'Spanish Is The Loving Tongue', and the big band version of 'George Jackson', rush released in 1971, and the *Desire* outtake, 'Rita Mae'. The version later issued in Australia and New Zealand (CBS S3BP 220502) is not so sonically supercharged. It was widely imported into the UK but was never formally released there or in the US. The album is now available on CD as a high-priced import. At first it was a double CD with cuts, now the whole thing is on three silver discs.

By the time this tour had wound its increasingly weary way around the USA, and when Dylan reached San Diego on 17 November 1978, he was a worn-out man, both physically and spiritually, his marriage in tatters, his music approaching the formulaic. 'Towards the end of the show someone out in the crowd knew I wasn't feeling too well. I think they could see that. And they threw a silver cross on stage. I brought it backstage and took it with me to the next town, out in Arizona. I was feeling even worse than I'd felt when I was in San Diego. I said 'I need something tonight that I didn't have before'. And I looked in my pocket and I had this cross'.

In a Tucson hotel room he had a vision much like Paul did on the road to Damascus. 'There was a presence in the room that couldn't have been anybody but Jesus. It was a physical thing. I felt my whole body tremble. The glory of the Lord knocked me down and picked me up.' Dylan put aside touring and recording to take instruction with the Vineyard Fellowship, whose preacher Hal Lindsey foretold a coming Armageddon in the middle east. As Dylan said in 1980, 'being born again is a hard thing. You're reborn, but like a baby. You're a stranger. You have to learn all over again'. And three years later, 'when I get involved in something, I get totally involved. I don't just play around on the fringes'. As his next run of albums showed categorically.

SLOW TRAIN COMING

US Release: 18 August 1979
UK Release:
CD Release: CBS CD 86095
CD Remaster/SACD Release:
Producer: Jerry Wexler/Barry Beckett

Columbia FC 36120
CBS 86095

Columbia 512349 6
Running Time: 47.02

SIDE ONE: Gotta Serve Somebody; Precious Angel; I Believe In You; Slow Train.

SIDE TWO: Gonna Change My Way Of Thinking; Do Right To Me Baby (Do Unto Others); When You Gonna Wake Up; Man Gave Names To All The Animals; When He Returns.

Bob Dylan: vocal, guitar, **Barry Beckett:** keyboards, percussion, **Micky Buckins:** percussion, **Tim Drummond:** bass, **Mark Knopfer:** guitar, **Pick Withers:** drums, **Muscle Shoals Horns, Carolyn Dennis, Helena Springs** and **Regina Harris:** vocals, arrangements by **Harrison Calloway**

Dylan took off the first five months of 1979. 'I went to Bible school'. If nothing else, it certainly pepped up his songwriting. When compared to *Street Legal*, his new lyrics were to the point and their meaning was as clear as springwater. All his listeners were damned unless they took preventative action. 'The songs that I wrote for the *Slow Train* album – I didn't plan to write them, but I wrote them anyway. After I had a certain amount of them, I thought I didn't want to sing them, so I had a girl sing them for me, Carolyn Dennis – I (would give) them all to her, and (have) her record them, and not even put my name on them. I wanted the songs out but I didn't want to do it. It would just mean more pressure.'

Dylan had had some kind of divine visitation in a hotel room in Tucson on 17 November 1978, 'I truly had a born-again experience, if you want to call it that. The glory of the Lord knocked me down and picked me up'. He embraced Christ as he had earlier embraced Woody Guthrie, with frightening single-mindedness and as a spur to his own creativity. Within days he was testing out instrumental versions of 'Slow Train Coming' and 'Do Right' at soundchecks. Now he had a sheaf of new songs, burning with conviction. Appropriately he went to the deep

South to record them, to the legendary Muscle Shoals studios in Sheffield, Alabama. Jerry Wexler rebuffed any attempts to evangelize him: 'Bob, you're dealing with a 62-year-old confirmed atheist. I'm hopeless, Let's make an album'.

Of the 1978 tour band only two of its backing singers survive here, Helena Springs – who had urged Bob down on his knees to pray – and Carolyn Dennis. Barry Beckett co-produced the album with Wexler and played keyboards alongside bassist Tim Drummond and the Muscle Shoals Horns. Dylan had seen Dire Straits, then a hot new British band, at the LA Roxy and flew guitarist Mark Knopfler and drummer Pick Withers over to complete the crew. Knopfler recalls 'the first night was pretty awful – it just didn't happen – although once we got into it, it was good. But all these songs are about God'.

The album was laid down in less than a week, from 30 April to 4 May. Mark remembers that 'Bob ran through a lot of these songs beforehand in a very different form, just hittin' the piano. Each song has its own secret and needs teasing out'. But what was no secret was that Bob was out to save your soul, using every resource in his armoury.

He gave a notorious interview to *Rolling Stone*. 'I've always thought there's a superior power, that this is not the real world and that there's a world to come. That no soul has died, every soul is alive, either in holiness or in flames'. Now he takes the Bible literally, both old and new testaments, and awaits the Second Coming. 'I don't think it's at hand. There's a lot of people walkin' around who think that the new kingdom's coming. And they're wrong'. Eventually the Messiah will come, but not yet. And peace is not on the agenda. 'You can reload your rifle and that moment you're reloading it, that's peace. It may last for a few years.'

Reviewers purred over how beautifully the instruments had been recorded and indeed how well Dylan was singing. The lyrics were something else. Paul Williams asked 'is he trying to convert me, or is he calling me a fool? Is he sharing his feelings with me or mocking me'. Sinead O'Connor later declared that this was the album that made her want to become a singer because it is 'sexy and funky as well as being religious'.

The cover is a heavily symbolic – laboured, even – woodcut by Catherine Kanner. A steam train straight out of the Wild West waits while men build tracks for it to run on and their womenfolk boil a pot. In the foreground a man wields a pickaxe in the shape of a cross. The back cover is far more appealing, a photograph of Dylan on his yacht, on a calm sea as evening falls. The CD digipack adds a photo of the Muscle Shoals crew off duty, and a startling shot of Dylan in a cowboy hat, lost in shadow and with his startling eyes catching the camera.

SLOW TRAIN COMING
BOB DYLAN

SIDE ONE
Gotta Serve Somebody (Dylan) 5.25

When Jerry Wexler began to put a running order together for the album, he at first left this out, which defies belief. Dylan 'had to fight to get it on the album'. Bob gives a nuanced vocal performance, from playful to scornful to impassioned, dancing with the beat. And the musicianship is to match, with sinister electric piano, Withers drumming up a storm, relentless guitar rhythm from Knopfler and a girl chorus who know their place in the mix this time around. As an opening track, it is the perfect calling card, addressing the unconverted.

Dylan later performed the song at the Grammy Awards Presentation and won the award for Best Male Rock Vocalist that same night. This is one of the greatest of Dylan's 'list songs' with a nod back to Memphis Slim's 'Mother Earth': 'you may own a city, even diamonds and pearls'. The Lord has not removed his sense of humour. Indeed the line about 'you can call me Zimmy' – the first reference in any of his songs to his birth name – is astounding, and some of the snares and delusions here, 'women in a cage', are wonderfully dismissive. But the catalogue he rolls out is wide enough to catch each and every one of his listeners on one hook or other.

Precious Angel (Dylan) 6.31

As Dylan later told Paul Zollo: 'it could go on forever. A lot of my songs strike me that way. That's the natural thing about them to me. They're not written in stone. They're on plastic'.

He sounds almost matter-of-fact as he sets out his stall, then gradually ups the emotional temperature until at the end he is almost howling. It starts like 'If Not For You' but the woman addressed here is an angel in more than the sexual sense. 'Lamp of my soul' as well as 'queen of my flesh'– quite an act to follow. This is a fierce and sole truth Dylan is evangelizing. Buddha and Mohammed are dismissed in the same line in favour of the Man – capitalized in *Lyrics* to make things clear – who 'died a criminal's death'.

This is far more of a restless farewell than 16 years before. Bob consigns his ungodly friends to the fire simply for showing concern. Knopfler almost makes his guitar talk. The jaunty arrangement and driving drums are reminiscent of how the Byrds used to remake Dylan songs in their own graven image.

I Believe In You (Dylan) 5.10
Sung by a man of flesh and blood, at the very edge but sweetly, at least at first. The cool musicianship only makes Dylan sound more distraught as he becomes impassioned. But this is a song from the apex of someone's spiritual life, the endless moment of holy zeal that creates both saints and lunatics.

Dylan portrays himself as an exile in his own land. It could just as well be written to a woman as to God, especially the line 'I believe in you, even on the morning after'. The only comparison in modern rock is the 1977 concerts by Richard and Linda Thompson, dressed in white robes and singing hymns to Allah that doubled as songs of sexual devotion. Like them, Dylan's most expressive and extreme renditions of this material was in live concert. In both cases these nightly displays of passion that shook anyone lucky enough to witness them, have been struck from the record. Here there is a lovely swaying beat and a guitar outro so liquid it almost melts. Jack White adapted the tune for the White Stripes' 2005 track 'As Ugly As I Seem'.

Slow Train (Dylan) 6.03
The song was first unveiled at a soundcheck towards the end of the 1978 tour, predating Dylan's enrolment in Bible classes with his new mentor Hal Lindsay at the Vineyard Fellowship. Dylan reckoned that 'just writing a song like that probably emancipated me from other kinds of illusion. On its own level, it was some kind of turning point'.

Rather like Ken Kesey and the Merry Pranksters with their mantra that you were either 'on the bus' or not, here you better get on this train or be crushed beneath its wheels.

Paul Williams has written about the song's 'fierce bright young penetrating howl of joy'. The way Dylan sings the song suggests that he can't wait for the train to hit the station and unleash Armageddon. Hard Rain, revisited. The more politically correct have objected to lines about 'foreign oil controlling American soil' and 'sheiks walking around like kings'. Indeed, such perceptions are largely responsible for the second Iraq war begun by elements in the Bush camp who attended to the same kind of evangelical scare-mongering that Dylan was under the sway of when he wrote this song. But, hell, it is exhilarating.

SIDE TWO
Gonna Change My Way Of Thinking (Dylan) 5.29
A song written to himself, like a penance. The backing is equally tough, as befits this urban blues, plus holy rolling organ. As in the last song, Dylan attests to a God-fearing woman whose ministry is more than just spiritual. 'She can do the Georgia crawl/she can walk in the spirit of the Lord'. But the lines about 'sons becoming husbands to their mothers' – pure D H Lawrence – are great as invective from the pulpit but make no real sense at all.

Lyrics also prints a set of alternative lyrics, with more references to the slow train coming and 'jumping on the monkey's back' and gives the 'track' the engine runs on a whole other sinister meaning.

Do Right To Me Baby (Do Unto Others) (Dylan) 3.54
Dylan starts by saying he 'don't wanna judge nobody', and Jesus warned about people looking at splinters in the eyes of others with a plank in their own, despite the jovial arrangement here. Except that the whole album is based on a fiercely judgmental world view with vocals to match. Here again there is a sexual ambiguity in this exchange, 'do right to me baby/and I'll do right to you'. 'Brother' would have been less troubling, especially given the fervent strictures against homosexuality that Dylan would deliver between songs when he took this material out on the road.

When You Gonna Wake Up (Dylan) 5.30
Dylan said 'that's a song you could write a song to every line in the song'. Which is odd, as many of the lines are simply the title repeated. The same idea as here lies behind Gurdjieff's philosophy, that mankind needs to awake from its entrenched mental habits. Dylan is more explicit about the means of enslavement, including Marxism that must have come as a shock to the New Left, for whom his earlier songs were a touchstone and Henry Kissinger, satirized in *Dr Strangelove*, and an eminence grise for a series of US administrations – and winner of the Nobel peace prize!

The line about 'spiritual advisors and gurus to guide your every move' is a bit rich coming from a man who at the time of writing this was part of a fringe Christian cult. Musically this is divine with growling bass, solid drumming, soulful organ and ecstatic brass.

Man Gave Names To All The Animals (Dylan) 4.27
Woody Guthrie wrote some children's songs, and here Dylan follows suit, a kid's song for adults with a sly reference to the serpent in Eden at the end. He leaves the rhyme word 'lake' for you to enter the silent rhyme word 'snake'. And it is already slithering close to the tree of knowledge. Musically, this is cod-reggae with a real bounce, and tight as a duck's *** (rhymes with pass).

When He Returns (Dylan) 4.31
Dylan sings as powerfully as at any time in his whole career over crashing piano chords from Barry Beckett, testifying like a hellfire preacher with the rhetorical command of John Milton: 'surrender your crown on this blood-soaked ground, take off your mask'. The second coming is no longer the joyous return of 'When The Ship Comes In' but something straight out of W B Yeats, a time of terror and dread. 'Truth is an arrow' and one that pierces not just the 'dust of rumours' this time around, but the very heart.

OUTTAKES:
30 April 1979, Muscle Shoals Sound Studio, Alabama: 'Trouble in Mind', later released as a single, minus one verse
2 May 1979, Muscle Shoals Sound Studio, Alabama: 'Ye Shall Be Changed'

'Trouble in Mind' 45 rpm single (with one verse edited out from studio take)
'Ye Shall Be Changed' *The Bootleg Series*.

SAVED

US Release: 20 June 1980   **Columbia 36553**
UK Release: **CBS 86113**
CD Release: Columbia 32742
Producer: Jerry Wexler and Barry Beckett   **Running Time:** 43.01

SIDE ONE: A Satisfied Mind; Saved; Covenant Woman; What Can I Do For You?; Solid Rock.

SIDE TWO: Pressing On; In The Garden; Saving Grace; Are You Ready

Bob Dylan: vocal, guitar, harmonica, **Tim Drummond**: bass, **Jim Keltner**: drums, **Spooner Oldham**: keyboards, **Fred Tackett**: guitar, **Terry Young**: keyboards and vocal: **Clydie King, Regina Harris, Mona Lisa Young**: vocals, special Guest Artist: **Barry Beckett**

Saved was recorded back in Muscle Shoals between 11 and 15 February 1980 after three months of relentless gigging with the road band who had played some of the most apocalyptic concerts of Dylan's whole career. No longer a 'stadium act' and playing not one song from before the conversion, these shows took place in human-sized venues, with hell-fire pronouncements from Bob between songs to rachet up the emotional temperature still further. Tapes from a 14-night residency at the Fox Warfield Theatre in San Francisco in November 1979 see a beguiling mixture of songs from *Slow Train Coming* and this one.

If *Saved* doesn't quite capture that musical fervour, it could be that – just like the Band in the middle of being booed on stage each night – the musicians had already given their all on stage to a largely hostile or uncomprehending audience. As tour manager Arthur Rosato told Heylin just two days after a show in Charleston and after three months on the road with a six-week break beckoning 'we didn't go home, we went straight into the studio'. They thought 'we never gonna get home'.

Although it sounds wonderful to contemporary ears, just one of many of Dylan's albums that have improved with age and distance, the storm of controversy over Dylan's typical all-encompassing purge of any songs not fit for the slow train – 'where time does not interfere' – resulted in this album being a commercial disaster.

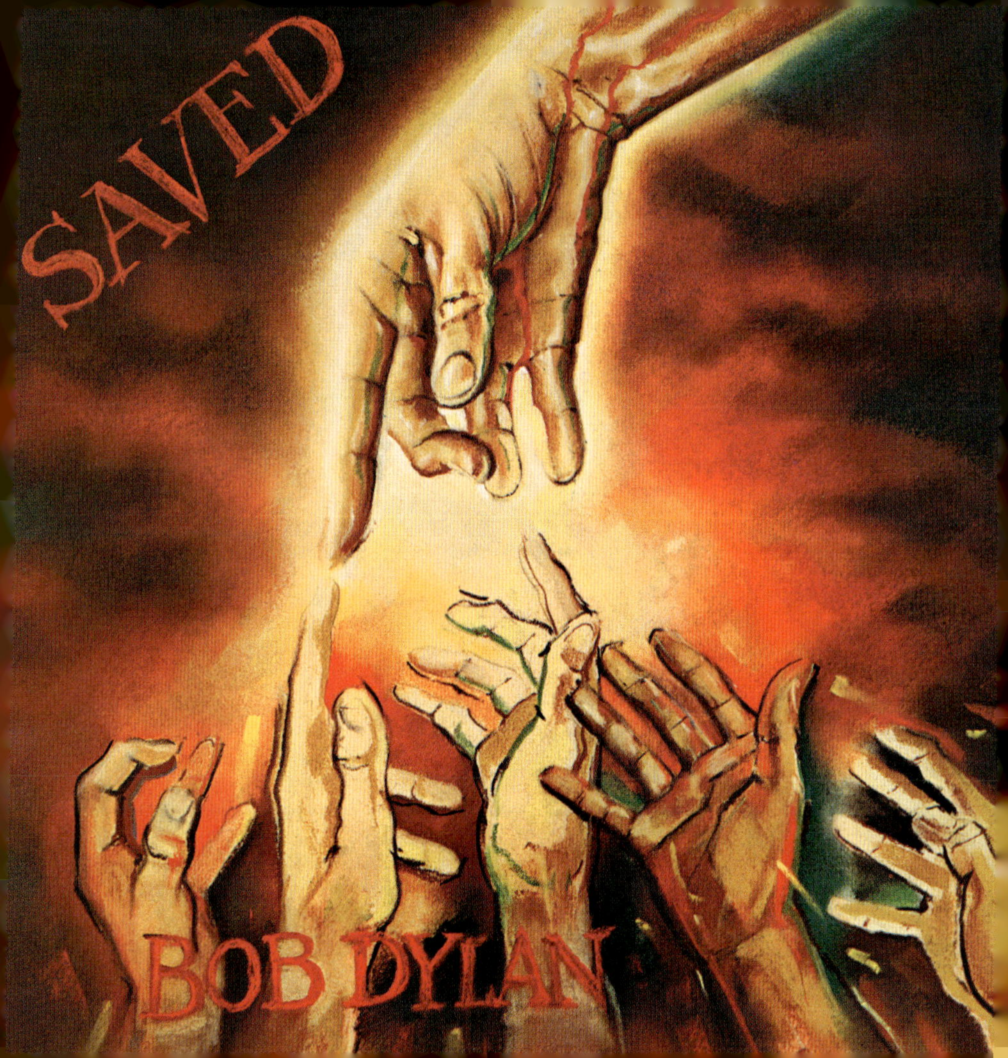
SAVED
BOB DYLAN

Quite aside from the appalling record sleeve, as Heylin points out, 'the sound itself has none of the textured quality of *Slow Train*'. The real problem lies with the miking of the drums. Rosato points out 'these drums that sound like boxes, just horrible': even as experienced a session man as Keltner dared not object. An incompetent engineer had taped up the drums. The band eventually took corrective action and removed the tape, but the damage was already done.

The lyrics here were more evangelically hard line than even those on the previous album. As Dylan put it, 'people didn't like those tunes, they rejected all that stuff when my show would be all off the new album', while acknowledging that 'I'm fortunate that I'm in a position to release an album like *Saved* with a major record company'. True: gospel and Christian-orientated albums tend not to sell through mainstream distributors, though they have a network all their own and a fervent audience, even without Dylan's add-on reputation.

Outside the tabernacles, the tastemakers were almost universally appalled. The general view was that there is a 'stridency and intransigence that is far less appealing than the more humane expression of faith on *Slow Train*', a hectoring quality that made this 'one of the most joyless gospel albums ever made'. For converts only. Much reference was made to the devil having the best tunes on the evidence herein. And no-one seemed to note the import of the quotation on the inner sleeve from Jeremiah. 'Behold, the days come, saith the Lord, that I will make a new covenant with the house of Israel and with the house of Judah'.

This could be read, through the prism of the New Testament, as a rapprochement between Christianity and Judaism, by whose tenets Dylan had been raised back in Hibbing, bar mitzvahs et al. Of course, it was Jewish nationalists who had urged the Romans to crucify Christ and like the disciples and Christ himself Judas too was a Jew, covertly fuelling much of the anti-semitism that had despoiled the Christian church through the centuries. Hence the additional resonance of that shout of 'Judas' back in 1966 and Dylan's mention of the Holocaust, briefly, in 'With God On Our Side'.

This album, fierce and bloody as it is, can be read as the zeal of a man who thinks he has come home at last; and the sense of drift and anomie in the following decade, the comedown when this proved to be a pipe dream. This is a partial excuse for the execrable cover painting, a pastel by Tony Wright. God stretches his very human hand to touch the fingertip of five other (all white) hands reaching up to a blood-red sky. The title and Dylan's name are roughly written, also in red, and half lost in flesh. The whole thing looks like a bad example of children's art. Inside the package are photographs of Dylan on stage with his gospel troupe taken by Arthur Rosato, two of which are so blurred as to be barely decipherable. It all looks extremely cheap and far from cheerful. From 1985, US issues used a less confrontational sleeve of Dylan live on stage as the front cover.

Columbia bosses were apparently appalled when the tapes reached them. This was nowhere near as user-friendly as the previous disc. They cancelled the album and arranged to record a tour date at Toronto on 19 April 1980 when the road show got back underway. Shorn of Dylan's inter-song harangues, this also lacked the sheer musical muscle of the original dates on the born-again freight train. Also, four of the seven songs shortlisted had already been included on *Slow Train Coming*. So the decision was reversed and *Saved* was issued as originally intended.

SIDE ONE
A Satisfied Mind (Red Hayes & Jack Rhodes) 1.57
Best known to folkies via Ian and Sylvia, and a strange song to start off with despite its familiar opening words 'how many times….' The three girls coo like doves and Dylan testifies with full force. The organ is particularly churchy and the double punch with piano suggests that this holy roller sound underlaid *Highway 61*, and Dylan's electric pomp, without anyone realizing it.

Saved (Dylan and Tim Drummond) 4.00
Starts almost like 'Jumping Jack Flash, with a reference to being blinded by the devil and born dead from the womb. What separates evangelical Christianity from other forms of that faith, Catholicism in particular, is this idea that to be made fit for heaven, the convert has to make a new commitment, to be born again in the blood of the Lord. A very personal transaction without the intervention of clergy. And Dylan certainly testifies here for all he is worth, over equally frantic musical backing.

Covenant Woman (Dylan) 6.02
Commentators differ as to whom exactly this woman is, but the consensus is Helena Springs, with whom Dylan split up shortly before the recording. Dylan sounds sad rather than ecstatic as he thanks her, from the bottom of her heart. Lines like 'I've been broken, shattered like an empty cup' reach out to any listener, whatever their faith, or lack of one. There is a stunning organ break, and some lovely soulful rhythmic guitar. In fact, from this distance, it sounds like a masterpiece.

What Can I Do For You? (Dylan) 5.54
In *Lyrics*, 'You' is capitalized, as if it weren't already clear that this was addressed to the Big Man. If Dylan had previously argued with his Dear Landlord, now he is abject as a believer must be. Good for him, but both the language here and the music are essentially pedestrian, a string of clichés, apart from the virtuouso harmonica break, that is among the best that Dylan has ever committed to vinyl – it sounds as if he is in the room.

Solid Rock (Dylan) 3.55
This also brings up a weird picture in the mind, of a bedraggled Dylan clinging onto a giant boulder. It is certainly a pale shadow indeed of the original live version that would shake the rafters of the hall, introduced under its full title of 'Hanging On To A Solid Rock Made Before The Foundation Of The World'. Dylan is quoted in *Biograph* 'well you don't hear things like that, full gospel, half gospel or otherwise'. Certainly even Led Zeppelin rarely blew up as wild a musical storm as this, not in terms of flying plectrums (it's quite restrained) but the sheer ferocity of the ensemble, thundering like, well, a runaway train. Live, the musical suspension of time after he would sing 'Hanging On' could last an aeon, or so it seemed.
Here the drums kick the band along, the bass rumbles and the three women sound like Tina Turner at her wildest, hell cats backing up their old tom.

SIDE TWO
Pressing On (Dylan) 5.11
The quiet after the storm, at least to start off, and now the girls are singing like sirens not banshees. The band embroider Dylan's fervent vocal delicately but are back on full power by the fade-out. Vocally, Van Morrison can summon up the same invincible sternness occasionally. All the invention is in the performance, the lyrics on the page read as evangelism by numbers. 'Don't look back' is hidden in there somewhere.

In The Garden (Dylan) 5.58
Bob Dylan: ''In The Garden' is actually a classical piece. I was playing at the piano, closed my eyes and it just came to me. I can hear it being played by a symphony orchestra or a chamber choir'. Another of the greatest songs of his career with a performance to match. These word-pictures of Jesus preaching, healing the sick and in Gethsemane, give the song a focus and its structure as a series of unanswered questions, to which the correct answer in every case is 'No.' Dylan is never happier than when pointing the finger at the unfortunate, whether Mr Jones, poor southern white trash, or unbelievers. But whatever creed or magic potion stops you screaming out at night in unspeakable agony, to misquote the Alabama Three, Dylan's fervour and the band following his every breath and change of mood, is exhilarating – and scary.

Saving Grace (Dylan) 5.01
At last some sweetness, like wild honey among the rocks. A beautiful tune, worthy of *The Basement Tapes* and another thank-you song to God. He admits that 'I've escaped death so many times', that ties in with the quote by his one-time PA Bernard Paturel, that 'before Sara, I thought it was just a question of time before Bob died'. He is honest enough to admit that even post-conversion, belief ebbs and flows: 'it gets discouraging at times, but I know I'll make it'. The band here sound very close to the Band, that rich attack of guitar, piano and organ, plus a flexible rhythm section, acting as one mind.

Are You Ready (Dylan) 4.41
Another series of questions, with some sweet lead guitar. Then the organ takes centre stage. 'Have you decided to be in heaven or hell?' There is only really one answer – Dylan is fully convinced he is right, and bound for glory.

SHOT OF LOVE

US Release: 12 August 1981

UK Release:
CD Release: Columbia 474689 2
Producer: Chuck Plotkin and Bob Dylan, plus
Bumps Blackwell on the title song, engineered by Toby Scott

Columbia TC 37496
Reissued with extra track PC 37496
CBS 85178
Running Time: 44.59

SIDE ONE: Shot Of Love; Heart Of Mine; Property Of Jesus; Lenny Bruce; Watered-Down Love.

SIDE TWO: The Groom's Still Waiting At The Altar (CD addition, not original vinyl); Dead Man, Dead Man; In The Summertime; Trouble; Every Grain Of Sand.

Bob Dylan: vocal, guitar, harmonica, piano, percussion, **Steve Douglas:** saxophone, **Tim Drummond:** bass, **Jim Keltner:** drums, **Danny Kortchmar:** electric guitar, **Carl Pickhardt:** piano, **Steve Ripley:** guitar, **Fred Tackett:** guitar, **Benmont Tench:** keyboards, **Clydie King, Regina McCrary, Carolyn Dennis, Madelyn Quebec:** vocals, **Donald 'Duck' Dunn:** bass, **Wm 'Smitty' Smith:** organ, **Ringo Starr:** drums, **Ron Wood:** guitar on 'Heart Of Mine'

According to Helena Springs, Dylan began to find 'a lot of hypocrisy in those Jesus people that he had gotten involved with'. Live, he was starting to re-integrate older, non-religious songs with his new material, but for those who caught these concerts when they hit the UK, there was no doubt as to where his heart still lay. And it wasn't with 'Blowin' In The Wind'. After two albums cut quickly in the same studios, *Shot of Love* is the result of a bewildering odyssey around the recording studios of Los Angeles, and a musical crew comprising the rhythm section and girl chorus from *Saved*, new guitarist Danny Kortchmar and Tom Petty's keyboard player Benmont Tench. Steve Douglas returns to play some masterful saxophone and on one track only for certain, are guest celebrities Ringo Starr and Ron Wood.

Dylan now shared production duties. Although the transcendent 'Every Grain Of Sand'

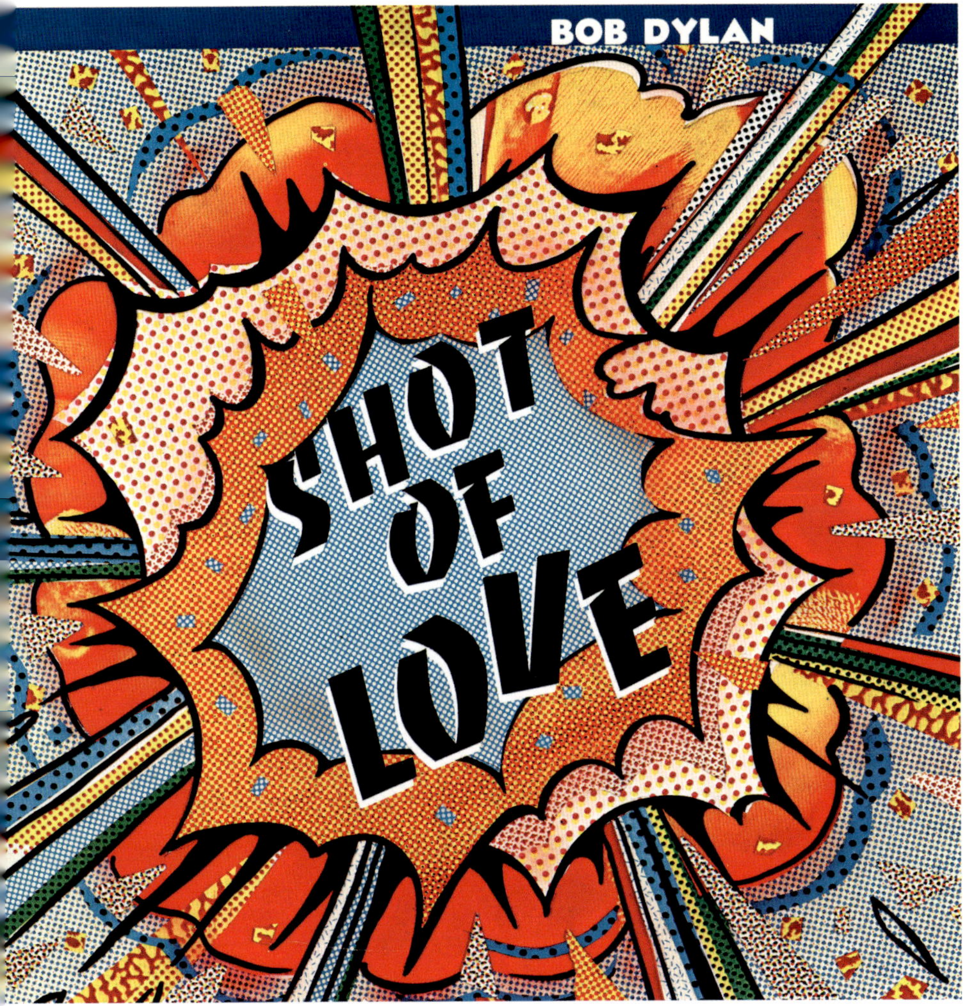
BOB DYLAN
SHOT OF LOVE

was first recorded as early as September 1980, many of the later outtakes suggest that Dylan may well have been contemplating a more apocalyptic hellfire and brimstone repertoire for his new album. The moving carnival first pitched up at United Western studio on 2 April 1981 and laid down some cover versions including 'Let It Be Me' and the lost song 'Fur Slippers', supposedly boasting 'some of the dumbest lyrics this side of country'. When a tape emerged of outtakes and instrumental tracks, they were 'playful meanderings'.

Dylan and crew returned home to Rundown later that month, but finally settled in May on Clover Studios farther down Santa Monica Boulevard where what Heylin calls the 'Springsteen-tested combination of producer Chuck Plotkin and engineer Toby Scott' laid down the bulk of the new album. This included polishing up some of the rough tapes first laid down at Rundown. But when Howard Alk, Dylan's collaborator on *Eat The Document* and other film projects, was found dead at Rundown, on New Years Day, 1982, Dylan soon cancelled his lease. From now on, he would be a rock'n'roll gypsy.

As to *Shot Of Love*, Dylan said 'the record had something that could have been made in the 40s or maybe the 50s. There was a cross element of songs on it. The critics, all they talked about was Jesus this and Jesus that, like it was some kind of Methodist record'. Although the sound level varies between tracks, it is certainly a lively and eminently listenable record, even if not quite up to Dylan's claim that it was the the 'most explosive' album he had ever made. Rough and ready, certainly, and it rocks like a bitch. 'Greasy kid's stuff', with an attitude. Co-producer Charles Plotkin was instructed to move away from the polished sound so beautifully captured at Muscle Shoals, and did so. But to leave songs as good as 'Caribbean Wind', 'Angelina', 'Yonder Comes Sin' and initially 'The Groom's Still Waiting At The Altar' on the cutting room floor still seems a little reckless.

The reviews were certainly entertaining. *Rolling Stone* heard 'hatred, confusion and egoism'. Michael Gray found Dylan's voice 'petulant and querulous, the music tired and the production thin'. For *Trouser Press*, Dylan made his faith 'seem like an affliction'. But this is nothing to the *NME*'s demolition job. 'Like thalidomide, R. D. Laing and Hughie Green, fate seems to have conspired to make Bob Dylan a totally redundant entity so far as the 1980s are concerned'.

The biblical quote this time around is from the New Testament, about hiding wisdom from the prudent and revealing it 'unto babes'. The album sleeve certainly reveals nothing, a design by Pearl Beach with the album cover at the epicentre of an explosion, in primary colours and with the cartoon-like energy of a pop-art canvas by Roy Lichtenstein. The back cover photo is of

Dylan having a close encounter with a rose. There are minor colour differences between the original UK and US sleeves. The Brazilian issue has a different back sleeve, the rear end of a car.

The album fared even worse than *Saved* on the Billboard chart, and when a wearying tour wound to its final end in Florida on 21 November 1981, the time had come for a rest. Dylan stayed at home for the whole of 1982 apart from a recording session backing up Allen Ginsberg and three duets with Joan Baez at a Peace Rally. On 16 February 1983, he made an unbilled appearance with Levon Helm and Rick Danko at the Lone Star Café, playing some rock'n'roll and country standards and two months later was back in the studio. But there was to be no more evangelizing.

SIDE ONE
Shot Of Love (Dylan) 4.21 (4.18 on CD sleeve)
Bob Dylan: vocals, guitar, **Clydie King**: vocals, **Danny Kortchmar**: electric guitar, **Steve Ripley**: guitar, **Tim Drummond**: bass, **Jim Keltner**: drums, **Carolyn Dennis, Regina McCrory, Madelyn Quebec**: vocals

This certainly starts the album with a bang. First Dylan and the girls – hello Clydie King, goodbye Helena Springs – sing a capella, then the band crash in with a killer riff. Dylan later raved over Bumps Blackwell, for whom this serves as an obituary. 'I gotta say that of all the producers I ever used, he was the best, the most knowledgeable and he had the best instincts. I would have liked him to do the whole thing but things got screwed up and he wasn't so-called "contemporary" – what came out was something close to what would have come out if he was really there'.

It certainly sounds rough and ready, like the best 50s rock – mother's milk to Dylan – with the singer rasping and sounding his old, contrary self. Dylan later said that this song outlined exactly where he was, 'spiritually, musically, romantically' and the keyword is ambiguous. But with a side order of humour. The lyrics are emotionally raw, a man in need: he needs love not stimulants. Even women are a betrayal: one 'mocked my God, humiliated my friends'. So the song leaves him in limbo, every certainty gone, even his faith. Here is the devil, 'swift, smooth and near'. Dylan sounds uncertain, alone and spiritually lost: 'my conscience is beginning to bother me today'. Welcome back.

Heart Of Mine (Dylan) 4.35 (4.29 on sleeve)
Bob Dylan: vocal, guitar, **Clydie King**: vocals, **Donald 'Duck' Dunn**: bass, **Wm 'Smitty' Smith**: organ, **Ringo Starr**: tom tom, **Chuck Plotkin, Jim Keltner**: drums, **Ron Wood**: guitar on 'Heart Of Mine'
'That's just a guitar song you know' said Dylan, and Honest Ron scratches like a chicken over a wonderfully loose Tex Mex rhythm section, with three percussionists. Almost a duet, and as Dylan reveals it was 'done a bunch of different ways, but I chose for some reason a particularly funky version of that – and it's really scattered.' 'We did it in like ten minutes'. In which case, ten minutes well spent.

Dylan also reveals 'I had somebody specific in mind when I wrote this, somebody who liked having me around'. Not a mention of God in this one.

Property Of Jesus (Dylan) 4.37 (4.33 on sleeve)
Bob Dylan: vocals, guitar, **Danny Kortchmar**: electric guitar, **Steve Ripley**: guitar, **Carl Pickhardt**: piano, **Tim Drummond**: bass, **Jim Keltner**: drums, **Carolyn Dennis, Clydie King, Regina McCrory, Madelyn Quebec**: vocals
This was allegedly written in response to some snide remarks about Dylan's new found faith by Mick Jagger; hence the chorus line about having a 'heart of stone'. Charity is off the agenda here with Bob back to one of the things he is best at, withering scorn: 'you've been captured but by whom?'

Lenny Bruce (Dylan) 4.35 (4.32 on sleeve)
Bob Dylan: vocals, guitar, **Clydie King**: vocals, **Benmont Tench**: keyboards, **Tim Drummond**: bass, **Jim Keltner**: drums, **Carolyn Dennis, Regina McCrory, Madelyn Quebec**: vocals
A slow piano-led gospel song to a dead martyr, but one with a heroin habit and a dirty tongue. Another tale of the good outlaw: 'Never robbed any churches'. This was written the night before it was recorded, though Lenny was already long dead and it sounds unfinished. Dylan's voice is spiky and slithery and the song could just as well be about himself: 'he fought a war on a battlefield where every victory hurts'.

Watered-Down Love (Dylan) 4.14 (4.10 on sleeve)
Bob Dylan: vocals, guitar, **Clydie King**: vocals, **Danny Kortchmar**: guitar, **Fred Tackett**: guitar, **Benmont Tench**: keyboards, **Jim Keltner**: drums, Carolyn Dennis, Regina McCrory, Madelyn Quebec: vocals
This sounds very innocent, white r&b, with a good chorus. After the endless word-play of *Street Legal*, it is good to see him writing a love song so concise, subjecting clever rhymes to the demands of the beat.

SIDE TWO
The Groom's Still Waiting At The Altar (Dylan) 4.05 (4.02 on sleeve)
(No musicians listed).
This wasn't present on the original release but got added later due to public demand, the only time one of his albums has been changed after release. It first saw the light of day on *Biograph*, where Dylan explained 'I listened back to the song and I felt too rushed. I felt we'd lost the original riff to the point where it was non existent. I listened back to it later and it sounded OK. But it wasn't really the way I wanted to play it'. It is a return to the *Highway 61* style, both the driving rhythm with sneering guitar and tinkling piano with surrealistic words.

Who is Claudette? Why is the cage burning? Hours of harmless fun can ensue. But there is a further ratcheting up of a feeling of apocalypse, 'curtain rising on a new age', and Christ still waits for his bride the church, to mark the end of the world.

Dylan attributed the ferocity of this take to Ringo and to guitarist Danny Kortchmar.. There is a live version to match, recorded the previous year during a thirteen-night residency at the Fox Warfield, with that night's guest Mike Bloomfield – his last live appearance before dying of a drugs overdose, just like Lenny Bruce.

Dead Man, Dead Man (Dylan) 4.04 (3.58 on sleeve)
Bob Dylan: vocals, guitar, **Clydie King**: vocals, **Fred Tackett**: electric guitar, **Steve Ripley**: guitar, **Steve Douglas**: alto sax, **Tim Drummond**: bass, **Jim Keltner**: drums, **Carolyn Dennis, Regina McCrory, Madelyn Quebec**: vocals
Loping white reggae with blasts of pure 50s rock'n'roll sax, and a song about Lazarus. This seems to be a riposte to his former mentors – 'dying on the vine' – who Dylan now suggests are in league with Satan. 'Do you have any faith at all?' Nothing like a convert betrayed.

In The Summertime (Dylan) 3.36 (3.34 on sleeve)
Bob Dylan: vocals, harmonica, **Danny Kortchmar**: electric guitar, **Steve Ripley**: guitar, **Benmont Tench**: keyboards, **Tim Drummond**: bass, **Jim Keltner**: drums, **Clydie King, Regina McCrory, Madelyn Quebec**: vocals

This seems to be a final, lonesome farewell and apology to Sara, post divorce. 'Did I lose my mind when I tried to get rid/of everything you see?' Dylan's voice plunges appealingly for the chorus and he plays lyrical harmonica. There's a sly reference to whatever problems arose when he went back on tour with the Band, 'before the flood' – just listen to the way he subtly emphasizes those three words like a private message. This is a lovely tribute to a love affair now forever closed, 'I'm still carrying the gift you gave'. A grace note to *Blood on the Tracks*.

Trouble (Dylan) 4.38 (4.32 on sleeve)
Bob Dylan: vocals, guitar, **Danny Kortchmar**: lead guitar, **Fred Tackett**: guitar, **Benmont Tench**: keyboards, **Tim Drummond**: bass, **Jim Keltner**: drums, **Carolyn Dennis, Clydie King, Regina McCrory, Madelyn Quebec**: vocals

Back to the coming Apocalypse. The Harry Smith Anthology too is full of such dire forbodings, as are the traditional sources it and Dylan have raided. It is a note that will recur through all Bob's later work, but never with so insistent a beat. He has certainly rediscovered his gift with a resonant phrase, 'stadiums of the damned' and the like. And once again it is a slow train coming round the bend, just 'put your ear to the train tracks'. You can already hear the rumble.

Every Grain Of Sand (Dylan) 6.12
Bob Dylan: vocals, harmonica, **Clydie King**: vocals, **Carl Pickhardt**: piano, **Benmont Tench**: keyboards, **Steve Douglas**: alto sax, **Tim Drummond**: bass, **Jim Keltner**: drums, **Carolyn Dennis, Regina McCrory, Madelyn Quebec**: vocals

This is the perfect riposte, a song of calm and spiritual resolution. Dylan 'felt like I was putting words down that were coming from somewhere else. Clydie sings this with me. I get chills when I hear her just breathe, something about the texture of her voice, so deep and so soulful. I think it's a first-take thing'.

This wonderful song, written during a time of 'deepest need', came to Bob on his Minnesota farm in the summer of 1980. There is a simple and equally heartfelt demo, resurrected on the *Bootleg Series* with Fred Tackett on guitar and Jennifer Warnes on backing vocals. No simplistic evangelizing here, but a truly holy vision, via William Blake in *Auguries of Innocence* seeing heaven in a 'grain of sand', of God in every aspect of his creation and the adept's flickering faith. 'Sometimes I turn, there's someone there, other times it's only me'. Bruce Springsteen cited this song when he inducted Dylan into the Rock'n'Roll Hall of Fame in 1986. And for Sheryl Crow it was 'the first religious song I heard which transcended all religions. I sang it at Johnny Cash's funeral. His family wrote to tell me how important that song had been to Johnny. The music to the song ebbs back and forth – its almost a waltz'. And once again, Dylan's harmonica breaks start exactly where words break off.

Peter Buck, who had long admired this song, used the same two chords, slowly repeating like a mantra, as the basis for another great song of reconciliation, REM's 'Everybody Hurts'.

OUTAKES
23 September 1980: Every Grain Of Sand
October 1980: Yonder Comes Sin
March 1981: Almost Persuaded, Tune, Rockin Boat, Borrowed Time, Gonna See Her, Wait And See, Angelina, Caribbean Wind
April 1981: All Dangerous To Me, Well Water, My Oriental Home, I Want To, Yes Sir No Sir, Is It Worth It?, High Away,(Ah Ah Ah), Child To Me, Wind Blowing On The Water, All The Way Down, More To This, Straw Hat, Instrumental Calypso, Walking On Eggs, All The Way Down, Shot Of Love, Caribbean Wind, Magic, Don't Take Yourself Away, You Changed My Life, Mystery Train, Need A Woman, Heart Of Mine
May 1981: Let It Be Me, Watered Down Love, Let Me See. Various studios

'Let It Be Me', 45 rpm single
'The Groom's Still Waiting At The Altar' 45 rpm single
'Every Grain Of Sand' (alternative version), 'You Changed My Life', 'Need A Woman', 'Angelina' on *The Bootleg Series*.

INFIDELS

US Release: 1 November 1983
UK Release:
CD Release: Columbia 460727 2
CD Remaster/SACD Release:
Producer: Bob Dylan and Mark Knopfler, engineered by Josh Abbey

Columbia QC 38819
CBS 25539

Columbia 512344 6
Running Time: 42.17

SIDE ONE: Jokerman; Sweetheart Like You; Neighbourhood Bully; License To Kill.

SIDE TWO: Man Of Peace; Union Sundown; I and I; Don't Fall Apart On Me Tonight.

Bob Dylan: vocal, guitar, harmonica, keyboards, **Alan Clark:** keyboards, **Sly Dunbar:** drums and percussion, **Mark Knopfler:** guitar, **Robbie Shakespeare:** bass, **Mick Taylor:** guitar, **Clydie King:** vocals on 'Union Sundown'

After Frank Zappa supposedly refused to take over production duties, Dylan entered the Power Station, New York in April 1983 for a month of sessions, meeting up again with Mark Knopfler, this time as co-producer, and with a crack musical unit, including former Rolling Stone Mick Taylor. They worked hard and meticulously, patiently taking each track in turn. Previously Dylan had always worked on the principle that 'I could always get away with just playing the songs live in the studio and leaving. But I decided (here) to take my time like other people do'. Then Dylan went back into the same studio alone in June. At which point the project changed direction.

Dylan explained that 'we put the tracks down and sang most of the stuff live. Only later when we had so much stuff, we recorded it over. Did you ever listen to an Eagles record? The songs are good, but every note is predictable, you know exactly what's gonna be there before it's even there. And I started to sense some of that on *Infidels*, and I didn't like it, so we decided to redo some of the vocals'.

But what he saw as a bit of scuffing up, others now see as a demolition job. The version of *Infidels* that now exists only in the imagination of the likes of Clinton Heylin was to comprise

BOB DYLAN
INFIDELS

nine songs, split into two conceptual suites. It sounds mouth-watering. Side one was to have consisted of 'Jokerman', 'License To Kill', 'Man Of Peace' and 'Neighbourhood Bully', four songs taking as their subject a world on the brink of catastrophe. Side Two would have contained the original takes of 'Don't Fall Apart On Me Tonight', 'Blind Willie McTell', 'Sweetheart Like You', ' I and I' and 'Foot Of Pride'. This was the full-on electric take of 'Blind Willie McTell', still officially unavailable. According to Clinton, 'on Side Two, Dylan begins to turn his gaze on how individuals might confront the End Time'. Armageddon is here. 'Foot Of Pride' is set during 'a plague that has left this whole town afraid'.

Much of this was due to end up on the cutting room floor. Re-recording a few vocals turned into a slash and burn demolition job. Dylan now agrees that he was wrong to do it. 'Lots of songs on that album got away from me. They hung around too long. They were better before they were tampered with. Of course, it was me tampering with them'.

The album that resulted now sounds masterly, especially in the beefed-up remaster. With the band at his disposal, it could hardly have been otherwise, though at the time *Melody Maker* considered it 'as stimulating as an evening at the launderette', and *Record Mirror* reckoned 'there is a lot to be said for early retirement'. The consensus now is 'Dylan is back in the rag-and-bone shop of the heart, making music of intensity and emotional directness'.

The front cover photo was taken by Sara Dylan of her husband through a car window, during a visit to Israel in September 1983 for the bar mitzvah of their son Jesse. The back cover is Dylan on the Mount of Olives. It was also reported that he had been spending time with the Lubavitchers, a Hassidic sect. Heylin quotes a rabbi: 'he's a confused Jew. We feel he's coming back'. Dylan himself is more equivocal. 'We're talking about Jewish roots. I ain't looking for them in synagogues.'

Its digital sound makes this Bob's first album specifically designed for CD even though copies postdated the vinyl issue and more care has been taken. The CD and cassette had a lyric sheet, the vinyl album didn't. The CD remaster doesn't either and is the only upgrade to receive mixed reviews: for *Record Collector*, 'on the brittle *Infidels*, there's a case for saying that less is more', that the reissue 'simply accentuates the most 80s (and dated) aspects of the production'. Others saw it as giving the already crystal-clear sound extra presence and depth. Real fans probably need both, plus a pirate copy of the many outtakes.

SIDE ONE
Jokerman (Dylan) 6.12

Having ended his previous album with a bona-fide masterpiece, Dylan starts this one with another. Written in the Caribbean, 'Jokerman came to me in the islands. It's very mystical. He hoodwinked the musicians, to attain exactly the performance he wanted, rough and urgent. Sly Dunbar tells the tale: 'Bob Dylan always does songs in different keys, like he'll change three, four different keys in a song, and he will change the lyrics on the fly, so when we cut 'Jokerman', we recorded it, then had a break overnight. In the morning he said "Could you just run 'Jokerman' for me again?" Nobody knew the tape was spinning, we were just running down the music and he said "OK that's it"'.

Opening with a clatter of drums from Dunbar, Dylan's urgent, nonsensical words are underpinned by Shakespeare's playful bass and embroidered by some scintillating guitar from Knopfler, like a second voice. The lyrics are suffused with a cornucopia of world mythologies, and the Book of Revelations. The 'harlot' here is the great Whore of Babylon and much else, while the opening lines allude to Ecclesiastes: 'cast your bread upon the waters, but after many days you will find it again'. And these are troubled waters here, with the (re)birth of Satan, 'dressed…in scarlet'.

Larry Sloman and George Lois later put together a superb video in which Dylan looks bemused as he sings the chorus. The words are printed out on the screen and appropriate images appended in rapid succession. 'You were born with a snake in both your fists' is glossed with a sculpture of a Minoan Serpent Goddess from ancient Crete. Ronald Reagan doubles as Jokerman. Maybe he is everyman, or the eternal priest/king of Joseph Campbell's book, *The Hero With A Thousand Faces*. As Dylan says, 'Songs are just thoughts. For the moment, they stop time…I'm a messenger. I get it. It comes to me so I give it back in my style'.

Sweetheart Like You (Dylan) 4.31

Dylan sings with huge tenderness over plangent keyboards, thwacked drums and chattering guitar. Again Christ is (mis)quoted about his father's house containing many mansions, and this song annoyed many in the women's movement, 'a woman like you should be at home/that's where you belong'. But then it is addressed to a floozy in some low drinking dive, or worse. And everything is symbolic. This was Dylan's first Top 60 single for some years. The outtake is even slower and gentler.

Neighbourhood Bully (Dylan) 4.33
Dylan said 'you (shouldn't) make it specific to what's going on today. The battle of Armageddon is specifically spelled out, where it would be fought and, if you want to get technical, when it will be fought'. One of the teachings of the Vineyard Church was that the middle east would be the locus for the final battle. Some of the more extreme neo-cons are still working towards setting it off. It is generally thought that the 'bully' here is the state of Israel, beset by enemies on all sides and criticized whatever it does. And, in the eyes of Dylan, no kind of bully at all.

The backing is loud and relentless, with a Velvet Underground-style love of repetition and simple rhythm guitar. No wonder Lou Reed chose another, cancelled track from this album 'Foot of Pride' to cover at the all-star tribute and gave it just this kind of upbeat, driving treatment.

License To Kill (Dylan) 3.31
This is 'Masters Of War' updated. In the previous song, a license to kill was given out to every 'maniac', to attack Israel. Now that this inbuilt lust for destruction has widened and will lead to the end of the planet, with dark forces directing the soldiery bought and sold and buried. Woman is the agent of peace here – tell that to Golda Meir – but seems powerless. Using the old dub trick of bass as the lead instrument, with drums and guitars setting out the beat and chord structure, this sounds like the first take it actually was. It does not so much end as come to a halt.

This side of vinyl comes in at under 19 minutes, short for Dylan. There's an absence at the centre where the full-on electric take of 'Blind Willie McTell' should be.

SIDE TWO

Man Of Peace (Dylan) 6.27
In St Paul's second letter to the Corinthians, chapter 11, 'even Satan disguises himself as an angel of light'. The subject here is also the Great Beast of Revelation, number 666. The band play on regardless, as if unconcerned by the apocalyptic tone of the lyrics with kingsnakes crawling and howling wolves, the blues reborn.

Union Sundown (Dylan) 5.21
A political song that seems to be arguing for protectionism and closed borders. The stomping music is straight out of the Magic Band, urgent and spiky, with a heavily echoed Dylan almost as driven as Mr Don Van Vliet. He portrays a Kafka-esque world where 'even your home garden/is gonna be against the law', and a world ruled by violence.

I and I (Dylan) 5.10
Bob Dylan: 'That was one of those Caribbean songs. A bunch of songs just came to me hanging around down in the islands'. There is a gentle undertow of reggae, the mysterious musical alchemy that turned the beat around on imported r&b 45s in Jamaica in the late 60s. Dylan fits neatly into the line of ganga-driven mystics from Marley to Ijahman to Lee Perry. 'I and I' is Jamaican patois for 'us'. In the last but one verse Spring comes 'smoking down the track', that slow train again.

Don't Fall Apart On Me Tonight (Dylan) 5.54
A love song, but one set in a world set for disaster where the streets are 'filled with vipers'. Dylan becomes the Mona Lisa. The imagery is back to *Highway 61* vintage, a millionaire 'with the drumsticks in his pants'. Knopfler uses his bottleneck to get an edgy slide effect with Dylan blowing away on his harmonica like a king.

OUTTAKES
April 1983, Power Station: Don't Fall Apart On Me Tonight, License To Kill, Man Of Peace, Jokerman, Don't Fly Unless It's Safe, Clean Cut Kid, Oh Susannah, Dark Groove, Sweetheart Like You (x8), Blind Willie McTell, This Was My Love (x2), Tell Me (x2), Foot Of Pride, Someone's Gotta Hold On My Heart (x2), Union Sundown, I and I, Julius and Ethel
May 1983, Power Station: Lord Protect My Child, Union Sundown 2, Death Is Not The End, Angels Flying Too Close To The Ground, Blind Willie McTell

'Angels Flying Too Close To The Ground' 45 rpm single
'Death Is Not The End' on *Down In The Groove*
'Foot Of Pride', 'Tell Me', 'Someone's Got A Hold Of My Heart', 'Lord Protect My Child', and 'Blind Willie McTell' (acoustic version) on *The Bootleg Series* .

REAL LIVE

US Release: 29 November 1984
UK Release:
CD Release: Columbia 467841 2
Producer: Glyn Johns

Columbia FC 39944
CBS 26334
Running Time: 52.23

SIDE ONE: Highway 61 Revisited**; Maggie's Farm**; I and I***; License To Kill*; It Ain't Me, Babe**.

SIDE TWO: Tangled Up In Blue**; Masters Of War**; Ballad Of A Thin Man**; Girl From The North Country***; Tombstone Blues*.

*St James Park, Newcastle, 5 July 1984
***Slane Castle, Slane, Ireland 8 July 1984

**Wembley Stadium, 7 July 1984

Bob Dylan: vocal, guitar, harmonica, **Colin Allen:** drums, **Ian McLagan:** keyboards, misspelt on the CD booklet, **Greg Sutton:** bass, **Mick Taylor:** lead guitar, **Carlos Santana:** additional guitar on 'Tombstone Blues'

Dylan said around this time that 'for me, none of the songs I've written has really dated. They capture something I've never been able to improve on, whatever their statement is. People say they're nostalgia, but I don't know what that means really. It's just another label'. Another record that now sounds far better than many supposed at the time, *Real Live* is a time capsule of the place these songs were at in 1984. In the case of 'Tangled Up In Blue' this was, lyrically at least, a very different place indeed.

Yet the general consensus is that this is 'an awful live album from a promising tour'. The guitar solos 'threaten to overshadow' the singer, and Dylan himself sounds 'like the very epitome of aged rock boredom'. Neither of these were true of a tour that, as a drawful of tapes attest, saw a revived Bob tearing through *Infidels* and his back pages like a teenager. The band play as well as you would expect with Allen, a veteran of Scottish belters Stone the Crows, and Taylor back on scintillating lead guitar, while Ian McLagan, whose rich organ stylings had underpinned the Faces and the Small Faces brings an Al Kooper-ish richness to the party.

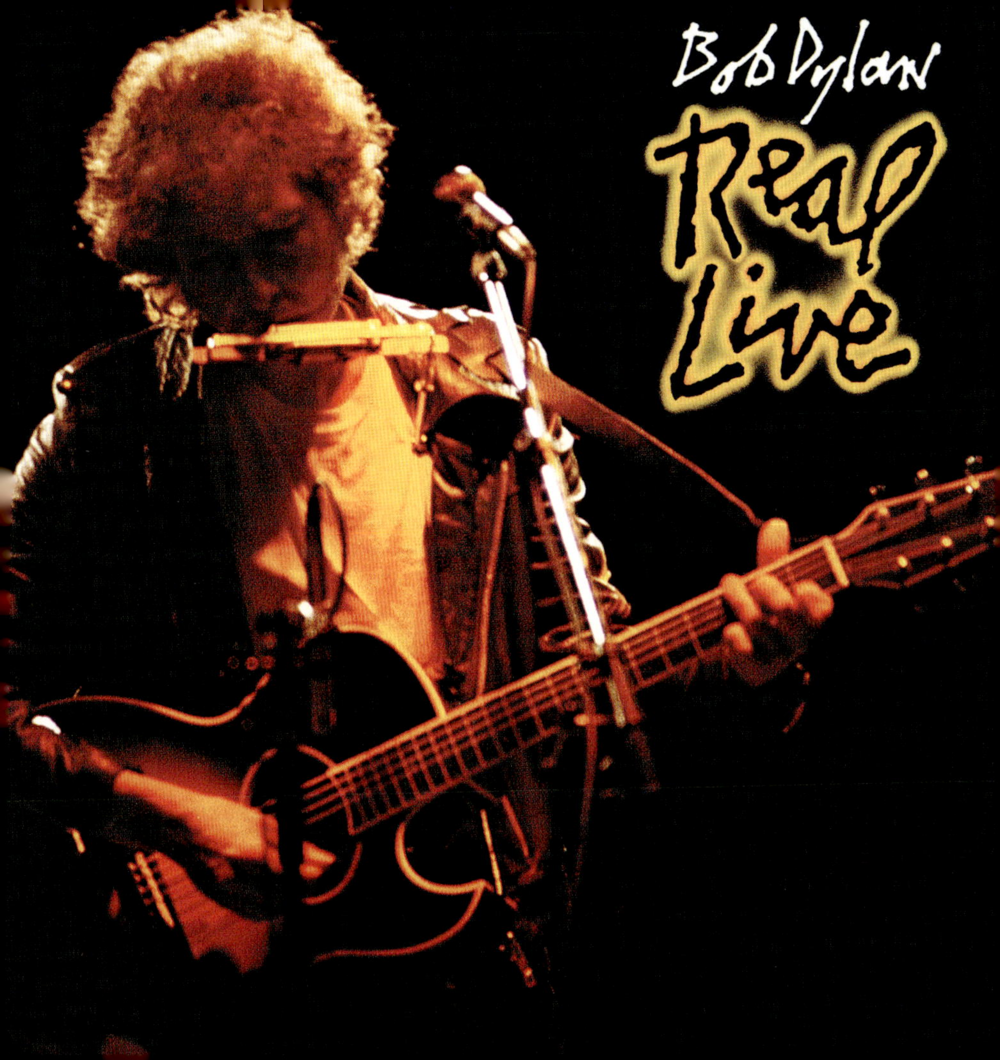
Bob Dylan
Real Live

The continuing debate is over track selection. Michael Gray asks how such 'poor stuff' can be chosen, time over time, for Dylan's concert recordings. 'You could hardly offer a worse live album from Dylan's 1984 tour of Europe than this. The choice of songs is hopeless, the choice of performances injudicious, the production inexcusably murky. How did the supposed ace producer Glyn Jones manage this?'

Comparing this with the bootleg CD *Les Temps Changent*, he has a point. It's not that *Real Live* is bad, just that it is only half the story. That double disc captures a concert held in Paris on 1 July with the same basic crew, full band versions of 'Jokerman' and 'Every Grain Of Sand' and solo takes of 'Hard Rain' and 'Its Alright Ma'. A *Bootleg Series* revisit is called for, as has already brought riches from the darkness, for the years 1964, 1966 and 1975. Columbia should treat Dylan's archives with the same kind of detailed devotion they have recently applied to Miles Davis.

The cover photographs, taken by Guido Harari, are of Dylan playing acoustic guitar with harmonica holder, lit by spotlights from behind as he faces an open-air crowd at night with monumental masonry in the background. Rome perhaps. Dylan played three consecutive nights there the previous month. There are also shots of the band, of special guest Carlos Santana (lost from the compact disc booklet) and of Bob looking quizzical in a straw hat. The CD had a brighter sound than the vinyl, and the Japanese CD issue sounds even better and also has a full lyric sheet.

SIDE ONE
Highway 61 Revisited (Dylan) 5.12
A Wembley roar, some chords on the organ and then we are into this dip into Dylan's back pages, but in a new edition. Taylor really flies on this one, in best *Let It Bleed* style, from when he was still a boy. There's a great bit of Chuck Berry rhythm guitar too. McLagan drives this and the next track from Wembley, barn-storming performances with Taylor and Dylan exchanging great guitar licks over the driving keyboards. The rhythm is completely different to the original recording, more relaxed.

Maggie's Farm (Dylan) 4.53
Tinkling keyboards and driving slide guitar, the originality of the song is ironed out so that we have standard blues rock, Brit style. It could go on forever.

I and I (Dylan) 6.04
The first of two songs from the new album, this lacks the rhythmic authenticity that Sly'n'Robbie would bring, their feeling for every beat, but Dylan really lives this one and turns it into a very personal drama. McLagan lays out a carpet of keyboards from which Mick Taylor launches into an aching solo that spurs Bob on to greater emotional honesty.

License To Kill (Dylan) 3.46
Another song from *Infidels*, and another great performance. Dylan snarls. The guitar is like Mott's version of 'All The Young Dudes' at one point. Taylor once again soars and the crowd roar. This intensifies for the next song that is some trick as it was recorded at the other end of England.

It Ain't Me, Babe (Dylan) 5.25
Back to basics, just Bob and his guitar and some virtuoso harmonica egged on by the crowd shows that all those years of smoking have not affected Dylan's lung power. The crowd sings the chorus. Dylan reconnects with the song, dramatizing it, bigging it up for a stadium audience.

SIDE TWO
Tangled Up In Blue (Dylan) 7.02
Bob Dylan comments elsewhere that: 'I changed the lyrics, to bring it up to date. The old ones were never quite filled in. I rewrote it in a hotel room somewhere. I think it was in Amsterdam. When I sang it the next night, it was right'. He went further on *Biograph*. 'I was never really happy with it. On *Real Live*, the imagery is better and more the way I would have liked it than on the original recording'. Most fans disagree, although this has a clumsy charm all of its own. In verse one, the spurned hero is last seen, 'rain pouring on his shoes/heading down for the old east coast'. Equally, if it is Sara that he rescues from a loveless marriage in verse two, then she was wed to a 'man four times her age'. He heads down for New Orleans 'where they

treated him like a boy' and picks up a waitress; 'she was working in the Blinding Light'. He gets on 'that train and rides', looking for someone, woman or man, where 'all of the beds are unmade'.

Masters Of War (Dylan) 6.34
Relaxed, rather as you imagine the Faces would have played it. Dylan sounds sympathetic, coming from a place of pity rather than anger. There is a lot of organ and lead guitar interplay, smooth and professional. It closes down, then starts up again, then ends for good.

Ballad Of A Thin Man (Dylan) 4.18
Straight into this. Dylan sounds unconnected and messes up the words. Surely they had a better version. This is Bob by numbers. Compared to the vitriolic 1966 renditions, this is a middle aged stroll. 'Earphones' have changed into a 'telephone' for no good reason.

Girl From The North Country (Dylan) 4.28
Back to acoustic guitar and mouth harp with two impressionistic solos, almost free jazz. Dylan sings as if he still cares, but it edges towards Roy Harper's parody of Bob's original, all long vowels and rustic twang.

Tombstone Blues (Dylan) 4.34
Carlos Santana guests, although you wouldn't really know it unless it said so on the sleeve. He had played support with his own band throughout the tour. This is shorter and snappier than the original studio take. Dylan almost growls 'well' or 'ah, yeah' at the end of each verse. The guitar work is sadly unimpressive. Again, there must have been better performances than this with three concerts to sample from. It ends the album on a drab note.

EMPIRE BURLESQUE

US Release: 8 June 1985
UK Release: June 1985
CD Release: Columbia 467840 2
Producer: Remix by Arthur Baker

Columbia FC 40116
CBS 86313
Running Time: 46.55

SIDE ONE: Tight Connection To My Heart (Has Anybody Seen My Love?); Seeing The Real You At Last; I'll Remember You; Clean Cut Kid; Never Gonna Be The Same Again.

SIDE TWO: Trust Yourself; Emotionally Yours; When The Night Comes Falling From The Sky; Something's Burning, Baby; Dark Eyes.

Bob Dylan: vocal, guitar, keyboards, harmonica, **Mike Campbell:** guitar, **Chops:** horns, **Alan Clark:** synthesizer, **Sly Dunbar:** drums, **Howie Epstein:** bass, **Anton Fig:** drums, **Bob Glaub:** bass, **Don Heffington:** drums, **Ira Ingber:** guitar, **Bashiri Johnson:** percussion, **Jim Keltner:** drums, **Stuart Kimball:** electric guitar, **Al Kooper:** rhythm guitar, **Syd McGuinness:** guitar, **Vince Melamed:** synthesizer, **John Paris:** bass, **Ted Perlman:** guitar, **Richard Scher:** synthesizer, synth horns, **Robbie Shakespeare:** bass, **Mick Taylor:** guitar, **Benmont Tench:** keyboards, **Urban Blight Horns:** horns, **David Watson:** saxophone, **Ron Wood:** guitar, **Peggi Blu, Debra Byrd, Carol Dennis, Queen Esther Marrow, Madelyn Quebec:** vocals

Things now get complicated. The best Dylan albums have always been those on which Bob alone or with a hand-picked gang of musicians, has worked quickly in one studio in real time and with a sympathetic producer. But the run of studio albums that follow are quite to the contrary until Daniel Lanois went back to basics and re-connected Dylan with his audience – twice. Meanwhile, Dylan went to all kinds of studios with all kinds of players waiting for inspiration to strike.

As he said in 1985, 'When I'm making a record, I'll need some songs, and I'll start digging through my pockets and drawers trying to find these songs. Then I'll bring one out, and I've never sung it before, sometimes I can't even remember the melody to it, and I'll get it in. Sometimes great things happen, sometimes not-so-great things happen'. As we have already

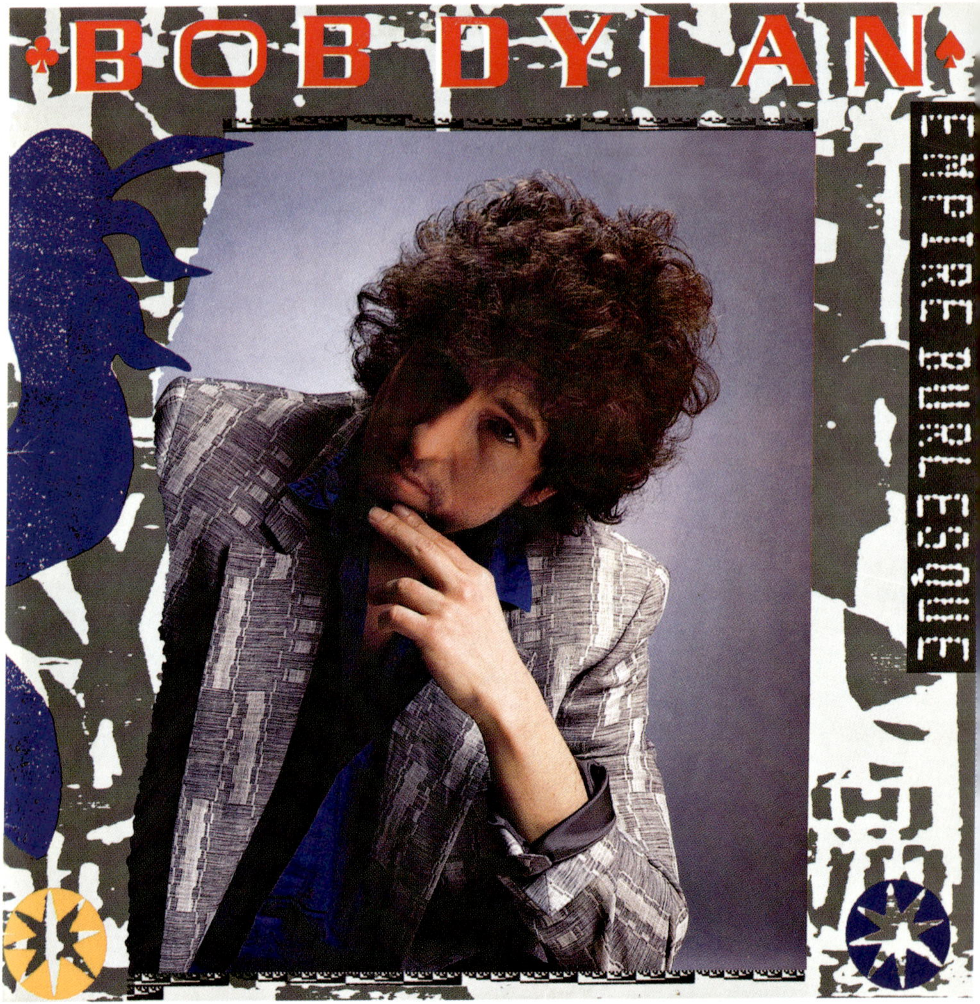
BOB DYLAN
EMPIRE BURLESQUE

seen, only *Saved* was road tested before recording. In the mid 80s – Dylan's artistic nadir – 'what I do now is record all the time. Sometimes nothing comes out and other times I get a lot of stuff that I keep. I recorded *Empire Burlesque* for a long time, I just put down the songs as I felt I wanted to put them down'.

As Heylin points out, albums of this era were compiled rather than planned. 1985's *Empire Burlesque* and 1986's *Knocked Out Loaded* are 'two volumes with the same depressing story to tell'. Their starting point was the same, a session at Delta Sound, New York in July 1984, straight after he returned from the European tour chronicled on *Real Live*. This produced 'Clean Cut Kid' for *Empire* and an instrumental sketch for *Knocked Out*'s 'Driftin' Too Far From The Shore'. Dylan would lay down a backing track and return to it later to add vocals.

Even less productive was a session at Intergalactic Studios on 24 July with the Al Green band. This proved a chaotic mis-match. 'Honey Wait' is an outtake from that day. With no charts and no fixed arrangements, the session dissolved in a shambles.

Ron Wood watched the chaos. 'All these guys from Memphis couldn't understand Bob's chord sequences. Every time he started off a new song he'd start in a new key, or if we were doing the same song over and over, every time it would be in a different key. The band were confused and one by one they left the studio'.

Dylan continued to drift in and out of recording studios like a lost soul. One day in November at LA's Oceanway Studio saw him attempt just two cover versions, Mungo Jerry's 'In The Summertime' – 'painfully bad' according to Heylin – and Allen Toussaint's elegiac 'Freedom for the Stallion'. In January 1985 he turned up in another Los Angeles studio, Cherokee, and one masterpiece resulted, the twelve minutes of 'New Danville Girl', driven onwards by drummer Don Heffington. This appeared only on *Knocked Out Loaded* in a revised and diluted form. Dylan moved straight back to New York and late February saw him at the Power Station, laying down the rest of the basic tracks.

He wasn't finished yet, he threw this mess of potage at dance music legend Arthur Baker to remix the tracks into some kind of sense. 'When it was time to put the record together I brought it all to him and he made it sound like a record'. Baker brought in the Urban Blight horns, percussionist Bashiri Johnson and Richard Scher on synth. Opinions differ as to what he achieved, though the Clean Cuts bootleg allows hard-core fans to compare before and after. Even before the remix, Dylan's voice has a pinched, speedy quality, less *Freewheelin'*, more the Chipmunks. What is lost in the remix, particularly on 'Emotionally Yours' is the presence of 'real' instruments. In the final version they have been levelled out, as if heard from another room. The general consensus is that in the cause of giving the disc a uniformity of sound, Baker laid 'a heavy-handed and unappreciative mix across tracks that had more worth than the final arrangements gave them credit'.

Ironically, the only track Baker did not remix was laid down by Dylan, totally solo, at these final sessions at the Power Station in March 1985. 'I'm the final judge of what goes on and off my records. There were nine songs I knew belonged on it and I needed a tenth. I finally figured out that the last song needed to be acoustic, so I just wrote it. I wrote it because none of the other songs fit that spot, that certain place'.

Arthur Baker certainly gave Dylan a contemporary sound that now is incredibly dated – all echo, reverb and booming synth drums – 'that made Jan Hammer sound like Merle Haggard'. High-tech gloss, fit for the MTV age. For Michael Gray it was a nadir, with Bob 'mewling his vocal way through a thick murk of formulaic riffs, licks and echo-laden AOR noises devised with a desperate eye on rock radio formats'. If this is true, it didn't work. Others looked beneath the glossy surface and found a series of poems about love, 'albeit love of the fractured, shattered and watered-down variety'. The recent *Rough Guide* reckons it an album 'ripe for favourable reassessment. Even simply as a period piece, *Empire Burlesque* has a certain charm, in a retro kind of way and the final track cuts to the bone.

Larry Sloman regards the whole album as inhabiting the terrain of 'Sweetheart Like You' from the previous album: 'Dylan as a denizen of hell, welcoming (and questioning) the presence of an innocent sweetheart. Love relationships, the hottest crucible of the spirit today, as Leonard Cohen has said'.

The cover matches the mood of its time, the high point of Reagan and Thatcher and only wimps eating lunch. Into the discos of which, Dylan intends to import the virus of despair via this carrier. In Ken Regan's photograph, Bob looks curly, quizzical and romantic, in a designer jacket and on the back the same straw hat as on the previous album. There is also a line drawing of a woman who looks very much like Sara. Gray is again on the attack. 'Dylan the perplexed fashion victim in Bruce Willis jacket'.

This was the first Dylan album to be issued simultaneously on vinyl and CD. The over production suits CD better and it all sounds very artificial, but that is exactly what Arthur Baker, and presumably Dylan, were looking for. Maybe the remix itself now needs a remix.

SIDE ONE
Tight Connection To My Heart (Has Anybody Seen My Love?) (Dylan) 5.22
Bob Dylan: vocal, keyboards, **Mick Taylor**: guitar, **Tad Perlman**: guitar, **Sly Dunbar**: drums, **Robbie Shakespeare**: bass, **Richard Scher**: synthesizers, **Carol Dennis, Queen Esther Marrow, Peggi Blu**: backing vocals
A girl chorus sing the chorus line, over and over, then in comes Dylan, moaning. There's a storm brewing and a man is getting beaten up in a 'town without pity'. Mick Taylor plays some great guitar that cuts through the aural murk. Dylan reverses the Christian sacrament, turning wine into blood: love has become an annoyance, and Bob sounds edgy.

'I'll go along with this charade until I can think my way out' has been appropriated from an early episode of *Star Trek*. It is a line delivered by Captain Kirk to Mr Spock who raises a creaky eyebrow. Other lines in this song come from old Humphrey Bogart movies. And the song provoked its own mini-movie, a very weird promo video directed by Paul Schrader in which Dylan wanders around Japan – picking up the allusion to *Madame Butterfly* – gets arrested, visits the red light zone and sees his double up on stage. He ends up with two women – and everybody lip syncs.

Seeing The Real You At Last (Dylan) 4.21
Bob Dylan: vocal, guitar, **Mike Campbell**: guitar, **Benmont Tench**: keyboards, **Don Heffington**: drums, **Rob Glaub**: bass, **Bashiri Johnson**: percussion, **Chops**: horns, **David Watson**: sax solo
This is a very adult, 'glad it's over', post-relationship song that some could take as autobiographical, bitter and about Sara. Even if once 'there was a nothing wrong with me/that you could not fix' – the *Nashville Skyline* years, maybe – there is now no more time for 'baby talk' in a time of troubles.

But this is a song that works against the grain of its surface meaning. Bob still seems obsessed with the subject of this song. She continues her allure, symbolized in Wild West imagery, 'you could ride like Annie Oakley/you could shoot like Belle Starr', her ghost presumably still knitting a bald wig for Jack the Ripper. Tom Petty's Heartbreakers plus brass bring a swagger to Dylan's voice and everyone sounds tough as hell.

I'll Remember You (Dylan) 4.14
Bob Dylan: vocal, piano, **Mike Campbell**: guitar, **Howie Epstein**: bass, **Jim Keltner**: drums, **Madelyn Quebec**: vocal
Straight into this hugely tender song of devotion, that could be an elegy for an old friend, or more likely a love song to a former girlfriend or ex-wife. There is a lovely line about the time when 'the wind blew threw the piney woods', ripe with regret. The original demo sounds tinny but Arthur Baker has polished it up for public consumption An uncredited organ player adds sweetness, and there is some heartfelt electric guitar. Madelyn sings along at the beginning as if she hadn't been given a lyric sheet – and indeed she hadn't.

Clean Cut Kid (Dylan) 4.16
Bob Dylan: vocal, guitar, **Ron Wood**: guitar, **Benmont Tench**: piano, **John Paris**: bass, **Anton Fig**: drums, **Carol Dennis, Queen Esther Marrow, Peggi Blu**: vocals
This one really rocks and rolls. Dylan returns to the subject matter of John Brown, a story about a boy being indoctrinated with patriotism and going off to war. Here it is Vietnam, from where he comes back anything but clean cut to jump to his death off the Golden Gate Bridge. Just like Stanley Kubrick's movie *Full Metal Jacket*, that showed a bunch of marines being brutalized by the military machine; the story continues here with the all-American boy sent back into civilian life without any brakes. The CD booklet puts trademark signs on all the corporations cited here, even the Rolls-Royce he steals and drives into a swimming pool, Keith Moon style.

The band stoke up the urgency, with Tench moving over to whorehouse piano to quote one commentator, and Ron Wood's dirtyass guitar. There's some great, uncredited harmonica that can only be Bob. The girl chorus could be straight out of a Phil Spector production.

Never Gonna Be The Same Again (Dylan) 3.08
Bob Dylan: vocal, keyboards, **Carol Dennis**: vocal, **Syd McGuinness**: guitar, **Alan Clark, Richard Scher**: synthesizers, **Robbie Shakespeare**: bass, **Sly Dunbar**: drums, **Carol Dennis, Queen Esther Marrow, Peggi Blu**: vocals
Another troubled love song with electric celeste, presumably mocked up on the synth, and a chugging, mid-period Rolling Stones feel. Hysterical guitar, an over-intrusive girl chorus and lyrics about a woman who is both living dream and nightmare. The original demo is so sharp it

hurts the ears, but somehow there is more presence in Dylan's voice, and the extraordinary up and down tune hits directly into the brain. But the song remains an enigma in any version, with Dylan a man obsessed.

SIDE TWO
Trust Yourself (Dylan) 3.28
Bob Dylan: vocal, guitar, **Madelyn Quebec**: vocals, **Mike Campbell**: guitar, **Benmont Tench**: keyboards, **Robbie Shakespeare**: bass, **Jim Keltner**: drums, **Bashirir Johnson**: percussion, **Carol Dennis, Queen Esther Marrow, Peggi Blu**: vocals

This could almost be Canned Heat with a singer on helium. Wonderfully repetitive, like the best rock music, and with some weird things going on under the surface. Dylan warns the woman this is directed towards that 'my love might only be lust', in a world of 'wolves and thieves'. Another song, like the one that preceded it, that seems only half written.

Emotionally Yours (Dylan) 4.30
Bob Dylan: vocal, piano, **Mike Campbell**: guitar, **Benmont Tench**: organ, **Howie Epstein**: bass, **Jim Keltner**: drums, **Richard Scher**: synth horns

This soundtracked a strange promo video with a mannequin spinning slowly on a turntable in time to the slow tempo here. Dylan confesses he feels lost, as if his whole life has never happened but the music is very sure of itself, with plangent lead guitar, almost hymnal synthesized strings and a see-saw chorus. The original take is bare, less concocted, faster and cuts to the heart.

When The Night Comes Falling From The Sky (Dylan) 7.30
Bob Dylan: vocal, guitar, **Madelyn Quebec**: vocal, **Stuart Johnson**: electric guitar, **Al Kooper**: rhythm guitar, **Robbie Shakespeare**: bass, **Sly Dunbar**: drums, **Bashirir Johnson**: percussion, **Richard Scher**: synthesizers, **Urban Bright Horns**: horns

Larry Sloman reckons this is 'touched by Jeremiah's fire…a scorching spirituality'. It is the one song here that Dylan has since endlessly recycled in concert. Apocalyptic is hardly the word for the lyrics, a world in darkness and nuclear winter, but they run counter to a particularly annoying mix, that sounds like it's coming out of a mobile phone. Go back to the original demo and it is even worse, shrill and headache-inducing. A real mess, so praise be to Baker, for at least getting this important song into a releaseable form.

There is a very odd video for this, with one girl in the crowd watching, the same one who played a mannequin in 'Emotionally Yours'. But nothing can rob this song of its power, with death in the wind and the Masters of War in charge of the planet. And yet another reading would be that it's a bitter falling-out-of-love song, with all this charnel-house imagery simply equating to Dylan's emotional state and that of his faithless beau. All he really wants is for her to reply to his love letter.

Something's Burning, Baby (Dylan) 4.54
Bob Dylan: vocals, **Madelyn Quebec:** vocals, **Ira Ingber:** guitar, **Vince Melamed, Richard Scher:** synthesizers, **Robbie Shakespeare:** bass, **Don Heffington:** drums
Another major song. If ever an album called for a simple, unplugged version…This seems to allude to Warren Zevon's 'Werewolves of London', turned bloodhounds here. The pace is sepulchral with martial drums and a slow duet. Another song about a man half in and half out of love, and as mysterious as only Dylan can be. 'I've had the Mexico blues since the last hairpin bend': endlessly resonant while making no sense whatsoever.

Neither does the album title – as usual – although there is a sense throughout that even the USA's hegemony is coming to an end in decadence, the 'burlesque' of the title. Everything is a stage play with the four riders of the apocalypse circling just out of sight.

Dark Eyes (Dylan) 5.07
Bob Dylan: vocal, guitar and harmonica
Now we enter the horror show for real, with just Dylan as nature intended. This is as close as we are ever likely to get inside his skull, and it is not a comfortable place to be, 'another world where life and death are memorialized'. The song takes us back to Gethsemane, but no paeons to Jesus here, just a cock crowing to mark Peter's betrayal. And something very sinister stirring, frightening even the beasts.

All completely stately with a very Irish melody line and Dylan sounding a little like Paul Brady. The tune's leaps and tumbles are vaguely reminiscent of 'Restless Farewell' with another flying arrow right on target.

Talking about this album, Leonard Cohen declared 'Nobody wants a happy song. The great songs have to embrace the whole world, and we know that this world is a butcher-shop'.

OUTTAKES:
24 July 1984: 'Honey Wait'
28 July 1984: 'Who Loves You More', 'Clean Cut Kid', 'Drifting Too Far From The Shore', 'Go 'Way Little Boy'
6 December 1984: 'New Danville Girl'
28 January 1985: 'Seeing The Real You At Last'
14 February 1985: 'Straight A's In Love', 'Waiting To Get Beat', 'The Very Thought Of You'
19 February 1985: 'When The Night Comes Falling From The Sky'
21 February 1985: 'Something's Burning Baby'
16 June: 'Freedom For The Station', 'In The Summertime'. Various studios

'Band Of The Hand (It's Helltime Man)' 45 rpm single
'When The Night Comes Falling From The Sky' alternative version on *The Bootleg Series*.

BIOGRAPH

US Release: 28 October 1985
UK Release: November 1985
CD Release: August 1997
Producer: Jeff Rosen

Columbia C5X 38830 5-LP box set
CBS 20-66509
Columbia 488099 2 3-CD box set
Running Time: 73.27, 71.55, 71.38

SIDE ONE: Lay Lady Lay, Baby Let Me Follow You Down, If Not For You, I'll Be Your Baby Tonight, I'll Keep It With Mine.

SIDE TWO: The Times They Are A-Changin', Blowin' In The Wind, Masters Of War, Lonesome Death of Hattie Carroll, Percy's Song.

SIDE THREE: Mixed-Up Confusion, Tombstone Blues, Groom's Still Waiting At The Altar, Most Likely You Go Your Way, Like A Rolling Stone, Jet Pilot.

SIDE FOUR: Lay Down Your Weary Tune, Subterranean Homesick Blues, I Don't Believe You (She Acts Like We Never Have Met), Visions Of Johanna, Every Grain Of Sand.

SIDE FIVE: Quinn The Eskimo, Mr Tambourine Man, Dear Landlord, It Ain't Me Babe, You Angel You, Million Dollar Bash.

SIDE SIX: To Ramona, You're A Big Girl Now, Abandoned Love, Tangled Up In Blue, It's All Over Now Baby Blue.

SIDE SEVEN: Can You Please Crawl Out Your Window?, Positively 4th Street, Isis, Caribbean Wind, Up To Me.

SIDE EIGHT: Baby I'm In The Mood For You, I Wanna Be Your Lover, I Want You, Heart Of Mine, On A Night Like This, Just Like A Woman.

SIDE NINE: Romance In Durango, Senor (Tales Of Yankee Power), Gonna Serve Somebody, I Believe In You, Time Passes Slowly.

SIDE TEN: I Shall Be Released, Knockin' On Heaven's Door, All Along The Watchtower. Solid Rock, Forever Young.

Dylan was rather disparaging when this sumptuous five-album box set came out and weighed down record store shelves. 'There's some stuff that hasn't been heard before but most of my

bob dylan *biograph*

3 - CASSETTE - DELUXE - EDITION

stuff has already been bootlegged, so to anybody in the know, there's nothing on it they haven't heard before. All it is, really, is repackaging, and it'll just cost a lot of money'. The CD version was ready just in time for Christmas.

Certainly, rare and unreleased tracks were outnumbered by music already available on album, but there was enough new material to provoke the interest of any fan. The book contained an excellent essay by Cameron Crowe, the *Rolling Stone* journalist who latterly became a movie scriptwriter, and there are extensive new interview quotes from Dylan himself. The whole thing is beautifully put together, even in the far meaner CD reissue, with a cornucopia of rare photos. It established a new market among wealthy baby boomers for the music of their youth, repackaged and enhanced.

On the cover, Dylan in a 1965 shot by Daniel Kramer, looks quizzical, flanked by two photographs of his later self. Inside are a slew of archive photographs, of Dylan's parents and of the young folk singer with Victoria Spivey, Joan Baez, his manager, Allen Ginsberg, Sara and the kids, Cheech and Chong and Bruce Springsteen.

Clinton Heylin waxes extremely acerbic on the 'awful' remix of 'Mr Tambourine Man', and the choice of a poor live recording of 'Knockin' On Heaven's Door' from the 1974 tour, rather than the studio version. There are wild rumours in collectors' chat rooms of various wrong takes supposedly issued erroneously on the original US CD version of this box set: the first issue presents the listener with a completely different take of 'I Don't Believe You', since replaced with the correct version. The original issue came in a proper 12 inch x 12 inch cardboard box with a booklet of equal size.

SIDE ONE/CD 1
Lay, Lady, Lay (Dylan) 3.17
From *Nashville Skyline,* a strange song to start this career overview that zigzags around in time without any real rhyme or reason.

Baby, Let Me Follow You Down (Ric Von Schmidt) 2.13
From *Bob Dylan*, it comes as a shock to hear the complete separation between voice and harmonica in one speaker and the guitar in the other, as if Dylan has very long arms.

If Not For You (Dylan) 2.41
From *New Morning*.

I'll Be Your Baby Tonight (Dylan) 2.45
From *John Wesley Harding*.

I'll Keep It With Mine (Dylan) 3.44
Previously unreleased, 'this rare tape, recorded for Judy Collins' was laid down as part of the sessions for *Another Side*. This song was supposedly written for and about Nico, and probably is why Collins never recorded it.

This is a magnificent find with Dylan accompanied just by his clunky piano style and what sounds like his boot stomping on the ground. It sounds very bare, especially to those long accustomed to the Fairport Convention arrangement, and Dylan has never sounded more alone, just like that train driver forever stuck out on the line.

SIDE TWO
The Times They Are A-Changin' (Dylan) 3.13
From the album of the same title, this side of the original LP does have a logic, drawn from just two adjacent albums, and ending on a previously unheard outtake that it is hard to follow with anything but the needle lifting off the vinyl.

Blowin' In The Wind (Dylan) 2.47
From *Freewheelin'*.

Masters Of War (Dylan) 4.31
From *Freewheelin'*.

Lonesome Death of Hattie Carroll (Dylan) 5.46
From *The Times They Are A-Changin'*.

Percy's Song (Dylan) 7.40
Previously unreleased, this was recorded in New York, in October 1963, towards the end of *The Times They Are A-Changin'* sessions. The melody line came from Paul Clayton. Bob Dylan recalled 'we played on the same circuit. When you're listening to songs night after night, some of them kind of rub off on you'. The song structure comes from the traditional song referred to in the lyric, that ends in much the same way, 'the only tune my fiddle would play/was "The dreadful wind and rain"'. Dylan has a thing about judges, although the one here does at least try to explain his sentence. Just Dylan and his guitar, and a coldly impassioned performance.

SIDE THREE
Mixed-Up Confusion (Dylan) 2.28
An alternative and inferior take of his first US single recorded at the same session in New York on 11 November 1962 with a pocket-sized electric band. Not as clattering as that released take, but still a tongue-in-cheek slice of rockabilly with what sounds like a tea chest bass and biscuit-tin drums, but isn't. Harmonica wasn't a usual component of early rock'n'roll, but it fits in well enough.

Tombstone Blues (Dylan) 5.56
From *Highway 61 Revisited*.

Groom's Still Waiting At The Altar (Dylan) 4.03
First issued as a single B-side and later added to *Shot Of Love* due to public demand.

Most Likely You Go Your Way (Dylan) 3.27
Live version from *Before The Flood*.

Like A Rolling Stone (Dylan) 6.08
From *Highway 61 Revisited*.

Jet Pilot (Dylan) 0.49
On the CD this is delayed and ends up on disc two, presumably for reasons of timings. Previously unreleased, this is from the *Highway 61* sessions, an early version of 'Tombstone Blues'. Again, the vinyl side does have a cheeky logic, centering on Dylan's first fully electric album with a later live version of one track from its predecessor and a song out of time, hailed in 1981 as a return to the glory days when it crept out as a B-side. Plus a precursor from back in 1962. And they sit together well. This is a unity completely lost on the CD that would have been far more appropriate if re-ordered chronologically, just like the subsequent *Bootleg Series*.

SIDE FOUR
Lay Down Your Weary Tune (Dylan) 4.35
Previously unreleased, this was recorded in New York on 24 October 1963, directly after 'Percy's Song'. Another bootlegger's favourite 'Eternal Circle' was laid down earlier the same day as the title track for the album from which this was excluded. Lovely all the same but it sounds like a poem set to music rather than a song.

'I wrote that on the West coast at Joan Baez's house. She had a place outside Big Sur'. Dylan was trying to recapture the feeling, and melody, of a Scottish traditional ballad he had heard on an old 78 rpm single. 'I wanted lyrics that would feel the same'. Chris Hillman recalls the Byrds hearing an acetate and then recording it for their second album. 'It is kinda like Dylan Thomas poetry, as if he wrote lyrics for popular music'.

Subterranean Homesick Blues (Dylan) 2.19
From *Bringing It All Back Home*.

I Don't Believe You (She Acts Like We Never Met) (Dylan) 5.30
A previously unreleased version, recorded live with the Hawks in Belfast on 6 May 1966. 'I thought we did rather well for the equipment we had to use. We were in territory that nobody had ever been in before'. In more ways than one…

Much the same as the Manchester version, slightly less driving, although at the time this was manna from heaven with the only previously official release from this cataclysmic tour a

B-side of 'I Want You' from Liverpool. Garth Hudson is the star of this particular take, like a madman who has hijacked a Wurlitzer. Plus Dylan of course, sounding pitiless.

The vinyl ends side four on a climax of two of Dylan's greatest ever songs. CD 1 comes to a close with this, and a kind of dying fall.

CD 2
Visions Of Johanna (Dylan) 7.31
Another previously unreleased version from the acoustic first half of that same tour, this was recorded at the first of two concerts at the Royal Albert Hall on 26 May, the penultimate show of the tour. He gets a bit tangled up over the lines about the watchman clicking his key chain, but this is a man on the edge. He doesn't so much perform this song as inhabit it.

Crowe notes the 'other-worldly quality' to this version and Bob too at this point it could be added. It is hushed and echoey, as if he is performing in a cathedral that in a way he is. Some fans tried desperately to write down every word, thinking they might never hear such wonders again.

Every Grain Of Sand (Dylan) 6.14
From *Shot Of Love*.

SIDE FIVE
Quinn The Eskimo (Dylan) 2.18
This previously unreleased version is taken from the *Basement Tapes* but it is missing from the double album from these sessions put together by Robbie Robertson and therefore denied the re-touched effect of most of that half-botched affair. It even seems to retain the rough but serviceable stereo of the original reels. Dylan has rarely sounded more laconic and this is a far more sinister affair than the jaunty Manfred Mann cover. It gives more credence to the common interpretation that this is about waiting for a drug dealer to come a-knocking. Then, 'everybody's gonna doze'. Down in the easy chair, maybe. It certainly segues nicely into the next track, if that is true....

Mr Tambourine Man (Dylan) 5.28
From *Bringing It All Back Home*.

Dear Landlord (Dylan) 3.15
From *John Wesley Harding*.

It Ain't Me Babe (Dylan) 3.33
From *Another Side*.

You Angel You (Dylan) 2.52
From *Planet Waves*.

Million Dollar Bash (Dylan) 2.32
From *The Basement Tapes*.

SIDE SIX
To Ramona (Dylan) 3.52
From *Another Side of Bob Dylan*.

You're A Big Girl Now (Dylan) 4.21
A previously unreleased version and an outtake from the final, revised *Blood On The Tracks*, from the original New York sessions. This was recorded on 25 September 1974.

Abandoned Love (Dylan) 4.27
Also previously unreleased, Crowe notes that the song was tested out with the Rolling Thunder Revue and recorded in New York in July 1975 for *Desire* but replaced in the final running order with 'Joey'. Dylan is still taking his band through the song here – Eric Clapton said that when playing with Dylan 'you listen hard and watch his hands for the changes. It may be your only take'.

This song was far too good to lose, a wonderfully mysterious tale with Scarlet Rivera and the crew giving it a touch of the orient. 'Everybody's wearing a disguise' and the song exemplifies the title of the album from which it was so carelessly rejected. For many of Bob's rivals this would be a career highlight.

Tangled Up In Blue (Dylan) 5.44
From *Blood On The Tracks*, surely all those who would want this would already have it. At the time it seemed a wasted opportunity to put more of the abandoned New York session out into the open.

It's All Over Now Baby Blue (Dylan) 5.39
This previously unreleased version, recorded live in Manchester on 17 May 1966. Now part of the *Bootleg Series*.

SIDE SEVEN
Can You Please Crawl Out Your Window? (Dylan) 3.33
First released as a 45 rpm single, this was laid down in New York in October 1965. There are two versions of this, one with Bloomfield and Kooper, the other – this one – with the Hawks. 'I was pressurized into doing another single. That's why that one came out, I think'.

It is great to hear this on an album, some of us wore the original single half to death. The first fruits of Robbie Robertson and the gang plus Dylan on disc and it still sounds full of a kind of malign life-force, best experienced from a great distance. It also opens one of the great vinyl sides of all time, now split over two CDs.

Positively 4th Street (Dylan) 3.52
Also first released as a 45 rpm single. Cut three months earlier in New York in July 1965, four days after Dylan went electric in public at Newport. The lyric is notoriously vitriolic, even for Dylan. It first surfaced on a 12-inch on the US Greatest Hits.

Isis (Dylan and Jacques Levy) 5.29
Recorded live in Montreal, 4 December 1975, with the Rolling Thunder Revue. It was first released on a stunning and now highly collectable four-song promotional 12-inch single to tie in with the Renaldo and Clara movie. Complete with the famous intro 'here's a song about marriage'. Rock music simply doesn't get better than this.

'Jet Pilot' placed here on CD.

CD 3
Caribbean Wind (Dylan) 5.52
Previously unreleased. This is a 1981 outtake from *Shot of Love*. 'I couldn't quite grasp what it was about after I finished it. I started it in St Vincent when I woke up from a strange dream in the hot sun. There was a bunch of women working a tobacco field on a high rolling hill. A lot of them were smoking pipes. I was thinking about living with someone for all the wrong reasons'. The song had first been heard in public at the Fox Warfield on 12 November 1980, but this later version has lost half of its original lines. The 1987 edition of *Lyrics* rewrote it further, so that 'were we sniper bait?' became 'did we snap at the bait'. Then *Lyrics 1962-2001* did a further and spectacular rewrite, bringing things back far closer to the original version. Bob admits here that 'sometimes you'll write something very inspired then you'll go back and try and pick it up, and the inspiration is just gone. I think there's four different sets of lyrics. I had to leave it'. Shortly after first performing it at the Warfield, he told Paul Williams that the song 'took the listener outside of time'. And it still does, to a movie of the mind.

Up To Me (Dylan) 6.16
This is a previously unreleased outtake from *Blood on the Tracks*. Dylan: 'I don't think of myself as Bob Dylan. Its like Rimbaud said, "I is another".' Another lost masterpiece that makes two in a row, and also about a mysterious and possibly deadly woman, just like 'Caribbean Wind'. A mixture of manufactured facts – Dylan as a postal clerk, for God's sake – unknowable characters like Dupree and Crystal, and poetic flights of fancy. Maybe this is about Charles Bukovsky or a lost scene from Chekhov. Then things come right back home with the narrator strumming a guitar and blowing through a harmonica around his neck. Just like Dylan.

SIDE EIGHT
Baby, I'm In The Mood For You (Dylan) 2.55
Previously unreleased, this was recorded in New York in July 1962 as part of the sessions for *Freewheelin'*. 'Probably influenced by Jesse Fuller', Dylan revealed. It is certainly playful.

I Wanna Be Your Lover (Dylan) 3.25
Previously unreleased, recorded in New York on 20 October 1965, this was laid down during the early sessions for *Blonde on Blonde*, with the Hawks. A parody of The Beatles' 'I Want To Be Your Man' that was also recorded by the Rolling Stones, this was briefly considered as a single.
'I always thought it was a good song, but it just never made it onto an album'. Prime stuff from the first flash of lysergic mayhem: a girl with bullets in her eyes, and a rainman, 'who leaves in the wolfman's disguise'. A world away from the cheeky young folksinger of the previous track.

I Want You (Dylan) 3.05
From *Blonde On Blonde*.

Heart Of Mine (Dylan) 3.42
A previously unreleased version recorded live in New Orleans in August 1981. The studio version appears on *Shot Of Love*. This starts with some dischord and the band gradually come into focus then settle into a lively groove across which Dylan's vocal dances. New Orleans has certainly worked its magic, you can almost hear the young Louis Armstrong tootling along to this good- time music.

On A Night Like This (Dylan) 2.57
From *Planet Waves*.

Just Like A Woman (Dylan) 4.54
From *Blonde On Blonde*.

SIDE NINE
Romance In Durango (Dylan and Jacques Levy) 4.38
A previously unreleased outtake of the song from *Desire*. Bob is on fire and the band respond in a rough and ready, south-of-the-border manner.

Senor (Tales Of Yankee Power) (Dylan) 5.40
From *Street Legal*.

Gonna Serve Somebody (Dylan) 5.24
From *Slow Train Coming*.

I Believe In You (Dylan) 5.09
From *Slow Train Coming*.

Time Passes Slowly (Dylan) 2.35
From *New Morning*.

SIDE TEN
I Shall Be Released (Dylan) 3.02
From *Greatest Hits Vol II*, a re-recording of a song from *The Basement Tapes* with Happy Traum.

Knockin' On Heaven's Door (Dylan) 2.30
From *Pat Garrett and Billy The Kid*.

All Along The Watchtower (Dylan) 3.02
Live version from *Before The Flood*.

Solid Rock (Dylan) 3.56
From *Saved*.

Forever Young (Dylan) 2.02
This previously unreleased version is a demo laid down in June 1973 for his publishers, played into an ageing reel-to-reel recorder. Not quite a case of leaving the very best for last, but this is totally unexpected and like peeking into Dylan's private chambers. It's very bareness, and – whisper it – bootleg quality give this early rendition a rough-grained authenticity that makes the sentiments all the more affecting. Dylan powers through it with a dramatic guitar chord at the end. It is full of feeling, yet totally devoid of sentimentality. A fine way to end what even now sounds like a chaotic, but fascinating mid-career summary.

KNOCKED OUT LOADED

US Release: 8 August 1986
UK Release:
CD Release: Columbia 467040 2
Producer: Sundog Productions, except for 'Got My Mind Made Up' produced by Tom Petty and Bob Dylan

Columbia OC 40439
CBS 86326

Running Time: 35.36

SIDE ONE: You Wanna Ramble; They Killed Him; Drifting Too Far From The Shore; Precious Memories; Maybe Someday.

SIDE TWO: Brownsville Girl; Got My Mind Made Up; Under Your Spell.

Bob Dylan: vocal, guitar, **Clem Burke:** drums, **T-Bone Burnett:** guitar, **Mike Campbell:** guitar, **Steve Douglas:** saxophone, **Howie Epstein:** bass, **Anton Fig:** drums, **Vito San Flippo:** bass, **Don Heffington:** drums, **Ira Ingber:** guitar, **James Jamerson Jr:** bass, **Philip Lyn Jones:** conga, **Al Kooper:** keyboards, **Sean Lynch:** drums, **Steve Madaio:** trumpet, **John McKenzie:** bass, **Vince Melamed:** keyboards, **Larry Meyers:** mandolin, **John Paris:** bass, **Tom Petty:** guitar, **Al Perkins:** steel guitar, **Raymond Lee Pounds:** drums, **Carl Sealove:** bass, **Patrick Seymour:** keyboards, **Jack Sherman:** guitar, **Dave Stewart:** guitar, **Benmont Tench:** keyboards, **Ron Wood:** guitar, **Milton Gabriel, Mike Berment** and **Brian Parris:** steel drums, **Peggi Blu, Carole Dennis, Madeline Quebec, Muffy Hendrix, Queen Esther Marrow, Annette May Thomas** and **Eliseca Wright:** vocals, **Childrens' Choir** on 'They Killed Him', **Tom Petty and the Heartbreakers** on 'Got My Mind Made Up'

Dylan described this album better than anyone. 'It's all sort of stuff. It doesn't really have a theme or a purpose'. Dylan had recently married his singer Carolyn Dennis in secret after the birth of their daughter Desiree, so he had other things on his mind at this point. There is no equivalent for 'Sad Eyed Lady' here, at least so far as we know. Each track has a different musical cast. Even Dylan became casual about turning up for an endless round of recording sessions. He reworked 'New Danville Girl', laid down back in December 1984 at Cherokee

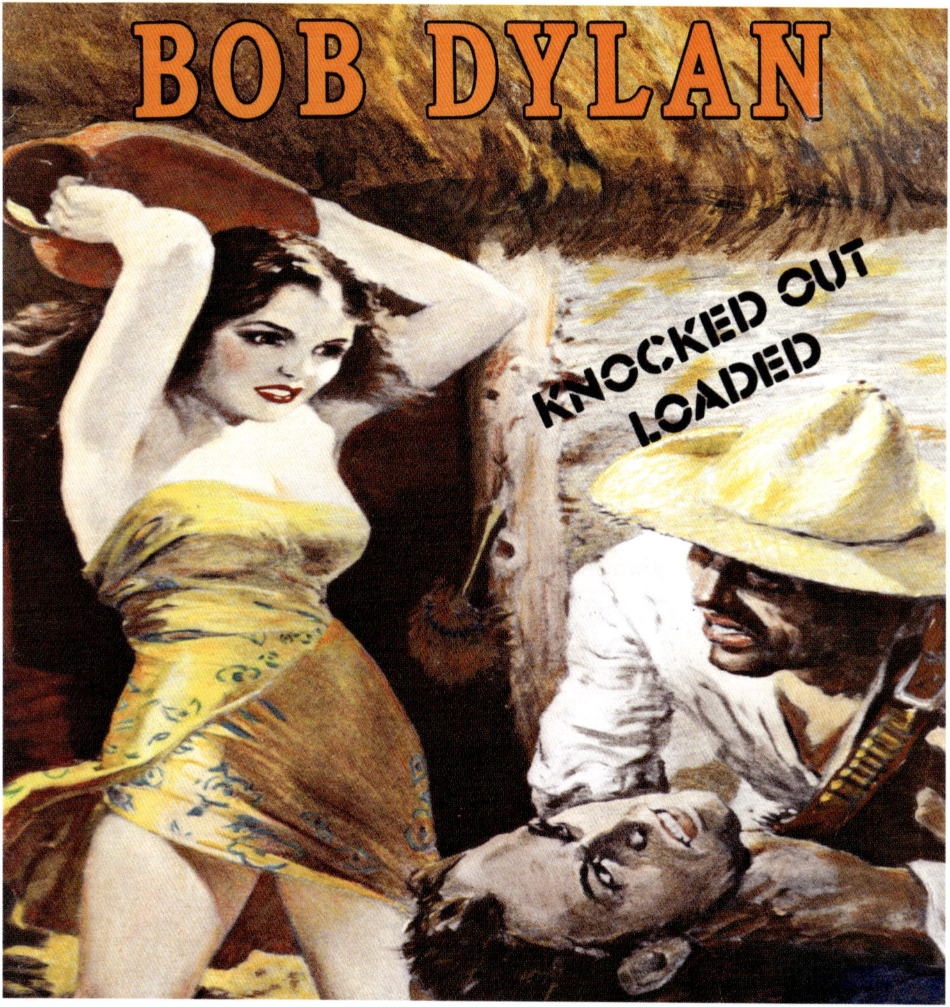
BOB DYLAN
KNOCKED OUT
LOADED

Studios. Two more demos for *Empire Burlesque* – 'Maybe Sunday' and 'Driftin' Too Far From Shore' – were also retooled.

Dylan then went on his travels seeking inspiration. He laid down 'Under Your Spell' with UK musicians including Dave Stewart at the Eurythmics Church, the band's recording studios in north London in November 1985. It was here that he gave a famously uncommunicative interview to Andy Kershaw for the *Old Grey Whistle Test* in late April 1986. He recorded three more tracks at Skyline Studios in Topanga Canyon, all cover versions, with old colleagues Al Kooper and T-Bone Burnette. Kooper said 'there were some really wonderful things cut at those sessions'. If so, they have yet to emerge.

In early May, he laid down 'Got My Mind Made Up' at Sound City Studios, Van-Nuys. The album was wrapped up – like a dodgy takeaway – back at Skyline in late May. And that was it.

Somehow it works as a picture of a man treading water. Michael Gray expected little from 'a title suggesting that its contents were thrown together' but by some miracle this 'third-rate assemblage of studio scrapings has a warmth and human fraility', everyone agrees on the standout track being 'Brownsville Girl'. The choir of kids was universally seen as a low point. In retrospect, the best new track laid down during this period, 'Band Of The Hand' recorded with the Tom Petty band in Festival Studios in Sydney in February 1986, was restricted to a film soundtrack, and put out briefly as a single.

There are no sleeve notes, but a long lists of special thanks, from Lou Reed to Jack Nicholson. Even the title is recycled from the old blues standard 'Junco Partner'. The cover is bizarre, a painting by Charles Sappington in primal colours. A barely clad girl is just about to smash a clay pot over the head of a bandit trying to throttle her lover in front of a cheap hovel, somewhere down Mexico way. It could be a scene from a bad movie. The cover is a reinterpretation of another Gregory Peck movie, not the black and white Gunfighter to which 'Brownsville Girl' refers, but *Duel in the Sun* (1946), a blaze of technicolour directed by King Vidor and co-starring Jennifer Jones. It looks like a homemade poster adorning an unauthorized showing of the film south of the border – it fits.

SIDE ONE
You Wanna Ramble (Herman Parker Jr) 3.14
Bob Dylan: vocal, guitar, **T-Bone Burnett**: guitar, **James Jameson Jr**: bass, **Al Kooper**: keyboards, **Raymond Lee Pounds**: drums, **Carol Dennis, Madelyn Quebec, Muffy Hendrix, Annette May Thomas**: backing vocals
A slice of refried rockabilly to start, the sort of thing that you might hear at a sound check, but hardly the kind of stuff that should open a Dylan album. Being Bob, you wonder if this is another 'Tired Horses', with Dylan's muse well and truly rambling at this point. Michael Gray dismisses this as 'tired r&b'. It gets louder in the middle briefly for no good reason.

They Killed Him (Kris Kristofferson) 4.00
Bob Dylan: vocal, guitar, **Jack Sherman**: guitar, **Vito San Filippo**: bass, **Al Kooper**: keyboards, **Steve Douglas**: saxophone, **Steve Madaio**: trumpet, **Carol Dennis, Madelyn Quebec, Muffy Hendrix, Annette May Thomas**: backing vocals, **The Childrens' Choir**
Gray regards this as 'wretched', and maybe Kristofferson should have stayed as janitor during the *Blonde On Blonde* sessions on this evidence. Here, the theme of the holy martyr, Christ and Ghandi and Martin Luther King, has none of the force of Dylan's gospel period. 'In The Garden', this is not. The entry of a children's choir takes the whole thing into the realm of parody.

Drifting Too Far From The Shore (Dylan) 3.39
Bob Dylan: vocal, keyboards, **Ron Wood**: guitar, **John Paris**: bass, **Anton Fig**: drums, **Peggi Blu, Carol Dennis, Madelyn Quebec, Muffy Hendrix, Annette May Thomas**: backing vocals
One of only two Dylan songs on a side of vinyl, this vies with his very worst, but despite the tinny production and mad drumming this is quite lively, especially Ron Wood's guitar, even if it does sound as if he has phoned it in from another studio. Dylan's keyboards are inaudible. His lyrics are more bitter than the reassuring female chorus would suggest, 'never needed to call you my whore', and it is this woman, not Dylan, who is drifting away. Not waving but drowning.

Precious Memories (Arranged by Dylan) 3.13
Bob Dylan: vocal, guitar, **Larry Meyers:** (mandolin), **Al Perkins:** steel guitar, **James Jamerson:** bass, **Raymond Lee Pounds:** drums, **Milton Gabriel, Mike Berment and Brian Parris:** steel drums, **Queen Esther Marrow, Carol Dennis, Madelyn Quebec, Muffy Hendrix, Annette May Thomas:** backing vocals
Another aural soup through which one can just about discern Dylan singing a gospel standard, to the accompaniment of steel drums.

Maybe Someday (Dylan) 3.17
Bob Dylan: vocal, guitar, **Mike Campbell:** guitar, **Howie Epstein:** bass, **Don Heffington:** drums, **Steve Douglas:** saxophone, **Steve Madaio:** trumpet, **Peggi Blu, Queen Esther Marrow, Carol Dennis, Madelyn Quebec, Muffy Hendrix, Eliseica Wright:** backing vocals
Dylan slags off some woman and it sounds like a private letter barely put to music, that should have been lost in the post. It is easy to see why this was rejected for *Empire Burlesque*, and even less comprehensible that it should be revived here. Especially when the likes of 'Blind Willie McTell' were still gathering dust. The production is dreadful – come back Arthur Baker, all is forgiven. It starts abruptly, and fades away for no good reason.

SIDE TWO
Brownsville Girl (Dylan and Sam Shepard) 11.00
Bob Dylan: vocal, guitar, **Ira Ingber:** guitar, **Carl Sealove:** bass, **Don Heffington:** drums, **Vince Melamed:** keyboards, **Steve Douglas:** saxophone, **Steve Madaio:** trumpet, **Eliseica Wright, Queen Esther Marrow, Peggi Blu, Carol Dennis, Madelyn Quebec, Muffy Hendrix:** backing vocals
Sam Shepard told Howard Sounes that 'we tossed around a bunch of ideas, none of them really got anywhere and then we just started telling stories to each other'. Dylan began one with the opening line, he must have queued to see *The Gunfighter* back in Hibbing. Directed by Henry King and released in 1950, this is now a cult classic, and is a savage tale of Gregory Peck as an ageing gunslinger coming back to find his estranged wife and kid. Finding himself up against all kinds of punks and psychos. One shoots him in a duel, but the dying Peck pleads with the sheriff not to string him up, but make him live the rest of his life with the memory of what he has done.

The result is a wonderfully tangled tale, with mariachi trimmings, that spans then and now and two women, one a memory, the other a saviour. Dylan might seem to have forgotten to sing from the evidence of the other tracks here, but he can sure narrate in the kind of half speech, half singing that Leonard Cohen has adopted in his later years. A dramatic monologue worthy of Gregory Peck in fact, and the new woman is similarly praised for providing a false alibi – 'it was the best acting I've seen anybody do'. Similarly, Henry Porter is bogus. But all this fits a degraded world where 'even the swap meets around here are getting pretty corrupt'.

Shepard was worried that the song was full of unusually long lines and about how Dylan would squeeze it all in, forgetting he was dealing with a master. 'The way he squashes phrasing and stretches it out is quite remarkable', he later admitted. Oddly, Dylan has since claimed that the song was a response to Lou Reed's 'Doin' The Thing That We Want To', that opens with the narrator going off to see a play, Sam Shepard's *Fool For Love*. Wheels within wheels, reflections of a mirror in another mirror.

There is another echo. Two of Dylan's heroes recorded a variant of the original title, Dock Boggs 'Danville Girl' that starts with a train ride – and Woody Guthrie 'Danville Girl No 2'. So this is 'Danville Girl No 3'. The original song had lines like 'I got off at Danville/got stuck on a Danville Girl/you can bet your life she was a pearl/she wore that Danville curl'.

One of the cancelled lines from 'New Danville Girl' was about 'watching shadows on an old stone wall', both a crude home cinema and Plato's central philosophical idea that life on earth was just a pale reflection of ideal forms somewhere in eternity. Even this track is a kind of Xerox, with the original, clearer demo laid down in November 1984 overlaid with a new vocal, with slightly different words, an over-zealous female chorus, and Steve Douglas's saxophone. And a change of location, though both Brownsville and Danville are archetypal place names from the Wild West, fitting a song which is 'suspended somewhere between history, fiction and myth' – to quote the *Rough Guide*.

Michael Gray also enthuses about an oasis in the Dylan desert at this point in time, 'intelligent and subtle, from a Dylan out from behind his 1980s wall of self-contempt and wholly in command of his incomparable vocal resources'. Well, he can do the equivalent to an ironic nod of the head, anyway. Bono makes even larger claims. 'It's a song that altered songwriting. It's a completely new kind of song and also has the spectacular line 'if there's an original thought out there I could use it right now'. 'Brownsville Girl' is a beautiful rhapsody about this. It's addressed to this other woman who seems to be his muse....Bob Dylan is there for every stage of your life'.

Got My Mind Made Up (Dylan and Tom Petty) 2.52
Bob Dylan: vocals, **Tom Petty:** guitar, **Mike Campbell:** guitar, **Benmont Tench:** keyboards, **Howie Epstein:** bass, **Stan Lynch:** drums, **Philip Lyn Jones:** conga, **Carol Dennis, Madelyn Quebec, Queen Esther Marrow, Elisecia Wright:** backing vocals
If only Dylan had recorded the whole album with the Heartbreakers. This one really rocks and brings Dylan's vocal back into focus. There is some great twangy guitar on this kissing cousin of 'Willie and the Hand Jive', the kind of stuff young Zimmerman terrified his school prom with back in Hibbing, just like that scene from *Back to the Future*.

Under Your Spell (Dylan and Carol B Sager) 3.55
Bob Dylan: guitar, **Dave Stewart:** guitar, **John McKenzie:** bass, **Clem Burke:** drums, **Patrick Seymour:** keyboards, **Muffy Hendrix, Carol Dennis, Queen Esther Marrow, Elisecia Wright, Madelyn Quebec:** backing vocals
'Don't know how much of this I can take' one line goes here, just before name-checking the album title, and some of his audience felt the same, with two possibly even worse albums to follow before the renewed glory of Oh Mercy.

Rough Guide describes this as 'pop lite co-written with Burt Bacharach's wife', but at least it makes you proud of the UK session crew who laid down the crisp backing before a female chorus was poured all over it in Topanga County. More is less.

DOWN IN THE GROOVE

US Release: 31 May 1988
UK Release:
CD Release: Columbia CK-460267
Producer: Engineered by Stephen Shelton and Coke Johnson, mixed by Stephen Shelton

Columbia OC-40957
CBS 460 267-1

Running Time: 32.07

SIDE ONE: Let's Stick Together; When Did You Leave Heaven?; Sally Sue Brown; Death Is Not The End; Had A Dream About You, Baby.

SIDE TWO: Ugliest Girl In The World; Silvio; Ninety Miles An Hour (Down A Dead End Street); Shenandoah; Rank Strangers To Me.

Bob Dylan: vocal, guitar, harmonica, **Mike Baird:** drums, **Eric Clapton:** guitar, **Alan Clarke:** keyboards, **Sly Dunbar:** drums, **Nathan East:** bass, **Mitchell Froom:** keyboards, **Myron Grombacher:** drums, **Beau Hill:** keyboards, **Randy Jackson:** bass, **Steve Jones:** guitar, **Steve Jordan:** drums, **Larry Klein:** bass, **Mark Knopfler:** guitar, **Danny Kortchmar:** guitar, **Madelyn Quebec:** keyboards, **Kevin Savigar:** keyboards, **Robbie Shakespeare:** bass, **Stephen Shelton:** drums, **Paul Simonon:** bass, **Henry Spinetti:** drums, **Kip Winger:** bass, **Ron Wood:** bass, **Peggi Blu, Alexandra Brown, Carol Dennis, Jerry Garcia, Willie Green, Bobby King, Clydie King, Brent Myland, Madelyn Quebec, Bob Weir, Full Force:** vocals

A shockingly brief album – hell, in the 60s one side of his vinyl outpourings would last almost as long as the brace here. And whereas they would be bursting with songs cast aside, here one has the feeling that he was desperately trying to cobble enough material together. As usual in such times of mental drought, Dylan set out to record an album of cover versions, *Self Portrait Vol 2*. The results are closer to *Dylan*, the only other album ever deleted from Bob's back catalogue. But here the cover versions, including some that got cut out, are generally better than his own material. Only two songs from this album enter the official canon of *Lyrics 1962-2001*.

Dave Alvin from the Blasters was briefly at Sunset Sound and remembers a 13-hour session, with some great rock'n'roll material including 'Red Cadillac And A Black Moustache' and Johnny Carroll's 'Rock With Me Baby', but it being ruined with choirs and the like, 'like changing the sound from Elvis Sun to Elvis RCA'. Dylan even apologized to him later for leaving this stuff off what

BOB DYLAN

Down In The Groove

would have been a far more interesting album.

It took six recording sessions to lay down this album, two consecutive days at London's Townhouse in August 1986 when he also cut his contributions to the soundtrack of *Hearts of Fire*, and a series of visits to Sunset Sound Studios in LA in April 1987, plus one final unspecified recording date in May. At least the tinny sound of the two previous albums is replaced, by and large, with a far closer approximation to a real band playing together in real time without any levers being pulled on the mixing desk to render it all into Venusian.

Dylan sings well throughout and at the time paid tribute to his most recent influences: 'Sinatra, Peggy Lee, I love all these people, but I tell you who I've really been listening to a lot lately is Bing Crosby. I don't think you can find better phrasing anywhere'. He also claims, with due cause here, that a good re-interpretation can be just as creative as a new song . 'I'm not saying I made a definitive version of anything with this last record, but I liked the songs. Writing is such an isolated thing. You have to get into or be in that place. In the old days, I could get to it real quick. I can't get to it like that no more'. He adds that 'those songs, they came in pretty easy'.

It is one of those albums that you can put on as background sound without being distracted. For Michael Gray, 'continued silence would have been more dignified than this'. *Q* magazine titled their review 'Why! There must be a reason for Dylan's new album. So tell us, Bob, what is it?'. The only explanation they can offer is that this is the result of 'a mischievous desire to take the p-ss out of his record company.

Nobody owns up to the cover photographs, a blurred shot of Dylan strumming acoustic guitar, and on what looks like the back of a truck, playing to an audience of one. Frankly bizarre. Whatever the critics think of the music, there are no quibbles about the sound quality, on either vinyl or CD. Once again, the album seems to have been over-cooked.

According to Clinton Heylin, the album, readied for release in autumn 1987, contained 'Got Love If You Want It' and Gene Vincent's 'Important Words'. Then Dylan swapped the latter for 'The Usual' from the movie soundtrack. Promo items were sent out that are now mildly collectable. The Argentinian issue to this day contains this slight aberration. Dylan had another rethink and pulled both for an *Empire Burlesque* outtake, 'Death Is Not The End', and 'Had A Dream About You, Baby'. The re-activation of the former gives some credence to Howard Sounes's supposition that this is an album about 'alienation, ageing and death'. In which case, it is well disguised. Dylan also jiggled the running order, that originally had placed the blasters on side one and the more reflective songs on side two.

SIDE ONE
Let's Stick Together (Wilbert Harrison) 3.08
Bob Dylan: vocal, guitar, harmonica, **Danny Kortchmar:** guitar, **Randy Jackson:** bass, **Steve Jordan:** drums
A Canned Heat-style boogie, with that female chorusline thankfully absent, and a great little rocking combo. If this album really is Dylan's Trojan horse, smuggling alienation in under the guise of a collection of songs that he probably sings in the bath, then this could be seen as about the death of creativity. 'You never miss your water 'til your well runs dry.'

When Did You Leave Heaven? (W Bulloc and R Whiting) 2.15
Bob Dylan: vocal, guitar, **Madelyn Quebec:** vocal, keyboard, **Stephen Shelton:** drums
Sombre chords on the synthesized keyboard and pounding drums, plus some rich electric guitar chords from Bob for this old Guy Lombardo hit. Short and sweet.

Sally Sue Brown (J Alexander/E Montgomery and T Stafford) 2.29
Bob Dylan: vocal, guitar, **Madelyn Quebec:** vocals, **Steve Jones:** guitar, **Paul Simonon:** bass, **Myron Grombacher:** drums, **Kevin Savigar:** keyboards, **Bobby King, Willie Green:** backing vocals
Another song that doesn't outstay its welcome but seems rather a wilful waste of a Sex Pistol and The Clash's bass player, outpowerd here by a squawking female singer. The male chorus is straight out of the Jordonaires. 'A track of no quality' sneers Ben Cruickshank. Well, it certainly ain't 'Sad Eyed Lady Of The Lowlands'.

Death Is Not The End (Dylan) 5.10
Bob Dylan: vocals, guitar, harmonica, **Clydie King:** vocals, **Mark Knopfler:** guitar, **Robbie Shakespeare:** bass, **Sly Dunbar:** drums, **Alan Clarke:** keyboards, **Full Force:** backing vocals
An *Empire Burlesque* outtake which addresses the greatest question of all, what becomes of us when we die. The song was later covered by another sin-wracked, hellfire hedonist, Nick Cave. Dylan sounds hushed, the backing choir works for a change and the musicians stay respectfully in the background. Unlike his born-again period, the chorus is sung in hope rather than joyous anticipation. This song becomes more apocalyptic when afforded a close listen.

Had A Dream About You, Baby (Dylan) 2.51
Bob Dylan: vocal, guitar, **Eric Clapton**: guitar, **Ron Wood**: guitar, **Kip Winger**: bass, **Beau Hill**: keyboards, **Mitchell Froom**: keyboards, **Henry Spinetti**: drums
An amazing band with two great guitar players and the sometime Mr Suzanne Vega on his vintage keyboards. A track recycled from *Hearts of Fire*, and it rocks along. A song of pure lust.

SIDE TWO
Ugliest Girl In The World (Dylan and /Robert Hunter) 3.31
Bob Dylan: vocal, guitar, **Danny Kortchmar**: guitar, **Randy Jackson**: bass, **Steve Jordan**: drums, **Stephen Shelton**: keyboards, **Madelyn Quebec, Carol Dennis**: backing vocals
The first of two writing collaborations with the Grateful Dead's main lyricist, the man responsible for the visionary poetry of 'Dark Star' and the roots poetry of *American Beauty* and *Workingman's Dead*. This is neither, and you'll soon be thinking that it is just a riff.

Silvio (Dylan and Robert Hunter) 3.06
Bob Dylan: vocal, guitar, **Nathan East**: bass, **Mike Baird**: drums, **Madelyn Quebec, Carol Dennis, Jerry Garcia, Bob Weir, Brent Myland**: backing vocals
Having three of the Dead in the studio and using them just for backing vocals seems a little wasteful. Dylan sings with raw energy, and the ghost of the Jordanaires again stalks the earth.

Ninety Miles An Hour (Down A Dead End Street) (H Blair and D Robertson) 2.56
Bob Dylan: vocal, guitar, **Madelyn Quebec**: vocal, keyboards, **Willie Green, Bobby King**: backing vocals
More death, or simply a cul-de-sac. Which musically, this is. Uninspired is the word.

Shenandoah (Arranged by Dylan) 3.37
Bob Dylan: vocal, guitar, harmonica, **Nathan East**: bass, **Madelyn Quebec, Carol Dennis, Peggi Blu, Alexandra Brown**: backing vocals
Dylan takes an arranging credit for this traditional song as performed by Odetta. Just a bass for company, plus four girl singers including his wife. The mandolin player goes uncredited. A song of the American frontier, and again the river could be Lethe, dividing the living from the dead.

Rank Strangers To Me (A Brumley) 2.57
Bob Dylan: vocal, guitar, **Larry Klein**: bass
One-time Mr Joni Mitchell on fretless electric bass, this was a song famously performed by the Stanley Brothers, from whom Dylan probably took 'Man of Constant Sorrow' on his first album. This is really spooky, another song about looking for a dead friend – maybe Jesus – among the living, among whom the singer now feels himself to be a ghost. Now another side of Dylan covering songs made famous by the Stanley or the Louvin Brothers, or even the terrifying Dock Boggs, really would have been something. As it is, just as the album gets interesting, it comes to an end.

OUTTAKES:
3 April, Sunset Sound Studios, California: 'Twist And Shout', 'Willie And The Hand Jive', 'Important Words', 'Got Love If You Want It', 'When Did You Leave Heaven?', 'Just When I Needed You Most' (some of these with Dave Alvin on guitar)

The sessions at London's Townhouse, held on 27 and 28 August 1986 that resulted in 'Had A Dream About You Baby' also produced 'The Usual', an alternative take of 'Had A Dream About You Baby', and 'Night After Night' all on the soundtrack album of *Hearts of Fire*; the soundtrack itself adds 'A Couple More Years'. The Argentinian version of *Down In The Groove* includes 'Got Love If You Want It'.

Just when Dylan's career seemed to have drifted too far from shore ever to see dry land again, despite having visited seemingly every recording studio in the known world, some rough demos by a few old friends, laid down in his garage in April and May 1988 and issued under the psudonym of the *Travelling Wilburys, Vol 1*, was released to massive sales and acclaim. A 1990 follow-up, Vol 3, was less successful, and Dylan's vocals were placed further back in the mix.

DYLAN AND THE DEAD

US Release: 6 February 1989
UK Release:
CD Release: Columbia CK 45056

Columbia OC 45056
CBS 4633811

Producer: Jerry Garcia and John Cutler,
engineered by John Cutler and Guy Charbonneau **Running Time:** 44.04

There is also a rare US-only CD picture disc

SIDE ONE: Slow Train*; I Want You***; Gotta Serve Somebody****; Queen Jane Approximately**.
* Sullivan Stadium, Foxboro, Massachusetts 4 July 1987
**Autzen Stadium, Eugene, Oregon, 19 July 1987
***Oakland Stadium, California 24 July 1987
****Anaheim Stadium, California 26 July 1987
Mixed at Club Front, San Rafael during November 1988

SIDE TWO: Joey*; All Along The Watchtower****; Knockin' On Heaven's Door****.

Bob Dylan: guitar, vocals, **Jerry Garcia:** guitar, **Micky Hart:** drums, **Bill Kreutzman:** drums, **Phil Lesh:** bass, **Brent Myland:** keyboards, **Bob Weir:** guitar

In the early summer of 1987 Dylan joined U2 at the legendary Sun studios in Memphis to lay down 'Love Rescue Me' for their album *Rattle and Hum*, a brief but very successful collaboration. Maybe it was inevitable then that joining up for six gigs in July 1987 with a similarly legendary rock band, the Grateful Dead, should be less eventful. Here were two of the prime movers in psychedelic rock. But unlike U2, then at the height of their powers, neither was the creative forces they had been 20 years before. Even so the 3-CD bootleg *The French Girl,* captures a splendid rehearsal session in May 1987, with all kinds of unexpected delights:

'The Ballad of Ira Hayes', 'John Brown', 'Tomorrow Is A Long Time', 'Stealin' and the Ian Tyson song of the title.

To the Dead's own bemusement, when they later provided live tapes for him to cherry-pick for an album, Dylan tested out possible selections on a cheap ghetto blaster. The Grateful Dead were masters of repackaging their own back pages and put together an interesting sequence that Dylan immediately trashed. Into the bin went three more fascinating oddities, 'Wicked Messenger' from New Jersey's Meadowlands, 'Ballad of Frankie Lee and Judas Priest' taped at Eugene, Oregon, and 'Chimes of Freedom' live at Anaheim.

Dylan writes in *Chronicles* about this strange year, a freak accident to his hand, a world tour with Tom Petty, and the Dead wanting him to sing old and obscure songs, like the above that he couldn't bring off emotionally. 'I felt like a goon.' But seeing a jazz singer in a bar gave him a clue about how to sing 'with natural power'. He rushed back to the Dead's rehearsal studio to try out this new vocal technique and 'something internal came unhinged'. These old songs became clear to him again and eminently singable, 'without having to be resticted to the world of words', whatever that means. All the more frustrating that these revivals have been left off the record by Dylan himself.

As Dylan admitted, ten years on. 'I was going on my name for a long time, name and reputation, that was about all I had. I didn't know who I was on stage'. Never more so than on the notorious Live Aid debacle that would have got him, Ron Wood and Keith Richard thrown off the stage at a down-at-heel folk club as Bob launched into a song in front of the watching billions that they had never even rehearsed.

Here again, there were rumours of tension between what one view would have as Dylan and his backing band, and another (many of the vociferous younger Deadheads) the Dead and their guest singer. Jerry Garcia told the *Golden Road* after the event, that 'you really have to pay attention to avoid making mistake, insofar as he's doing what he's doing and everybody else is trying to play the song'. Any deviation from Dylan's own view of how to play a song was simply not tolerated. 'In that sense, he de facto became the leader of the band.'

So was Bob just being crassly insensitive to everyone else on stage – the Dead being almost supernaturally aware of what each other was playing, hence their legendary status as a jamming band? 'He's funny. He has a chameleon quality. It's not as though we're fighting with him. But he doesn't have a conception about two things that are very important in music, starting and ending a song'. This was to become even more apparent during the *Never Ending*

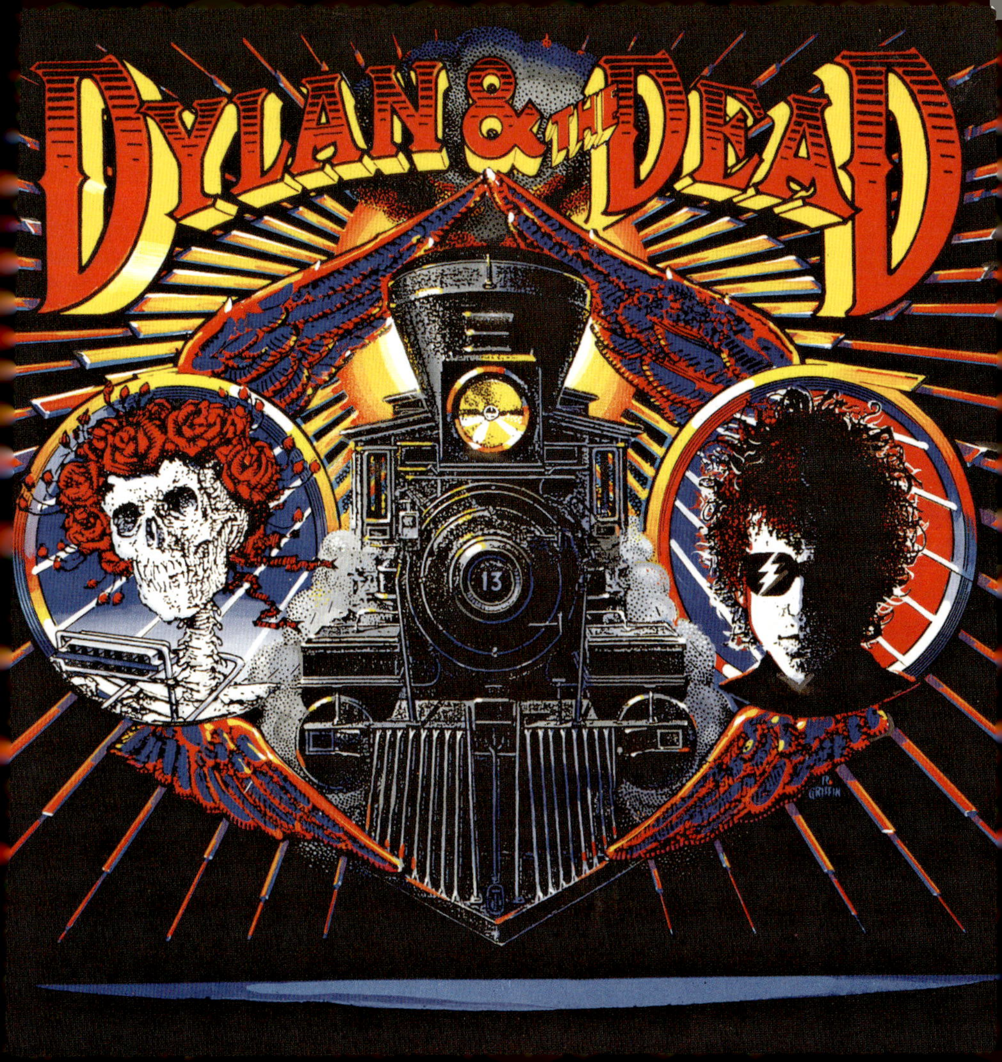
DYLAN & THE DEAD
13
R. GRIFFIN

tour, especially when Bob began to fancy himself as a lead guitarist.

Record Collector magazine failed to sympathise. 'Dylan sounds totally disinterested; there is not a trace of passion in these seven leaden readings from his back catalogue'. The Dead boogie gently, 'with little regard for the material. There are brief moments when something interesting is about to happen, but they soon fade away'. For Michael Gray, Dylan 'can't remember the words to any of these songs, the vocal sound is miserable, and the Dead lumpenly uninspired'. Later overviews were more charitable of an album 'everybody loves to hate, but also oddly endearing', even if the vocals are 'rotten'. For the *Rough Guide*, this is 'one of the most despised discs in rock history, but now sounds like a perfectly decent Grateful Dead covers album with the added bonus of the man who wrote the songs as a guest vocalist'.

But how different from the Grateful Dead's own genius at delving into their own tape archives in the 'Dicks Picks' series and the like, beautifully packaged and annotated and in 3 and 4-CD bite sized chunks. At under 45 minutes here they barely get going. And the Dead think in two-hour sections, not just a jumble of odd tracks. Bootlegs of individual concerts from this month put the Dylan section in its place as part of a longer concert and develop a flow from song to song that is totally lost on the official chronicle. Yet another album crying out for the Jeff Rosen treatment.

Nothing wrong with the cover, though, by Dead loyalist Rick Griffin, and his usual conjoining of bright colours, fairground calligraphy and a sinister undertow. A visual counterpart of *Blonde On Blonde* era Dylan, indeed. Here, a threatening black steam train, number 13, thunders towards the viewer as steel spikes splay outward. The archetypal Dead skeleton, wreathed in roses, poses with a harmonica holder. Dylan circa '66 stares out with a lightning flash on one of his shades – both are attached by eagle wings, like a hells' angel motif. The back cover is the back of the train, thundering away in a cloud of steam. Inside is a lovely shot of Dylan encircled by the Dead, taken by Herb Greene. Garcia gazes at him fondly, like a proud uncle.

Even so, somehow Dylan sounds trapped in these songs, and with this band. In *Chronicles* he describes a panic attack he suffered a few months later onstage with the Heartbreakers. Dylan 'cast my own spell to drive out the devil'. It was like being born again, again, in front of 30,000 people. 'Instantly it was like a thoroughbred had charged through the gates'. He came to see that as being as close as he had been to retiring for good instead of being at the end of his personal story, 'I was actually in the prelude to the beginning of another one'. The immediate result would be choosing his own tour band for what has become known as the 'never ending tour' and a new burst of songwriting that would result within two years of the recording of *Oh Mercy*.

SIDE ONE
Slow Train (Dylan) 4.54
A song that had not previously featured on a live Dylan album before, and it chugs along nicely, though with none of the born-again zeal of that extraordinary year of live brimstone and treacle, late-1979 to late-1980.

Garcia provides ornamentation like the electrified bluegrass picker he really is, and Myland gives good keyboard, while the Dead rhythm section is as effective as you would expect, even if their incendiary live peak circa 1968-1972 is by now a distant memory. Even the later band could enter a zone of total improvisation, usually coming out of the double drum solo, but Dylan does little to provoke them into greatness.

I Want You (Dylan) 3.59
A comfortable jog trot.

Gotta Serve Somebody (Dylan) 5.42
Another of the born-again songs, live on disc for the first time. But the Dead do not take to a reggae rhythm like ducks to water, more like swans sliding on the ice, and Dylan sings without conviction or wit or any obvious attempt to impart meaning to the 'meaningless ring' of the syllables he dutifully trots out here.

Queen Jane Approximately (Dylan) 6.30
Another song never before committed to a live album by Dylan. An album highlight, with Gerry and his drug-crazed crew playing with 'impeccable sensitivity'. Richard Williams admired the 'wasted majesty' of this version. There is lovely piano from Myland, and for once singer and musicians do really seem to be responding to each other, rather than engaging in a dialogue of the deaf.

SIDE TWO

Joey (Dylan/J Levy) 9.10

Dylan is far from modest about a song that is generally poorly regarded. But not by Jerry: 'That's a tremendous song, and you'd only know that singing it night after night. Garcia got me singing that song again. He said that's one of the best songs ever written. Coming from him, it was hard to know which way to take that. It got me singing that song again with them (the Dead). It keeps on getting better'. Not on the evidence here, a rendition even more sepulchral than on *Desire*. Even so, its composer proudly claims that '"Joey" has a Homeric quality to it that you don't hear every day. Especially in popular music'.

Well, it certainly goes on a bit, though not as long as the *Odyssey*. And if Dylan can indeed hold a candle to the blind bard with his startling way with a metaphor, this song is an exception. For more than one commentator, this performance is a 'twilight zone of bad taste'. What is missing is dramatic tension, so prevalent during the Rolling Thunder Revue era.

All Along The Watchtower (Dylan) 6.17

This sticks closely to the Hendrix arrangement, as did the Band, without the musical fireworks of his cover version, but Garcia takes flight with some fluid guitar and Weir kicks ass in the bass department. Dylan seems to wake up at last.

Knockin' On Heaven's Door (Dylan) 6.35

This should be heaven to a jamming band like the Dead, but Dylan sounds strangulated, and one of the most fluid four-handed percussion sections in all rock music are reduced to a dull plod. Just when Garcia is about to get going on one of his benign lead guitar breaks, Dylan comes back in with a bored-sounded vocal. Funereal rather than elegiac.

Any differences between Dylan and Garcia were soon resolved. When Jerry died in 1995, Dylan gave him a heartfelt tribute. 'To me he wasn't only a musician and friend, he was more like a big brother who taught and showed me more than he'll ever know. There's a lot of space and advances between the Carter Family and, say, Ornette Coleman, a lot of universes, but he filled them all without being a member of any school'. Ten years later, Rhino released a double CD, Garcia Plays Dylan, with lengthy and loving re-interpretations, all recorded live – Garcia's natural habitat – between 1973 and the year of Garcia's death, with various combos, from the Dead to Legion of Mary.

OH MERCY

US Release: 22 September 1989
UK Release:
CD Release: Columbia CK 45281
Producer: Daniel Lanois

Columbia OC 45281
465800-1
CD Remaster/SACD Release: 512343 6
Running Time: 39.03

SIDE ONE: Political World; Where Teardrops Fall; Everything Is Broken; Ring Them Bells; Man In The Long Black Coat.

SIDE TWO: Most Of The Time; What Good Am I?, Disease Of Conceit; What Was It You Wanted; Shooting Star.

Bob Dylan: vocal, guitar, harmonica, piano, organ, **Malcolm Burn:** keyboards, bass, mercy keys, **Willie Green:** drums, **Tony Hall:** bass, **John Hart:** saxophone, **Daryl Johnson:** percussion, **Larry Jolivet:** bass, **Daniel Lanois:** dobro, lap steel, guitar, omnichord, **Cyril Neville:** percussion, **Rockin' Dopsie:** accordion, **Alton Rubin Jr:** drums, **David Rubin Jr:** scrub board, **Mason Ruffner:** guitar, **Paul Synegal:** guitar, **Brian Stoltz:** guitar

From the *Dead* to *Oh Mercy* is – as those two concepts suggest – as stunning a musical rebirth as even Dylan has achieved at roughly ten years intervals throughout his career. Thus the late 50s saw him transform himself from a light crooner to a Guthrie clone, the late 60s from a wired-up rocker to a crafty mountain man uttering gnomic mantras, the late 70s from a chemical pierrot in face paint to a stern evangelist. Ten years on, we would have *Time Out Of Mind* coming after a return to acoustic blues and trad folk with the same aural magician, Daniel Lanois – Eno's assistant and disciple – again setting the controls for the heart of the sun. Maybe the time is almost ripe for him and Dylan to get together again amidst the sodden ruins of the Big Easy and conjure some more musical voodoo.

In 1989, Dylan re-signed a new album deal with Sony. *Oh Mercy* was taped from 7 to 24 March 1989 with overdubs added in early April in Daniel Lanois's Studio-On-The-Move, temporarily located at 1305 Soniat, complete with swamp grass and stuffed crocodiles, plus a multiplicity of vintage instruments and recording equipment. In *Chronicles*, Dylan writes fondly about this place of musical alchemy, a Victorian mansion close to Lafayette Cemetery – you can feel the ghosts of old New Orleans coming through on the music here – 'parlour windows, louvered shutters, high Gothic ceilings, walled-in courtyard'. It sounds like a hidden world, with heavy blankets darkening and soundproofing the windows. A place where day was night and night day. Hot and steamy.

There was a musical crew to match. Dylan writes of his first sighting of Lanois, noir all over, 'a balck prince from the black hills. He was scuff proof'. His guitarist Mason Ruffner was of the same type, cool and sharp, 'had a high pompadour, a gold tooth smile with a tiny guitar inlaid'. The more musically laid-back Brian Stoltz had played with the Neville Brothers for years. And on one memorable night, Rockin' Dopsie and his Cajun Band set up in the big parlour and jammed with Dylan on a new and unrehearsed song, 'Where Teardrops Fall' that went straight onto the record.

As Lanois told *Mojo*, 'on day one of recording, he showed up with a few pieces of paper, no instruments, not much of anything. I basically gave him a package price. For $150,000 he got everything: musicians, equipment, mixing…the works'. Though things went well from the start, Bob was not used to 'the stripped down sound I wanted. There were a few moments when he got discouraged. The way I was working, overdubbing and stacking tracks was not even a consideration for him'. They only worked at night, though Lanois would sometimes subtly speed up the 'different musical tempo after dark'. So this is a very carefully wrought artefact, as far as you could get from, say, the production of *Blood on the Tracks*.

Dylan gives a blow-by-blow account of these magical weeks in chapter four of *Chronicles*: the sobbing saxophone break here is played by John Hall, who Dylan flashes on as an exact lookalike for Blind Gary Davis, 'who I'd known and followed round years earlier'. Dylan knows he is in the right place at the right time with the right people. 'Felt like I had turned a corner, and was seeing the sight of a god's face'. Suddenly Dylan had focus, a relaxed time frame, a crack musical crew and a determined producer. He also had a folder of great new songs, ripe for uncomfortable listening.

Having gashed his hand so badly, 'no feelings in the nerves', and also having just learnt that his yacht had capsized in the Caribbean, Dylan had even considered giving up art and going into business – rather like Rimbaud. But one night he was sitting with his guitar at his kitchen table, 'nothing on the hillside but a shiny bed of lights', and wrote 20 verses or so that became 'Political World'. 'I thought I might have broken through to something'. Over the next few weeks he roughed out almost two dozen new songs. He felt as if he had been woken up.

BOB DYLAN
OH MERCY

'A song is like a dream, and you try to make it come true. They're like strange countries that you try to enter.' Lanois and crew helped him on the journey.

Lanois later told Nigel Williamson how Dylan worked on these drafts, largely in the studio. 'Dylan overwrites. He keeps chipping away at his verses. I've seen the same lyric turn up in two or three different songs as he cuts and pastes them around, so it's not quite sacred ground'. But Lanois did exactly this, giving Dylan a sacred place in which to turn these words into music.

We have U2 to thank for all this, their own music transformed as had Talking Heads been before them by Eno and his young Canadian apprentice. 'Bono had heard a few songs and suggested that Daniel Lanois could really record them right. Daniel came to see me when we were playing in New Orleans last year and we hit it off.' He immediately recognized a fellow spirit, a pro who was always open to the unexpected. 'Daniel just allowed the record to take place any old time, day or night. You don't have to walk through secretaries, pinball machines and managers and hangers-on in the lobby, and parking lots and elevators and arctic temperatures. Some people expect me to bring in a Bob Dylan song, sing it and they record it. Other people don't work that way – there's more feedback.' Feedback in more ways than one, Lanois concocted a whole musical universe around Dylan's wracked vocals, full of echo and mystery, making him half man half myth.

David Henderson later described the vocals here as sounding like Dylan is 'crouched next to you in the back seat of a broken down car'. Fingering a cut-throat razor, one could add. He certainly doesn't sound friendly.

Lanois, no mean guitar player himself, recalls that 'Bob liked to get something in the name of spontaneity, and then we'd spend a lot of time on details. Some vocals were worked on and lyrics were changed. It was fascinating to see the transformation some of the songs made. They would begin as one story and at the end of the night they would be something else'. And Dylan in turn has always found a conventional recording studio 'very foreign to me. The controls, the tape itself, the machinery is something that never really interested me enough to gain control over, one way or another. Daniel got me to do stuff that wouldn't have entered my mind'.

Especially in the early hours, just like back in Nashville in 1966, when inspiration strikes. 'Most are stream-of-consciousness songs, the kind that come to you in the middle of the night'. But he denies that these songs are particularly bleak. 'It could but then again it needn't be. A lot of that might have to do with the different textures of instrumentation on it rather than the songs themselves'. If you say so, Bob. 'When we finished recording, it felt like the studio could have gone up in a sheet of flame'.

The album drew hugely favourable reviews, both for Dylan's renewed lyrical sharpness and for the way these new songs were 'swathed in the warm sensurround sound hallmarked by Daniel Lanois'. Dylan himself compared it to the Sun sound down in Memphis. 'On Sun records, the artists were singing for their lives, and sounded like they were coming from the most mysterious place on the planet'. *Oh Mercy* is now seen as a masterpiece for its tenderness and wisdom, with Dylan looking back in sorrow rather than anger, singing as if suffused with unbearable knowledge. As the *Rough Guide* puts it, the 'unflinching theme of this album is life and love seen from the perspective of middle age, reconciled to a world of fraying morality'.

The cover is as artful as the music within, a photograph of New York graffiti street art by 'Trotsky'. A man and woman are dancing, or maybe fighting. The album title is picked out in the same primary colours. Dylan appears on the back, all eyes and bare flesh, having just emerged from a pool and donned a straw hat.

SIDE ONE
Political World (Dylan) 3.48
Bob Dylan: vocal, guitar, **Daniel Lanois**: dobro, **Mason Ruffner**: guitar, **Brian Stolz**: guitar, **Tony Hall**: bass, **Cyril Neville**: percussion, **Willie Green**: drums

A calling-on song, this sets out the terrain of a world in need of the mercy of the album title, a dystopia where people play out their private lives against 'cities of lonesome fear', and where unseen forces call the shots. The Masters of War are still in charge, though more subtly. As Dylan said at the time, 'it's all been neutralized, nothing threatening, nothing magical, nothing challenging. For me I hate to see it. It's like 'conscience' is a dirty word'. He wrote the song during a 'heated presidential race', but the world here 'is more like an underworld'. He wrote at least double the verses used here, perhaps sensibly omitting lines like 'comes out of the blue/moves towards you/like a knife cutting through cheese'.

Musically, it is rough and urgent, with clattering percussion and Lanois's edgy dobro tangling up the listener's nerves. Dylan's voice is echoey, like rockabilly from hell.

There was a strange video, directed by John Cougar Mellancamp, where beautiful women in an opulent restaurant are totally ignoring Dylan up on the podium.

Where Teardrops Fall (Dylan) 2.33
Bob Dylan: vocal, piano, **Daniel Lanois**: lap steel, **Paul Synegal**: guitar, **Larry Jolivet**: bass, **Alton Rubin Jr**: scrub board, **John Hart**: saxophone, **Rockin' Dopsie**: accordion
This is far gentler, almost a waltz, with lilting steel guitar and a schmaltzy saxophone solo at the end. 'It was just a three-minute ballad, but it made you stand straight up…like someone had pulled the chord to stop the train'.

Dylan sounds like Tom Waits' older brother in this picture of love as a charm against the outside world. They walk past rivers of blindness, and the lines about banging the drum slowly come from 'Streets of Laredo', the song of a cowboy who has died of a sexually transmitted disease. Dylan summons the romantic cliché 'roses are red, violets are blue', but is only driven to revisit his loved one because of boredom, when 'time is beginning to crawl'. And yet he hasn't sung with such quiet lust since 'Lay Lady Lay'.

Everything Is Broken (Dylan) 3.15
Bob Dylan: vocal, guitar, harmonica, **Daniel Lanois**: dobro, **Malcolm Burn**: tambourine, **Brian Stolz**: guitar, **Tony Hall**: bass, **Daryl Johnson**: percussion, **Willie Green**: drums
Dylan sings almost joyfully about a deconstructed world, that turns out to be what he sees and feels whenever his loved one is away. Hence the joy, perhaps. The words delight at their own cleverness, and Dylan's vocal takes pleasure at the simple rhythms here, almost like a nursery rhyme. This has the same tense rhythmic thrust of post-Velvets Lou Reed, another misanthrope.

Dylan wrote it in 'quick choppy strokes'. It is a catalogue of needless waste, provoked by a memory of sitting on the beach at Coney Island and seeing a General Electric portable radio, broken in the sand. The song originally had a ray of hope, with the lines 'I'm crossing the river going to Hoboken/maybe over there, things ain't broken'. Then he took it out.

This was first cut in March 1989 as 'Broken Days'. By April, after the overdubbing process, Dylan had completely rewritten the song, and given it a new title. They laid it down 'with plenty of tremelo…with the full band on the floor' watching each others' every move. There is a fretful feel to both words and music, driven by those edgy bongos, with Lanois again adding texture with his jangling dobro. The matching video, filmed by Jesse Dylan and much aired on MTV, had his dad looking spectacularly ill at ease.

Ring Them Bells (Dylan) 3.01
Bob Dylan: vocal, piano, **Daniel Lanois**: guitar, **Malcolm Burn**: keyboards
Bob told Paul Zollo 'somebody once came in and sang it in my dressing room. To me. To try to influence me to sing it that night (laughter). It could have gone either way, you know'. So which way did it go? 'It went out the door and didn't come back'.

That spirit of mischief is totally lacking from this song, quiet and holy, as spiritual as anything on *Saved*, with churchy organ and Bob himself on percussive piano. Dylan reckons that Daniel is more 'than a sound man. He was like a doctor with scientific principles'. He praises Lanois's input, that 'captured the essence of it on this, put the magic into its heartbeat and pulse. He definitely captured the moment. He might have captured the whole era'.

This is 'The Chimes of Freedom' revived, a heavenly vision on earth. But the bells are ringing for the lost and the helpless. Dylan's voice is tender and fierce, both at once. And he looks forward to divine judgment, not mercy.

Man In The Long Black Coat (Dylan) 4.35
Bob Dylan: vocal, 6 string and 12-string guitar, harmonica, **Daniel Lanois**: dobro, **Malcolm Burn**: keyboards
This was composed entirely in the studio, and the atmosphere of chirpin crickets at the start is reproduced electronically. Echoed electric guitar chords, and harmonica like a summons to a gunfight are set to the strains of a slow waltz. The way Lanois uses stereo here is inspired, like a movie soundtrack. Dylan writes of how 'a peculiar change crept over things. The dread intro gives you the impression of a chronic rush. It's cut out from the abyss of blackness'.

Then along comes the Clint Eastwood figure, death or something worse. Dylan's voice has never been so deep, or rasping. Just listen to the way he sings 'he had a face like a mask'. He could be a stand-in for that hellfire preacher, with every conscience 'vile and depraved'. Dylan elsewhere describes him as 'someone whose body doesn't belong to him. Someone who loved life but couldn't live.'

The basic story of a young innocent tempted to his doom is straight out of folklore, Mr Fox or the House Carpenter. Beware the bogieman. Lanois has excelled himself in giving this song the soundstage it deserves, unsettling as that might prove. But the Deep Purple reference is probably unintended. This would have made a wonderful video.

SIDE TWO
Most Of The Time (Dylan) 5.04
Bob Dylan: vocal, guitar, **Daniel Lanois:** guitar, **Malcolm Burn:** keyboards,
Tony Hall: bass, **Cyril Neville:** percussion, **Willie Green:** drums

This album just gets better and better. Here is a perfect example of what Lanois called 'that Louisiana swamp sound'. After 'working this song to a standstill' at an earlier session – during which Dylan wanted a ticking clock and a big band arrangement – this was a first take. Even Dylan could not have repeated the sorrow in his voice as he sings about coping after a busted love affair. The bass swoops down to earth, undermining any self-delusion, and Lanois adds celestial guitar, while percussion clatters. Another song about time slipping away, and resilience.

The last two lines are heartbreaking with the chorus line undermining his seeming carelessness. Then the band play on.

The video is simply the band playing, filmed by multiple cameras, and featuring a different performance than on the record. Howard Devoto says 'everyone knew it should have been the single'. For the singer David Gray: 'You get this feeling of a man with a deep sense of longing, thinking of someone he lost long ago. It's not a pop song but it's getting that way. I talked to Lanois about that album and he said Dylan spooked him, he felt Dylan was inhabiting him like some ghost'.

What Good Am I? (Dylan) 4.46
Bob Dylan: vocal, guitar, piano, **Daniel Lanois:** dobro, **Malcolm Burn:** mercy keys

Dylan is stage centre, interrogating his very soul in the midnight hour. There is a wonderfully hushed quality to this track, with tinkling mercy keys (perhaps inspiring the album title), sensitive dobro playing and one of Bob's most intimate ever vocals, plus a series of unanswered questions.

He wrote the song all in one go after seeing Eugene O'Neill's *Long Journey Into Night*, stopping into a club on 4th Street to catch a gig by Guitar Shorty, then watching the cops moving on a homeless man – 'only a hobo' – and feeling powerless to intervene. 'Sometimes you see things in life that turn your heart rotten and you try to capture that feeling without naming the specifics.'

Disease Of Conceit (Dylan) 3.43
Bob Dylan: vocal, piano, organ, **Mason Ruffner**: guitar, **Brian Stolz**: guitar, **Tony Hall**: bass, **Willie Green**: drums

Another late-night song, with an echoing title line. If a man has as much money and fame as Dylan and can still ache like he does on this song, what hope is there for any of us? The antithesis of celebrity culture with a lonesome guitar break. Dylan uses only the most hushed part of his voice, but is nimble when needs be, contracting long lines to fit the music.

Dylan writes that the song has 'gospel overtones', and that he wrote it after watching the fall of TV evangelist Jimmy Swaggart, Jerry Lee Lewis's cousin. 'I wondered what the harlot might have looked like that lured this famous preacher into rolling in the muck'. He admits that conceit is not really a disease, 'more of a weakness'. Among the cancelled lines – fortunately – are 'I'll hump ya and I'll dump ya and I'll blow your house down. I'll slice your cake before I leave town'. His next album was to be full of this kind of stuff, but the order of the day here is solemnity.

What Was It You Wanted (Dylan) 5.02
Bob Dylan: vocal, guitar, harmonica, **Daniel Lanois**: guitar, **Malcolm Burn**: bass, **Mason Ruffner**: guitar, **Brian Stolz**: guitar, **Cyril Neville**: percussion, **Willie Green**: drums

Yet more quiet music with a side order of betrayal. We're back to Judas in the garden betraying Christ with a kiss. Another series of unanswered questions in the final line reminds us of Travis Bickle as portrayed by Robert De Niro looking into the mirror. 'Are you talking to me?' And seeing only himself.

The music ebbs and flows like the ocean with stately harmonica and insistent electric guitars. As Bob writes in *Chronicles*, 'the way the microphones are placed makes the atmosphere seem texturally rich, jet lagged and loaded – quaaludes, misty'. They had to keep the song 'level and the right side up'. In the end, even Barry White couldn't hold a candle to this.

Dylan wrote the song quickly, back in his kitchen: 'I heard the lyric and melody together in my head, and it played itself in a minor key'. He adds that one has to have been the object of attention to write this or maybe even to understand it. Having people continually tapping you on the shoulder and asking for an autograph, or worse. 'Sometimes you just have to bite your upper lip and put your sunglasses on'.

Shooting Star (Dylan) 3.13
Bob Dylan: vocal, guitar, harmonica, **Daniel Lanois:** omnichord, **Brian Stolz:** guitar,
Tony Hall: bass, **Willie Green:** drums
To complete the most introspective side of any Dylan album ever, Bob looks to the heavens. And sees more New Testament echoes, the last temptation and the Sermon on the Mount. 'The song came to me complete, full in the eyes like I'd been travelling on the golden pathways of the sun and just found it. It was illuminated' – with the fires of Hades. These are the End Times with a 'fire truck from hell' on the loose. And he still doesn't even raise his voice.

Dylan wrote 'I didn't write it so much as I inherited it'. Here in New Orleans, gazing up at the heavens at night has long been a poetic act. 'I'd seen a shooting star from the backyard of our house, or maybe it was a meteorite.' It puts man in his place, but also suggests transcendence. One could compare John Keats' 'Bright Star' sonnet, or the final poem in Seamus Heaney's North, where in a time of civil war, he manages to miss the 'comet's pulsing rose'.

OUTTAKES
28 February 1989: 'Born In Time'
7 March 1989; 'Ring Them Bells', 'What Good Am I?'
8 March 1989: 'Most Of The Time', 'Disease Of Conceit'
12/13 March 1989: 'Most Of The Time 2', 'God Knows' (x2), 'Dignity'
14/ 15 March 1989: 'Everything Is Broken', 'Shooting Star' (x2)
21 March 1989: 'What Was It You Wanted?'
28 March 1989: 'Political World'
30 March 1989: 'Series Of Dreams' (x2)
All recorded by Daniel Lanois at Studio-On-The-Move, Emlah Court, New Orleans

'Series of Dreams' on *The Bootleg Series*
'Dignity' on *Greatest Hits Vol 3*
'Most Of The Time' (demo) on single of the same title.

See chapter 4 of *Chronicles Volume One*, which deals with this album's writing and recording.

UNDER THE RED SKY

US Release: 11 September 1990
UK Release:
CD Release: Columbia 467 188 2

Columbia C 46794
CBS 467188 1

Producer: Don Was, David Was and Jack Frost, engineered and mixed by Ed Cherney

Running Time: 35.33

SIDE ONE: Wiggle Wiggle; Under The Red Sky; Unbelievable; Born In Time; TV Talkin' Song.

SIDE TWO: 10,000 Men, 2x2; God Knows; Handy Dandy; Cat's In The Well.

Bob Dylan: vocals, acoustic guitar, harp, piano, accordion, **Kenny Aronoff:** drums, **Rayse Biggs:** trumpet, **David Crosby:** vocals, **Paulinho Da Costa:** percussion, **Robben Ford:** guitar, **George Harrison:** rhythm guitar, **Bruce Hornsby:** piano, **Randy Jackson:** bass, **Elton John:** piano, **Al Kooper:** keyboards, **David Lindley:** slide guitar, bouzouki, **David McMurray:** saxophone, **Jamie Muhoberac:** organ, **Slash:** guitar, **Jimmie Vaughan:** guitar, **Stevie Ray Vaughan:** guitar, **Waddy Wachtel:** guitar, **Don Was:** bass, **Sweet Pea Atkinson, Sir Harry Bowens, Donald Ray Mitchell** and **David Was:** vocals

With new producers Don and David Was, Dylan returned to his Los Angeles recording haunts, Oceanway on 6 January 1990, then Culver City and the Complex in March, with overdubs at the Record Plant in April. The January session that produced four album tracks and featured legendary Texan guitarist Stevie Ray Vaughan and his brother Jimmie, while other guest celebrities included slide maestro David Lindley, the Dead's latest keyboard player Bruce Hornsby, guitarist Slash from Guns n'Roses and old touchstone Al Kooper. Those providing overdubs included Dave Crosby, George Harrison and Elton John.

Born Donald Fagenson in Detroit, Was met David Weiss in high school and together they formed Was (Not Was) in 1991 in LA. He brought some of his tough r&b sensibility to the new record. As he told Pete Doggett, 'it was done very quickly, including the songwriting', so quickly that he laid down his original vocals in two days. But, as Was told Heylin, the real fireworks occurred at the mixing session. 'He breaks out his papers again and says he's going to redo the vocal.' Behaviour enough to make any producer 'lose his mind!'. 'The moment before he sings it, he's still writing'. Was found a working method early with Dylan, to mess everything up: 'if something was too beautiful, if it looked like it was trying to please, then it was against his purposes'. 'He's not going to go out there and put his arm around Trisha,he's not going to do that sh-t'. That attitude suffuses this odd album.

When asked whether the title referred to the first Iraq war, he hinted that he had a wider Armageddon in view. 'No, not really. That record was released before the hostilities began. But it's relevant, I'd say, but so are the songs I wrote 30 years ago'.

If the last album was inhabited by the ghosts of Jonathan Swift and John Donne, satire and love poet, this was more in the world of Edward Lear and Burl Ives, with a side order of rap. Dylan had been listening to the likes of Ice-T. 'The kind of music that Danny and I were making was archaic. With Ice-T and Public Enemy, who were laying down the tracks, a new kind of performer was bound to appear. And one unlike Presley. One doing it with hard words, and working 18 hours a day'. Eminen probably fits the bill here, another angry white boy from the other side of the tracks, just like the young Dylan, or Beck.

Robert Christgau headlined his review 'Dylan's back' – presumably from the solipsism of *Oh Mercy* or maybe the dog days of the 80s.' Kenny Aronoff's drumming provides a lot of what Dylan was lacking in heft'. Michael Gray welcomes a 'rougher and less unified sound. The core of the album is an adventure into the poetic possibilities of nursery rhymes'. Heylin describes a far greater work than *Oh Mercy* – without justifying this extraordinary claim – 'a single edifice, every girder in its assigned place'. For Tim Riley 'apart from the faceless vocals, the songs seem all juiced up with nowhere to go'. All agree on one thing, that this is a return to gutbucket r&b, cross-hatched with the riddling charms of *The Basement Tapes*.

Current girlfriend Carole Childs is thanked, and the album is dedicated to 'Gabby Goo Goo', aka Desiree Gabrielle Dennis-Dylan, Bob's then secret daughter, born 31 January 1986. There were no sleeve notes, but album buyers were offered a limited edition of Dylan's own notes to all the songs here, available via Entertainment Connections. The cover photographs are credited to Camouflage, and indeed this is an album of masks and disguises. Bob crouches on the scrubby waste ground of the Mojave Desert, California, with a town in the background menaced by a range of hills. The monochrome image is made even more sinister by Dylan's name being picked out in red over a lowering sky. On the back sleeve, Bob is dressed in trainers and jogging clothes sitting on a short flight of steps leading up to a graceful house, with an American flag in the plant pot.

BOB DYLAN
under the red sky

SIDE ONE
Wiggle Wiggle (Dylan) 2.09
Bob Dylan: vocal, guitar, **Slash:** guitar, **David Lindley:** guitar, **Jamie Muhoberic:** organ, **Randy Jackson:** bass, **Kenny Aronoff:** drums
Repeated chords, played by a guitar army, then muscular drumming leads into a playful Bob, singing a riddling song, like the more childish aspects of Harry Smith's Anthology. And the key is sex, the one mystery kids can't penetrate, man and woman wiggling like a 'bowl of soup' and a 'big fat snake', 'til it comes'. Froggy went a courting, and this is exactly what happened. But the line about vomiting fire suggest that these nursery tales have a bitter aftertaste.

Under The Red Sky (Dylan) 4.09
Bob Dylan: vocal, acoustic guitar, **George Harrison:** slide guitar, **Waddy Wachtel:** guitar, **Al Kooper:** keyboards, **Randy Jackson:** bass, **Kenny Aronoff:** drums
The title song looks back to memories of Hibbing and the *Highway 61* sound slowed down. Another nursery rhyme for adults with the children baked in a pie and a time when narrative ends – 'the man in the moon went home and the river went dry'. But the 'key to the kingdom' is hidden somewhere in these childish mysteries. Is that blind horse quietly grazing waiting for the riders of the Apocalypse to mount up? And is the sky red with blood?

Unbelievable (Dylan) 4.07
Bob Dylan: vocal, acoustic guitar, harmonica, **Waddy Wachtel:** guitar, **Al Kooper:** keyboards, **Randy Jackson:** bass, **Kenny Aronoff:** drums
Refried rockabilly with nonsense lyrics and the riff from 'Gimme Some Lovin'. And sinister lyrics in which everything is broken. Paul Williams reckons this is about the end of the 80s high times, during which the promised land of milk and honey sold itself for money. This is 'Subterranean Homesick Blues' with a hangover. An earlier draft had a line about the end times, 'that time has finally come' as well as more overt images of judgment and retribution.

In the video, Bob is a chauffeur, his passenger a live pig, the car registration is LSD, Bob also gets driven by a young rocker, and two women enter the fray. It is as incomprehensible as the song it soundtracks. 'Don't come back with stories untold.'

Born In Time (Dylan) 3.39
Bob Dylan: vocal, accordion, **Bruce Hornsby**: piano, **Robben Ford**: guitar, **Randy Jackson**: bass, **Kenny Aronoff**: drums, **Dave Crosby**: backing vocals

Williams reckons this a 'great love song'. Another commentator thinks it could be a father thinking of his daughter. It certainly takes us back to the home comforts of *New Morning*, with a bitter edge. 'You hanged the flame, you'll pay the price.' This is a memory conjured up in monochrome and 'in the lonely night'. Both tune and accompaniment are gorgeous, a swaying, harmonic lament.

Another song about time slipping away, with some kind of disaster waiting in the wings, 'where the ways of nature will test every nerve'.

TV Talkin' Song (Dylan) 3.03
Bob Dylan: vocal, guitar, **Bruce Hornsby**: piano, **Robben Ford**: guitar, **Randy Jackson**: bass, **Kenny Aronoff**: drums

Never before can Speakers' Corner in London's Hyde Park have inspired such a song of paranoia about media control. Maybe it was Tom Paine reborn, up there preaching. Heylin describes the original take as 'one of the most disturbing songs in Dylan's post-evangelist output', with the crowd ending up hanging one of the preachers from a lamp-post, just like Mussolini, then Dylan pulling back to himself watching this safely on a screen, just like 'Black Diamond Bay'.

The version here, despite its musical urgency, seems a lot of fuss and bother about nothing. Don Was felt this last-minute vocal, added during the final mix, was a revision too many: 'I think it lost something.' Best cloak these apocalyptic forebodings in fables. 'No ambiguity' as one commentator puts it.

SIDE TWO
10,000 Men (Dylan) 4.21
Bob Dylan: vocal, guitar, **Jimmie Vaughan**: guitar, **Stevie Ray Vaughan**: guitar, **David Lindley**: slide guitar, **Jamie Muhoberic**: organ, **Randy Jackson**: bass, **Kenny Aronoff**: drums

We are back unsafely in the world of folklore: 'Nottamun Town,' before he turned it into 'Masters Of War' or nursery rhyme, that repository of history and nightmare. Here are the soldiers the grand old Duke of York marched up and down the hill, all coming to get you.

There is something of the truly terrifying Howlin' Wolf in the sound here, a spooked blues straight out of Dante's *Inferno*. Everyone here is trapped in their own circle of hell.

The whoosh at the beginning is the sound of the multitrack firing up as Was suddenly realizes that Dylan is composing a song then and there. And it was never revised or dubbed over from this one-and-only take. At the heart of the song is a poisoned love affair with the two participants being needlessly nice to each other and Dylan asking who's your lover now: 'let me eat off his head so you can really see'.

2 x 2 (Dylan) 3,37
Bob Dylan: vocal, guitar, **Elton John**: piano, **David Lindley**: bouzouki, **Randy Jackson**: bass, **Kenny Aronoff**: drums, **Paulinho De Costa**: percussion, **David Crosby**: backing vocals

We're back with *The Basement Tapes* here, parodying one or other strain of Americana, here the simple-minded Sunday School fable, counting upwards, crossed with Shirley Ellis's 'The Clapping Song', where everybody went to heaven in a 'little row boat'. There's a playful break on electric piano by Elton, and Crosby duets, faintly. But look closer and there are disturbing resonances, lovers lost in the 'foggy dew' of folk song terror, and poison and jail and black cats crossing the path and the great flood coming. The lyrics still sound unfinished. There are at least two variant takes, one of which rhymes 'one' with 'thy will be done', straight out of the Lord's Prayer. Paul Williams reckons the words 'are not made for consumption by the conscious mind'. Others might consider them nonsense, and not in a good way.

God Knows (Dylan) 3.02
Bob Dylan: vocal, piano, **Stevie Ray Vaughan**: lead guitar, **Jimmie Vaughan**: guitar, **David Lindley**: slide guitar, **Jamie Muhoberic**: organ, **Randy Jackson**: bass, **Kenny Aronoff**: drums, **Paulinho De Costa**: percussion

Dylan tried to lay down this song for *Oh Mercy*, but it eluded him. According to Don Was, 'we rehearsed it a few times before (but) that was the one we had difficulty with'. Heylin considers that apart from a 'fade in mid-flight' this would be a masterpiece of delivery and diction the equal of anything on the previous album. But it is anyway, everything the last song was not, sung and played with growing venom and with lyrics to match. And two of the greatest guitarists on the planet in the backing crew.

Handy Dandy (Dylan) 4.03
Bob Dylan: vocal, guitar, **Waddy Wachtel**: lead guitar, **Jimmie Vaughan**: guitar, **Al Kooper**: organ, **Don Was**: bass, **Kenny Aronoff**: drums, **Paulinho De Costa**: percussion, **Sweet Pea Atkinson, Sir Henry Bowens, Donald Ray Mitchell** and **David Was**: backing vocals
This is 'Like A Rolling Stone' for the nursery, in a mirror, with Kooper overdubbed back on the organ and a red hot drummer. An earlier take featured lots of Stevie Ray on electric slide and no organ at all, but this is more sedate, more ominous. Some people think this is about Prince – it has the musical self-assurance of the Minneapolis midget – others a self portrait. He is also Mr Fox with flashing teeth, and in the line of mythic gunslingers and riverboat hustlers, Ramblin' Gambling Willie reborn. This beau might seem impregnable, but 'something in the moonlight still hounds him'.

Cat's In The Well (Dylan) 3.21
Bob Dylan: vocal, piano, **Stevie Ray Vaughan**: guitar, **Jimmie Vaughan**: guitar, **David Lindley**: slide guitar, **Jamie Muhoberic**: organ, **Don Was**: bass, **Kenny Aronoff**: drums, **David McMurray**: saxophone, **Rayse Biggs**: trumpet
This takes the album out on a sprightly note, with a hot band, obscene lyrics – 'back alley Sally is doing the American jump' – and as Heylin puts it 'the apocalypse revisited in 6/8 time'. 'The world is being slaughtered, and it's a bloody disgrace', pun intended. There is an echo of 'Rocks and Nails', where it's squirrels that bring to mind women, with those big bushy tails. Here it's a wolf stalking that poor pussy. The music is pure rock'n'roll, uptempo like Little Richard and a great not-a-note-wasted guitar solo.
    Song and album close with Bob calling on the Lord to 'have mercy on us all', and a final clatter of drums. Like a coffin closing, it was the last original song – apart for a live on TV premiere for *Oh Mercy* outtake 'Dignity', and a slew of official bootlegs – that Dylan would offer the world until time had gone out of mind.

OUTTAKES:
January/ March 1990: 'Handy Dandy', 'TV Talkin' Song'

THE BOOTLEG SERIES VOLS 1-3

US Release: 26 March 1991
UK Release:
The 5-LP set was released in Europe only and contains the full version of 'Series of Dreams', catalogue number COL 468086 1
Produced and compiled by: Jeff Rosen

Columbia C3K 47382   3 CDs in 12" box set
Columbia 488100

Running Time: 77.15, 76.50, 77.01

CD 1: Hard Times In New York Town; He Was A Friend Of Mine; Man On The Street; No More Auction Block; House Carpenter; Talking Bear Mountain Picnic Massacre Blues; Let Me Die In My Footsteps; Rambling, Gambling Willie; Talkin' Hava Negeilah Blues; Quit Your Low Down Ways; Worried Blues; Kingsport Town; Walkin' Down The Line; Walls Of Red Wing; Paths of Victory; Talkin' John Birch Paranoid Blues; Who Killed Davey Moore?; Only A Hobo; Moonshiner; When The Ship Comes In; The Times They Are A-Changin'; Last Thoughts on Woody Guthrie.

CD 2: Seven Curses; Eternal Circle; Suze (The Cough Song) ; Mama, You Been On My Mind; Farewell, Angelina; Subterranean Homesick Blues; If You Gotta Go, Go Now (Or Else You Got To Stay All Night) ; Sitting On A Barbed Wire Fence; Like A Rolling Stone; It Takes A Lot To Laugh, It Takes A Train To Cry; I'll Keep It With Mine; She's Your Lover Now; I Shall Be Released; Santa-Fe; If Not For You; Wallflower; Nobody 'Cept You; Tangled Up In Blue; Call Letter Blues; Idiot Wind.

CD 3: If You See Her, Say Hello; Golden Loom; Catfish; Seven Days; Ye Shall Be Changed; Every Grain Of Sand; You Changed My Life; Need A Woman; Angelina; Someone's Got A Hold Of My Heart; Tell Me; Lord Protect My Child; Foot Of Pride; Blind Willie McTell; When The Night Comes Falling From The Sky; Series Of Dreams.

There now followed a long songwriting drought, broken by this 3-CD/5-LP trawl through the archives, two albums of traditional material, an appearance on MTV's *Unplugged*, and a live recording of an evening in which Dylan's peers joined him to cover his old songs, for good and

BOB DYLAN
the bootleg series
volumes 1-3
[rare & unreleased]
1961-1991

ill. But new Dylan compositions would have to wait for 1997's *Time Out Of Mind* and *Love and Theft*, issued four years later, both full of echoes from dead men.

As Dylan said this same year, 'there was a time when the songs would come three or four at the same time, but those days are long gone. Once in a while, the odd song will come to me like a bulldog at the garden gate and demand to be written. But most of them are rejected out of my mind right away. You get caught up in wondering if anyone really needs to hear it. Maybe a person gets to the point where they have written enough songs. Let someone else write them'.

So his record company looked back instead. *The Bootleg Series* was beautifully annotated by John Bauldie of the *Telegraph*. This described the excitement that Greil Marcus' five-page December 1969 article in *Rolling Stone* about the range of Dylan's unofficial recordings had sparked off among collectors, and the 'feverish underground' of tape trading and amateur scholarship that resulted. So here were 58 songs new to the canon, concentrating on Dylan the songwriter, and the prelude to a series of live concert recordings – the first of which, the fabled 1966 Manchester show, would appear four years later.

And indeed this was manna from heaven, 23 of these tracks new even to hard core collectors. Unlike *Biograph*, nothing here had previously seen an official release. But it could have been even better. The original idea, to tie in with Dylan's 50th birthday, was to release 10 separate CDs, one a month from March to December. This was soon trimmed down to a 4-CD set – like the Byrds retrospective also from Sony – and then trimmed further to three silver discs.

Clinton Heylin's article on all this is a sustained howl of pain. How on earth could an original track listing, which already had ignored 'New Danville Girl', be trimmed of vital songs like the alternative 'Its All Over Now, Baby Blue', the acoustic 'She's Your Lover Now', and 'Ain't Gonna Go To Hell For Anybody'. Easily, some might say. He makes a more cogent point, that there is no thematic sense to the three discs, other than an almost chronological running order. And it seems a shame not to go the whole way and gather together in one place all the *Blood on the Tracks* outtakes, or the early New York sessions for *Blonde On Blonde*. And most of the last-minute omissions were of later material, leaving the compilation weighted unfairly towards Dylan's first two years in New York.

But this is to kick a gift horse unfairly. The material here is stunning, and the inclusion of 25 songs laid down between November 1961 and October 1963 opens up a huge swathe of Dylan's early work, outside the three official albums they surround. These were times when Bob was an outsider from the entertainment industry – even if signed up to one of its major record labels – with songs about debauched bootleggers, mothers that drowned their own children, Cadillacs, floods, union hall fires, darkness and cadavers. The cultural hangover from the 50s was still in deep freeze, a few Beat poets and bohemian folkies and cool jazzers excepted: 'a certain rude rhythm was making it all sway'. And the richness of Dylan's early acoustic repertoire was part of this outlaw defiance.

Now, with inner-city rap on one side and drug-fuelled dance music on the other, the art of traditional songwriting, as shown on these three CDs in all its varied glory, from ballads to impressionistic chansons, was in remission. And Dylan's back pages here, plus a growing interest in Americana, post punk, acted on young songwriters just as the Harry Smith Anthology had done on the youthful Robert Zimmerman.

Here was almost four hours of music that no one else on earth could have created. The critical reaction was enthusiastic, even if some found three discs hard going. One comparison of material that 'only seems to improve with age' was with the Beatles' six-CD Anthology series, 'only ten – no, one hundred – times better'. And everyone noticed the considerable upgrades in sound from bootleg versions that had slipped out over the previous 20 years.

The cover was a monochrome shot of Dylan in the studio in the mid 60s. The substantial booklet boasts another pot-pourri of photos, from a cherubic boy with Suze Rotolo to a much older man resting on a sign that reads 'Don't Climb the Pyramids'.

CD 1

Hard Times In New York Town (Dylan) 2.17
Recorded live in a Minnesota hotel room, Minneapolis 22 December 1961
Bob Dylan: guitar, vocals
Taken from the 'Bonnie Beecher' tape, this is based on the traditional 'Down on Penny's Farm', transplanted to the big city. Where 'Talking New York is exuberant and funny, this is defiant and bitter – despite the hokey accent at the begnining – and you do wonder why he hasn't fled a place where they 'kick you when you're up and knock you when you're down'. The song opens up into a panorama of the whole United States, and it has never sounded so vast.

He Was A Friend Of Mine (Trad arr Dylan) 4.03
Outtake from Dylan's first album, recorded 20 November 1961.
Bob Dylan: guitar, harmonica, vocals
The source was 'Shorty George', recorded by Leadbelly, learnt via Eric Von Schmidt. But Dylan injects his own brand of youthful melancholy. Bob moans, his lonesome guitar ebbs and flows like the sea, and the harmonica is like a lonesome train whistle. The Byrds later turned this into a lament for John Kennedy.

Man On The Street (Dylan) 1.54
Outtake from *Bob Dylan*, recorded 22 November 1961.
Bob Dylan: guitar, harmonica, vocals
This adapts the melody of the traditional song 'The Young Man Who Wouldn't Hoe Corn', learnt via Pete Seeger. Written in August 1961, and inspired by seeing a policeman jab a dead street-sleeper with his club, Dylan sounds quizzical and does a perfect hillbilly impression. The verse structure is based on Brecht's 'Litany Of Breath'. This compounds a line from the opening song that 'when someone disappears you never even know'.

No More Auction Block (Trad, arr Dylan) 3.02
Recorded live at the Gaslight Café, Greenwich Village late 1961
Bob Dylan: guitar, vocals
A song of freed slaves; probably learnt from Odetta. He later adapted the tune for 'Blowin' In The Wind' – 'I took it off a song that's a spiritual and "Blowin' In The Wind" sorta follows the same feeling'. Fourth in a line of sad or depressing songs – not much Chaplin hereabouts – Dylan has tragedy in his voice, rather than release.

House Carpenter (Trad arr Dylan) 4.08
Outtake from *The Freewheelin' Bob Dylan*, recorded 19 March 1962.
Bob Dylan: guitar, vocals
Child Ballad 243, Joan Baez regularly sang this, but never like this. Dylan sounds ancient and pitiless as the ocean, his urgent guitar driving like a whip. Bob inhabits both merman, and infatuated wife. 'What are those hills, they look as dark as night?', 'Those are the hills of hellfire my love, where you and I will unite'.

Talking Bear Mountain Picnic Massacre Blues (Dylan) 3.44
Outtake from *The Freewheelin' Bob Dylan*, recorded 25 April 1962.
Bob Dylan guitar, harmonica, vocals
At last some levity, if only for the bored way he sings 'yippee', or rhymes casket and picnic basket. Deliciously deadpan, but there is a hint of a protest song in the last verse. Taken from a deliciously macabre story he read in a newspaper. The Hudson Belle was chartered by a Harlem social club for a fathers' day treat. Hundreds of counterfeit tickets were sold, and a fracas broke out with many people injured. The ship never left its berth. Dylan's first topical song, and according to Badly Drawn Boy, his funniest, especially the line when Bob supposedly scrambles to shore; insensible and 'bald'. 'Dylan's great at going that one step further than anyone else.'

Let Me Die In My Footsteps (Dylan) 3.33
Outtake from *The Freewheelin' Bob Dylan*, recorded 25 April 1962.
Bob Dylan: guitar, vocals
Included on the original version of *Freewheelin' Bob Dylan*.
Dylan was travelling through the mid-west, 'and they were making this bomb shelter right outside of town, one of these sort of Coliseum-type things. I guess I wrote the song in my head back then, but I carried it with me for two years until I finally wrote it down'. He sings more in pity than anger, and with a young man's hunger for life, 'where the mountain streams flood'. As 'Blind Boy Grunt', he later played harmonica with Happy Traum on lead vocal on this same song that appeared on *Broadside Ballads Volume 1* in 1963.

Rambling, Gambling Willie (Dylan) 4.11
Outtake from *The Freewheelin' Bob Dylan*, recorded 24 April 1962.
Bob Dylan: guitar, harmonica, vocals
Included on the original version of *Freewheelin'* and based on the life of gambler Will O'Conley, up on Cripple Creek. Dylan heard the Clancy Brothers singing the traditional outlaw song 'Brennan On The Moor' and 'I wrote some of my own songs to some of the melodies that I heard them do'. But even they lack Dylan's relish and sense of rhythm, or his sheer joy in singing here. Joyful harmonica, too, and guitar that rings like a bell.

Talkin' Hava Negeilah Blues (Dylan) 0.50
Outtake from *The Freewheelin' Bob Dylan*, recorded 25 April 1962.
Bob Dylan: guitar, harmonica, vocals
Robert Shelton wrote, this 'burlesques the folk music craze and the singer himself'. 'Here's a foreign song I learned in Utah'. And he spends the short song trying to pronounce its title: with a yodel at the end.

Quit Your Low Down Ways (Dylan) 2.37
Outtake from *The Freewheelin' Bob Dylan*, recorded 9 July 1962.
Bob Dylan: guitar, vocals
Peter, Paul and Mary covered this the following year, on an album to which Dylan wrote the sleeve notes. Based on Kokomo Arnold's 'Milk Cow Blues' – 'Mama if you can't quit your sinnin', please quit your low down ways' – and it's deliciously fake, with a sheer exuberance which has certainly disappeared over the years.

Worried Blues (Trad arr Dylan) 2.37
Outtake from *The Freewheelin' Bob Dylan*, recorded 9 July 1962.
Bob Dylan: guitar, vocals
A rare example of Dylan's finger-picking guitar style, although the words frankly aren't up to much, what few there are, but his voice cracks appealingly on 'I've got trouble in my mind'. Sheer pastiche.

Kingsport Town (Trad arr Dylan) 3.27
Outtake from *The Freewheelin' Bob Dylan*, recorded 14 November 1962.
Bob Dylan: guitar, harmonica, vocals, unknown second guitarist
This is based on Guthrie's 'Who's Going To Shoe Your Pretty Little Feet', a song that Dylan used to perform back in Dinkytown. Here he assumes an Okie accent to match, elongating the vowels and singing through his nose in a way half the buskers of the time would soon be imitating, badly. Only Bob can suddenly sound as tender and seductive as he does here, kissing 'your Memphis mouth'.

Walkin' Down The Line (Dylan) 2.52
Recorded at the Witmark Studios, New York, 1963.
Bob Dylan: guitar, harmonica, vocals
Dylan recorded this same song for *Broadside* magazine in late 1962. This sprightly recording comes from a session when he copyrighted some of his early compositions for his music publisher, that would make a more-than-satisfying album in their own right. This song was covered by the likes of Glen Campbell and Ricky Nelson.

Walls Of Red Wing (Dylan) 5.01
Outtake from *The Freewheelin' Bob Dylan*, recorded 24 April 1963.
Bob Dylan: guitar, harmonica, vocals
The tune comes from the Scottish song 'The Road And The Miles To Dundee'. Red Wing is a boys' reform school in Minnesota, but this sounds like an exercize, not lived experience. It plods until the pen portrait of the sadistic guard suddenly brings it to life, as Dylan's imagination takes hold.

Paths of Victory (Dylan) 3.17
Outtake from *The Times The Are A-Changin'*, 12 August 1963.
Bob Dylan: piano, harmonica, vocals
Dylan performed this on a rare and early TV appearance on a folk music special in March '63. Bauldie describes it as 'possibly the most Guthrie-esque song that Woody never wrote'. Um-pah piano, and Dylan sounds hopeful.

Talkin' John Birch Paranoid Blues (Dylan) 4.24
Recorded live at Carnegie Hall, New York 26 October 1963.
Bob Dylan: guitar, harmonica, vocals
Live version of the song dropped at the last minute from *Freewheelin'*, and in whose cause he walked out of the Ed Sullivan show – 'hootenanny television' – when he was told not to sing it. 'And there ain't nothing wrong with this song'. Dylan skewers the US far right with sarcasm at a time of paranoia over reds in the bed. The audience respond to his every quip, and singing about a toilet bowl was almost another taboo at the time. Plays some harmonica too.

Who Killed Davey Moore? (Dylan) 3.08
Recorded live at Carnegie Hall, New York 26 October 1963
Bob Dylan: guitar, vocals
Boxer Davey was knocked out by Sugar Ramos in March 1963 and died two days later. Bob premiered this song 18 days later at his Town Hall concert. It's cleverly adapted from the nursery rhyme 'Who Killed Cock Robin?' with its insistent rhythms. Everyone claims innocence. Dylan crams as many words as possible into each verse, a real performance piece.

Only A Hobo (Dylan) 3.28
Outtake from *The Times They Are A-Changin'*, recorded 12 August 1963.
Bob Dylan: guitar, harmonica, vocals
This appeared in *Broadside* a few months earlier. The song is an update of John Wallace Crawford's poem 'Only A Miner Killed' that became a popular song, 'Only a miner killed – oh! Is that all/one of the timbers caved; great was the fall'. Here, Dylan evokes little real passion. He also recorded this, as Blind Boy Grunt, for *Broadside Ballads Volume 1*.

Moonshiner (Trad arr Dylan) 5.05
Outtake from *The Times They Are A-Changin'*, recorded 12 August 1963.
Bob Dylan: guitar, harmonica, vocals
A traditional southern mountain ballad but no one had ever sung it quite like this before, almost literally becoming the man in question. John Bauldie ties this extraordinary performance to Dylan's description of his own songs as 'exercises in tonal breath control'. Never has addiction sounded so, well, addictive.

When The Ship Comes In (Dylan) 2.54
Piano demo for Witmark Music Publishing Company, Witmark Studios New York 1962
Bob Dylan: piano, vocals
An early run through, with rough-and-ready piano rather than guitar, for a song that subsequently appeared on *The Times They Are A-Changin'*. It lacks the joyousness of the album take. As well as a host of Biblical echoes, this draws on Brecht's revenge song 'The Black Freighter' and namesake Dylan Thomas' poem 'Fern Hill', 'though I sang, in my chains, like the sea'.

The Times They Are A-Changin' (Dylan) 2.58
Piano demo for Witmark Music Publishing Company, Witmark Studios New York 1963.
Bob Dylan: piano, vocals
Another curiosity, recorded before the album version with piano rather than guitar and at a sepulchral pace. 'I wanted to write a big song, some kind of theme song, with short concise verses that piled up on each other in a hypnotic way'.

Last Thoughts on Woody Guthrie (Dylan) 7.08
Recorded live at Town Hall, New York 12 April 1963
Bob Dylan recites his own poem, rushing and mumbling, and from the page rather than by memory – you can hear him rustling the manuscript – hence the occasional fluff. Guthrie died in 1967, so this is not an obituary, more a farewell to Dylan's own past, a tribute and a valediction. So a whole CD gone and not an electric instrument in sight. Somehow, despite so many delights this all sounds like apprentice work with a leavetaking at the end. It doesn't flow as a listening experience, more a collection of odd tracks thrown together. But the next CD is pure gold with Dylan's songwriting in full flow.

CD 2
Seven Curses (Dylan) 3.46
Outtake from *The Times They Are A-Changin'*, recorded 6 August 1963.
Bob Dylan: guitar, vocals
First recorded as a Witmark demo and later taped at the Carnegie Hall concert on 26 October of the same year for the withdrawn live album *Bob Dylan In Concert*. Many think this version incomparable, tapping into the cold, implacable heart of folklore. It is an ancient tale which Shakespeare adapted in *Measure for Measure*. There is no humour, no Pompey or mocking Lucio here. Dylan's source was 'Anathea', as performed by Judy Collins who said 'I see what Dylan has always done is to connect with this inner, subterranean river of the subconscious'.

Eternal Circle (Dylan) 2.38
Outtake from *The Times They Are A-Changin'*, recorded 24 October 1963.
Bob Dylan: guitar, vocals
Bob played an early version of this to Tony Glover in June '63. It's a new kind of song, hypnotic, quickly sketching in a dramatic mis-en-scene, using the song structure almost as a frustrating device. Sexy too, and already showing Dylan's ability to telescope poetry into a phrase, seeing the girl as if 'through a bullet of light'.

Suze (The Cough Song) (Dylan) 1.57
Outtake from *The Times They Are A-Changin'*, recorded 24 October 1963.
Bob Dylan: guitar, harmonica
A nice interlude. This instrumental, though not the coughing, draws on Jimmie Tarlton's 'Mexican Rag' and was later adapted as 'Nashville Skyline Rag'. Bob makes those strings ring. The 'Suze' is surely Suze Rotolo.

Mama, You Been On My Mind (Dylan) 2.56
Outtake from *Bringing It All Back Home*, recorded 9 June 1964.
Bob Dylan: guitar, vocals
Occasionaly Dylan would sing this as a duet with Joan Baez who changed the title to 'Daddy' when she recorded it on her own. There is also a ponderous Witmark demo version, and Dylan reprised it with George Harrison in 1970. This is part of his new writing style; imagistic, sensual (at least in the way he sings it here) and a world away from the folk tradition.

Farewell, Angelina (Dylan) 5.26
Outtake from *Bringing It All Back Home*, recorded 13 January 1965.
Bob Dylan: guitar, harmonica, vocals
For years this was available only via Baez's sultry version, and this version not even imagined. Dylan sings most mysteriously and Bauldie describes this as 'a clear step forward in his writing style, with surreal symbolic lyrics used to create atmosphere and mood as much as to tell any literal tale'. The tune comes from the traditional 'Wagoner's Lad' and the playing card imagery is like 'Rambling, Gambling Willie', as re-imagined by Max Ernst.

Subterranean Homesick Blues (Dylan) 2.55
Outtake from *Bringing It All Back Home*, acoustic take, recorded 13 January 1965.
Bob Dylan: guitar, harmonica, vocals
'Quiet on the set' orders Tom Wilson. Another welcome surprise. Bauldie describes Bob's 'extraordinary skip-rope monotone' on this solo take, maybe a guide vocal for the musicians who were about to electrify it and folk music forever. For which we must wait until the next song.

If You Gotta Go, Go Now (Or Else You Got To Stay All Night) (Dylan) 2.54
Outtake from *Bringing It All Back Home*, recorded 15 January 1965.
Bob Dylan: guitar, harmonica, vocals, **Al Gorgone:** guitar, **Kenny Rankin:** guitar, **Paul Griffin:** keyboards, **Joseph Macho Jr:** bass, **Bobby Gregg:** drums
Dylan first performed this in concert in autumn 1964, and it always drew laughter. But this is the rocked-up studio version and much faster that emerged first as a now extremely rare single released in Holland in August 1967. Dylan's voice has learned how to sneer and the band make him sound a whole load tougher. Fairport Convention had a top 20 hit with it, having translated the risqué lyrics into French.

Sitting On A Barbed Wire Fence (Dylan) 3.52
Outtake from *Highway 61 Revisited*, recorded 15 June 1965.
Bob Dylan: guitar, vocals, **Mike Bloomfield:** guitar, **Al Kooper:** organ, **Paul Griffin:** organ, **Harvey Brooks:** bass, **Bobby Gregg:** drums
A joyous strut, in blues form, even though as Dylan admits, not much more than 'just a riff'. Here is the electric Dylan in all his new-found glory with the line about the Arabian doctor ready to be transplanted to 'Just Like Tom Thumb's Blues'. Gorgeous interplay between Bloomfield, Kooper and Dylan's dancing harmonica.

Like A Rolling Stone (Dylan) 1.35
Outtake from *Highway 61 Revisited*, studio rehearsal 15 June 1965.
Bob Dylan: guitar, vocals, **Mike Bloomfield:** guitar, **Al Kooper:** organ, **Harvey Brooks:** bass
Another extraordinary discovery. Dylan played this brief snippet in stately waltz time to get his musicians in the mood. There is a vulnerability here that in the finished take is gone entirely. As Bob puts it, 'the song was written on an old upright piano in the key of G sharp, then later at Columbia recording studio transferred to the key of C'. The chorus came to him first.

It Takes A Lot To Laugh, It Takes A Train To Cry (Dylan) 3.21
Outtake from *Highway 61 Revisited*, recorded 15 June 1965.
Bob Dylan: guitar, vocals, **Mike Bloomfield**: guitar, **Al Kooper**: organ, **Paul Griffin**: organ, **Harvey Brooks**: bass, **Bobby Gregg**: drums
Originally called 'Phantom Engineer' and one of his many songs about trains, it lacks the nagging, haunted quality of the final take, but you can almost picture the runaway train, hurtling down the tracks. And it has variant words, 'don't the ghost child look good, mama, sitting on his madman's knee'.

I'll Keep It With Mine (Dylan) 3.38
Outtake from *Blonde On Blonde*, recorded 27 January 1966.
Bob Dylan: piano, vocals, **Robbie Robertson**: guitar, **Al Kooper**: organ, **Rick Danko**: bass, **Bobby Gregg**: drums
This was written at least 18 months earlier and a simpler take, with Dylan on piano, appears on *Biograph*. It starts the same here, then Wilson breaks in on the monitor, puzzled, and the band – but only two fifths of the Band – drift in the background like smoke. This is pure magic, largely because it is so obviously meant to remain unheard. For nu-folk supreme Devendra Banhart, ''I'll Keep It With Mine'was written for Nico and like all of Dylan's tunes its perfect'. There is surviving film footage of the Byrds at a party, 'and you can see Dylan and Nico making out'.

She's Your Lover Now (Dylan) 6.09
Outtake from *Blonde On Blonde*, recorded 21 January 1966.
Bob Dylan: guitar, vocals, **Robbie Robertson**: guitar, **Garth Hudson**: organ, **Richard Manuel**: piano, **Rick Danko**: bass, **Sandy Konikoff**: drums
The original title of this song about a ménage à trois in hell was 'A Little Glass Of Water'. Four fifths of the Hawks drive this like fury. It is possibly about the poseurs ligging around Warhol's Factory. The lines about standing in a bar 'with a fish head and a harpoon and a fake beard plastered on her brow' is about as far out as popular song has ever gone. This breaks off early – as if even Dylan has run out of spite, and worked himself into incoherence. This adds dramatic tension to what is probably the most extreme song that has possessed even him. There is also a complete, semi-acoustic take – Bauldie prints out the missing verse, though *Lyrics* ignores it.

I Shall Be Released (Dylan) 3.54
Recorded autumn 1967, outtake from *The Basement Tapes*.
Bob Dylan: guitar, vocals, **Robbie Robertson**: guitar, **Garth Hudson**: organ, **Richard Manuel**: piano, vocals, **Rick Danko**: bass, vocals, **Levon Helm**: drums, vocals
From the Hawks to the Band, and this couldn't be more different, moving from jealous spite to compassion and hope, sung as if from the dark side of the moon. This is the original *Basement* demo in rough-and-ready stereo with Richard Manuel supplying his trademark bruised falsetto. From the fatalism in both voices you know this is going to be a life sentence.

Santa-Fe (Dylan) 2.08
Recorded autumn 1967, outtake from *The Basement Tapes*.
Bob Dylan: guitar, vocals, **Robbie Robertson**: guitar, **Garth Hudson**: organ, **Richard Manuel**: piano, **Rick Danko**: bass, **Levon Helm**: drums
Helm joined in the *Basement* session only towards the end, this track was the first clue that there was far more to these lost sessions than even the double album's worth selected by Robbie Robertson in 1975. Lyrically weird, like something Dylan wrote in his sleep.

If Not For You (Dylan) 3.32
Alternative version, *New Morning* outtake, recorded 1 May 1970.
Bob Dylan: guitar, vocals, **George Harrison**: guitar, **Charlie Daniels**: bass, **Russ Kunkel**: drums
This is the first extract to emerge from the studio session that Dylan and Harrison shared: both subsequently cut this track for *New Morning* and *All Things Must Pass*, separately. Harrison's guitar weeps softly and Bob takes this real slow.

Wallflower (Dylan) 2.48
Recorded New York City, 4 November 1971.
Bob Dylan: guitar, **Ben Keith**: pedal steel, **Russell Bridges**: bass, **Kenneth Buttrey**: drums
Recorded at the same sessions that Dylan cut the 'George Jackson' single. He also sung backing vocals on this song for Doug Sahm and Band, released in 1972. Patti Smith sympathized with this song when young, as a wallflower herself. A waltz with a Nashville lilt, despite the recording venue. The harmonica player – surely Dylan himself – is uncredited, but swings.

Nobody 'Cept You (Dylan) 2.39
Outtake from *Planet Wave*, recorded 2 November 1973.
Bob Dylan: guitar, vocals, **Robbie Robertson**: guitar, **Garth Hudson**: organ, **Richard Manuel**: piano, **Rick Danko**: bass, **Levon Helm**: drums
A highlight of early dates in Dylan's 1974 US tour with the Band, and only left off the album at the last minute, to be replaced with 'Wedding Song'. This sounds tentative, but a far more subtle and convincing testimony to domestic harmony, with a wife like the 'old familiar chime' of a hymn, who keeps the strangers at bay.

Tangled Up In Blue (Dylan) 6.50
Outtake from original New York studio session of *Blood on the Tracks*, 16 September 1974.
Bob Dylan: guitar, vocals, **Tony Brown**: bass, unknown guitar player, probably **Charles Brown III**, **Eric Weissberg** or **Barry Kornfield**
The pronouns have been changed around on the Minnesota version from 'he' to 'I', with some variant lyrics, like time spent 'loading luggage onto a truck'. Gaz Coombes of Supergrass is one of many who prefers this earlier version, 'more emotional, more contemplative', 'slow, downbeat' whereas the album version is 'more bouncy'.

Call Letter Blues (Dylan) 4.27
Outtake from original New York studio session of *Blood on the Tracks*, 16 September 1974.
Bob Dylan: guitar, vocals, **Charles Brown III**: guitar, **Eric Weissberg**: guitar, **Barry Kornfield**: guitar, **Thomas McFaul**: keyboards, **Tony Brown**: bass, **Richard Crooks**: drums
Another New York outtake, replaced by the musically similar 'Meet Me In The Morning', recorded three months later. But the released version lacks the pain of lines like 'Well children cry for mother, I tell them "Mother took a trip"'. This is a far more significant song than the simple blues form makes it sound, with one of the three verses excised from *Lyrics* about call-girls in the doorway – hence the title – giving him the eye, but 'my heart's just not in it'.

Idiot Wind (Dylan) 8.52
Outtake from original New York studio session of Blood on the Tracks, 19 September 1974
Bob Dylan: guitar, vocals, **Tony Brown**: bass
Again replaced at the last minute by a Minnesota take of what is almost a different song, with

different mood and slightly revised lyrics. Here Dylan sings more in sorrow than in the white heat of anger without the consolation of anything other than strummed guitar and simple bass. He throws the I Ching, and a hound dog bays. His wife leaves her bags behind and the chauffeur collects them, then resigns – which sounds like a page from a diary. Some sweet day, all these outtakes will join together on one album, but you couldn't really follow this.

CD 3
If You See Her, Say Hello (Dylan) 3.44
Outtake from original New York studio session of *Blood on the Tracks*, 16 September 1974.
Bob Dylan: guitar, vocals, **Charles Brown III:** guitar, **Eric Weissberg:** guitar, **Barry Kornfield:** guitar
Another CD, another original New York take. You can hear Dylan's sleeve hitting the guitar, though the other three credited here are supernaturally quiet. This was probably too emotionally naked for release first time around, but it opens a disc that gives the lie to virtually every official release through *Blood on the Tracks*, showing what could have been. And now is.

Golden Loom (Dylan) 4.25
Outtake from *Desire*, recorded 30 July 1975.
Bob Dylan: guitar, vocals, **Scarlet Rivera:** violin, **Rob Stoner:** bass, **Howie Wyeth:** drums, **Emmylou Harris:** backing vocals
This weird song draws on alchemy and the writings of Carl Jung. Maybe Robert Graves too, whose 'grammar of poetic myth' *The White Goddess*, Dylan read in those early New York days. Bob said 'once you see what's under the veil, what happens to you? You die or go blind'. Scarlet and Emmylou both sound like female deities in the spirit of the song. And the music sways.

Catfish (Dylan and Jacques Levy) 2.48
Outtake from *Desire*, 28 July 1975.
Bob Dylan: guitar, vocals, **Eric Frandsen:** slide guitar, **Rob Stoner:** bass, **Sugarblue:** harmonica
In praise of baseball pitcher Catfish Hunter. A more acceptable tribute than that to Joey. Bob reveals his secret life as a sports fan. This is so laid back it is almost comatose in the J J Cale vein. He even allows someone else to play harmonica.

Seven Days (Dylan) 3.59
Recorded live Tampa, Florida 21 April 1976 by Rolling Thunder Revue.
Bob Dylan: guitar, vocals, **T-Bone Burnett:** guitar, **Steven Soles:** guitar, **Mick Ronson:** guitar, **Bobby Neuwirth:** guitar, **David Mansfield:** mandolin, **Scarlet Rivera:** violin, **Rob Stoner:** bass, **Howie Wyeth:** drums, **Gary Burke:** congas
All the ragged glory of Rolling Thunder, and a kissing cousin of 'Six Days On The Road'. Dylan had gatecrashed Eric Clapton's recording sessions for *No Reason To Cry*. Clapton recalls 'he was just hanging out. He was living in a tent in the bottom of the garden'. He offered this song to Eric who declined it, but Ron Wood later covered it on *Give It Some Neck*.

Ye Shall Be Changed (Dylan) 4.07
Outtake from *Slow Train Coming*, recorded 27 May 1979.
Bob Dylan: guitar, vocals, **Mark Knopfer:** guitar, **Barry Beckett:** keyboards, **Tim Drummond:** bass, **Pick Withers:** drums
The first born-again song here, and a picture of the Resurrection of the Dead, as so often painted by Stanley Spencer, with the same disturbingly fleshy sense of dead men rising, bursting 'out of their clothes'. Dylan has obviously forgotten to add a tune at this point. The verses are a trifle uncomfortable, to the unconverted at least, with Dylan now jabbing his finger at the unrighteous, which tends to include most of his old audience. You don't need to go to Russia or Iran to find fanaticism. Just look closer to home.

Every Grain Of Sand (Dylan) 3.37
Publishing demo for Special Rider Music, 23 September 1980.
Bob Dylan: piano, vocals, **Fred Tackett:** guitar, **Jennifer Warnes:** background vocals
Early version of the song which appeared on *Shot Of Love*, that rivals the official take, a song of elegiac beauty and a real front porch affair. Lee Renaldo salivates over this version, 'recorded down home in Bob's house, this leaves space for the dogs outside barking and the screen door slamming'. Dylan's voice sounds sore, or is he just being transported to a realm not of this earth?

You Changed My Life (Dylan) 5.13
Outtake from *Shot of Love*, recorded 23 April 1981.
Bob Dylan: guitar, vocals, **Danny Kortchmor**: guitar, **Steve Ripley**: guitar, **Benmont Tench**: organ, **Tim Drummond**: bass, **Jim Keltner**: drums, **Clydie King**: backing vocals
Another song of spiritual change, shrill and rushed, as if trying to convince himself rather than his listeners. There are some odd images here, eating 'with pigs on a silver tray'. A song to God, who is obsessively addressed and who 'came in like the wind, like Erroll Flynn'.

Need A Woman (Dylan) 5.43
Outtake from *Shot of Love*, recorded 4 May 1981.
Bob Dylan: guitar, vocals, possibly **Fred Tackett**: guitar, **Benmont Tench**: organ, **Tim Drummond**: bass, **Jim Keltner**: drums, **Clydie King**: backing vocals, **Regina McCrary, Carolyn Dennis**: backing vocals
You can hear the damage being self-inflicted on Dylan's voice here. No wonder there's a 'fire inside my nose'. He sings without joy and over an aural sludge. The lyrics are a string of clichés, all evil eyes and promised lands and 'ain't no fire you can't walk through'. Ry Cooder substantially rewrote this song for *The Slide Area*, with Bob's blessing. 'He didn't care. It was all the same to him'.

Angelina (Dylan) 6.57
Outtake from *Shot of Love*, recorded 4 May 1981.
Bob Dylan: guitar, vocals, possibly **Fred Tackett**: guitar, **Benmont Tench**: organ, **Tim Drummond**: bass, **Jim Keltner**: drums, **Clydie King, Regina McCrary, Carolyn Dennis**: backing vocals
Nothing prepares you for this. One of the great discoveries, recorded at Clover Studios, towards the end of lengthy sessions for a scrappy album and he left this off! Dylan is suddenly back in focus, his musicians entranced and the lyrics are like a new language. This is trance music, 'in the valleys of the giants where the stars and stripes explode', performed in holy quiet. A love song, in 3-D.

John Bauldie describes it as 'part Cocteau film, part Braque painting, totally surreal, it defies logic and heads off for the deepest, darkest parts of poetic mystery'.

Someone's Got A Hold Of My Heart (Dylan) 4.33
Early version of 'Tight Connection To My Heart', outtake from *Infidels*, recorded 25 April 1983.
Bob Dylan: guitar, harmonica, vocals, **Mick Taylor**: guitar, **Mark Knopfer**: guitar, **Alan Clark**: keyboards, **Robbie Shakespeare**: bass, **Sly Dunbar**: drums
A rewritten version was later re-recorded for *Empire Burlesque*, but lacked the easy grace of this. The music somehow exactly fits the texture of his voice, spot on. Bauldie points out how Dylan sings words to tie in with their meaning, so his voice 'seems to wind around the words "wind around" or be as wide as "wide", or as easy as "easy"'.

Tell Me (Dylan) 4.24
Outtake from *Infidels*, recorded 21 April 1983.
Bob Dylan: guitar, harmonica, vocals, **Mick Taylor**: guitar, **Mark Knopfer**: guitar, **Alan Clark**: keyboards, **Robbie Shakespeare**: bass, **Sly Dunbar**: drums, **Full Force**: backing vocals
This lopes, not quite reggae but with the emphasis on the wrong beats, slide guitar that tickles the palate, backing singers who for once know their place – and swing. A strange love song – 'do you have any morals/do you have any point of view' – but Bob sounds frisky, and coos seductively.

Lord Protect My Child (Dylan) 3.56
Outtake from *Infidels*, recorded 3 May 1983.
Bob Dylan: guitar, harmonica, vocals, **Mick Taylor**: guitar, **Mark Knopfler**: guitar, **Alan Clark**: keyboards, **Robbie Shakespeare**: bass, **Sly Dunbar**: drums
Slow jazz chords on the piano and some subtle slide guitar, as Dylan takes his time to deliver a heartfelt song to a young son. A more uncertain, less memorable update of 'Forever Young'. Although this would still have been a highlight of many of Dylan's most recent albums, the four remaining songs are truly manna from heaven. In the half decade that followed they would keep the devout more than satisfied.

Foot Of Pride (Dylan) 5.56
Outtake from *Infidels*, recorded 25 April 1983.
Bob Dylan: guitar, harmonica, vocals, **Mick Taylor**: guitar, **Mark Knopfer**: guitar, **Alan Clark**: keyboards, **Robbie Shakespeare**: bass, **Sly Dunbar**: drums
Who said Dylan had left surrealism behind? Sly drives the band from the back, this rolls like a juggernaut, with a great chorus and lyrics that sound like a hellfire preacher on LSD. Errol Flynn sounds far more at home here, along with manly women, cast-down businessmen, Miss Delilah and the 'beautiful people', all ripe for divine retribution.

The equally vengeful Lou Reed performed a spirited version at the 'Bobfest' in 1992. There is something of the Velvet's rhythmic thrust to this too that must have attracted another writer who could celebrate 'bodies piled up in mounds'.

Blind Willie McTell (Dylan) 5.51
Acoustic version, outtake from *Infidels*, 5 May 1983.
Bob Dylan: piano, vocals, **Mick Taylor**: guitar
Why on earth wasn't *Infidels* a double album? It would have rivalled *Blonde On Blonde*. There's still time. And this would have been the pinnacle. One of Dylan's greatest ever songs, here sung in holy hush, although the full electric version remains on the shelf. No matter, Taylor's acoustic guitar suggests a whole orchestra and this is surely Bob's finest-ever keyboard recital, making the notes dance.

McTell who, born in Georgia in 1901, was a legendary 12-string player performed at medicine shows and carnivals. His most famous song, laid down in 1929, was 'Statesboro Blues'. He also recorded as 'Georgia Sam', namechecked on 'Highway 61 Revisited'. Alan Lomax recorded him in the 40s, but he died in obscurity in 1959. The reference here to staring out of the old St James Infirmary is taken from the lament of that name that Blind Willie recorded as 'Dying Crapshooter's Blues'.

Dylan sings this with some of the sweetness of the man he is commemorating. His Christ, almost. As Martin Carthy told *Mojo*, this song 'blows this massive hole through the romantic notion of the South, its about corruptability. It's everything a song should be. I love the position of the narrator, sitting in a New Orleans hotel room contemplating the whole history of the south, the murder and the magnolias, but not with anger for a change. It's a rumination'.

When The Night Comes Falling From The Sky (Dylan) 5.37
Recorded New York City 19 February 1985, original version.
Bob Dylan: guitar, vocals, **Little Steven**: guitar, **Roy Bittan**: keyboards, **Robbie Shakespeare**: bass, **Sly Dunbar**: drums

An earlier, clearer and very different take to the version that appeared on *Empire Burlesque*. This is crystal. That is mud. But it jogtrots where the later version has developed a kind of wracked majesty. Tinkling along are two of Springsteen's E Street Band, although Stevie Van Zandt is just as well known these days for his appearances as one of Tony's made men in The Sopranos. And Bob does almost sound like the man he once might have alluded to unfairly in the line about imitators stealing him blind. You can almost imagine him pulling a girl out of the audience to dance with him.

Series Of Dreams (Dylan) 5.52
Outtake from *Oh Mercy*, recorded 23 March 1989.
Bob Dylan: guitar, vocals, **Daniel Lanois**: guitar, 12-string guitar, bass, percussion, **Mason Ruffner**: guitar, **Glen Fukunaga**: bass, **Roddy Colonna**: drums, **Cyril Neville**: talking drum, remix by **Rick Chertoff** and **Bill Whitman**, New York January 1991, additional musicians **Peter Wood**: keyboards, **Rick DiFonzo**: guitar

We leap forward four years to the most recent track included here that Lanois considers 'a fantastic, turbulent track that I felt should have been on the record but he had the last word'. Urgent, mysterious and sung by a man who seems to have moved beyond the temporal world. Where has that eager young boy at the start of this box set gone? And could he have even imagined the strange and varied places that his voice and innate genius would lead him into. John Bauldie describes how 'images are vaguely perceived or half-remembered, incoherent, disconnected'. Ultimately, they refuse to allow such mysteries 'to be translated into any kind of literal sense'. This is also true for so many of the wonderful songs on these three CDs. It outperforms the greatest hits collections of virtually any of his contemporaries.

GOOD AS I BEEN TO YOU

US Release: 3 November 1992
Europe Rlease: December 1992
CD Release: Columbia 472710 2
Producer: Production supervised by Debbie Gold, recorded and mixed by Micajah Ryan

Columbia CK 53200
Columbia 472710
Running Time: 55.33

SIDE ONE: Frankie & Albert; Jim Jones; Blackjack Davey; Canadee-I-O; Sittin' On Top Of The World; Little Maggie; Hard Times.

SIDE TWO: Step It Up And Go: Tomorrow Night; Arthur McBride; You're Gonna Quit Me; Diamond Joe; Froggie Went A Courtin'.

Bob Dylan: vocals, guitar, harmonica (on 'Sittin' On Top Of The World' and 'Tomorrow Night' only)

Early in June in 1992, during a short break in the Never Ending Tour, Dylan went into the Acme Recording Studios in Chicago with David Bromberg to record an album's worth of cover versions. He had already started to slip them into his live sets. It was a natural progression from *Self Portrait* and *Knocked Out Loaded*. He laid down a whacking 26 songs, mixing child ballads like a spooked rendition of 'PollyVaughan' with the work of his favourite songwriters. Everthing from Jimmie Rodgers to Blind Willie McTell to Tim Hardin and a bone-chilling version of Bromberg's own 'Catskill Symphony', about a man coming back to life after a long hibernation and finding all his friends gone. Maybe this is exactly how Dylan felt himself after so many of the Greenwich Village crew had been lost in transit.

The sound of the four tracks that have emerged is what session engineer Blaise Barton described as 'sort of bluegrass, mainly acoustic with some fiddle or mandolin'. Some had a brass section overdubbed, or even the full might and fury of a South Side choir. Fifteen tracks were selected and mixed down for release, but Dylan scrapped the lot and started again.

Dylan had already used his garage come recording studio in the grounds of his post-modern mansion in Malibu to lay down rough-and-ready solo material for tribute albums and the like. 'Pretty Boy Floyd' and 'Old Man' were already done and dusted. In late July, he had

bob dylan

GOOD AS I BEEN TO YOU

decided to augment the new album with a couple more songs, recorded here at home too, suddenly he realized that this was where his heart truly lay. All the Bromberg material was shelved and replaced by nakedly solo renditions of traditional songs, all supposedly first takes. By early August the whole album was in the can.

Dylan later said 'my influences have not changed, and any time they have done, the music goes off to a wrong place'. He recorded *Good As I Been To You* 'so that I could personally get back to the music that's true for me'. This one-time prophet of times a-changin' has always paid homage to previous generations of traditional singers. 'There was a bunch of us, me included, who got to see all these people close up, people like Son House, Reverend Gary Davis, or Sleepy John Estes. Those vibes will carry into you forever, really, so it's like those people, they're still here for me. They're not ghosts in the past. They're continually here.'

Dylan has twice spoken about the 'old songs' in a startling and memorable way that should be written in gold letters above the Smithsonian. Talking to Nora Ephron in 1965, when he seemed to be beaming in his own songs from another planet, he declared 'folk music is the only music where it isn't simple. It's never been simple. It's weird, man, full of legend, myth, bible and ghosts. I've never written anything hard to understand, not in my head anyway, and nothing as far out as those old songs. They were out of sight'. And a year later, in the *Playboy* interview, he went still further. 'Traditional music is based on hexagrams. It comes about from legends, bibles, plagues and it revolves around vegetables and death. There's no one that's going to kill traditional music. It doesn't need to be protected. In that music is the only true, valid death you can feel today off a record player.'

Twenty-six years later, Dylan sings in a weird monotone, without drama or emphasis. His pinched vocals, seemingly strained by the rigours of never ending gigs, could even be mistaken for an ancient Appalachian lady, sitting on her front porch chewing tobacco and singing into a hand-held tape recorder. Andy Kershaw declared that he would play the original recordings of songs murdered by Bob on this album. Ben Cruikshank reckons 'railway station buskers' could do a better job.

Even Michael Gray admits that the vocals show a sad decline, 'a dropping away of his once unerring ability to place and control each syllable and each breath'. But there is so much more going on here. Dark and surreal, this could be an 'inspired, lost work from some opium-thralled folk-archivist'. There is something about this album that chills the soul, as Heylin puts it, a 'world-weariness that is no longer affected, coming from a man who has been on the road too long'.

The cover is to match, a monochrome snap by Jimmy Wachtel of Bob in a rough leather jacket and half shaven, looking up to heaven, or somewhere equally beyond the realm of words. And the music, more field recording than polished professional offering, reminds Paul Williams of stories of Dylan jamming on old songs in private, moments in time 'remembered in awe by the people who happened to be there'. Now he has sat down (albeit in familiar surroundings) and committed some of them to tape. Some tell a story, others imply one, but all encode violence, or sexuality, or joy or defiance in a simple ballad structure.

Dylan does not credit any of the sources he has used. Williams describes Bob as a 'song scholar' but one who 'has not gone out of his way' to rework these songs as found. So he becomes a vehicle for the original arrangement, mostly learnt from a recorded source. Thus in his take of 'Arthur McBride', learnt from Planxty's Paul Brady, Dylan adapts an Irish accent. Although he plays harmonica only on two tracks, his guitar playing here is sparkling. And the deliberately basic recording conditions, without any production tricks to sweeten up the sound, mean that rather than being buried under frantic girl backing singers or fighting against pick-up rock bands, both Dylan's voice and guitar are almost in the room – truly spooky.

SIDE ONE
Frankie & Albert (Trad arr Dylan) 3.50
This was recorded, among many others, by Mississippi John Hurt on the Harry Smith Anthology. Frankie, a feisty woman, shoots her true love Albert dead for dallying with Alice Bly. She goes to the scaffold singing the catchy chorus. And nothing is revealed. Maybe that is the point, with Dylan deliberately draining his voice of expression, to simply become a vehicle for this song of love and revenge. You have to work at this album for the subtle delights like the playful way he sings 'rooty toot toot' as the gun goes off.

Jim Jones (Trad arr Dylan) 3.55
A 19th-century broadside ballad, as if sung by a convict transported by sea to Australia. This is from the singing of Mick Slocum of the Original Bushwackers who recorded this in 1975 and copyrighted the tune, or John Kirkpatrick's recording made a year later. Dylan sings with relish and an astounding vulnerability.

Blackjack Davey (Trad arr Dylan) 5.50
There is a live tape of Dylan singing Guthrie's arrangement of this ancient song as far back as 1961, about a young wife who runs off with her gypsy lover. She takes off her gloves of Spanish leather. There is something eager and disturbing about Dylan's deadpan narration. Paul Williams reckons all is down to 'the inflection in his voice, the way he's inside the song, the charm and conviction of the storyteller. Lust in his voice – the girl's lust, not the gypsy's. How does he do that?'

Canadee-I-O (Trad arr Dylan) 4.24
Most likely from Nic Jones' version on his 1980 album *Penguin Eggs*, about a female stowaway, all for love. Dylan melts into the song and his voice swoops around the melody as he tells this romantic tale of cross-dressing with a happy ending.

Sittin' On Top Of The World (Trad arr Dylan) 4.30
The first blues song of the set, and whatever the copyright says, this was written by two of the Mississippi Sheiks who recorded it back in 1930. Dylan played harmonica on a 1962 version by Big Joe Williams. And he plays great harp here too as he boasts through his tears.

Little Maggie (Trad arr Dylan) 2.55
The source is probably Tom Paley's 1953 recording on *Folk Songs from the Southern Appalachian Mountains*. Dylan speaks with great respect of the New Lost City Ramblers in *Chronicles*. He sings this with relish, pounding his guitar. Gun-toting Little Maggie is a real mountain girl with a 'rifle on her shoulder, six shooter in her hand'.

Hard Times (Trad arr Dylan) 4.35
Written by Stephen Foster whatever the official attribution. This late 19th-century standard is pure music hall, not a traditional song at all. Its words would fit any depression, including the one that hit the west in the early 90s. Dylan relishes the tune and almost moans at times.

SIDE TWO
Step It Up And Go (Trad arr Dylan) 2.57
Recorded by Brownie McGhee in 1941 under the pseudonym Blind Boy Fuller No 2. Dylan probably knew it via the Everly Brothers, but it is an old jug band song often called 'Bottle Up And Go'. Dylan gives it his all in a gruff-voiced, middle-aged kind of way. For Paul Williams this is perhaps the key to the whole album, 'it reminds us that the guitar is a rhythmic instrument as much as a melodic one, and that there is a strong rhythmic element in the performance of all these songs'. But he doesn't exactly set the woods alight.

Tomorrow Night (Trad arr Dylan) 3.44
Actually written by Sam Goslow and Will Grosz, and a hit for Lonnie Johnson in 1947. Dylan probably knew it from Elvis Presley's Sun recording. Now this is singing! Dylan croons and you can almost imagine the orchestra behind him, all in monogrammed uniforms. For Williams, this is 'pure situation. No story'. And yet old stager Dylan knows exactly how to locate the emotional heart of the song. The deliberate pause between 'surrender' and 'to me' is 'rich in sexuality'. It is much the same situation and mood, as 'Lay, Lady, Lay'.

Arthur McBride (Trad arr Dylan) 6.22
Taught to Dylan by Paul Brady backstage during a gig at Slane Castle: Paul recorded it in 1976 on *Andy Irvine/Paul Brady*. Dylan's voice is very, very strange here. It is a real outlaw song with the recruiting sergeant bloodily outwitted in the end. Bob finds great relish in impersonating his imprecations.

You're Gonna Quit Me (Trad arr Dylan) 2.48
Written and recorded by Blind Blake in 1927. Dylan had sat at the feet of the Rev. Gary Davis as he performed this around Greenwich Village in the 60s. There is a ragtimey feel to it, but sung in the oddly muted way that every song on this album is treated.

Diamond Joe (Trad arr Dylan) 3.17
Cisco Houston recorded it on the *Hard Travelling* LP, and this cowboy ballad was also in the repertoire of Dylan's friend Ramblin' Jack Elliott. Joe is another John Wesley Harding, not taking much account of the law. Jerry Garcia recorded it too, on *Almost Acoustic*.

Froggie Went A Courtin' (Trad arr Dylan) 6.24
Mike and Peggy Seeger are among countless others to record this, on 1977's *American Folk Songs For Children*. This is among the great flood of British songs that crossed the Atlantic and survived up in the mountains and out on remote farms. This was supposedly first a political satire from the time of Elizabeth I, dealing with her many suitors. The adventurer Sir Walter Raleigh was her 'fish', the French Ambassador her 'ape' and the Duc d'Alencon her 'frog'. Here, the animals and reptiles and insects have been Americanized.

For Paul Williams: 'we're not so much interested in the story as in the chain of images the storyteller conjures up'. Dylan similarly set out a succession of poetic images in songs from 'Hard Rain' to 'Series Of Dreams'. Probably the highlight of the album, Dylan sings these nonsense lyrics with total seriousness with a metaphorical twinkle in his eye. Everything gets eaten, including the cornbread. Bob doesn't even crack on the last line – 'if you want any more, you can sing it yourself'. The song just ends with a slight flourish on the guitar.

OUTTAKES (cut previously in same home studio)
'Pretty Boy Floyd' on *Folkways, A Vision Shared*
'People Get Ready' on *Flashback*

30TH ANNIVERSARY CONCERT CELEBRATION

US Release: 24 August 1993
UK Release: Columbia 474000 1 3-LP set
Producer: Jeff Rosen and Don Devito

Columbia C2K 53230 2-CD set
Sony 474000 1 2-CD set
Running Time: (75.21) (73.05)

SIDE ONE: John Mellancamp: Like A Rolling Stone, Leopard-Skin Pill-Box Hat; Stevie Wonder: Blowin' In The Wind; Eddie Vedder/Mike McCready: Masters Of War.

SIDE TWO: Lou Reed: Foot Of Pride; Tracy Chapman: The Times They Are A-Changin'; June Carter/Johnny Cash: It Ain't Me, Babe; Willie Nelson: What Was It You Wanted; Kris Kristofferson: I'll Be Your Baby Tonight

SIDE THREE: Johnny Winter: Highway 61 Revisited: Ron Wood: Seven Days: Richie Havens: Just Like A Woman; The Clancy Brothers and Robbie O'Connell with special guest Tommy Makem: When The Ship Comes In: Mary Chapin Carpenter/Rosanne Cash/Shawn Colvin: You Ain't Going Nowhere.

SIDE FOUR: Neil Young: Just Like Tom Thumb's Blues, All Along The Watchtower: Chrissie Hynde: I Shall Be Released; Eric Clapton: Don't Think Twice, It's All Right.

SIDE FIVE: The O'Jays: Emotionally Yours; The Band: When I Paint My Masterpiece; George Harrison: Absolutely Sweet Marie; Tom Petty & The Heartbreakers: License To Kill, Rainy Day Women #12 & 35.

SIDE SIX: Roger McGuinn: Mr Tambourine Man; Bob Dylan: It's Alright, Ma (I'm Only Bleeding); Bob Dylan, Roger McGuinn, Tom Petty, Neil Young, Eric Clapton, George Harrison: My Back Pages; Everyone: Knockin' on Heaven's Door; Bob Dylan: Girl Of The North Country.

Bob Dylan: vocals, guitar, **Kenny Aronoff:** drums, **Randy Ciarlante:** drums, vocals, **John J Cascella:** accordion, keyboards, **Steve Cropper:** guitar, **Donald 'Duck' Dunn:** bass, **Howie Epstein:** bass, lap steel guitar, **Ron Fair:** piano, **Anton Fig:** drums, **Lisa Germano:** violin, **John David Grissom:** guitar, **Booker T.Jones** (organ), **Jim Keltner:** drums, **Al Kooper:** organ,

BOB DYLAN

The 30th Aniversary Concert Celebration

Kerry Marx: guitar, **Jeffrey G. Meyers**: bass, **Pat Peterson**: vocals, percussion, **Mickey Raphael**: harmonica, **G. E. Smith**: guitar, mandolin, bass, **Benmont Tench**: keyboards, **Michael B. Wanchie**: guitar, **Don Was**: bass, **Reggie Young**: guitar, **Jerry Barnes, Katrice Barnes, Leotis Clyburn, Gynice Colemen, Dennis Collins, Sheryl Crow, Cissie Houston, Gary Houston, D. Keith John, Brenday White King, Curtis King, Sue Medley, Rose Mithcam, Christine Ohlman**: vocals

On 16 October 1992, Columbia Records hosted an evening at Madison Square Garden to 'Celebrate The Music Of Bob Dylan', a three-and-a-half hour show broadcast live on pay-TV. It also later appeared on video and laserdisc. With backing from Booker T and the MGs, plus the events music director, G. E. Smith, a succession of Bob's friends and fans took turns to do their party pieces, as outlined above and caught on this album.

Things did not go entirely to plan. Neither Van Morrison nor Elvis Costello – slated to sing 'Positively 4th Street' – turned up. Sinead O'Connor chose to challenge the audience then sing 'War', written by the wrong Bob, Marley not Dylan, and leave the stage in tears. John Hammond Jr had rehearsed 'I'll Be Your Baby Tonight', but Kris Kristofferson pulled rank, so the son of Dylan's first producer sang Jesse Fuller's 'See That My Grave Is Kept Clean', a highlight of Bob's debut album. This was significant, as the evening was supposed to commemorate the 30th Anniversary of Dylan signing to the record company (pulling a veil over his brief dalliance with Asylum).

Dylan began his brief set with 'Song To Woody', also premiered on that debut album, but it is omitted here, supposedly because of technical difficulties over the miking of Bob's guitar. After the television cameras were switched off, he returned for the solo version of 'Girl From The North Country' that closes the album. He looked 'spruce and dapper', and this is reflected on the cover. Dylan's name is picked out over photographs of guest stars: Clapton, Wonder, Neil Young, Chrissie Hynde, George Harrison, Tom Petty et al. The back cover is a great action shot of most of the above on stage with Dylan, duelling guitars.

SIDE SIX
Bob Dylan: It's Alright, Ma (I'm Only Bleeding) (Dylan) 6.21
Performed solo in his latest, querulous voice, like a man preparing to be sick, and notably cavalier with pitch and tune, he drags out the last word of each verse. The reference to the president standing naked getting an ironic cheer during an election year. Described variously as 'coruscating' and 'brisk', this holds the current land speed record for the fastest recorded run through (almost literally) of this song.

My Back Pages (Dylan) 4.40
Bob Dylan, Roger McGuinn, Tom Petty, Neil Young, Eric Clapton, George Harrison:
Eight guitarists fight for space on stage and McGuinn, Petty, Young, Clapton, Bob and Harrison all sing a verse each. Dylan later re-recorded his vocal for the 'live' album. There is a piercing guitar break from Young.

Everyone: Knockin' on Heaven's Door (Dylan) 5.38
With Clapton wailing away on lead, this has never sounded more like an anthem. Dylan's vocal is a thing of wracked magnificence, mourning a generation.

Girl Of The North Country (Dylan) 5.12
Bob Dylan
Sung as it should be, totally alone and after the cameras have all been switched off. Now it's the west wind a-blowing, the tune re-invented and a labyrinthine harmonica solo to bring the night to a close. *Q* magazine describes Dylan here as 'caressing the words tenderly and immersing himself in the memory, this was a man forever moving forward, for once allowing himself the indulgence of nostalgia. A tight smile and low bow and he was off'.

WORLD GONE WRONG

US Release: 26 October 1993
CD Release: Columbia CK 57590
UK/Europe Release: December 1993
Producer: Bob Dylan

Columbia C 53200

Columbia 474857 1
Running Time: 43.58

SIDE ONE: World Gone Wrong; Love Henry; Ragged & Dirty; Blood In My Eyes; Broke Down Engine.

SIDE TWO: Delia; Stack A Lee; Two Soldiers; Jack-A-Roe; Lone Pilgrim.

Bob Dylan: vocals, guitar and harmonica

World Gone Wrong was again recorded in Dylan's home studio, supposedly in a couple of afternoons in May 1993. It is a raw album – full of images of violence. Following criticisms of the previous album and its lack of details of source material, Dylan provided comprehensive, if not fully comprehensible, liner notes, in the wrong order. There was a more equal distribution between what old 78s used to list as 'race' and 'hillbilly' classics. He told Craig McGregor, 'I only listen to the old music: the old blues singers and the old country singers'. As he said on the album's release, 'singers in the 50s and 60s were just one step removed from the early ones, and you could hear that. But you can't hear it anymore, it's so polluted and unclean. Even *World Gone Wrong* is a step or two removed. People should go to those old records and find out what the real thing is, because mine is still second generation'.

That may be, but nobody else would have got away with releasing even this approximation in a world of remixes and multi-track studios and computer-assisted vocals. As Robert Wyatt wrote in *Mojo*, 'hear this man do it and take courage. How great it could be if everybody struggling to find their own voice were able to stop struggling and, well, use their own voice'. Dylan has always had 'the nerve to draw on history as a living stew-pot.' Paul Williams notes how his voice and guitar are 'inseperable partners' here. *Select* hears only a 'p-ssed up busker on the London Underground making it up as he goes along'.

Others saw beneath the surface, and regarded this as Dylan's one-man version of the Harry

BOB DYLAN world gone wrong

Smith Anthology with him doing all the voices. Michael Gray finds the album 'less Gothic' than its predecessor. Others find it more varied and an easier listening experience. For Paul Williams it is 'so warm it makes the previous albums seem cold and distant'. It is an album that provides the ante-room in terms of mortality and decay for the next time he would enter a recording studio, to make *Time Out Of Mind*.

On the cover Dylan is caught by photographer Ana Velez in a café in Crouch End, just opposite Compendium Books – for so many years the best place in London to track down Beat publications and rare Dylan tapes – dressed in a top hat like a hip undertaker and almost out-performed by an extremely ugly painting of man in spiritual torment.

SIDE ONE
World Gone Wrong (Trad arr Dylan) 3.57
A few seconds of dead air and Dylan sings, as if from the grave, this devastatingly lonely song about 'strange things' happening. The lines about not having a home could be straight out of 'Like A Rolling Stone'. Dylan learnt this from the Mississippi Sheiks, and they could be writing about today, 'evil charlatans' and the celebrity culture, 'irrationalist bimbos and bozos, the stuff of legend'. Bob wants to return to the 'fundamental', whatever that means.

Love Henry (Trad arr Dylan) 4.24
A 'perverse tale' learnt from Tom Paley. Dylan sees the Lord here as a medieval equivalent of modern day 'corporate man', though this is more usually seen as a variant of the 'Pretty Polly' murder ballad. And it is the man who gets murdered. Dylan sings like Anthony Perkins looks at the end of *Psycho*, eyes bright with madness.

Ragged & Dirty (Trad arr Dylan) 4.10
Dylan writes that this comes from a record by Willie Brown, although his version also owes something to a Sleepy John Estes 1929 recording. A song of the depression with a lovely guitar figure. 'Schmaltz and pickled herring', Bob glosses, and it sure does have the 'heavy moral vocabulary' he claims. A woesome lover, and you can hear the ghost of Dylan's young self in this performance, through a series of refracting mirrors.

Blood In My Eyes (Trad arr Dylan) 5.04
Bob learnt this from the Mississippi Sheiks, 'rebellion versus routine seems to be their strong theme' and they now fit these 'New Dark Ages'. Another haunted song with a jaunty tune and a chorus about an excess of desire that he makes sound extremely sinister. Bob is certainly in better voice than the first time he was good to us by raiding his dusty 78s.

Broke Down Engine (Trad arr Dylan) 3.23
Learnt from a disc by Blind Willie McTell, 'it's about trains, mystery on the rails' but on a deeper level, 'it's about variations of human longing – the low hum in meters and syllables'. Dylan shows more signs of life here than in the whole of the previous album. It's easy to recognize that young hobo with a guitar and a harmonica rack down at the Gaslight. A cheerful tune at last, despite the undertones of evil living.

SIDE TWO
Delia (Trad arr Dylan) 5.42
The way he sings 'All the friends I ever had are gone' breaks the heart. You suddenly feel that for all the fame and money and women, this is a man totally lost. He becomes the song, his tender, wrecked voice and strummed guitar the vehicle to carry it, and only parses this as a combination of variant originals. Another murder ballad and a song about 'counterfeit loyalty', the usual vengeful judge, and the luckless gambler Delia six foot under. A masterpiece.

Stack A Lee (Trad arr Dylan) 3.50
There is some sprightly and welcome harmonica to break the spell, though Dylan sings this tale as if on his death bed. Not a shred of verbal expression except the dry-as-dust comment that the six white horses that take Billy to the graveyard fail to bring him back.

    This tale of a bar-room fight that ends with a shot through the head comes from the version by Frank Hutchinson. Dylan declares in his notes that 'no man gains immortality thru public acclaim'. Quite the opposite, if the 1966 tour is taken into consideration. He spends longer describing this track than singing it. Stagolee, as he is more usually known, is 'in a cell, no wall phone – he is not some degraded existentialist dionysian idiot'. And Billy here has more life than anyone on TV, supposedly, even when dead.

Two Soldiers (Trad arr Dylan) 5.46
He learnt this direct from Jerry Garcia. 'A battle song extraordinaire', as is Bob's vocal here, quite indescribable. Bob sees this Civil War tragedy as a remnant of that old, weird America, 'before Chaplin, before *The Wild One*' (ie Marlon Brando in leathers) 'before the Children of the Sun' – the hippies, presumably – 'before the celestial grunge, before the insane world of entertainment exploded in our faces'. This from a man who followed Nirvana onto *Unplugged*, and headed a three-and-a-half hour celebrity love-in in his own honour. But listen to the song, and he means every word. Dylan moans the words like a wolf with his tongue pierced on a barbed wire fence, emitting its final breath.

Paul Williams thinks that his comments here, 'Are you any good at what you do? Submerge your personality' is the key to the whole album. 'No album he ever made came closer to telling the truth about his private world.'

Jack-A-Roe (Trad arr Dylan) 4.56
Back to ancient balladry. This was learnt from Tom Paley; 'the young virgin follows her heart and in it the secrets of the universe', and gets married in the end. A song that 'gets inside reality'. It certainly sounds like an echo from something deep inside the earth. You really need a lyric sheet to grasp exactly what he is singing here, as his diction is lost in action. 'Tense strumming' on the guitar and slight reverb on his vocal – 'my kind of sound is very simple, with a little bit of echo, and that's about it'.

Lone Pilgrim (B. F. White/A. M. Pace) 2.44
Taken from an old Doc Watson song. No more 'blood in my eyes' and the tears are wiped away too, in this lovely spiritual. 'There won't be songs like these anymore, factually there aren't any now'. And none of the Pop Idol clan could ever sing a line like 'my soul flew to mountains on high' so quietly, or with such joyful tranquillity.

OUTTAKES:
'You Belong To Me' on soundtrack to *Natural Born Killers*
This enigmatic song was offered for inclusion in the soundtrack to *Natural Born Killers*. The film version had actors voices dubbed over part of the track, but the original take circulated shortly afterwards.

BOB DYLAN'S GREATEST HITS VOL 3

US Release: 15 November 1994　　**Columbia CK 66783**
UK Release: 477805-2
Also came out in France as a double vinyl album.
Producer: none, but mastered by Vic Anesini.　　**Running Time:** 77.26

Although none of the tracks here is a hit in any real sense, this first selection for 24 years shows the depth and power of Dylan's albums since *Pat Garrett*, even if his closest thing to a hit single during this time, 'Baby Stop Crying', is not included. The tracks are not in chronological order but make for a good listening experience. Any critical discussion centred on what was seen as a disastrous and modish remix of 'Dignity' – from those who had heard the original on bootleg – and a far more welcome retooling of 'Silvio'. For Michael Gray, its 'posturing edge' has been removed, resulting in 'an amiable, light, poised little thing. It is still not worth including'. Nothing is included here from *Dylan*, *The Basement Tapes*, *Saved* or *Empire Burlesque*.

This CD flows nicely, although the remake of 'Dignity' sounds heavy-handed with over-emphatic drums, like a cart horse clattering down the road. 'Silvio' sounds like a whole layer of audio gunk has been scraped off – maybe the same trick could be applied to other mid-80s recordings in the fullness of time. Here, Dylan is suddenly stage centre, rather than sending his vocal in from the wings. The cover has Dylan looking pensive in a photo by Ken Regan and inside in a neatly piped jacket.

Tangled Up In Blue (Dylan) 5.42 from *Blood on the Tracks*.
Changing Of The Guards (Dylan) 6.36 from *Street Legal*.
The Groom's Still Waiting At The Altar (Dylan) 4.04 from *Shot Of Love*.
Hurricane (Dylan/Jacques Levy) 8.35 from *Desire*.
Forever Young (Dylan) 4.58 from *Shot Of Love*.
Jokerman (Dylan) 6.16 from *Infidels*.
Dignity (Dylan) 5.58 outtake from *Oh Mercy*, remixed.
Silvio (Dylan/Robert Hunter) 3.07 from *Down In The Groove,* remixed.
Ring Them Bells (Dylan) 3.03 from *Oh Mercy*.
Gotta Serve Somebody (Dylan) 5.25 from *Slow Train Coming*.
Series of Dreams (Dylan) 5.54 from *Bootleg Series Vols 1-3*.
Brownsville Girl (Dylan/Sam Shepherd) 11.04 from *Knocked Out Loaded*.
Under The Red Sky (Dylan) 4.10 from *Under The Red Sky*.
Knockin' On Heaven's Door (Dylan) 2.31 from *Pat Garrett and Billy the Kid*.

The original running order had 'True Love Tends To Forget' and 'Tight Connection To My Heart', replaced by 'Changing Of The Guard' and 'Series Of Dreams'.

BOB DYLAN'S GREATEST HITS VOLUME 3

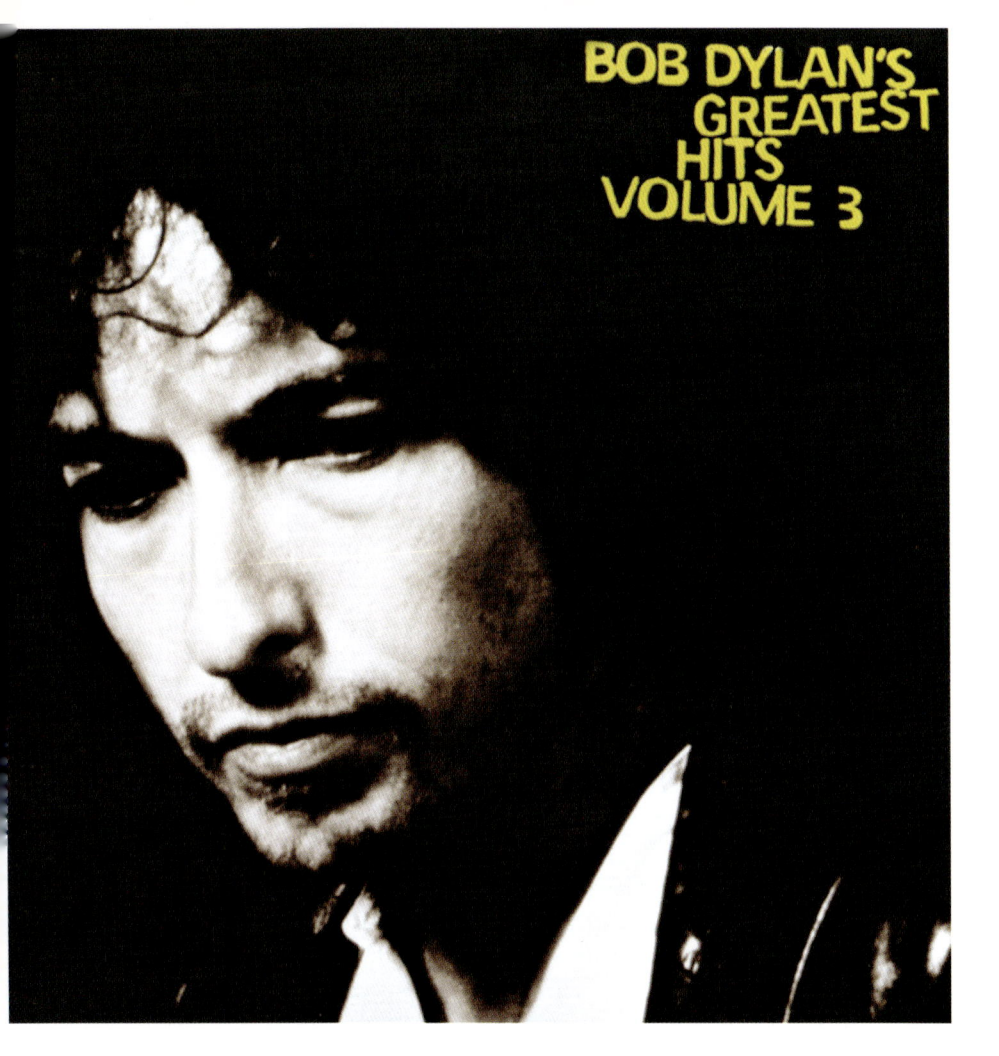

MTV UNPLUGGED

US Release: 25 April 1995
Reissued as Columbia 67000 S1,
with extra track, 'Love Minus Zero'
UK/Europe Release: Columbia 478374 2
Producer: Jeff Kramer and Jeff Rosen

Columbia CK 67000

Running Time: 69.23

SIDE ONE: Tombstone Blues; Shooting Star; All Along The Watchtower.

SIDE TWO: The Times They Are A-Changin'; John Brown; Desolation Row.

SIDE THREE: Rainy Day Women #12 & 35; Love Minus Zero/No Limit; Dignity.

SIDE FOUR: Knockin' On Heaven's Door; Like A Rolling Stone; With God On Our Side.

Bob Dylan: vocal, guitar, harmonica, **Bucky Baxter:** pedal steel, dobro, **Tony Garnier:** bass, **John Jackson:** guitar, **Brendan O'Brien:** Hammond organ, **Winston Watson:** drums

Dylan and his tour band recorded their set for *Unplugged* on 17 and 18 November 1994 at the MTV studios in New York, from which both the show – now available on both video and DVD, including a version of 'Love Minus Zero/NoLimit' not broadcast at the time – and album were plucked, seemingly at random. Left aside were worthwhile performances of rare songs like 'Hazel', 'My Back Pages', 'Tonight I'll Be Staying Here With You' and 'Absolutely Sweet Marie' – with some great pedal steel – and in particular a stunning version of 'I Want You'.

On both sets, Bob used his tour band with plugged-in bass plus Brendan O'Brien on Hammond organ. The sound is semi rather than all acoustic and thus broke the cardinal rule of the show, but quiet all the same. Dylan had planned to appear alone, as he had on those two wonderful BBC broadcasts some 30 years before, but was talked out of this by MTV executives. Maybe they feared skeletal versions of obscure songs written by dead men, as he had just committed to two slices of vinyl. The show aired on 14 December in the US and nine days later in Europe.

The results were generally seen at the time as a huge return to form, to a voice, a band and a set list from the glory days. Some begged to differ. Andy Gill thundered about what he

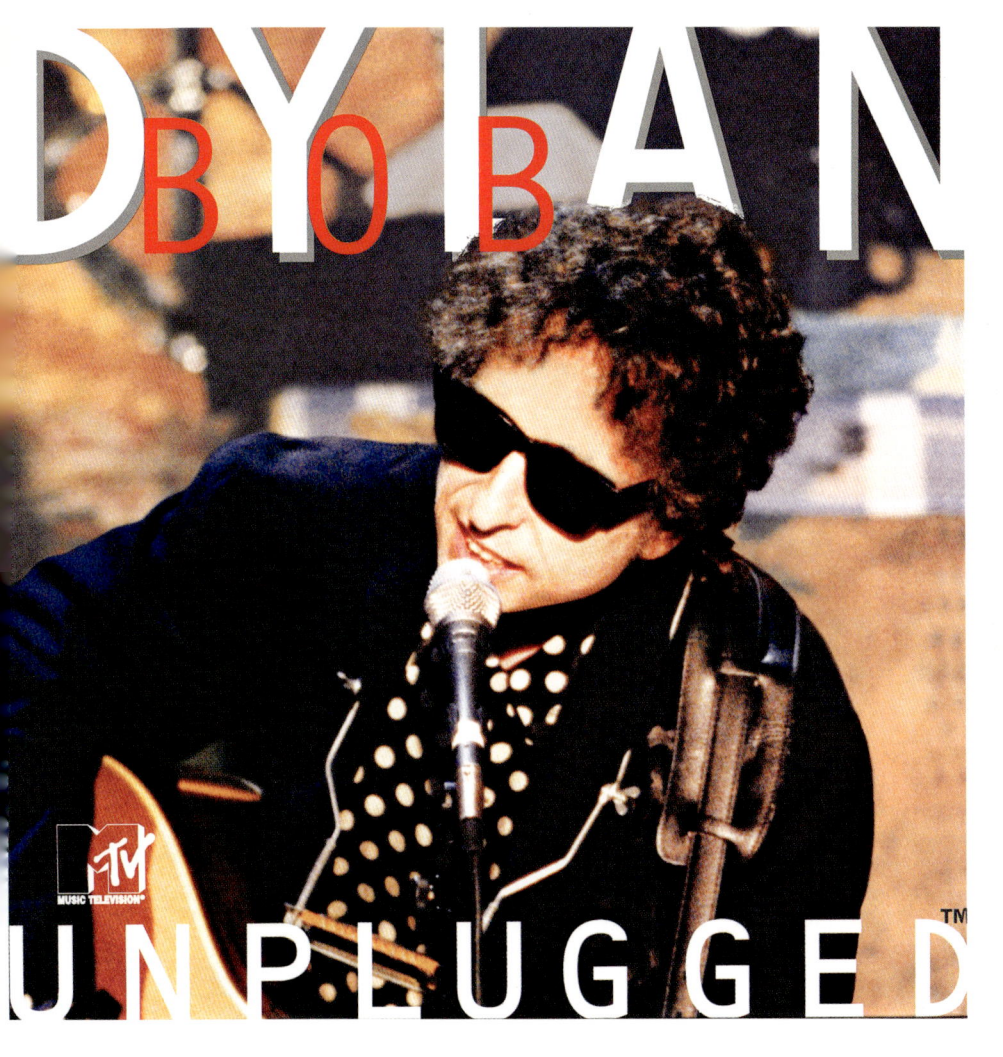

BOB DYLAN

MTV UNPLUGGED

saw as 'shameful dullness and yawnsome predictability. No one else, not even Guns n'Roses would treat Dylan songs in such cavalier fashion'. But that surely is the point. For Michael Gray, it remains the 'dreariest, most contemptible, phoney tawdry piece of product ever issued by a great artist'. When the DVD emerged in 2004, one expert reckoned 'it reveals a performance far more coherent and controlled than anyone allowed for at the time'.

It now sounds easy on the ear, mellow and mellifluous, though perhaps a trifle lacking in passion. There are no ragged edges here. Bob would have liked to do old folk songs with acoustic instruments, but there was a lot of input from other sources as to what would be right for the audience. One new thing is the Dead-inspired (acoustic) guitar duels between Dylan himself and John Jackson that close many of the songs here, though not to the tedious length these tinklings could stretch out to in performance. The album cover is a photograph taken by Frank Micelotta of Dylan on set in his polka dot shirt.

SIDE 1
Tombstone Blues (Dylan) 4.54
It's that lovely *Highway 61* organ sound again gone rustic, as has Dylan's slightly hoarse voice. There is a wonderfully lived-in quality to this version, hardened on the road and with a cheerful vibe, quite contrary to the spirit of the original where tombstone signified a living death, as well as the habitat of Belle Star. Now it sounds a comfortable place to be either way.

Shooting Star (Dylan) 4.06
Rough Guide calls this 'lovely and wistful', although there is a note of underlying desperation too. Dylan even plays a short acoustic guitar break. During the long fade out, pedal steel makes a nice contrast with a fine harmonica break, then the organ breaks in like Garth Hudson lying well down on his easy chair. The crowd go predictably wild and the band goes – in real time – into…

All Along The Watchtower (Dylan) 3.37
Miles away both from the usual Hendrix-inspired arrangement, let alone the spooky original, this time round it is relaxed, like the Band on valium. Dylan tries out a different melody line in the third verse, that again leads into a polite freak-out.

SIDE 2
The Times They Are A-Changin' (Dylan) 5.48
A complete makeover, now sung with the wisdom of middle age, contemplative and almost melancholy where the original was brisk and a call to action. Again the organ is the key instrument here, a bit like Procol Harum, a far from idiot wind, blowing around Dylan's slow, measured vocal. Subtle drumming too. Bob makes the line about 'the present now will later be past' resonate as the baby boomers this was written for start celebrating their 50th birthdays.

John Brown (Dylan) 5.27
An anti-war song from 1963, never before on album – as the clued-in audience obviously realize from the reaction at the end – and the biggest surprise of the whole set. Dylan suddenly sounds urgent, and he brilliantly acts out both mother and damaged son. The band take a back seat, their backing almost subliminal, then break out between verses. They are far more sympathetic to their master than some of the journeymen Dylan has used for swathes of the Never Ending tour.

Desolation Row (Dylan) 8.18
Another surprise, and one of only three songs that Dylan ran through on both recording dates. This is an undramatic rendition, almost throwaway, to a swaying accompaniment with Dylan sotto voce. The vibe is relaxed, like something down Tijuana way. Verses five, six and nine are missing in action here. Then in the last verse, Dylan suddenly sounds desperate, as if Desolation Row is not quite the nice place it has sounded like for most of the song. The guitars briefly catch fire then wind up to an arpeggio.

SIDE 3
Rainy Day Women #12 & 35 (Dylan) 3.29
A bit more life here with thwacked drums, although this sounds more like an invite to a drinks party than the drugs scene from *Blow Up*. He cackled in Nashville, here he sings with a smile in his voice. Dylan brings his harmonica to the party and the band really take of but without any great sense of abandon.

Love Minus Zero/No Limit (Dylan) 5.22
Gentle, and Dylan has a real country burr in his voice. This does sound unplugged. Just the way he emphasizes the word wall is worth the price of the CD. More evidence of Dylan as a post-modern crooner.

Dignity (Dylan) 5.31
Uptempo and sung with real spirit, as befits the newest song here, at least in terms of release. And he brings out the needle-sharp lyrics of what increasingly sounds like yet another cast-aside masterpiece. Glen Dundas prints an amusing photograph of Dylan, sandwiched between boxer Frank Bruno and Ron Wood meeting Prince Philip in 1986: in fact it is his son Prince Charles. This probably outweighs even the album outtake and appeared as the lead track on three separate CD singles too, with a wealth of bonus live material.

SIDE 4
Knockin' On Heaven's Door (Dylan) 5.31
More emotional than the album version, maybe because Dylan feels closer to the event now, and with an excellent elongated harmonica break. European copies of both LP and CD were originally issued with an overdubbed three seconds of the audience whistling and clapping, but this was removed on later copies and an offer made to replace originals free of charge.

Like A Rolling Stone (Dylan) 9.10
All the need and hurt of the original have gone, what is left is perhaps the most dispensible remake of the whole concert, and overstays its welcome. Manchester 1966, this is not. The band also sounds like they're going through the motions here. Paul Williams describes it as 'anti-climactic, the song lacks feeling and the band never finds the groove' not even the organ player, so excellent elsewhere. Dylan's voice is weird here, enunciating ev-er-y syll-ab-le. Williams thinks it's so that no-one can accuse him of mumbling, as many did in live performances of the time.

With God On Our Side (Dylan) 7.08
Another highlight, again replacing the starkness and urgency of the acoustic original for this regretful and slow take, with bowed bass, weeping pedal steel and rich organ chords. 'Splendid and stately', but in a spirit of glasnost, he omits the verses about the German holocaust and about learning to hate the Russians that must have come especially hard on the descendant of Soviet emigrants. Why didn't Dylan add O'Brien to his tour band immediately?

Paul Williams was intrigued by the way Dylan rested part of his backside on a stool for many of the songs here – perhaps under orders from the TV bosses, for whom this was all part of the unplugged ethos. He seems unusually relaxed for a TV appearance, maybe because he is shielded from the TV lights and the viewers too. At the end of the DVD he shakes hands with some of the select audience in what looks like a staged gesture.

DVD Release: Columbia 202435 9, 73 mins. Contains four songs – 'Tombstone Blues', 'John Brown', 'Desolation Row' and 'Love Minus Zero'/'No Limit' – not on the original broadcast.

COL 486936 1

BOB DYLAN TIME OUT OF MIND

TIME OUT OF MIND

US Release: 30 September 1997
CD Release: Columbia 486936 2
UK Release: 1998 Columbia
Producer: Daniel Lanois

Columbia CK 68556

COL 486936 2-LP set,
Running Time: 72.52

Love Sick; Dirt Road Blues; Standing In The Doorway; Million Miles, Tryin' To Get To Heaven; 'Til I Fell In Love With You; Not Dark Yet, Cold Irons Bound; Make You Feel My Love; Can't Wait; Highlands.

Bob Dylan: vocal, acoustic and electric rhythm lead guitar, harmonica, piano, **'Bucky' Baxter**: acoustic guitar, pedal steel, **Brian Blade:** drums, **Robert Britt:** Martin acoustic and Fender Stratocaster, **Cindy Cashdollar**, slide guitar, **Jim Dickinson:** keyboards, Wurlitzer electric piano and pump organ, **Tony Garnier:** electric bass and acoustic upright bass, **Jim Keltner:** drums, **David Kemper:** drums, **Daniel Lanois:** guitar, mando-guitar, firebird, Martin 0018, Gretch gold top, rhythm and lead, **Tony Mangurian:** percussion, **Augie Meters:** Vox organ combo, Hammond B3 organ and accordion, **'Duke' Robillard:** guitar, electric L5 Gibson, **Winston Watson:** drums

Dylan spent a cold winter snowed in on his Minnesota farm and began to write an album's worth of songs, that shared some common themes. 'They just naturally hung together, because they share a certain scepticism. They're more concerned with the dread realities of life than the bright and rosy idealism popular today.' He told Jeff Kramer 'I'm not going to record them', but he made rough demos. In January 1997 he booked a return visit to Dr Daniel Lanois. This time around they convened not in the fading splendours of a New Orleans mansion but in the Criteria Studios in Florida, booking in from 13 to 28 January 1997.

The musicians were largely different too. Lanois played guita, and there was a core band of bassist Tony Garnier from Dylan's tour band, legendary drummer Jim Keltner, spooky organist Augie Meyers from the Sir Douglas Quartet and another veteran, Jim Dickinson, on other keyboards. The rest of the musicians came and went: steel guitar player Bucky Baxter was another member of the tour band. Dylan played a lot of guitar and piano himself. And he took the rare step of gifting Columbia a written statement of intent. 'Daniel and I talked about these songs and how they should sound long before we recorded them.' People tended to concentrate on his lyrics, but here 'the music itself has just as far-reaching an effect, and it was meant to be that way. It's definitely a performance record instead of a poetic, literary type of thing. You can feel it rather than think about it'.

Rockabilly specialist Duke Robillard was booked in for the last nine days of recording, invited by Bob personally. They had met when Duke was playing with the Fabulous Thunderbirds in LA. *Isis* interviewed him. Recording sessions lasted up to 12 hours at a time, 'basically non stop'. People were playing in real time, and facing each other. 'Everybody's role was to listen and respond. Everybody was part of the whole.' It was a very spontaneous form of music making. 'Every song went through several complete transformations. We didn't do anything the same way twice.' Dylan's vocals were all done live. And enough was recorded, both here and during a mysterious spell in California, to fill at least another album.

The sessions also were filmed by Daniel's brother Bob. The studio had been dressed like a stage set to keep things special 'with homestyle lampshades and couches like some sort of parlour, hush lighting so that eveyryone would feel comfortable. We played in the middle of this'.

Another, anonymous musician, filled in some more gaps. The acoustic demos, that Dylan reworked in the studio, often were extremely beautiful in their own right. In the studio, there would be enough musicians to make up three separate bands, all playing at once, but it worked because 'the musicians only played small parts, soloing was not called for'. They generated many reels of tape. And most songs generated a host of outtakes, like a stripped-down 'Standing In The Doorway' with just Dylan and Meyers, and 'Not Dark Yet' and 'Can't Wait', both with radically different lyrics. The lengthy 'Highlands' was recorded three times in its entirety. As to Dylan's old time lyrics, they were 'designed to create a mood. The record is set in another time, the south, Missouri, Mississippi. It's steamboat, civil war, very Mark Twain kinda stuff'. The sound too was exactly 'what Bob wanted'. And they were just working together on sequencing the album 'when he got ill'.

Dylan spoke about this new album just before the illness that almost made the release of *Time Out Of Mind* posthumous. 'I think it might be shocking in its bluntness. There isn't any waste. There's no line that has to be there to get to another line'. As he had said some years back, when he was recording *Oh Mercy* with the same producer, 'everybody works in the shadow of what they've previously done. But you have to overcome that'. And the title sums up brilliantly the nature of the songs here, looking back, and compacting past, present and future. In some ways he has rediscovered the multi-faceted nature of *Blood on the Tracks*, as if rewritten by a man starting to feel his age.

Lanois was omnipresent, tweaking the soundstage. As Peter Doggett put it, 'almost every track steams with the humid discomfort of a swamp', Dylan fights his way through, sounding parched. His voice is a shadow of what it was, a 'cruelly muted rasp' that sounds as if it is scraping blood from his throat. Lanois accentuates this by using compressors, making Bob sound like an 'uneasy ghost'. And half the songs here are structured around the 12-bar blues format and 'summon up the ghosts of Slim Harpo and Muddy Waters'. And Blind Willie McTell.

The critical reaction was ecstatic, even at times hysterical, as if Dylan had survived a near-death experience and then written about his brush with mortality, whereas it was really about a failed love affair – or nothing connected with his own life at all. Robert Christgau, having made this very point, adds 'the timelessness people hear in it is what Dylan has long aimed for – simple songs inhabited with an assurance that makes them seem classic rather than received'.

Even so, comments at the time like '73 minutes of genius' and 'Dylan is at his creative peak' are not too far from the truth. For Greil Marcus, this is 'as bleak and blasted as any work an artist in any field has offered in ages'. It dares to deal with mortality and is 'shocking in its bitterness'. The narrator of these stories begins by walking dead streets and ends with him traversing 'streets of an almost deserted city'. Although Marcus doesn't mention it, this is a familiar trope from surrealist painting – just think de Chirico, or writers like David Gascoyne or Iain Sinclair, walking the city streets by night. Greil does reference the movie *Sullivan's Travels*, that later inspired *Oh Brother Where Art Thou*: the hero there finds too that 'the rags of poverty and anonymity don't merely hide the signs of wealth and celebrity, but dissolve them'.

One listener at least to this album, bought a few days before I saw him give a 'back-from-the-brink' performance in the unlikely environs of a Bournemouth leisure centre, like John Milton reading *Paradise Lost* in a music hall, wondered at a man to whom all the baubles and temptations of this world were endlessly available, and who still sounded so utterly wretched.

Marcus puts it rather better, 'it's less the island of one man's broken heart than a sort of half-world, a devastated, abandoned landscape where anyone might end up at any time, so long as that time is now'. To obtain exactly this effect, Lanois 'treated the voice almost like a harmonica when you overdrive it through a small guitar amplifier'. As Dylan told *Newsweek*, 'it is a spooky record, because I feel spooky. I don't feel in tune with anything',

A few professional grouches have since revalued the album downwards. For Michael Gray, it was 'riddled with lazy writing and sludgy music bordering on the kind of nightclub jazz that many of us had looked to Bob Dylan to vanquish'. However, a musician as astute as Elvis Costello, son of a dance-band singer, declared 'it might be the best thing he's ever done'. Writing in *Mojo*, Costello preferred the sound to the more effete *Oh Mercy*. In concert, Dylan's voice can now be a little too abrasive – look who's talking – but here the discreet production tricks highlight his mastery of phrasing: 'you're not listening to sweet-voiced singing, you're listening to get the feeling he's singing about'. Elvis, another man recording under a pseudonym, traces all the roots of this album back to the Harry Smith Anthology. Music history transcends geography. 'I mean, what's Bob Zimmerman doing living in Duluth? That's in itself a story, he had to get there from somewhere. That's folk music explained.'

On the cover Dylan plays acoustic guitar, surrounded by recording equipment in a slightly blurred photograph that looks as if taken in a space capsule. In one inside shot, he sits cradling a cane while two old men behind him look bemused. The back cover photo has a fresh-faced Dylan, certainly not a man who looks as if he has just had a close shave with mortality. But the cleverest touch is the disc itself, a reproduction of the 'Viva-tonal' Columbia label from the 20s, when the defiantly retro music would feel right at home.

Love Sick (Dylan) 5.21

What sounds like the rustlings of a ghost, then we're straight into an aural soup of unease. Dylan sounds like something from beyond the grave, wearily traversing the streets 'that are dead', missing his woman. But she infects his heart and his brain. Farfisa chords stab like a heart monitor, alongside soft electric piano and the ghost of pedal steel. Its like slowed down psychedelia, or 'I Put A Spell On You' played in a madhouse. Bob's voice is like 'choking phlegm', the beat claustrophobic, as he sings about betrayal – 'did I hear someone tell a lie' – and time passing. The pace is funereal, and gives you the chills.

On the closing line about wanting 'to be with you' his voice cracks, and the instruments play some kind of closing benediction. Or maybe it is the moment of release from this mortal coil, the rest of the album is a dying man looking back over the events of his life. It's that kind of record, as far from pop culture as you can possibly get.

As Marianne Faithfull points out, 'being love sick and sick of love are two entirely different things. And yet obviously the same to an old romantic like Mr D'. Someone else could make this sound sappy, but the way Dylan sings, 'very intense and strong and not at all detached – it's a statement, and a great one, about love'.

Dirt Road Blues (Dylan) 3.36
Like so many of the songs here, this is based on a grab bag of phrases from songs laid down on shellac years before Dylan was born, then given a personal twist. Charley Patton recorded 'Down the Dirt Road Blues' in 1929, and Arthur Crudup 'Dirt Road Blues' in 1945. But musically this is pure rock'n'roll, even if one expert described it as 'rockabilly at the end of a tunnel'. And another as sounding like a chance meeting between Carl Perkins and deep Mississippi blues, or just as if 'Charley Patton had lived long enough to make it to Sun studios in the 50s'.

Dylan plays Elvis to Duke Robbilard's Scotty Moore, plus slap bass and clickety-clack drums. But the thrilling music, like 'Highway 61 Revisited' with a dirty face, masks lyrics about a man ill at ease, under a shadow of his own making and putting up barriers 'to keep myself from everyone'.

Ironically, it was something in the Mississippi fog that Bob contracted when out cycling. Histoplasmosis, a swelling of the heart, almost made this album his last. It was eventually cured by a voodoo priest in Louisiana allegedly.

Standing In The Doorway (Dylan) 7.44
We're back to slow introspection, a slow country shuffle with solemn organ and guitar filigrees, not a million miles away from 'Sad Eyed Lady', but grown weary. Dylan stands alone, listening to the bells tolling and telling his confession, 'blues wrapped around my head'. A song that sounds so wretchedly personal is built on other men's bones. William Harris's 1928 song 'Bullfrog Blues' contains the line 'I left you standin' here in your back door crying'. Dock Boggs' 'Danville Girl' has the line 'smoking a cheap cigar', and 'let me drink when I'm hungry/let me drink when I'm dry' and is recycled from 'Moonshiner Blues', recorded by Bob when he was a young man. Now he sounds impossibly old.

No blues singer ever came up with a phrase like 'even if the flesh falls off of my face'. And there's a smirk on the face of the sphinx – a Gay guitar is not what you think, but a flashy guitar brand favoured by country singers in the 50s. Buddy here is either the one who might spare a dime, or Buddy Holly: the man who Dylan felt passed a musical torch to him when he saw his last ever show, and whose spirit Bob later told the Grammy awards ceremony he felt looking down on him during these sessions.

Dylan passes the torch on to a younger generation, as did Holly. Singer Jonathan Rice finds that 'at the heart of his writing there's just this constant, impenetrable loneliness. Someone has to do that so that the rest of us can be happy'.

Million Miles (Dylan) 5.52
A 'steamy blues shuffle', this has the same apocalyptic sense of betrayal as 'This Wheel's On Fire', slowed down to a funeral march. But it still swings and Dylan has vengeance in his voice. The evil cousin of 'One Too Many Mornings'. The reference to 'that's alright mama', another song Bob once covered in a spirit of joyful youth, brings to mind the primal growl of Arthur 'Big Boy' Crudup and Elvis's first Sun single. Maybe *Time Out Of Mind* is Dylan's equivalent of the great modernist poem The Waste Land, contemporary despair evoked through a mess of images and echoes. But even T. S. Eliot's voice never rasped quite like this. Even William Burroughs didn't sound so catatonically dry. It's the voice of a serial killer.

Tryin' To Get To Heaven (Dylan) 5.22
The band ups the pace, from funereal to dead slow, and Dylan seems to perk up a bit, even if just to deliver an 'unashamed admission of mortality', to a tune that could break your heart. Dylan is no longer knocking on heaven's door; it's not even in sight here.

The life here is drained, vampire-like, from a whole slew of blues song, its title probably taken from the American folk song 'The Old Ark's A-Moverin'': 'look at that sister comin' long slow/she's trying to get to heaven fo' they close the do''. This is 'Blind Willie McTell' with a hangover, a picture of the old south, 'riding in a buggy with Miss Mary-Jane' and shaking the sugar down.

There is an extraordinary harmonica break, like the best of Dylan, where it carries on the sense of the lyrics into a place where language no longer works.

'Til I Fell In Love With You (Dylan) 5.18
More vintage r&b, with Dylan's voice echoing loneliness like his late friend Roy Orbison without the falsetto, and the band recorded almost subliminally, so that instruments appear

and disappear in the aural mist. Dylan's lyrical concision is at its best here, clipped and poetic, not a word wasted, using rhyme as a springboard. 'Well my house is on fire, burning to the sky/I thought it would rain but the clouds passed by'.

Not Dark Yet (Dylan) 6.29
This song is at the emotional heart of the album, a man railing against the mutability of life, just like his namesake in 'rage, rage against the dying of the light'. It also echoes Slim Crithchlow's 'Girl From The Red River Shore', collected by the Lomaxes: 'she wrote me a letter and she wrote it so kind'. Dylan Thomas never recited over a backing as luminously beautiful as this, a rich blend of organ and heavenly guitar and muffled drums.

As Nigel Williamson puts it, even 'Jackson Browne has never chronicled the disintegration of a relationship with quite such harrowing frankness'. And let's face it, such delight at his own misery too, the way that a broken love affair leaves us feeling, oddly, like lords and ladies of our own universe. But it is about far more than that, about being trapped in the one body and lifetime we are given: 'I was born here and I'll die here against my will'. Emmylou Harris considers it the greatest song ever written about growing old. 'For those of us entering that door, it brings up things we didn't know we were capable of feeling. He put the poetry into that experience.'

Cold Irons Bound (Dylan) 7.16
This echoes the Irish ballad 'The Constant Farmer's Wife': 'bound down by strong irons, their sins to prevail'. But he is not going down easy. Drums clatter, and Dylan snarls like a cornered alley cat in a vocal performance that won him a Grammy for Best Male Rock Vocal Performance.

As Howard Devoto puts it, Lanois's production 'showcases the grain of Dylan's voice better than any other album. The voice way up front, the instrumentation stripped back and way down in the mix'. The reference to the 'winds in Chicago' highlights the musical debt here to the kind of clattering electric blues he shocked Newport with back in 1965.

Make You Feel My Love (Dylan) 3.33
That last song at least offered a memory of joy, and Bob gets almost sentimental, singing from a higher register of his voice – though still through a sandpaper throat – and the backing is

based on that old familiar organ'n'piano blend. Still set at dead slow. Dylan implores, the music sounds almost churchy at the end, but maybe this is only the eye of storm.

Can't Wait (Dylan) 5.47
Here 'the air burns'. Dylan sounds like Howlin' Wolf, his head 'caught in a trap', though as Paul Williams points out, he also sounds like a 'sly dog'. The music is more sprightly, and Dylan has a hint of threat in his voice, buoyed up by the slowed-down blues beat, swamp rock with teeth. What Nick Johnstone described as 'big, echoey chambers, swampy, haunting loping drums, the lonesome guitars and Dylan's voice, old, gnarled, corroded'.

If the Johnny Cash of *Nashville Skyline* appealed to Dylan with his homey side, this is a homage to the darker shadows of the man in black, who 'walked the line' because he knew all too well where he walked to when he strayed.

Live in concert, the song intensified its air of sardonic anger, not that far away in tone from some of the more extreme born-again material. A line like 'the lonely graveyard of my mind' is pure *Blonde On Blonde*, slowed down and with a switchblade, and the gate he stands beside here, 'breathing hard', could well be that one he stood outside back then, waiting for 'Absolutely Sweet Marie'.

Highlands (Dylan) 16.32
Dylan says the riff comes from a Charley Patton song. The lyrics certainly take off from Robert Burns' poem 'My heart's In the Highlands, my heart is not here/my heart's in the Highlands, a chasing the deer'. And it starts with pure blues guitar, then the band lope in, one by one. Dylan's voice suddenly sounds wistful, and he takes us on a long and deliberately inconsequential shaggy dog story, much like 'Brownsville Girl', or one of Neil Young's more impressionistic pieces. That's Young whose music he is forced to turn down. And there is a sudden reference to Erica Jong too, whose 1990 short story 'Any Woman's Blues' has its heroine looking at a canvas 'I painted to his design (he had scribbled a rough sketch on a napkin)'. Many think that the line 'the party's over' is about the 60s. Certainly Dylan sounds mildly happy here just to be keeping going, dreaming of the Highlands, or heaven, or whatever, and 'that's good enough for now'. As Greil Marcus puts it, the songs here 'are like watching people pass through revolving doors. You have as much right to expect someone to reappear as quickly as she vanished as to expect never to see her again'. The waitress turns her back, and suddenly 'the air is now so mean

you're as relieved as the singer when he slips out of his chair'. But the Monty Python atmosphere of this song says otherwise, ending this album of deathly songs. As Bob said in 1963, 'what made the real blues singers so great is that they were able to state all the problems they had, but at the same time they were standing outside themselves. And in that way, they had them beat'.

OUTTAKES:
'Mississippi', held over to *Love and Theft*
'Girl From The Red River Shore'
'No Turning Back'
Other reputed outtakes include a 27-minute 'Highlands' and a 'stunning' 'Not Dark Yet'.

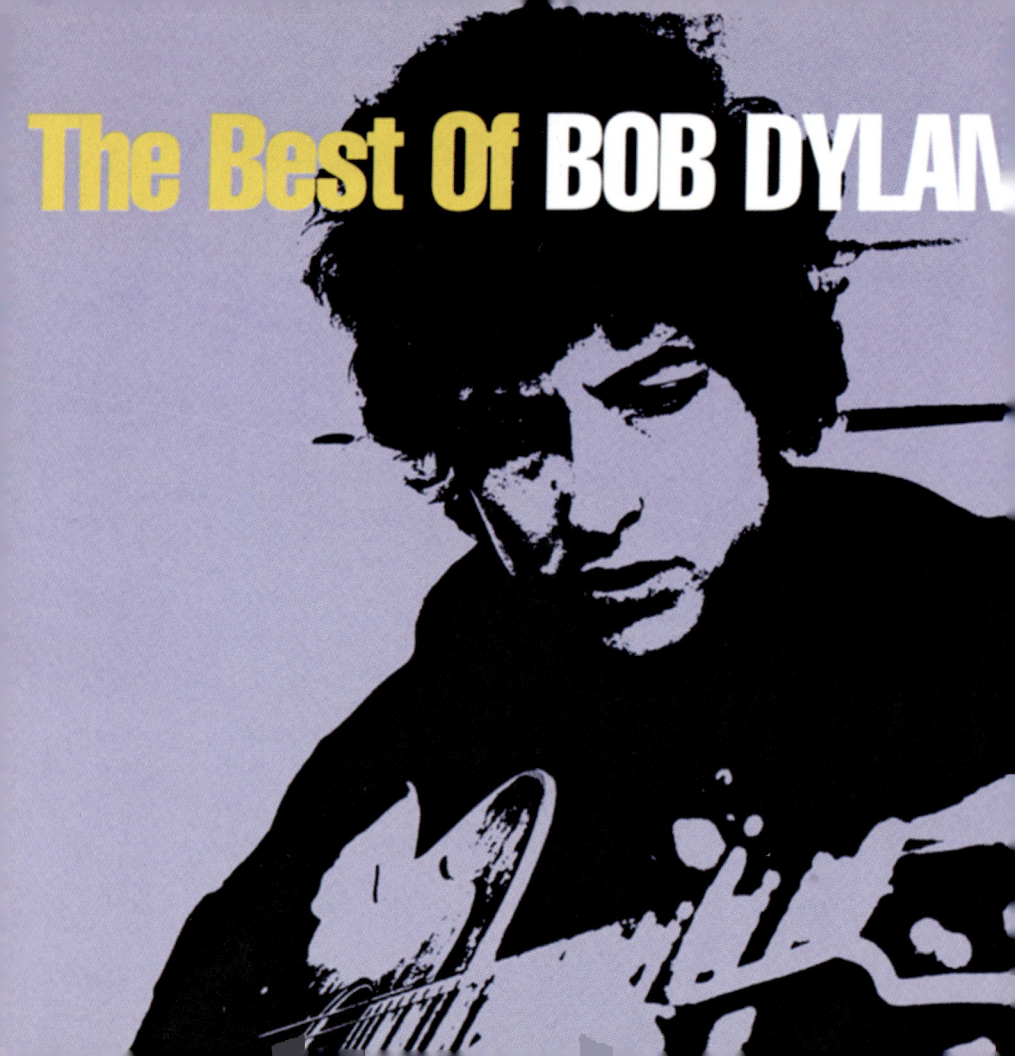

The Best Of BOB DYLAN

THE BEST OF BOB DYLAN

UK Release: 1997 (UK only)   **CD Release:** Sony TV 28CD
Running Time: 76.21

Blowin' In The Wind; The Times, They Are A-Changin'; Don't Think Twice, Its Alright; Mr Tambourine Man; Like a Rolling Stone; Just Like A Woman; All Along The Watchtower; Lay, Lady, Lay; I Shall Be Released; If Not For You; Knockin' On Heaven's Door; Forever Young; Tangled Up In Blue; Oh Sister; Gotta Serve Somebody; Jokerman; Everything Is Broken; Shelter From The Storm

Michael Gray found this an unnecessary compilation, one dictated by the company's TV ad department that cuts across his back catalogue, and adds nothing to it. Worst of all, in his view, are the claims of digital remastering and Super Bit Mapping. On the earlier, acoustic material, this gives an 'alarmingly poor idea of how those originally sounded', and this provokes disquiet at its silent rewriting of audio history.

There is one previously unreleased track, a rough-and-ready outtake of 'Shelter From The Storm', from the New York sessions for *Blood on the Tracks*. The cover utilizes archive photographs, one of them superimposed over Dylan's original typescript for 'Subterranean Homesick Blues'.

Blowin' In The Wind (Dylan) 2.48 from *Freewheelin'*.
The Times, They Are A-Changin' (Dylan) 3.15 from *The Times They Are A-Changin'*.
Don't Think Twice, Its Alright (Dylan) 3.40 from *Freewheelin'*.
Mr Tambourine Man (Dylan) 5.29 from *Bringing It All Back Home*.
Like a Rolling Stone (Dylan) 6.11 from *Highway 61 Revisited*.
Just Like A Woman (Dylan) 4.56 from *Blonde On Blonde*.
All Along The Watchtower (Dylan) 2.34 from *John Wesley Harding*.
Lay, Lady, Lay (Dylan) 3.21 from *Nashville Skyline*.
I Shall Be Released (Dylan) 3.05 from *Greatest Hits Vol 2*.
If Not For You (Dylan) 2.44 from *New Morning*.

Knockin' On Heaven's Door (Dylan) 2.32 from *Pat Garrett and Billy The Kid*.
Forever Young (Dylan) 4.58 from *Planet Waves*.
Tangled Up In Blue (Dylan) 5.44 from *Blood on the Tracks*.
Oh Sister (Dylan) 4.02 from *Desire*.
Gotta Serve Somebody (Dylan) 5.26 from *Slow Train Coming*.
Jokerman (Dylan) 6.17 from *Infidels*.
Everything Is Broken (Dylan) 3.16 from *Oh Mercy*.
Shelter From The Storm (Dylan) 6.00 outtake from *Blood on the Tracks*.

All aurally enhanced by Super Bit Mapping
'Shelter From The Storm' is an outtake that first surfaced on the soundtrack to *Jerry Maguire*, and here appears on an official release for the first and so far, the only time.

BOB DYLAN LIVE 1966: THE BOOTLEG SERIES VOL 4, THE 'ROYAL ALBERT HALL' CONCERT

CD Release: 13 October 1998
Also issued on vinyl as a limited edition 2LP set on heavyweight vinyl, with a 12 inch booklet, in conjunction with Classic Records,
UK Release:
Producer: concert recording by Mr M Claydon, electric concert mixed by Michael H. Brauer, Steve Berkovitz, produced by Jeff Rosen

Columbia Legacy C2K 65759 2-CD

Columbia C2K 65759 –1
Columbia Legacy COL 491485 2

Running Time: (48.17) (47.05)

CD 1: She Belongs To Me; Fourth Time Around; Visions Of Johanna; It's All Over Now, Baby Blue; Desolation Row; Just Like A Woman; Mr Tambourine Man.

CD 2: Tell Me, Mama; I Don't Believe You (She Acts Like We Never Have Met); Baby, Let Me Follow You Down; Just Like Tom Thumb's Blues; Leopard-Skin Pill-Box Hat; One Too Many Mornings; Ballad Of A Thin Man; Like A Rolling Stone.

Bob Dylan: vocals, guitar, harmonica, piano on 'Ballad Of A Thin Man', **Rick Danko:** bass, background vocal on 'One Too Many Mornings', **Garth Hudson:** organ, **Mickey Jones:** drums, **Richard Manuel:** piano, **Robbie Robertson:** guitar

When the most legendary bootleg double album of all time finally saw the official light of day, Andy Kershaw spoke for everyone when he declared 'I still can't believe they've finally put it out. I just keep staring at my copy'. The concert held at Free Trade Hall, Manchester on 17 May

1966, a wholly acoustic first half, and a second half with the Hawks, finally has the full Legacy treatment, with vastly improved sound and a separate booklet with all the right vintage photographs, and an insightful article by Dylan's old friend Tony Glover. Bouquets all round.

It was thought for years that this was from one of Dylan's final two 1966 tour dates (as it proved, due to a skidding motorbike) at the Royal Albert Hall in London, with the Beatles and the rest of rock royalty watching and Dylan denying that any of his songs might have anything to do with drugs, or the like. But the unofficial Dylan industry went to work, and found that this was in fact the Royal Albert Hall, Manchester, aka the Free Trade Hall, now closed and shuttered. But no-one who had been there could mistake where that fateful shout of 'Judas' had come from and, in what still seems little short of miraculous, the majestic Martin Scorsese TV documentary actually shows footage of the event in question. Andy Kershaw outted the culprit in a fascinating BBC radio documentary, revised and rebroadcast in September 2005, to tie in with the first showing of *No Direction Home*.

Not so well known is the strange history of how this concert finally got released. As *Record Collector* explained, some Bobcats allege that Jeff Rosen and his team have in some way perverted the sound of this hallowed tape. When Sony first announced the project in 1995, then temporarily abandoned it, the projected discs soon surfaced on the bootleg market as *Guitars Kissing And The Contemporary Fix*, with various glitches edited out. This was again worked on, levelling out the sound levels on the mono first disc, editing out a break during 'Mr Tambourine Man', and adding the brief snatch of the National Anthem at the end. The whole concert has been sonically repositioned and Dylan's voice tweaked, in particular his between-songs comments. 'The new release adds another dimension and captures the slightly distorted, almost grunge-like rasp of an over-stretched amplification system in a vast hall'.

Columbia admit that the Nagra tapes, taken straight from the PA, ran out during the two longest songs, 'Desolation Row' and 'Visions of Johanna' and that the omissions had to be patched in from a different source. You can only really hear this on headphones. The acoustic disc runs slightly faster than bootleg copies by around two per cent. The meticulous Pete Doggett tested this against his piano and his ears, and considers the bootleg version is truer to real life. But the the full dramatic pause between 'Ballad of a Thin Man' and 'Like A Rolling Stone' is presented on disc for the first time. The electric half comes from a three-track tape recorded by separate microphones in front of the stage by London company IBC, who recorded four of these cataclysmic concerts for a possible live album. Three to go, then.

The Bootleg Series Vol. 4
BOB DYLAN LIVE 1966

The "Royal Albert Hall" Concert

As to the performances on the night, Doggett finds the acoustic set tame in comparison to others on the tour, in particular the cathedral harmonica sound of Melbourne, 'on which Dylan sounds so stoned that it's remarkable he's still alive'. Here, 'Mr Tambourine Man' doesn't 'spiral into the decadent madness' that it did even on other UK gigs. As to the electric half, this is simply 'the greatest rock concert of all time'.

The best way into the performances is via soundscapes from Dylan's own mind at this time, beyond logic or humanity. He told a Beverly Hills press conference 'They can't hurt me. Sure they can crush you and kill you. They can lay you out on 42nd and Broadway and put the hoses on you and flush you in the sewers and put you on the subway and carry you out to Coney Island and bury you out on the Ferris Wheel. But I refuse to sit here and worry about dying'.

As he said to *Rolling Stone* in 1969, 'I was on the road for almost five years. It wore me down, I was on drugs. A lot of things just to keep you going. My songs were long, long songs. That's why I had to start dealing with a lot of different methods of keeping myself awake, alert'. And as he commented in *Biograph*, 'back then, the sound systems were not sophisticated like they are today. We used to carry our own sound truck just to boost up the sound in those halls. There were hardly any monitors at all. You could never really hear yourself. I thought we did rather well with the equipment we had to use. We were in territory that nobody has ever been in before'.

As well as the excellent essay here that starts off with the riots at the premiere of Stravinsky's *Rite Of Spring*, there is a full account of this wild night in C. P. Lee's excellent book *Like The Night, Bob Dylan and the Road to Manchester Free Trade Hall* (1998), written by an eye witness. He précised it for *Uncut*. 'My prevailing memory of that night is fear. Nothing had prepared me for the noise, the animosity of that night. It was directly confrontational, in your face. I did really think at the time that I'd just seen something totally historic'. There were lots of very angry people in the crowd that night. But the first half reassured the folkies that he had not abandoned them. And then they switched on the amps, the music went into overdrive, the booing started, 'and then the confrontation occurred'.

I remember talking to the visionary poet Barry McSweeney shortly before he drank himself to death, a man who named a poetry press after the bootlaces Dylan was wearing that night, and he recalled turning round at the Newcastle gig and headbutting the man behind him who had been booing the electric set. It was that kind of tour, as passionate in some ways, although fought for ultimately lower stakes than the civil rights struggle, that Dylan was seen by some to have abandoned and betrayed with his new drug music. But this was seeking a new way of freedom, too, not between the races but in the space of one's own skull.

As to the rest of the CD package, the front cover is by Jerry Schatzberg of Dylan looking inscrutable. The booklet boasts a wonderful range of shots by a whole slew of lensmen including Barry Feinstein and Don Hunstein from the 1966 tour – plus the Newport Folk Festival fracas with Dylan in his polka dot shirt. There is an outtake from the session for the first album cover, the right way round at last, and a poignant monochrome shot with Pete Seeger. The man who poses with grubby street urchins from behind dark shades is living in a different cosmos.

CD 1
She Belongs To Me (Dylan) 3.27
Polite applause, then Dylan sings with yearning in his voice, but sounding about a million miles away from the audience. His vocal is slightly echoey, with careful acoustic guitar, and he drags the odd word out, oddly. It is the harmonica that is truly extraordinary, dancing around the beat and virtuoso in its range, but somehow lost and lonely. The applause is more emphatic at the end.

Fourth Time Around (Dylan) 4.37
A long harmonica intro, then Dylan sings with quiet venom. He emphasizes every last syllable that makes it all the nastier. Like a gangster laying out slowly and formally exactly what he intends to do to you.

Visions Of Johanna (Dylan) 8.09
How could anyone boo when they had earlier heard this, maybe the greatest acoustic delight they would ever experience in live concert for the rest of their tiny lives. Bob told *Biograph* that 'I still sing that song every once in a while. It still stands up now as it did then, maybe more in some kind of weird way'. Here, stripped of Nashville's finest, and moaning like a whipped hound, it is a naked thing indeed.

It's All Over Now, Baby Blue (Dylan) 4.46
Dylan retunes, then into this, a more urgent affair, still to a stunned silence with not a boo to be heard. Rarely can the human voice have sounded so romantically vulnerable, delivering laureate-level poetry to the masses with not a hint of condescending to them. But beamed down from another planet. And his harmonica breaks sound like the wind blowing across an Arctic plain.

Desolation Row (Dylan) 11.32
Well they certainly know this one, and Dylan gives them it to them slow and sinister, after coughing briefly. He sings softly, and misses not a word. Then he see-saws his harmonica break just before the last verse, almost making you feel sea sick, and his voice comes back suddenly angry. The applause at the end is prolonged, broken by Dylan starting the intro to the next song, without a word.

Just Like A Woman (Dylan) 5.53
Still it goes on. This is sung in a kind of holy quiet, with Dylan a priest of the imagination. Just listen to the way he intones 'aches', then goes into the passage about dying of thirst, sounding so wounded, so much in pain. In a tiny but significant change, the estranged couple are now introduced 'by' not 'as' friends. And the harmonica break at the end is spectacular, improvising off the melody line like a maestro.

Mr Tambourine Man (Dylan) 8.52
More prolonged applause, still not a word of acknowledgment, then into the final mono delight of this CD, again sung wistfully and in full voice, with his guitar jingle-jangling. Bob coughs a couple of times, almost trips over his words at one point, but otherwise sounds immortal. Once again he breaks the words with harmonica arabesques, leading into what sounds like a lonesome train whistle as he bids his folk audience farewell. They clap as if forever, and the record fades.

CD 2
Tell Me, Mama (Dylan) 5.10

Then this! Jon Spencer of the Blues Explosion reckons that this is 'raw, it's down and dirty rock'n'roll. Hell, its punk rock, man'. Steve Jackson in *Uncut* reckons 'even the way the record starts, you can hear the audience chatting, you can even hear the footsteps of the musicians on the wooden boards, and Dylan's Cuban heels shuffling about. It's very, very quiet and sedate. Garth Hudson's just getting warmed up, playing wee organ bits, Dylan starts strumming the intro and then the drummer just counts in and there's this incredible explosion'.

It was described elsewhere as if someone tipped a whole canteen of cutlery onto the stage. The Hawks with their stand in, brutal drummer, bring out every ounce of malevolence and joy in their singer's voice. They sound like the hardened pros they already were, but even Ronnie Hawkins never howled like this.

This is a song he never got round to recording, even as an outtake, and you really need the transcript in *Lyrics* to understand what exactly he is singing about. Not that it makes any sense even then, all 'grave-yard whips' and 'we bone the editor'. Certainly the line about 'something is tearing up your mind' cuts through the air here, and is like a red rag to some of the bullheads in the audience. Although there is also warm applause. Jackson worries that this version would lose the bootleg's clarity of sound, 'but in many ways it has enhanced it'.

I Don't Believe You (She Acts Like We Never Have Met) (Dylan) 6.07

A few solo harmonica toots, then Dylan says, his voice dripping with sarcasm, 'It used to be like that, and now it goes like this'. Nervous laughter from some of the crowd, then into this portrait of the morning after. After the end of the world perhaps, in this rendition. Dylan's piercing harmonica goes well with the fairground organ and precise, pointed lead guitar. Bob drags out the words, like a contortionist, and still manages to accentuate every syllable, like that acoustic troubadour from before the break, who is still here on stage, if you just switched off the band.

The Hawks cascade music down on the heads of the crowd, to match, full of confidence and with not an ounce of compassion. Jungle drums at the end.

Baby, Let Me Follow You Down (Dylan) 3.46

Another bout of tuning up, and the first sound of trouble from the crowd. Dylan breaks his harmonica intro as a slow handclap starts up, then resumes without a word although you can just picture his face. Then Danko thunders in on bass, and any audience noise is obliterated. Dylan howls, Robertson wails and Hudson is the madman at the organ, running up and down the keyboard. Manuel's brief keyboard break is like a sudden shaft of sanity, then the whole band pile back in, and Bob is out there at the front of his gang, his fists metaphorically raised. Cheers of delight from the enlightened half of the audience.

Just Like Tom Thumb's Blues (Dylan) 6.50

Still it comes. A bone-crunching intro and Dylan's voice is sharp enough to cut your ears. Much like that scene in Bergman's *Hour of the Wolf* when the monochrome images could slit an unwary eyeball. But this Bosch-like vision is in glowing stereo with every instrument picked out, in a way that somehow eluded the hugely superior studio technology of the 80s. You can still taste the sweat and smell the fear, almost. Robbie accentuates the riff at the end, and the band thunders to a close.

More applause, then shouts and more slow handclaps, but Dylan is insistent on reading out the title of the next song very slowly then someone shouts something inaudible and the crowd grow nastier. Truly frightening, like the prelude to a lynching. Then someone counts the next song in.

Leopard-Skin Pill-Box Hat (Dylan) 4.50

Dylan sounds surprisingly chirpy, feeding off the bad vibes. The Hawks make the music dance, with Robertson's ego-less lead guitar, not a note wasted, and Mickey Jones the secret weapon here, pounding those bass drums like a demon. Then Robbie comes back, wailing.

One Too Many Mornings (Dylan) 4.23

More tuning up to cool down the crowd, but the shouts start again, rise to a crest and Robertson seems to be playing along. Dylan mumbles nonsense, the crowd quieten to hear what he is saying and he utters the immortal words 'if you only just wouldn't clap so hard'. Cheering from some, this is like the bloodiest possible United/City derby. Manchester is used to civic unrest, from the Peterloo Massacre onwards. But what Dylan is offering them is this regretful, almost melancholic outburst of musical feeling, with wonderful tinkling from Manuel, and those trademark Band vocal harmonies, already in place here. Not that anyone notices at the time. The 'restless, hungry feeling' is encoded in the backing music now, as well as Dylan's voice, and the way he almost shouts 'you're right from your side and I'm right from mine' couldn't be better judged in the circumstances.

Ballad Of A Thin Man (Dylan) 7.55
More audience unrest, with the band not exactly quick to start another number, and Dylan mute, then Robertson leads into the luminous guitar intro to this stately reading. Hudson plays a blinder on organ and Bob howls another kiss-off song that again seems perfectly targeted tonight. Except that there are lots of Mr Jones out there, one possibly with a knife. Or something even more wounding.

Like A Rolling Stone (Dylan) 8.02
Fumblings at the microphone, something not quite audible from the crowd, then the clearly heard and notorious shout of 'Judas'. Dylan replies in total shock 'I don't believe you, you're a liar', then either 'a f-cking liar' to him, or 'play f-cking loud', to his band. Either applies. And they come in like Armageddon, with the most stunning, passionate music imaginable, driven again by those thunderous bass drums. Their employer suddenly sounds liberated, as if nothing worse could now happen, like a first-world-war captain leading his troops over the top into the concentrated gunfire of the enemy and somehow surviving to fight another day. Eight minutes of careful venom, sung almost lovingly, shredding even the 45 rpm version, with the six men on stage in total musical harmony. Robertson makes that syncopated five note riff into a symphony and carries the song away at the end with clipped precision.

    A final 'thank yooooou' from Bob, mixed boos and cheers with no-one calling for an encore, then the sounds of silence apart from a buzz of chatter and departing boot-heels and the sudden shock intrusion of 'God Save The Queen' adds a final, surreal touch. Manchester would not see anything like this again.

THE BEST OF BOB DYLAN VOL 2

US Release: 8 May 2000 (CD only)   **CD Release:** COL 498361 9
Running Time: (77.24) (18.30)

Things Have Changed; A Hard Rain's A-Gonna Fall; It Ain't Me Babe; Subterranean Homesick Blues; Positively 4th Street; Highway 61 Revisited; Rainy Day Women # 12 & 35; I Want You; I'll Be Your Baby Tonight; Quinn The Eskimo (The Mighty Quinn); Simple Twist Of Fate; Hurricane; Changing Of The Guards; License To Kill; Silvio; Dignity; Not Dark Yet

A digitally remastered affair, fresh as a new coat of paint, with an interesting choice of tracks, including something brand new, and a bonus disc with two stunning live performances. The CD package features vintage photographs by Ken Regan and David Gahr, one of which is superimposed over what looks like the manuscript of *Tarantula*.

Things Have Changed (Dylan) 5.08 from the *Wonder Boys* soundtrack. The best thing here comes first. Dylan won an Academy Award for this song, and he actually turned up to thank them for being brave enough to honour a song that 'doesn't pussyfoot around or turn a blind eye to human nature'. It was the first thing he wrote after his serious illness and it is both light-hearted and savage. 'People are crazy and times are strange…I used to care but times have changed'.

Mojo reckoned it a 'decidedly wry shrug of ambivalence from the edge of old age, informed by Dylan's brutally dry humour and a fleeting mood of teenage abandon'. He considers various ways to pass the time, which includes taking dancing lessons, dressing in drag and steering a female stranger around in a wheelbarrow. It contains the telling line 'I've been trying to get as far away from myself as I can'. The song played over the closing titles of *Wonder Boys*, starring Michael Douglas. It was the first time Dylan had written something specifically for a movie since *Pat Garrett*.

A Hard Rain's A-Gonna Fall (Dylan) 6.52 from *Freewheelin'*.
It Ain't Me Babe (Dylan) 3.38 from *Another Sideof Bob Dylan*.

The Best Of BOB DYLAN
volume 2

Subterranean Homesick Blues (Dylan) 2.22 from *Bringing It All Back Home*.
Positively 4th Street (Dylan) 4.08 single release.
Highway 61 Revisited (Dylan) 3.15 from *Highway 61 Revisited*.
Rainy Day Women # 12 & 35 (Dylan) 4.33 from *Blonde On Blonde*.
I Want You (Dylan) 3.06 from *Blonde On Blonde*.
I'll Be Your Baby Tonight (Dylan) 2.42 from *John Wesley Harding*.
Quinn The Eskimo (The Mighty Quinn) (Dylan) 2.47 from *Greatest Hits Vol 2*.
Simple Twist Of Fate (Dylan) 4.18 from *Blood on the Tracks*.
Hurricane (Dylan) 8.33 from *Desire*.
Changing Of The Guards (Dylan) 7.03 from *Street Legal*.
License To Kill (Dylan) 3.31 from *Infidels*.
Silvio (Dylan/Robert Hunter) 3.05 from *Down In The Groove*, remix from *Greatest Hits Vol 3*
Dignity (Dylan) 5.35 outtake from *Oh Mercy*, mercifully remastered, with the disco drums from an earlier compilation gone into the dumper. This version sparkles.
Not Dark Yet (Dylan) 6.27 from *Time Out Of Mind*.

CD 2 Special Limited Edition
Highlands (Live Version) (Dylan) 11.18
Recorded live at Santa Cruz on 16 March 2000. Recorded with his tour band, with Dylan sounding like one of the muppets, a generally boxy feel and over-loud whoops from the audience that suggests this is not from the mixer tape. Maybe Dylan has begun to do what Van Morrison did to pad out some of his CD singles and is bootlegging the bootleggers. There's some nice mandolin and the version sounds sadder and more urgent than the studio take. The lonesome way he sings the line 'I've got new eyes, everything seems so far away' is heartbreaking. But those whoops make it a difficult listen, particularly on headphones.

Blowin' In The Wind (Live Version) 7.10
Recorded live at Santa Cruz, again on 16 March 2000
More in-your-face audience reaction as Bob plunders his back pages for this softly sung and largely unplugged rendition, with some nice vocal harmonies. It could almost be a lost *Basement Tape* version with onlookers.

THE ESSENTIAL BOB DYLAN

US Release: 31 October 2000
UK/Europe: 21 May 2001 Sony Music TV
STVCD 116 2CD set, 36 tracks

Columbia C2K 85168 2 CD set, 30 tracks

Running Time: (77.32) (77.38)

CD 1: Blowin' In The Wind; Don't Think Twice It's Alright; The Times They Are A-Changin'; It Ain't Me Babe; Maggie's Farm; It's All Over Now, Baby Blue; Mr Tambourine Man; Subterranean Homesick Blues; Like A Rolling Stone; Positively 4th Street; Can You Please Crawl Out Your Window?, I Want You; Just Like A Woman; Rainy Day Women #12 & 35; All Along The Watchtower; Quinn The Eskimo (The Mighty Quinn) ; I'll Be Your Baby Tonight; Lay, Lady, Lay; If Not For You; I Shall Be Released; You Ain't Going Nowhere; Knockin' On Heaven's Door

CD 2: Forever Young; Tangled Up In Blue; Shelter From The Storm; Hurricane; Changing Of The Guards; Gotta Serve Somebody; Blind Willie McTell; Jokerman;
Tight Connection To My Heart (Has Anybody Seen My Love) ; Silvio; Everything Is Broken; Dignity; Not Dark Yet; Things Have Changed

The most comprehensive greatest hits compilation currently in the marketplace. Supposedly available only for a limited period. The *Independent* reckoned it was a 'sprawling 36-track odyssey whose range and depth simply beggars belief'. As to the stand-out track, well 'virtually all of them'. The two great discoveries of the last compilation to come along, a mere five months before, are here too. The 'Dignity' outtake is the welcome remix, while 'Things Have Changed' has moved from start to finish and still sounds wonderful.

There is a short essay by Patrick Humphries, stressing how Dylan spans from then to now: 'Dylan straddles these times effortlessly, times he single-handedly changed'. The cover is from a contemporary photograph by David Gahr, plus the near-instant reprise by a shot taken by Ken Regan also used in *The Best of…Volume 2*. Far more spectacular are two colour images from 1966 by Jerry Schatzberg and Daniel Kramer.

CD 1
Blowin' In The Wind (Dylan) from *Freewheelin'*.
Don't Think Twice, Its Alright (Dylan) from *Freewheelin'*.
The Times They Are A-Changin' (Dylan) from *The Times They Are A-Changin'*.
It Ain't Me Babe (Dylan) from *Another Side of Bob Dylan*.
Maggie's Farm (Dylan) from *Bringing It All Back Home*.
It's All Over Now, Baby Blue (Dylan)) from *Bringing It All Back Home*.
Mr Tambourine Man (Dylan)) from *Bringing It All Back Home*.
Subterranean Homesick Blues (Dylan)) from *Bringing It All Back Home*.
Like A Rolling Stone (Dylan) from *Highway 61 Revisited*.
Positively 4th Street (Dylan) single release.
Can You Please Crawl Out Your Window? (Dylan) single release.
I Want You (Dylan) from *Blonde On Blonde*.
Just Like A Woman (Dylan) from *Blonde On Blonde*.
Rainy Day Women #12 & 35 (Dylan) from *Blonde On Blonde*.
All Along The Watchtower (Dylan) from *John Wesley Harding*.
Quinn The Eskimo (The Mighty Quinn) (Dylan) original *Basement Tape* version, from *Biograph*.
I'll Be Your Baby Tonight (Dylan) from *John Wesley Harding*.
Lay, Lady, Lay (Dylan) from *Nashville Skyline*.
If Not For You (Dylan) from *New Morning*.
I Shall Be Released (Dylan) from *Greatest Hits Vol II*.
You Ain't Going Nowhere (Dylan) from *Greatest Hits Vol II*.
Knockin' On Heaven's Door (Dylan) from *Pat Garrett and Billy The Kid*.

The Essential BOB DYLAN

CD 2
Forever Young (Dylan) from *Planet Waves*.
Tangled Up In Blue (Dylan) from *Blood on the Tracks*.
Shelter From The Storm (Dylan) from *Blood on the Tracks*.
Hurricane (Dylan/Levy) from *Desire*.
Changing Of The Guards (Dylan) from *Street Legal*.
Gotta Serve Somebody (Dylan) from *Slow Train Coming*.
Blind Willie McTell (Dylan) from *The Bootleg Series Vols 1-3*.
Jokerman (Dylan) from *Infidels*.
Tight Connection To My Heart (Dylan) from *Empire Burlesque*.
Silvio (Dylan/Hunter) from *Down In The Groove*.
Everything Is Broken (Dylan) from *Oh Mercy*.
Dignity (Alternate Version) (Dylan) from *Touched By An Angel* soundtrack album.
Not Dark Yet (Dylan) from *Time Out Of Mind*.
Things Have Changed (Dylan) from *Wonderboys* soundtrack.

"LOVE AND THEFT"

US Release: 11 September 2001   **Columbia CK 85975 (standard CD),**
Columbia COL 86076 (2-CD limited edition),
Columbia CH 9034 Hybrid CD/SACD
(released September 2003)

UK Release: **Columbia COL 504364** 2 (standard CD),
Columbia COL 504364 9 (2-CD ltd. edition)
Columbia COL 504364 1 (2-LP set)

Europe Release: September 2003   **Columbia 512357 CD/SACD issue,**
with 12-page booklet

Producer: Jack Frost, a pseudonym for Bob Dylan   **Running Time:** 57.32

Tweedle Dee & Tweedle Dum; Mississippi; Summer Days; Bye And Bye; Lonesome Day Blues; Floater (Too Much To Ask); High Water (For Charley Patton); Moonlight; Honest With Me; Po' Boy; Cry A While; Sugar Baby

Bob Dylan: vocal, guitar, piano, **Larry Campbell:** guitar, violin, banjo, mandolin, **Tony Garnier:** bass, **David Kemper:** drums, **Augie Meyers:** Vox organ, B3, Accordion, **Clay Meyers:** bongos, **Charlie Sexton:** guitar

Although it was released on 9-11, just as the world went mad, and new masters of war from third world caves declared their own form of Islamic Armageddon, all 12 tracks of the new album were recorded four months earlier. Dylan booked in from 9 to 25 May 2001 at Sony Music Studios, New York with his tour band, plus Augie Meyers on keyboards.

You could not really get much further from the swampy profundities of *Time Out Of Mind*. This was a comedy hour in comparison, though there were dark shadows if you looked hard enough. And after 9-11, people sure were, even if one reviewer described it as 'a Third Millenium Nashville Skyline'. As Dylan said of *"Love and Theft"* – the quotation marks are deliberate – 'I didn't want to get caught short without uptempo songs. A lot of my songs are slow ballads. I can gut wrench a lot out of them. But if you put a lot of them on a record, they'll fade into one another'. Its title comes from an obscure academic tome written by Eric Lott, published by the Oxford University Press: *Love and Theft: Blackface Minstrelsy and the American Working Class*.

Just before the album release, Bob confessed a love of the minstrel tradition to Edna Gunderson. Even 'Desolation Row' is 'a minstrel song through and through. I saw some ragtag minstrel show in blackface at the carnivals when I was growing up, and it had an effect on me, just as much as seeing the lady with four legs'. The minstrel show was essentially a form of lampoon, from contemporary pop songs to Shakespeare's plays, anything was fair game. Just like here. Certainly the album recreates a slew of vintage Americana. Bob even pays homage to, or maybe parodies, the place where jazz meets music hall, that he briefly visited on the scat singing of 'If Dogs Run Free' from *New Morning*. Dylan swings. It is certainly a world away from the confrontational young turk of Manchester '66.

But such a strategy also confronts the status quo. As Peter Doggett described it, Dylan's response to the madness of the planet as it hits the 21st century is 'to cloak himself in the comforting ghosts of Muddy Waters, Howlin' Wolf, Hoagy Carmichael and Bill Monroe, and then indulge in the kind of manic, despairing, coal-black humour he last displayed on *The Basement Tapes*'. Are these song fuelled by word play, or world weariness, that is the question. 'In the wake of the World Trade Centre attacks, the knife-edge humour and bleak surrealism make perfect sense'. As Dylan said to the LA Times, 'any day above ground is a good day'.

Other critical heavyweights piled in to read profundities into what might equally be the equivalent of a wink and a grin. Greil Marcus imagines an eccentric old man round the corner who goes for long solitary walks, muttering to himself, and writes and plays his own eccentric songs 'with a phoney-looking toothpaste smile'. It is an album of 'shifting stories'. But not quite as even Marcus could imagine. With chilling irony, the review, published on 8 September, talks of 'the window Dylan's new music itself opens up in time'. And of how the phrase 'I don't care' drops off its line 'like a body falling out of a window, with the same thud'.

Dylan pondered in his press release whether this album was another '*Oh Mercy*, or *Blood on the Tracks*, or whatever? Probably not. 'I think of it more as a greatest hits album, without the hits'. One rude voice among a paeon of rhetoric – 'a stylistic scree', 'a curiously

Columbia 504364 9

BOB DYLAN

"Love And Theft"

anachronistic vernacular' and the like – was that of Alexis Petrides. This is 'as cranky and erratic an album as 2001 is likely to see'. The problem with Dylan trying on for size the 'jazz-inflected ballad favoured by 1940s crooners' is that he is no Bing Crosby. Bob's voice has deteriorated into 'a mucoidal, otherworldly husk', a dead ringer for Papa Lazarou from The League of Gentlemen. When he sings about meeting a girl in the moonlight, it sounds less like a romantic situation, more 'the soundtrack of a public information film warning children not to talk to strangers'. So is this wit clothed in an enigma (or perhaps vice versa), or 'just rambling, obtuse nonsense? That debate, like much of *Love and Theft*, is best left to the Bobcats'.

Well, here goes. This is a self-consciously post-modern work, hence the quotation marks around its title, gathering echoes and phrases and sounds and reshaking the kaleidoscope. Like David Bowie, an early admirer, Dylan uses William Burroughs' idea of cut-up writing to forge – in both senses – some kind of sense. Bob himself described this record as 'an electronic grid, the lyrics being the sub-structure that holds it all together'. This brings us to the knotty problem of plagiarism. This caused no little controversy with *Good As I Been To You*, with at least one other musician suing him for (supposedly) appropriating their arrangements of public-domain material.

Here the debate enters the realm of the ludicrous. Chris Johnson, a 29-year-old Minnesotan working in Japan, came by chance on Dr Junichi Saga's book *Confessions of a Yakuza*, based on conversations with a dying gangster, and found that great chunks of its prose had been recycled in the lyrics of Dylan's new albums, almost word for word. Thus (Saga first) 'My mother was the daughter of a wealthy farmer, died when I was eleven, I heard that my father was a travelling salesman' compared with 'My mother was the daughter of a wealthy farmer/my father was a travelling salesman, I never met him'. There are many more examples. Dr Saga does not seem unduly concerned, indeed the controversy caused his book to be reprinted. Dylan maintained radio silence. The album picks up all kinds of references to vintage American traditional songs too. It is, after all, called "Love and Theft", and one song title, 'Floater', even refers directly to the way that folk music recycles key lines endlessly. But the whole thing is decidedly odd.

Best take the cover as a form of stand-up comedy, with Dylan looking back at the viewer deadpan, modelling his new moustache that makes him look shifty. Other photographs show Bob staring at Augie Meyers' electric organ, reading a Mexican newspaper, and posing in a long black leather coat. Trust nothing, trust no-one. The whole album could even be a lampoon of *Time Out Of Mind*, just as *The Basement Tapes* brought surrealism out of Paris and the drug-induced mind, and put it firmly on the back porch. But a cold wind is blowing.

CD 1
Tweedle Dee & Tweedle Dum (Dylan)
When the record fades up, the party has already started. This is literally nonsense, two characters from Lewis Carroll's classic of that genre *Alice in Wonderland*. But as with Carroll, the sinister is never far away. 'Two big bags of dead man's bones' took on an even more horrific meaning on the day of release. As in any fable, the two warring twins could be anyone, Bush and Al Gore, two sides of Dylan's own psyche, even born again Christianity and fundamentalist Islam that, after all, both do come from the same mother's knee. Elvis sang a piece of unrelated fluff called 'Tweedle Dee' but took it straight, not with the biting irony Dylan invests here. Musically, it's like *Highway 61 Revisited*, sung and played by half-wits.
Nothing is accidental on this album, least of all the mention of *A Streetcar Named Desire*. Dylan said of Tennessee Williams, author of that sultry, Southern epic: 'A few years back he died in New York City in a hotel room all by himself. And nobody found him until the next day. He was there because he couldn't get a job'.

Mississippi (Dylan) 4.46
Dylan abandoned this song having demo-ed it for his previous album. It had since been premiered in a more anthemic form on a Sheryl Crow album. According to Bob, 'Lanois thought it was pedestrian. Took it down the Afro-polyrhythm route – multi-rhythm drumming, that sort of thing. Polyrhythm has its place, but it doesn't work for knifelike lyrics trying to convey majesty and heroism. I thought too highly of the expressive meaning behind the lyrics to bury them in some steamy cauldron of drum theory'. Here the bass is playing a triple beat, 'and that adds up to all the multi-rhythm you need'.

The version here has a certain stately magnificence but fits in not at all with the punning, faux-naïve tone of the rest of the album, *Self Portrait* replayed in a madhouse. This is serious through and through and drags a vocal to match, with Dylan sounding close to tears. And it is not exactly cheerful stuff – 'days are numbered' and 'the emptiness is endless, cold as the clay' – but Dylan allows us a brief glimpse of hope. He will look at his lover ''til my eyes go blind', and asks her to extend a hand.

Summer Days (Dylan) 5.21
Pure rockabilly here, back to the days of his youth. A bit of western swing too. There is great snare drumming and a dancing, vibrato-free guitar all over the shop. Dylan gets into the spirit of what is his most carnal album since way back: 'I've got eight carburettors', baby. And great one-liners are studded all over the songs like diamonds. 'You're a worn out star'. Hardly. 'You can't repeat the past...of course you can': the keynote to this whole album.

Bye And Bye (Dylan) 4.53
This borrows its melody line from Billie Holiday's carefree 'Having Myself A Time' that Bob might have heard on the radio during his Minnesota boyhood. It starts with a silly joke, sitting on his watch so that he can be on time, but then hints of foreboding emerge, a man 'walking on briars'. The final verse carries references to civil war and a baptism of fire, all to the same shuffle beat, jovial organ riff (Garth Hudson in the play pen) and clipped guitar. Dylan's vocal is unreadable, conversational yet gamey, perhaps a hint of the Japanese Godfather at the end.

Lonesome Day Blues (Dylan) 3.16
Bone-crunching Chicago blues with Dylan sounding as tough as leather and the band hard as nails. This shares the title of a Blind Willie McTell song, but not its content. It speeds up as it goes, tells some family tales and sounds like a winning general lecturing his prisoners. 'I'm gonna teach peace to the conquered'. And through it all blows an idiot wind, gaining in intensity, 'whisperin', then making the leaves rustle, suddenly 'things are fallin' off of the shelf'.

Floater (Too Much To Ask) (Dylan) 6.05
The tune is based on 'Snuggled On Your Shoulder', first recorded by Bing Crosby in 1932, an elegant western swing number, but 'a squall is setting in'. And Dylan warns, the gangmaster again, that 'I'm not quite as cool or forgiving as I sound'. More family tall tales, by this floater – or drifter – who has recently experienced the death of his mother and is soon to revisit his younger days in prose in *Chronicles*.

High Water (For Charley Patton) (Dylan) 5.00
Charley Patton composed 'High Water Everywhere' straight after the great 1927 Mississippi Delta flood, as recreated in *Oh Brother Where Art Thou?*. Patton was born in Mississippi in1891

and died there in 1934, a man who relentlessly enjoyed life and sang about it in 'a hoarse, hollering vocal delivery, at times incomprehensible' with driving guitar. This is real down-home stuff with a chattering banjo, and a sideways glance at Appalachian favourite 'The Cuckoo' which US world-music pioneers Kaleidoscope turned into an anti-war song back in the late 60s.

Part of this new tempest and flood is a wave of doctrinaire ignorance, and there is also a side swipe at Creationism: George Lewes was a rational scientist and a supporter of Darwin. Now evolution seems to be going in reverse, 'I'm putting out your eyes'. If even the affable Big Joe Turner, who fronted the Basie orchestra and recorded 'Corrina, Corrina', is getting dark thoughts, the times really are out of joint.

Moonlight (Dylan) 4.05

An affectionate parody of a pre-war romantic tune, like some of the stuff The Beatles did on *Magical Mystery Tour*. The band play a soft-shoe shuffle with lots of lap steel. Greil Marcus notes in a scholarly fashion that this is 'less like Hoagy Carmichael than Jeanette MacDonald and Nelson Eddy's "Indian Love Call". It's a parlour from the 19th century that comes into view'. But one with blood running down the walls. Here the clouds are 'turning crimson', notwithstanding the 'songbird's sweet melodious tone' with which this opens.

Honest With Me (Dylan) 3.25

Another Chicago style blues, and indeed set there, though rarely do the likes of Muddy Waters sing about a woman with a face 'like a teddy bear'. More medicine show imagery – 'the Siamese twins are comin' to town' – or is this warring Tweedledee and Tweedledum again? There is one joke that you get only if you read the song in *Lyrics*. 'I'm going off into the woods, I'm hunting bear' is re-spelt 'hunting bare', picking up the 'stark naked' of the previous line.

This new song plunders wholesale lines from an old Civil War ballad supporting the south. And the Armageddon awaiting the USA is again prefigured: 'when I left home the sky split open wide'. 'Some things are too terrible to be true.'

Po' Boy (Dylan) 5.49

Mellow guitar and lovely, old timey melody with Dylan singing like a bird and going back to his childhood, a 'poor boy in a red hot town', and more fictional family memories, even if he does seem to confuse the plot of *Othello* with *Hamlet*.

On one level this is literally just a joke, and a knock, knock one at that, as kids play, punning Freddy and ready. Another is about finding a strange man in your wife's bed. 'Seven Drunken Nights' recast. There is something infinitely sad in Bob's voice, the tears of a clown. As Howard Devoto, hardly known for his own jovial nature, puts it: 'Bob loves his bad jokes and these are such good bad jokes. But it's also an incredibly sad song. All those teetering, absurdly packed long lines'.

Cry A While (Dylan) 3.06
Another electric blues that starts like a slowed down 'Rainy Day Women'. Dylan rasps, the drums and bass thump, and an amped-up guitar plays exactly the right notes, like early Taj Mahal. The rhythm seems to stop and start and the band put not a foot wrong.

More gangster (or even gangsta) chic, a tough and masculine world straight out of Raymond Chandler where everyone is backstabbing someone else, and – in the best joke of the whole album – a pounding on the wall 'must have been Don Pasquale making a 2am booty call'.

Sugar Baby (Dylan) 5.05
A muted close to a lively record. This is in the orbit of some of the weirder alt country bands to emerge around this point in time, like Lambchop or Bonnie 'Prince' Billie. It shares its title and air of menace with a song of the same name written and sung by Dock Boggs, an east Virginia miner with a stone face and a short fuse. But it is fused here with a line from a medieval English mystery play: 'look up, look up', set during the nativity. The closing lines come almost verbatim from another old mountain song, 'The Lonesome Road', and that title could describe this song as a whole. Lyrically, this is a rag bag of odd phrases, seemingly recycled from other places, and full of bone-dry humour, much like Samuel Beckett set to music. 'Every moment of existence seems like some dirty trick.'

It is another 'Dark Eyes', a closing song in which Dylan drops all his masks and stares at his audience directly. He and his band did exactly that the last time I saw them in concert, to have those piercing eyes and Buster Keaton face staring straight through you was extremely daunting. But there are flecks of humour here too. 'These bootleggers, they made pretty good stuff' could either be about illicit stills up in the Appalachians, or some of the people who trade in his back pages. And one line in particular hits home in the aftermath of Ground Zero. 'You've always got to be prepared but you never know for what' But truer to this weird album is what is currently the final line of almost 600 pages of the latest collected *Lyrics*. 'Might as well keep going on'.

CD 2 (Limited edition bonus disc)
I Was Young When I Left Home (Trad, arranged Dylan) 5.24
Live Minneapolis 22 December 1961.

Bob Dylan: vocal, guitar
Right back to the beginning and a young man singing to a couple of friends in Bonnie Beecher's apartment. The guitar cuts like a knife and that absurdly young voice sounds wistful and regretful and utterly lost.

The Times They Are A-Changin' (Dylan) (Alternate Version) 2.57
Live New York, 23 October 1963
Bob Dylan: vocal, guitar
Much slower than the released version, less militant, more inward and worth the price of the whole package just by itself. This still has the power to 'vibrate your walls'.

BOB DYLAN LIVE 1975: THE BOOTLEG SERIES VOLUME 5, THE ROLLING THUNDER REVIEW

US Release: 26 November 2002
Columbia C2K 87047 2-CD set
3LP box set, Classic Records/Columbia CK 87047-1-R (140g vinyl),
CK 97047-1-Q (200g vinyl)
With 70pp booklet and blue vinyl 45 rpm single 'Tangled Up In Blue'/'Isis'
Producer: Jeff Rosen and Steve Berkovitz, original recordings supervised by Don DeVito

UK Release: Columbia 510140 2
2-CD set, lesser quality of paper and print than US issue.
Running Time: (51.02), (50.56)

CD 1: Tonight I'll Be Staying Here With You*****; It Ain't Me Babe**; A Hard Rain's A-Gonna Fall*****; The Lonesome Death of Hattie Carroll****; Romance in Durango**; Isis; Mr Tambourine Man***; Simple Twist Of Fate**; Blowin' In The Wind****; Mama, You Been On My Mind**; I Shall Be Released***

CD 2: It's All Over Now, Baby Blue*****; Love Minus Zero/No Limit*****; Tangled Up In Blue****; The Water Is Wide****; It Takes A Lot To Laugh, It Takes A Train To Cry****; Oh, Sister****; Hurricane*; One More Cup Of Coffee (Valley Below)****; Sara***; Just Like A Woman****; Knockin' On Heaven's Door**

Recorded at
*Memorial Auditorium, Worcester, Mass 19 November 1975
**Harvard Square Theatre, Cambridge, Mass 20 November 1975
***Boston Music Hall 21 November 1975 (first show)
****Boston Music Hall 21 November 1975 (second show)
*****Forum de Montreal, Canada 4 December 1975

BOB DYLAN LIVE 1975
The Bootleg Series Vol. 5

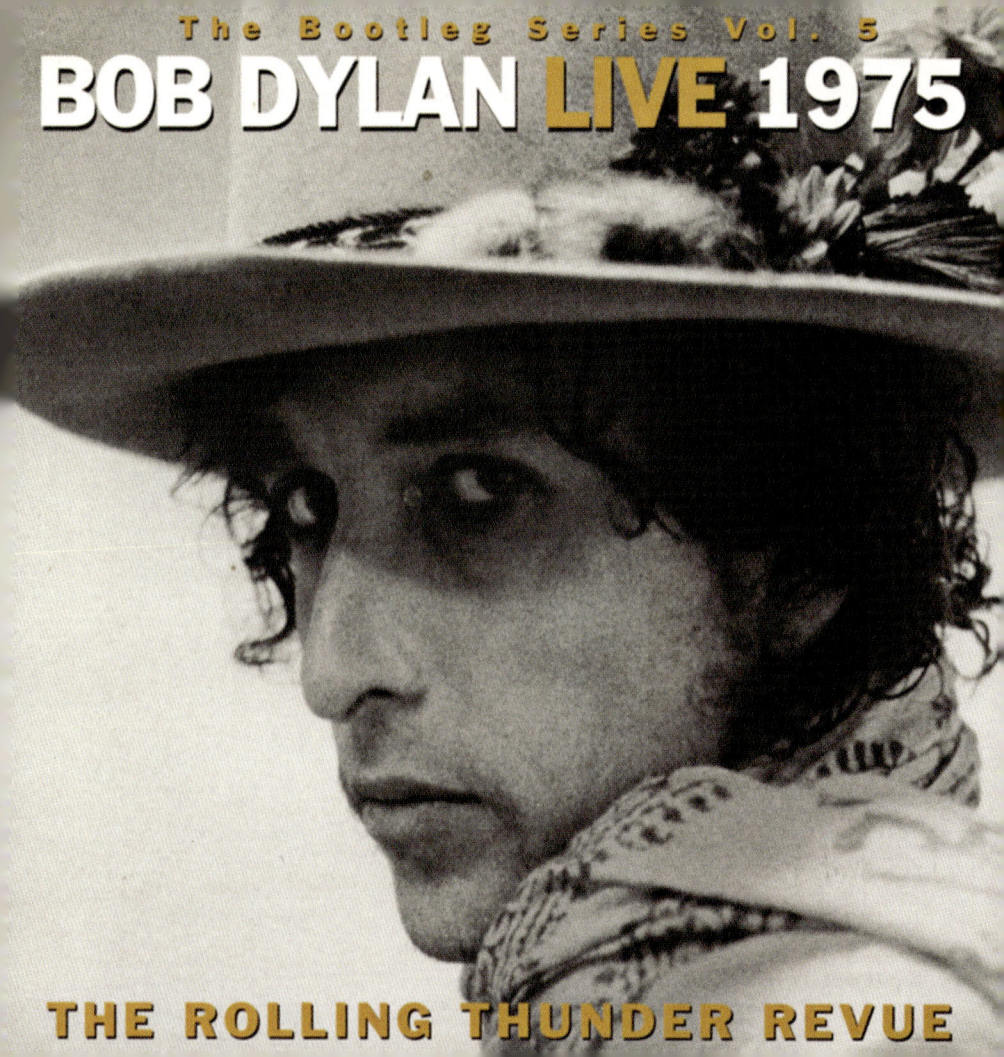

THE ROLLING THUNDER REVUE

Bob Dylan: vocal and guitar, **Ronnee Blakely:** vocal, **T-Bone Burnett:** guitar, **David Mansfield:** steel guitar, mandolin, violin and dobro, **Bobby Neuwirth:** guitar and vocal, **Scarlet Rivera:** violin, **Luther Rix:** drums, percussion and congas, **Mick Ronson:** guitar, **Stephen Soles:** guitar and vocal, **Rob Stoner:** bass, **Howie Wyeth:** piano and drums, **Joan Baez:** vocals on 'Blowin' In The Wind', 'Mama You Been On My Mind', 'I Shall Be Released' and 'The Water Is Wide', **Roger McGuinn:** vocals on 'Knockin' On Heaven's Door'

This is a composite experience, drawn from five separate concerts by this souped-up gypsy band taped on 24-track, capturing the music in all its ragged glory. It presents a cross section of the first leg of the Rolling Thunder Revue, playing intimate venues where possible and literally upending the folk rock rulebook. Rather like the parallel experiments of Ashley Hutchings on the other side of the Atlantic – a torch picked up with musical abandon by Jah Wobble – the bass is at the heart to things here, the rest of the band take their cue from Rob Stoner, or play off against him. His loss from the 1978 world tour was palpable. But here this Greenwich Village pick-up band – Neuwirth's 'punk street thugs' – is in full flow, a totally different experience to the harder, more desperate sounds of the second leg of the tour in early 1976, as captured on *Hard Rain*.

Dylan had found Stoner playing bass with Bobby Neuwirth and added drummer Howie Wyeth and gypsy fiddler Scarlet Rivera for *Desire*. For the road band, Neuwirth added himself, boy genius David Mansfield, lanky Texan guitarist T-Bone Burnett, singer/writer Stephen Soles and rock guitar star Mick Ronson, plus Luther Rix on percussion. Young and sparky, they gave Dylan a musical springboard.

The idea for this rough-and-ready approach, playing venues where they could look the audience in the eye at first, at least, until economics intervened, had come to Dylan in Corsica, some six months earlier. 'The sun was going down and the moon was sapphire. I was sitting on a donkey cart, bouncing around on the road there and that's when it flashed on me that I was gonna go back to America and get serious'. He decided to put together an old timey medicine show. Indeed, in a chronological coincidence, it connects directly with the anarchic spirit and updated minstrel songs of *Love and Theft* as a blood brother, 26 years apart. As Dylan said at the time, 'ever see those Italian troupes that go around Commedia dell-arte. Well, this is just an extension of that, only musically'. Hence the white face paint and stage costumes.

As Larry Sloman's excellent liner notes reveal, the name supposedly came from a native American shaman, or real thunder over Dylan's Malibu home, or the carpet bombing of

Cambodia by Nixon. This third possibility was strengthened when Neuwirth named the backing band Guam after the US base from which these bombers flew.

The musicians travelled between gigs, stretched along the north eastern seaboard, by bus and camper vans. They would book small theatres under an assumed name then turn up incognito. One particularly weird night Dylan performed at first in a hideous Bob Dylan mask, then tore it off to reveal a more palatable visage and everything was filmed. As Dylan later confirmed, 'that tour was always intended to be a movie. It always existed on more than one level. That's why the costumes, all the make-up, something to make it a little different, to put it in a time setting, of which the movie would seem to revolve around'.

All kinds of celebrity guests turned up – Joan Baez's duets with Bob were a nightly feature. Ramblin' Jack Elliot and Roger McGuinn were other near-permanent members with guest appearances from Joni Mitchell, Arlo Guthrie and Gordon Lightfoot. Allen Ginsberg and Sara Dylan were also along for the ride. Although it is excellent musically, the double-CD format here does scant justice to the three-hour stage show.

First Guam would play a six-song set, then actress/singer Ronnee Blakely would sing a couple, then the guests who went along that night, on one memorable occasion a duo of Ginsberg and Rick Danko. Ramblin' Jack was always the last guest spot, then Dylan came on stage to duet with Neuwirth on 'When I Paint My Masterpiece', a nightly highlight. Bobby would introduce Bob to the crowd by saying 'here's another old friend' and predictably they raised the roof. Then Dylan played six songs with the band, usually culminating with 'Isis' before the intermission. The second half started with an acoustic duet between Bob and Joan, then Baez's own spot, with maybe a couple from McGuinn. Then it was Dylan for eight songs, with the band gradually joining him and a mass encore by everyone on Woody Guthrie's 'This Land Is Your Land'.

But the music here is pure, undiluted Bob – with Baez, McGuinn and Guam all filling in the background – and thus the shape and tension of these extraordinary concerts is lost. This is a Fellini-esque recolonization of American myth and history: no coincidence that the tour kicked off in Plymouth. Here were a new bunch of Pilgrim fathers, come to resettle the nation in a blizzard of face paint and cowboy boots and cocaine and flowery hats and that was just the men! Many of the participants later turned to Jesus. The Rolling Thunder Revue has become, in retrospect, a swansong for excess and companionship, pure 60s. And the music is to match, setting fire to a bunch of classic songs.

The Rolling Thunder Revue was intended to last forever, though its original spirit didn't survive Christmas. The energy levels of the Never Ending Tour would never reach the ones here. Reviews of this blast from the past were generally ecstatic now that this tour was finally in the public domain. Some saw it as a match for Manchester 1966, even if that were a pitched battle between band and audience, and this a nightly love-in.

As Peter Doggett puts it, 'Dylan never sung like this again, before or after, song after song is delivered in a majestic fury of emotion, totally without restrictions yet under complete control'. Other reviews mentioned his 'impassioned intimacy', 'the most excited Dylan performance ever' and a 'sprawling band' playing with surprising sensitivity. By scrambling up the gig chronology, we get the pure essence of these stunning shows, white-hot Dylan reinventing his past. And with packaging to match, with lots of Ken Regan's backstage photos, the whole ramshackle crew onstage, Dylan and Ginsberg at Jack Kerouac's grave and the imprisoned Rubin Carter. Plus the sumptuous tour logo, hand painted with antique script, like a holy icon.

There are two excellent eyewitness tour accounts, Sam Shepard's *Rolling Thunder Logbook* (1977) and Larry Sloman's *On The Road With Bob Dylan* (1978, reprinted 2002).

CD 1
Tonight I'll Be Staying Here With You (Dylan) 3.55
The band crash, angular and clattering, like a punk band with a violin, and Dylan half-shouting, hoarse and angry as he sexes up a song once noted for its air of complicit domesticity. The new words, 'throw my ticket in the well, throw my mattress out there too', suggest that this will be a one night stand at best. It certainly throws the listener in at the deep end of this wild concert experience.

It Ain't Me Babe (Dylan) 5.25
Another remake, urgent and sprightly, as Dylan dances across the lyrics, to the strains of pedal steel. This has been variously described as a 'steamroller overhaul' and a new 'twitchy flamenco/country crossover style', but there are really no handy musical reference points. Dylan has done it again, creating a new sound. And his harmonica solo is driven, like a madman dancing on hot coals. The audience go berserk.

A Hard Rain's A-Gonna Fall (Dylan) 5.17
Again this is a complete respray job, a holy acoustic icon taken at a 'Highway 61 Revisited' jogtrot, fast and violent, with a carnival of noise behind him. Judas squared. Andy Gill thinks Status Quo, but those boogie merchants could never have rocked as hard as this, peppered with slide guitar, and everyone in overdrive. Just as the melancholy, measured recorded version was totally appropriate for its time, so this fits the twitchy 70s, with monetarism ready to smash apart the post-war welfare consensus and dirty little wars in global backwaters.

The Lonesome Death of Hattie Carroll (Dylan) 5.25
Whatever Dylan thought up in that Corsican twilight, it was certainly not a reprise of the tried and tested renditions with the Band a year before. If that were heritage, this is a gleeful smashing up of holy relics. Another holy cow led to slaughter, with an arrangement led in by Stoner's bass, then drums clatter as they do to perfection during this tour and at one point tap like a judge's gavel, a lovely touch, plus a dub-like trance of rhythm instruments, and Dylan again sounds righteously angry. This is actually far more respectful to the spirit of this song with Zanzinger now long released into the community, than a polite Joan Baez-style warbling. This burns.

Romance in Durango (Dylan/Levy) 5.22
'This is Scarlet Rivera joining us. Remember Durango, Larry?' If he does, he doesn't put it in his book, probably just as well for what has been described as 'like a party in a Mexican bordello' with lots of tinkling on mandolin and dobro, and Rivera adding those piercing top notes. If she could sometimes sound too sickly sweet on *Desire*, at these concerts she played like a banshee, a musical equivalent of her truly creepy spider web face paint. You wouldn't want to invite the Rolling Thunder boys and girls home.

Isis (Dylan/Levy) 5.11
Comparatively restrained when compared to the two versions, video and audio, on the bonus disc, but still an aural assault. The album version is the palest shadow compared to this, with what Andy Gill calls its 'nice air of shifty, mischievous intrigue'. Chunka chunka rhythm and Rivera providing primary colours on fiddle, then they all clatter in between the verses, led by Bob's piercing harmonica, the aural equivalent of Dylan's flashing eyes in the movie. He

sounds matter of fact, then querulous, then driven, then resigned, then exultant. You're not sure at the end whether he is thanking the band, the audience or himself. Even on its hugely delayed 2002 release date, this was still the wildest track of the year.

Mr Tambourine Man (Dylan) 5.28
The band go offstage, probably to take some class A drugs, and Bob is left with just an acoustic guitar and his naked voice, but the jumped-up rhythms continue through this urgent rendering. You could even dance to this. He indulges in some harmonica pyrotechnics at the end.

Simple Twist Of Fate (Dylan) 4.26
In this rearrangement of the original running order, this is the first chance to pause for breath, a fragile, acoustic delight. Dylan's voice rises and falls for dramatic effect.

Blowin' In The Wind (Dylan) 2.41
Even at this distance, the crowd's excitement at seeing the one-time king and queen of folk reunited on stage is palpable. And by the miracle of sound technology, the next reissue will feature them in their pomp. But here there is a slightly elegiac air, especially when they start with this old chestnut, sung throughout in unison. Andy Gill speaks for most commentators nowadays – with whom Baez's stock has crashed through the floor – that 'for once she enhances a performance, where her earnest descant operates at a pleasingly piquant angle to Dylan's ebullient, country drawl'. The song is no longer hopeful, or wistful, or anything really, just a bunch of words and a good tune.

Mama, You Been On My Mind (Dylan) 3.04
Joan Baez dedicates this song to a lady called Mama sitting in the front row. She is the rather creepy gypsy woman who dresses Baez in a white dress and prattles on in the interminable movie based around this tour. Their two voices coil around each other like snakes, joined in this bluegrass-style country strut by walking bass, quiet drums and chunky guitar, plus banjo and pedal steel. You can almost see them queueing up for their time at the mike. This is playful, with the best bit coming when the instruments all briefly drop out, leaving the former lovers almost chuckling at each other.

I Shall Be Released (Dylan) 4.45
Some badinage with the audience, then gentle pedal steel and the two sing with tenderness and melancholy. Gill and others sneer at Baez's 'inexplicably bad harmonies that are mannered to the point of camp'. Others of us hear her singing with rare passion, at what remains her finest musical hour. A lovely relaxed guitar break, and the two vocals yearn as one. 'Bobby will be back', Joan reassures the audience. And he is, in a different country and two weeks later.

CD 2
It's All Over Now, Baby Blue (Dylan) 4.31
Just Dylan at the microphone again. In a weird reverse of musical history, Bob's vocal takes on the ironic, clipped and rhythmic tones of Brian Ferry, one of the more eccentric of his interpreters. Dylan's harp playing here verges on the inspired.

Love Minus Zero/No Limit (Dylan) 3.17
Dylan sounds hushed, accentuating the consonants and drawing out every ounce of poetry. Somehow even here he is urgent, his acoustic guitar driving him onwards. This is not just a performance, more an event, with another masterclass in folk harmonica at the end.

Tangled Up In Blue (Dylan) 4.41
With the album this comes from still fresh in the record racks, the audience whoop recognition. Another magnificent rendition, with a few slight verbal alterations, but just the same atmosphere as the originals, both nostalgic and hopeful. And yet another harmonica break that brings its own rough poetry at the end.

The Water Is Wide (Traditional) 5.16
Baez returns for this, though *Folk Roots* later opined that her voice here is a 'strident blare, that should have been erased at birth'. But it does exactly what is needed, straining for transcendence in this old spiritual with ethereal pedal steel suggesting the heaven that this song and performance, strains towards. You can almost taste the tears here, a love song in all but words – the bough breaks – finishing with both singing 'I'. And who could imagine two such egos ever settling down together.

It Takes A Lot To Laugh, It Takes A Train To Cry (Dylan) 3.12
'Here's an autobiographical song', Dylan says mysteriously. The band are back from their refreshments and this chugs along the tracks as the words would suggest. One early idea for the revue was to travel between gigs by train, rather than on the road. The guitar breaks here are rough and ready, but with much the kind of piercing, almost amateurish spirit of Steve Jones a year or so later, plugged into the spirit of the song – and the times.

Oh, Sister (Dylan/Levy) 4.05
Someone shouts out demanding a protest song and ever the way, Dylan replies with this, that does indeed seem to protest, but at something private and to be kept in the family. The band are at their most relaxed, still with rough edges but heartbreaking violin and some heartfelt vocal harmonies that are stretched out almost to the point of pain on the word 'saved'. Then everyone goes silent for a moment. Although *Desire* was not yet in the shops, the audience must have known that a treat was in store.

Hurricane (Dylan/Levy) 8.15
'If you've got any political pull at all, you can get this man back on the streets.' The whole crew paid him a visit in prison, and played a benefit show back in New York which eventually succeeded. Played with 'righteous urgency' and exuberant fiddle around Dylan's half-shouted vocals, they sound like a street gang put to music. Eight minutes, and not a second wasted. Whereas the re-recorded, censored version drags somewhat, this is enough to get the audience in Worcester, Massachusetts to rise to their feet and storm Trenton jail. Well, the man did call out for a protest song, even if in it came two days later and in another town.

One More Cup Of Coffee (Valley Below) (Dylan/Levy) 4.06
'We love you Bobby', and who couldn't for this south-of-the-border meditation, as Dylan's vocal strains to the top edge of his range, and gypsy fiddle circles from around the camp fire. Again that wonderfully dysfunctional drums'n'bass reverses the beat, like a white Sly and Robbie. At the end, Rivera's violin is like a spent firework, spiralling down to earth.

Sara (Dylan) 4.38
A solid rhythm, no syncopation here, and the band lay back as Dylan sings like a demon. You

can almost picture the audience's mouths dropping open to hear for the first time so openly autobiographical a song. This is a man singing as if his life depended on it, with a woman's voice coming in for the chorus, presumably Ronee playing at being Emmylou. Fervent clapping from the crowd that goes on and on.

Just Like A Woman (Dylan) 4.31
Dylan responds to a shouted request, and this is certainly more than just karaoke. One commentator describes this version as 'routine' that only goes to show how you should trust your own ears, not those of others. Passionate and wild round the edges, with bass and drums like a heartbeat. The band goes down the scale in unison, then comes back up again and makes the hairs rise on the back of the neck. You're never sure exactly which guitarist is playing what, but if not actually Mick Ronson, the egoless lead lines here are true to his now-departed, slightly shambolic spirit.

Knockin' On Heaven's Door (Dylan) 4.21
Sweet with pedal steel, and Roger McGuinn on melancholic second vocal. You can almost smell the blood Bob wipes metaphorically off his face. This is more celebration than lament with the band's essential optimism breaking through, not least on the mass chorus. For the irreligious among us, Scarlet's soaring violin and the rambunctious band bring us probably as close to heaven as we will ever get. 'Thanks for coming, we'll be in the area for a few days, maybe see you tomorrow night' Bob signs off as the master of ceremonies in this rock'n'roll circus.

Bonus DVD:
Tangled Up In Blue (Dylan) 4.33 From *Renaldo and Clara*.

Isis (Dylan/Levy) 4.10. Recorded at the Forum de Montreal, Canada 4 December 1975.

Isis (Dylan/Levy) 5.21. From *Renaldo and Clara*. This is audio only, with a still of Dylan sitting on a stool onstage. He prefaces it with, 'this is a song about marriage' and dedicates this version to Leonard. Cohen, presumably, because this is from the Montreal show.

MASKED AND ANONYMOUS

US Release: 21 July 2003 **CD Release:** Columbia 512556 6, limited edition 2-CD set
Producer: Jeff Rosen **Running Time:** 66.31

CD 1: Magokoro Brothers: My Back Pages; Shirley Caesar: Gotta Serve Somebody; Bob Dylan: Down In The Flood (new version); Grateful Dead: It's All Over Now, Baby Blue; Sophie Zelmani: Most Of The Time; Los Lobos: On A Night Like This; Bob Dylan: Diamond Joe; Articolo 31: Come Una Pietra Scalciata (Like A Rolling Stone); Sertab: One More Cup Of Coffee; Francesco de Gregori: Non Dirle Che Non E' Cosi (If You See Her, Say Hello); Bob Dylan: Dixie; Jerry Garcia: Senor (Tales Of Yankee Power); Bob Dylan: Cold Irons Bound (new version); Dixie Hummingbirds: City Of Gold

CD 2: 'The Reissue Series Sampler', limited Edition disc containing seven previously issued tracks from forthcoming SA-CD reissues that feature CD upgrades and play in any CD machine. All I Really Want To Do; Love Minus Zero/No Limit; Stuck Inside Of Mobile With The Memphis Blues Again; Tangled Up In Blue; Gotta Serve Somebody; Moonlight; Cold Irons Bound

Bob Dylan: vocal, guitar, **Larry Campbell:** guitar, vocal, **Tony Garnier:** bass, **George Recile:** drums, **Charlie Sexton:** guitar, vocal

Recording dates of live concert 18 July 2002, stage 6 of Ray-Art Studios, Canoga Park, California, nine appear in the movie, plus a deleted scene of 'Standing in the Doorway' and an unbroadcast 'If You See Her, Say Hello'. Four of these appear on this CD. The others include 'Amazing Grace', 'I'll Remember You', 'Drifter's Escape' and 'Watching The River Flow'. The film was released six days later, on 27 July 2003.

In February 2002, there were reports in the trade press that Dylan was to take part in a new movie, based supposedly on a short story by Enrique Morales titled *The Wings of Destiny*. Morales, an Argentinian writer living in Paris, later denied that this was anything to do with him. The screen writers Sergei Petrov and Rene Fountaine are said to be pseudonyms for Dylan and

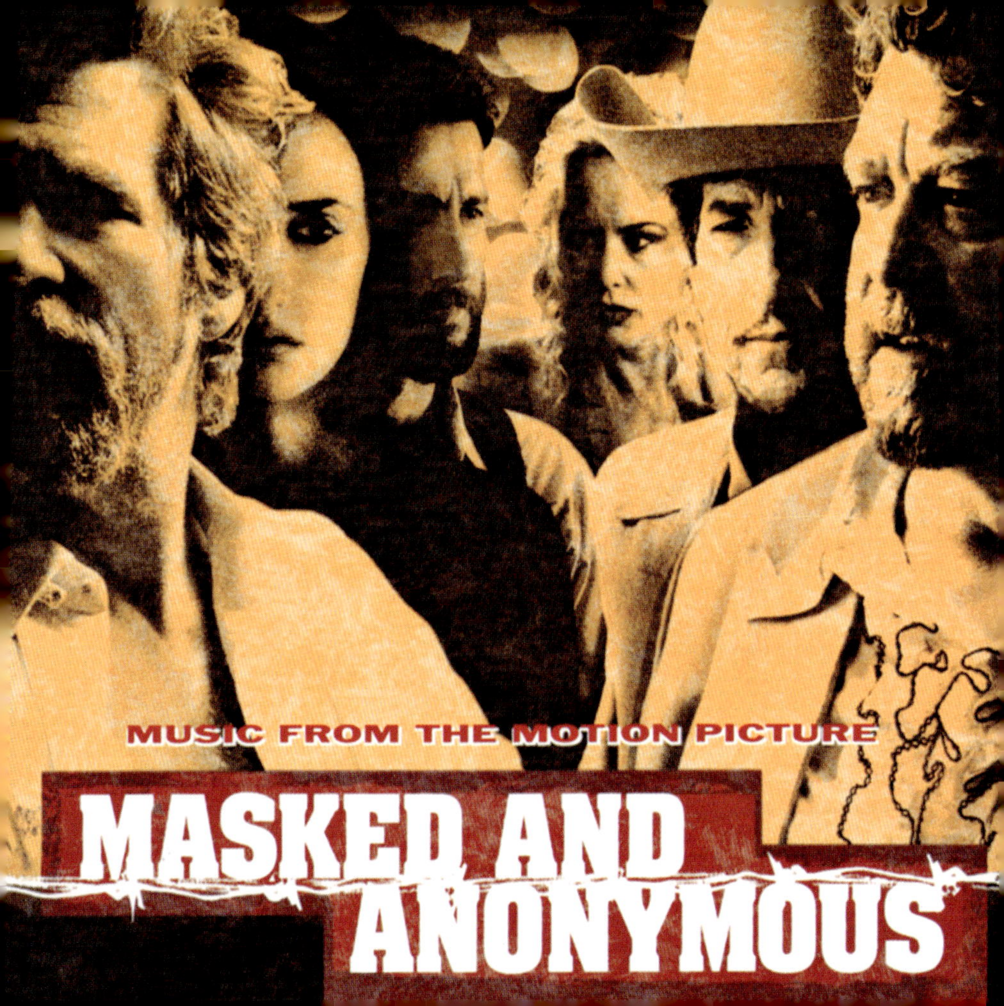
MUSIC FROM THE MOTION PICTURE
MASKED AND
ANONYMOUS

the film's director Larry Charles, from *Seinfeld*.

In the movie, set in a 'mythological Third World America', Dylan plays Jack Fate, an 'ageing rocker' who is released from prison to play a charity concert. In a film that is endlessly self-referential, his Never Ending tour band are renamed 'Simple Twist Of Fate'. Charles had very specific ideas about how to shoot the performance scenes. 'We went back to the old Johnny Cash television show, to Grand Ole Opry shows with Hank Williams'. The CD booklet is illustrated with stills from the film, starring Hollywood heavyweights like John Goodman, Penelope Cruz and Jessica Lange. Apart from Dylan himself, it is a fascinating and highly listenable compilation of his songs performed in different languages and styles, from gospel to hip-hop.

Bob Dylan; Down In The Flood (Dylan) 3.36

The Basement Tapes song retooled by a more straightforward but purposeful band, and even more 'propulsive', to quote Alan Light's sleeve notes. We've gone full circle, to an album package that tells you what you're hearing. But he's right, as he is when he urges us to 'listen to the way he leans purposefully into the rasp in his voice'. But it is a version now missing any sense of the Apocalypse.

Bob Dylan: Diamond Joe (Trad arr Dylan) 2.32

A 'playful string band version' of a different song to that of the same title on *Good As I Been To You*. This paeon to whisky is a cousin to 'Cotton Eye Joe' with the same propensity to dance. Dylan sounds positively upbeat, with not a trace of irony or disaster waiting in the wings. What's gone wrong?

Bob Dylan: Dixie (Trad arr Dylan) 2.13

In the movie, Dylan is handed a list of protest songs the network wants him to sing, Lennon's 'Revolution', Neil Young's 'Ohio', Pete Townshend's 'Won't Get Fooled Again', and ignores them all to play this old chestnut. Quite why is a man who hails from the frozen north of America so taken with the culture of the south? On screen, when Dylan stumbles over the start of the second verse, he shoots a glance to Larry Campbell, looking for a prompt. Inconsequential, far more revolutionary and true to the protest spirit is Articolo 31's extraordinary cut-up version of 'Like A Rolling Stone', using the bare bones of the original to infuse new urgent flesh and adding a female chorus to answer 1965-era Dylan's questions. And the rhythms get you moving too.

Bob Dylan: Cold Irons Bound (Dylan) 5.44
A 'graveyard stomp' with Dylan revisiting one of the key tracks from *Time Out Of Mind*, and 'summoning up the ghost of Howling Wolf'. It might even be better than the studio version, the tour band showing their innate power with a rhythm section almost to rival Rolling Thunder. Drums clatter, guitars chatter and Dylan goes to the lowest range of his voice to portray vengeance.

He has certainly learnt how to hold himself like a classic bluesman. The callow boy of the first album would be well impressed.

DVD Release: Partner Entertainment BBCDVD 1511, 100 minutes.

BOB DYLAN LIVE 1964

The Bootleg Series Vol. 6

CONCERT AT PHILHARMONIC HALL

BOB DYLAN LIVE 1964: THE BOOTLEG SERIES VOL 6, CONCERT AT PHILHARMONIC HALL

US Release: 30 March 2004
Columbia/Legacy C2K 86882
2-CD 3-LP box set, Classic Records/Columbia
July 2004: C2K 86882 – 140 (140g vinyl),
C2K 86882 – 200 (200g vinyl) With 12" booklet
Producers: Original concert recording
31 October 1964, Philarmonic Hall, New York,
album produced by Jeff Rosen and Steve Berkovitz

UK/Europe Release: 29 March 2004
Columbia/Legacy COL 512358 2

Running Time: (63.56), (40.20)

CD 1: The Times They Are A Changin'; Spanish Harlem Incident; Talkin' John Birch Paranoid Blues; To Ramona; Who Killed Davey Moore?; Gates Of Eden; If You Gotta Go, Go Now (Or Else You Got To Stay All Night); It's Alright, Ma (I'm Only Bleeding); I Don't Believe You (She Acts Like We Never Have Met); Mr Tambourine Man; A Hard Rain's A-Gonna Fall.

CD 2: Talkin' World War III Blues; Don't Think Twice, It's All Right; The Lonesome Death Of Hattie Carroll; Mama, You Been On My Mind; Silver Dagger; With God On Our Side; It Ain't Me, Babe; All I Really Want To Do.

Bob Dylan: vocal, guitar, harmonica, **Joan Baez:** vocal

As Princeton's Sean Wilenz outlines in the excellent CD booklet, it is a measure of Albert Grossman's confidence in his new folk star that he should book as grand a venue as Philharmonic Hall. Opened two years earlier as part of the Lincoln Centre and now renamed the Avery Fisher Hall, its imperial grandeur made it the most prestigious venue in America even if its acoustics were dire. In just three years, Dylan had graduated upwards from handing round a basket for small change to solo concerts at the Town Hall, then Carnegie Hall and now a 'cavernous, gilded theatre', home to Leonard Bernstein and the New York Philharmonic. In these august surroundings both star and his audience looked like 'a bizarre insurrection of the hipster beatnik young'. They now probably own half of America between them.

Robert Shelton's review describes how 'an audience that overflowed onto stage seats greeted him reverently'. Bob's 'ability to shape a meaningful programme added up to a frequently spellbinding evening by the brilliant singing poet laureate of young America'.

Dylan walked on stage, without introduction and singing strange new songs before the interval. Reassuring ones, and Joan Baez too, in the second half. Wilenz, then 13, remembers one song, possibly name-checking Arthur Koestler's *Darkness at Noon*, as 'ominous and overpowering'. It was the first time that this, and some of the other key songs of the yet-to-be-recorded *Bringing It All Back Home*, were given a public airing. They took up the verbal experiments on *Another Side*, and took them right to the wire. In Dylan's own words, these new, abstract songs are 'insanely honest, not meanin' to twist any head and written only for the reason that I myself, me alone, wanted and needed to write them. I've conceded the fact there is no understanding of anything'.

The album was professionally recorded and even given a catalogue number, Columbia 2302. Presumably cut down to a single slice of vinyl. But at this point Dylan was moving so quickly that within three months he was back in the studios with an electric band, and a live acoustic album would already have been out of date. And what is sketched out here comes into its full glory on side two of his next album

Live 1964 brings us Dylan at a tipping point. On these two discs he is forever frozen in time between coffee-houses and rock gigs, between protest and visions. Caught when he was still at one with the audience, 'the last strains of a self-aware New York bohemia before it became mass marketed', still just in touch with a fast-vanishing America sung by Guthrie and written up by Jack Kerouac.

He wrote a prose poem for the Philharmonic concert programme, 'Advice for Geraldine on her Miscellaneous Birthday'. Ironically, it warned against 'going too far out in any direction', for people will feel 'something's going on up there that they don't know about'. But this was exactly what listening to this concert brings back, a man up on stage already pointing out a new direction for society, way out past the Gates Of Eden.

You can almost see it in some of the photographs here. The front cover is a lovely colour full-face photograph by Hank Parker, augmented by on-stage shots by Daniel Kramer. There's Dylan posing in front of joke-shop masks and with an arcade game rifle, plus with Joan Baez and Allen Ginsberg, and playing both autoharp and – in an empty coffee shop with a tough-looking John Sebastian – a bass guitar. The ghost of electricity is blowing in the wind.

CD 1
The Times They Are A-Changin' (Dylan) 3.29
Rustles, then cheers, in glowing stereo. The show was divided into two halves by a 15-minute interval. The first half was 'for innovation as well as some glances at where Dylan had already been'. This was his usual opening number at this time, and took on a new resonance in the light of some of the songs about to be unveiled that night. Dylan sings it with spirit, still sounding absurdly young, but no longer angry. More like a man who has already won the war.

Spanish Harlem Incident (Dylan) 3.07
It's great to hear a live version of this with Dylan's voice cawing like a crow and more than usually piercing harmonica, plus strummed guitar. Had Dylan got to West Point as once he intended, this would have sounded good.

Talkin' John Birch Paranoid Blues (Dylan) 4.06
The song notoriously banned from the Ed Sullivan show after a CBS executive turned cold and ordered him to sing something different. Maybe it was the reference to a toilet bowl. Dylan earned much street cred as a result, and introduces it tonight 'with a mixture of defiance and good humour' as 'Talking John Birch Paranoid Blues', emphasizing the fourth word. 'It's a fictitious story'. His storytelling draws genuine laughter. And this time round he is looking under the rose bush too, and interrogates the mailman with a hop and a skip, who punches him out. It doesn't stop him, he gets himself a magnifying glass, just like Sherlock Holmes. 'Them reds did it, the ones on Hootenanny'. Cue affectionate applause.

To Ramona (Dylan) 6.02
Dylan giggles. 'Who cares?'. Obviously he does, judging from this tender rendition and the way he caresses the peerless melody to just a simple guitar. He makes the humble harmonica into an instrument worthy of this setting, playing it slow and with feeling, a true maestro.

Who Killed Davey Moore? (Dylan) 4.46

This always went down well live, the song about a young featherweight boxer who fell into a coma and died after losing a title bout to Sugar Ramos. Phil Ochs composed a long narrative song, describing the fight in detail. Dylan's take was more inventive, basing it on a nursery rhyme, largely sung on one note to build up the tension, and blaming everyone. He first sang this song only three weeks after the boxer died, just like a broadside ballad.

On the line about boxing not being permitted in Cuba, you will hear scattered applause, maybe some of the *Sing Out* crowd, who would be so affronted at Newport less than a year later. But Dylan is already leaving such simplicities behind. 'Its got nothing to do with boxing. Its got nothing to do with nothing. But I fit all these words together, that's all'. Wilenz posits that his laughter in the middle of the long intro, without mentioning exactly what song he is about to play, might be the result of mild intoxication, whether through Beaujolais, pot, or youthful fame. He is certainly high on himself: 'this has been taken out of a newspaper, nothing has been changed except the words'.

Gates Of Eden (Dylan) 8.32

Dylan introduces the second ever public performance of this song with the laconic 'this is called "A sacrilegious lullaby in D minor"' He even plays the correct chord – 'Now in all seriousness'. The audience laugh, not knowing what to expect – 'This is a love song'. And then he hits them with nearly nine minutes of pure poetry, wailed out across the silent auditorium. This is slightly slower and more emphatic than the studio version. No-one stirs, but you can almost picture jaws dropping and eyes widening.

Dylan sings with sad majesty and a frightening sense of focus. After the song, he plays the intro to the next song, then stops and declares 'I hope that didn't scare anybody, it's Halloween and I've got my Bob Dylan mask on. Just masquerading'.

If You Gotta Go, Go Now (Or Else You Got To Stay All Night) (Dylan) 4.06

Then straight into this, a welcome change of mood, before the second epic of the night. Everyone laughs, first because it is a genuinely funny song and secondly out of relief having stayed quiet for the cathedral intensity of the previous song. They really catch fire when they realize exactly what taboos he is knocking down here. Casual sex is okay among the bohemian crowd, and it is obvious here that Dylan is not talking to a virgin 'You know I'd have a guilty conscience' he sings, but that is exactly the point, there is nothing here to be ashamed of.

As Wilenz puts it, 'Dylan was doing with words what Elvis had done with his pelvis'. A girl shouts out something incomprehensible at the end. 'Anything you say' he rejoins. 'I hope I never have to make a living.'

It's Alright, Ma (I'm Only Bleeding) (Dylan) 11.26
Dylan introduces the next song as 'It's Alright Ma, It's Life And Life Only' as if it's going to be another light-hearted affair. The audience giggle, and he adds, 'yes, it's a very funny song'. Then having misdirected the innocents, he launches into a song with a verbal ambition no rock group of the time could even come close to. The images unwind like a waking portmanteau distopia, a protest song on LSD. Even though he muffs a line, for a heartstopping second, this even puts the recorded version in the shade, using words like weapons. It just goes on and on and on, sparing no-one.

Robert Shelton wrote after the event of a song 'played out against dramatic modal guitar figures…the demonic visions of a sensitive modern musical poet'. It sums up how profoundly this song must have affected the lucky souls here, hearing this straight from his creative furnace.

I Don't Believe You (She Acts Like We Never Have Met) (Dylan) 4.01
Dylan retunes his guitar, giving everyone pause for breath, then jokes that the next song is about 'all the people who say they've never seen you. I swear everyone has met somebody who claims they never saw them. Hi!' He is so taken with his own cleverness that he loses the song completely, goes on as if to verse two, then asks for help. A Bronx voice shouts out 'I can't understand' and he is off, like a greyhound out of the traps. Champion harmonica too. Dylan acts out the song like a pro.

Mr Tambourine Man (Dylan) 6.33
A few random toots on the mouth organ, then on to another virtually new, totally amazing song, though lots of the audience already recognize it. Shelton describes it as an 'introspective, symbolist piece that moved in and out of the listener's comprehension'. It is the entry ticket to wonderland, the only price for which is maybe your mind. It sounds particularly naked tonight, though Bob's voice has a frightening surety and he takes this at an unhurried pace. Warm applause at the end.

A Hard Rain's A-Gonna Fall (Dylan) 7.44
The torrent of words tonight comes to a temporary halt with this, the oldest song he will perform in this half. Strummed guitar, then he changes his mind and sings this instead and there is an almost relieved torrent of clapping. A universe away from the Rolling Thunder version from 11 years later and finally released a year or so before – such is the digital Dylan back catalogue now, a succession of frozen hours – this is slow, dignified, with emphatic guitar and nothing plugged in other than Bob himself into the wellsprings of his own imagination.

After this stunning first half, presumably artist and audience headed off separately for a drink. But the evening's delights were far from over.

CD 2
Talkin' World War III Blues (Dylan) 5.51
No preamble, and straight into a classic talking blues, much like the record, though the record player is now playing Martha and the Vandellas' 'Leader of the Pack' that would be news to the Shangri Las. You can feel the relief of the audience now safely back on familiar territory. This is already a period piece from two years before, when World War III seemed a distinct possibility. And it is now Carl Sandberg who supposedly delivered the tongue twister at the end.

Don't Think Twice, It's All Right (Dylan) 4.34
More good-natured banter from the audience. 'Please, what?' Dylan asks, affably. Then he takes the melody of another classic to the limits, almost parodying himself, like a hound baying. He toys with the rhymes, almost in childish wonder, then whoops through his harmonica.

The Lonesome Death Of Hattie Carroll (Dylan) 6.58
'This is a true story, right out of the newspapers again: it's like conversation, really'. He sings with apparent tenderness, then muted anger but again this already sounds dated in the view of what has already gone down tonight. You feel that he could sing this in his sleep by now. It will take the Rolling Thunder Revue to reinvest this with venom. But it gets one of the biggest reactions of the night.

Mama, You Been On My Mind (Dylan) 3.36
The concert needs something extra, and it arrives in the shape of Joan Baez that takes the

crowd by surprise. The golden couple of folk, still pretending at least to be an item, sing a love song to each other, with Baez singing 'Daddy' here, cosily. She also goes 'shooka shooka' during an instrumental break, like the girl groups Dylan had slagged off three songs earlier. Their voices intertwine well, like an expert pair of figure skaters. Then comically fall apart.

Silver Dagger (Traditional) 3.47
'Percy's Song' someone calls out earlier. 'We're going to do one of Bob Dylan's earlier songs', Joan quips, then goes into this old chestnut with Dylan weaving around her vocal on harmonica, scatting the part and effortlessly upstaging his former patron.

With God On Our Side (Dylan) 6.18
More audience laughter, then back to Bob with Baez providing harmony vocals. From this distance, a little Baez goes a long way, at least until after she began to deconstruct her own madonna image. And Bob already sounds 'weary as hell' with his own song. But the audience cheer to the rafters.

It Ain't Me, Babe (Dylan) 5.11
The final duet with Baez tonight and the most fervent on Bob's part, although he giggles half way through.. The voices are so incongruous you can hardly blame him, like a duchess and a tramp. There is a fascinating account of Dylan's relationship with Joan Baez – both musically and personally – and with her sister Mimi, and Mimi's husband Richard Farina, by David Hajdu in his book *Positively 4th Street* (2001).

All I Really Want To Do (Dylan) 4.02
Time for an encore. The crowd bark out requests. He mugs his way through 'All I Really Want To Do', sounding like Tiny Tim for a second. He will never sound quite so friendly again. It is the opening song from his most recent album, that he has otherwise ignored, until the last song with Baez.

Is this a good natured goodbye to Joan, or to his audience, or even to part of himself. After a bad natured tour of the UK (backstage at least), he will next appear in public at Newport brandishing an electric guitar.

NO DIRECTION HOME; THE SOUNDTRACK. BOOTLEG SERIES VOL 7

US Release: 30 August 2005
UK/Europe:
Producer: Jeff Rosen, Steve Berkovitz, Bruce Dickinson and Martin Scorsese

Columbia Legacy C2K 93937
Columbia/Legacy 520358-2
Running Time: (72.13), (72.22)

CD 1
When I Got Troubles; Rambler, Gambler; This Land Is Your Land; Song To Woody; Dink's Song; I Was Young When I Left Home; Sally Gal; Don't Think Twice, It's All Right; Man Of Constant Sorrow; Blowin' In The Wind; Masters Of War; A Hard Rain's A-Gonna Fall; When The Ship Comes In; Mr Tambourine Man; Chimes Of Freedom; It's All Over Now, Baby Blue.

CD 2
She Belongs To Me; Maggie's Farm; It Takes A Lot To Laugh, It Takes A Train To Cry; Tombstone Blues; Just Like Tom Thumb's Blues; Desolation Row; Highway 61 Revisited; Leopard-Skin Pill-Box Hat; Stuck Inside Of Mobile With The Memphis Blues Again; Visions Of Johanna; Ballad Of A Thin Man; Like A Rolling Stone,

This two-CD package proudly describes itself as the companion soundtrack to Martin Scorsese's two-part feature film. Only two of the tracks are already on album. But this is not a soundtrack in the traditional sense. The film's structure plays fast and loose with time. The compilers of this collection used the songs in the film (including unearthed footage from the UK 1966 tour) as a reference point, finding alternative takes, rare live performances and unreleased tracks that amplify the pivotal sequences in the film and avoid duplication. As it came out first, it also made anticipation of the TV documentaries all the keener.

There is a typical sleeve note from the Rolling Stones' one-time manager and spin doctor

BOB DYLAN
NO DIRECTION HOME : THE SOUNDTRACK
A MARTIN SCORSESE PICTURE

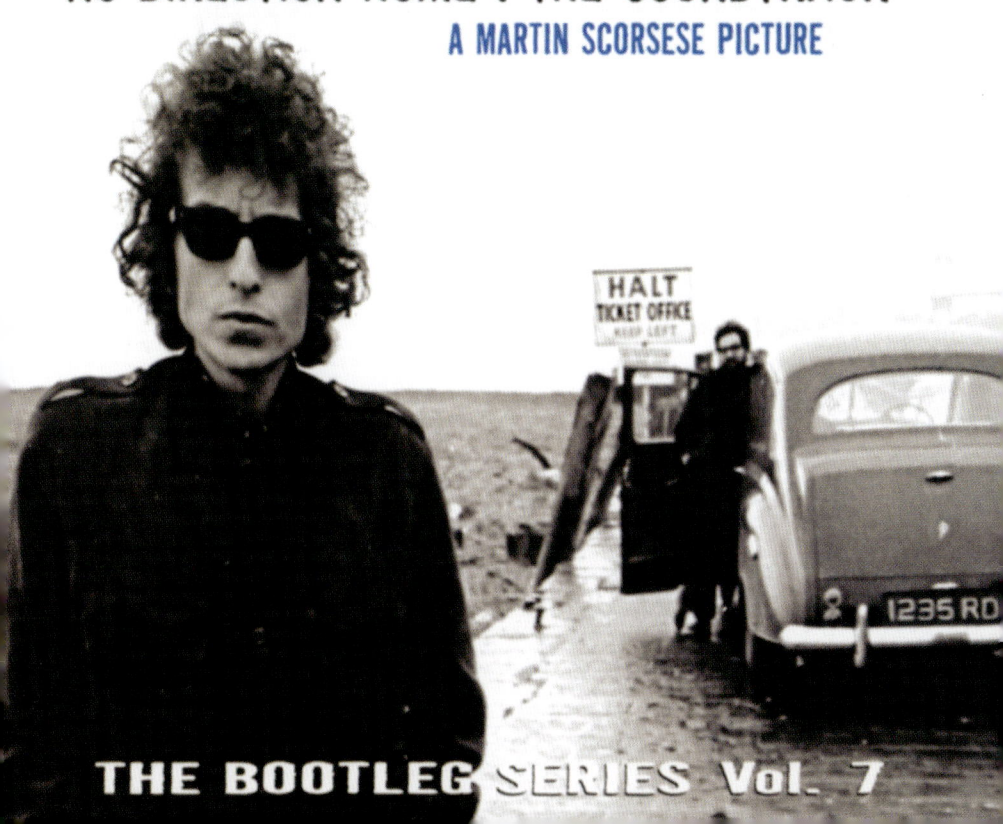

THE BOOTLEG SERIES Vol. 7

Andrew Loog Oldham, whose lower case back cover musings were seen at the time as a direct cop from Dylan. He's still at it. 'in england and france, better known as europe, there was dylan before there were beatles and stones. 43 years later, dylan still moves the goalposts, sets the game and chronicles dem bells, our lives hath seen shakespeare again'.

The cover is the famous photograph by Barry Feinstein of a windswept and extremely hacked-off Dylan on the road to nowhere, posing by a bleak ferry crossing point as Pennebaker waits in the Austin Princess. The numberplate of which has been cunningly altered to 1235 RD, an in-joke referring to 'Rainy Day Women'. On the back of the CD package is an extremely cherubic Dylan singing in a stairwell. Inside are even greater treasures. The cover of Bringing It All Back Home before its 'psychedelic' treatment; baby Bob; piles of film canisters and reel-to-reels; the angry young Dylan in his work shirt; onstage at Newport '65; wearing his *Blonde On Blonde* scarf; holding a battered cross a decade and more before the conversion. And, most poignant of all, bareheaded and riding his motorcycle, pre-crash. It almost matches the extraordinary act of cultural archaeology that is Scorsese's four hour-plus TV movie.

CD 1
When I Got Troubles (Dylan) 1.30
A 1959 home recording of what was probably young Bob's first original song. Very mellifluous too. It could be the young Paul McCartney. The guitar playing is clumsy but spirited, the lyrics self-involved and down from the start, but the singing is sweet, like Ricky Nelson. John Harris reckons this 'might pass for a pre-war field recording or a hilariously lo-fi off-cut from Harry Smith's Anthology'.

Rambler, Gambler (Trad arr Dylan) 2.28
In August 1960, Cleve Petterson bought a new Radio Shack tape recorder in Minneapolis and tested it out on a local wanabee and truant from the nearby university. Dylan's voice has deepened by about two octaves and this unexceptional take on a variant of the folk tune 'Wagoner's Lad' is already recognizably Dylan with a rapidly improving guitar technique.

This Land Is Your Land (Woody Guthrie) 5.59
Live at Carnegie Chapter Hall, 4 November 1961, this is the Guthrie anthem that would climax the Rolling Thunder Revues. Rudimentary harmonica, and a mournful rendition by Woody's young clone, but with a wistfulness all of his own. Genius has descended.

Song To Woody (Dylan) 2.41
Dylan's earliest composition from his debut album and a farewell to the master, creatively speaking. A pivotal moment in the documentary – Dylan says he had to write this song because he needed to get these sentiments out of his head and into the air.

Dink's Song (Trad arr Dylan) 5.03
Minneapolis, Minnesota 22 December 1961
This and the next song were recorded by Bob's friend Tony Glover three days before Christmas and much bootlegged as the 'Minnesota Hotel Tape'. But here it is direct from the master reel. 'Dylan is already a wonderful interpretative singer of traditional songs' says Eddie Gorodetsky in the sleeve notes.

I Was Young When I Left Home (Dylan) 5.25
Minneapolis, Minnesota 22 December 1961
'I kinda made it up on a train. It must be good for somebody, if not for me.' This is hugely poignant and has a strong autobiographical context, even though Dylan never lost touch in the way the protagonist does here. It is an early example of Bob reworking floating lyrics from traditional songs into his own personal expression. The lonesome guitar jangles so hard it almost hurts the ears.

Sally Gal (Trad arr Dylan) 2.38
Outtake from *Freewheelin' Bob Dylan*.
'70086 take one', the great John Hammond intones and his latest protégé is away, playing harmonica like a clucking chicken on heat, then some hackneyed lyrics that he sings as the nonsense they are, but with great spirit. 'An exuberant romp…the folkie equivalent of finishing your set with "Not Fade Away"' is how the notes describe it. And he sure can whoop.

Don't Think Twice, It's All Right (Dylan) 3.36
Demo for Whitmark Music, March 1963.
Bob's music publisher Lou Levy would virtually lock him in a room with a tape recorder to sing his latest songs into, so they could be transcribed for sheet music. The songs were pressed onto discs and sent to other performers, and it was in this way that Dylan's name began to spread. But it is more than a technical exercise, it is sung with real feeling to a limpid guitar accompaniment.

Man Of Constant Sorrow (Dylan) 3.24
The attribution would surprise the Appalachian singers who were singing this before its supposed author was born, but he remakes it in his own image, and makes us believe he has experienced so much. Taken from the 1963 TV show *Folk Songs* and *More Folk Songs*.

Blowin' In The Wind (Dylan) 4.23
Live at the Town Hall, New York 12 April 1963
'Here's a song I wrote which has been recorded. It doesn't sound much like the way I sing it. But the words are the same. That's the important thing.' He rescues it from Peter, Paul and Mary with this melancholy version, prefaced with lonesome harmonica and tonight 'less a political anthem, more like a lover's question'.

Masters Of War (Dylan) 4.43
Live at the Town Hall, New York 12 April 1963
'I believe in the Ten Commandments. The first one, I am the Lord thy God, is a great commandment, if it's not said by the wrong people'. He sings this briskly, almost matter of fact, but full of a young man's anger. The crowd go wild.

A Hard Rain's A-Gonna Fall (Dylan) 8.23
Live at Carnegie Hall, New York 26 October 1963
He introduces this song by explaining that something is going to happen, by implication not necessarily the Cuban missile crisis of '62 as referred to in Nat Henroff's *Freewheelin'* sleeve notes. The different tones he can get from his acoustic guitar hereare amazing and he sings with both dread and compassion. This live recording is pin sharp.

When The Ship Comes In (Dylan) 3.37
Live at Carnegie Hall, New York 26 October 1963
'Nowadays there are crueller Goliaths', but they will be slain too. Including over-zealous hotel clerks, brought clattering down here by the boy Bob with his sling of words. He knew his bible even back then.

Mr Tambourine Man (Dylan) 6.43
Columbia Studios, New York 9 June 1964,
Ton Wilson sounds drunk, or very ironic, telling these two Guthrie fanciers to get closer to the mike. The first complete take of the song, though Bob and his partner in crime Ramblin' Jack Elliott mangle some of the lyrics. An outtake from *Another Side*, one album early, supposedly the version sent to the Byrds who then invented 'folk rock' with its help! It must be – the pace is near identical, even if McGuinn, Clark and Crosby glide vocally where these two stumble appealingly.

Chimes Of Freedom (Dylan) 8.04
Live at the Newport Folk Festival, Rhode Island 26 July 1964
A majestic, driving version of this mystical vision, at the last Newport that Dylan attended to near-unanimous acclaim. His voice is hard as teak. Next year, he would be back to bury it. 'The loose-limbed enthusiasm of a man with lightning in his pocket.'

It's All Over Now, Baby Blue (Dylan) 3.33
Outtake from Bringing It All Back Home, Columbia Recording Studio, New York City 16 January 1965.
A slight but sweet melodic variant, it also served as the acoustic encore after the controversial electric set at Newport in 1965, supposedly a kiss off to any folk fans who could not follow him into the maelstrom.

    The first of the two CDs in this package has contained not the slightest trace of electricity, except in the force of Dylan's delivery. Things will change.

CD 2
She Belongs To Me (Dylan) 4.08
Outtake from *Bringing It All Back Home*, Columbia Recording Studio, New York 14 January 1965
Bob Dylan: vocal, guitar, **Bruce Langhorne**: guitar, **William E Lee**: bass
Slower and more limpid than the released version, and lacking drums, with bass guitar ticking out the pulse. This song was originally called 'Worse Than Money'. Liquid guitar patterns from Langhorne, and a typically gorgeous vocal from Dylan, until you listen a little closer to the words. It's either about a spoilt beautiful woman, or the muse.

Maggie's Farm (Dylan) 5.03
Live at the Newport Folk Festival 25 July 1965.
Bob Dylan: vocal, electric guitar, **Michael Bloomfield**: electric guitar, **Barry Goldberg**: organ, **Al Kooper**: organ, **Jerome Arnold**: bass, **Sam Lay**: drums
Peter Yarrow announces in an extremely serious tone 'the person who is coming up now has…changed the face of folk music to the large American public because he has brought to it the point of view of a poet'. What we actually get is a street urchin – 'let's go' – with Paul Butterfield's tough band and his tongue stuck in a barbed-wire fence. Bloomfield plays a blinder. This is tight and nasty, and does indeed fit the disdainful poetry of this song far better than just an acoustic guitar ever would. 'He's got a limited amount of time.' Too true, and the rest of this astonishing CD will trace what happened over the next 12 months.

It Takes A Lot To Laugh, It Takes A Train To Cry (Dylan) 3.35
Outtake from *Highway 61 Revisited*, Columbia Recording Studios, New York 15 June 1965. Original title 'Phantom Engineer'.
Bob Dylan: vocals, electric guitar, **Michael Bloomfield**: electric guitar, **Al Gorgoni**: guitar, **Al Kooper**: organ, **Frank Owens**: piano, **Joseph Macho Jr**: bass, **Bobby Gregg**: drums
This is take 8 of what Kooper calls the 'up tempo' draft, much in the style of the previous song. Al resurrected this arrangement on *Super Session*, an album like *Hamlet* without the prince. The engineer in the last verse will indeed end up cancelled. 'Bloomfield continues to turn the blues idiom upside down.'

Tombstone Blues (Dylan) 3.36
Alternate take (take 9) from *Highway 61 Revisited*, Columbia Recording Studios, New York 29 July 1965.
Bob Dylan: vocal, electric guitar, **Michael Bloomfield:** electric guitar, **Paul Griffin:** piano, **Bobby Gregg:** drums, **Joseph Macho Jr:** bass, **Al Kooper:** organ
Comedy time. This wild outtake features some background vocals by the boys in the band, overdubbed on another take by the Chambers Brothers. But what really distinguishes this is the fuzztone bass that sounds as if it had crept in from a Spike Jones session. You can hear the organ better here, and Bloomfield wails. Does he really sing 'John the blacksmith'? Dylan cracks up, and who can blame him.

Just Like Tom Thumb's Blues (Dylan) 5.45
Alternate take (take 5) from *Highway 61 Revisited*, Columbia Recording Studios, New York 2 August 1965.
Bob Dylan: vocal, electric guitar, **Michael Bloomfield:** electric guitar, **Al Gorgoni:** guitar, **Paul Griffin:** piano, **Bobby Gregg:** drums, **Harvey Brooks:** bass, **Al Kooper:** organ
This early take lacks the 'smeared Crayola bleary sunrise sound' of the album version apparently. It's great to hear all the ingredients of the finished take, not quite yet cooked through, with prominent electric piano and languorous guitar, and a less urgent vocal. And the words just needed a bit of tweaking; 'the cops don't need you here' is one word too many.

Desolation Row (Dylan) 11.40
Alternate take (take 1) from *Highway 61 Revisited*, Columbia Recording Studios, New York 29 July 1965.
Bob Dylan: vocal, acoustic guitar, **Harvey Brooks:** bass, **Al Kooper:** electric guitar
Recorded in the middle of the night, and it has that distant vibe. For John Harris, 'the delicate acoustic riff is replaced by a doleful blues figure – Kooper plays guitar like the young Lou Reed'. Kooper himself writes that this version 'marries the song with the punkiness of the rest of the album. Too bad the drummer had already gone home when we cut it'. But this drags where the released version struts. Even so, worth the price of admission just for the cancelled lyric about the Kafka-esque 'them' spoon feeding Casanova 'the boiled guts of birds'.

Highway 61 Revisited (Dylan) 3.40
Alternate take (take 6) from *Highway 61 Revisited*, Columbia Recording Studios, New York 2 August 1965.
Bob Dylan: vocal, electric guitar, **Michael Bloomfield**: electric guitar, **Al Gorgoni**: guitar, **Paul Griffin**: piano, **Bobby Gregg**: drums, **Harvey Brooks**: bass, **Al Kooper**: organ
Percussive electric piano and Bloomfield on heart-stopping slide guitar – he pulls off some brief solos here too – with urgent drumming. But something is missing. At the end of this take, Kooper removes the police siren he wears around his neck to give drug-taking hippies the fright of their lives, and suggests that Dylan adds it to his harmonica rack. It's like giving a baby a new rattle, and sure enough on the finished take Dylan has put it to brilliant use.

Leopard-Skin Pill-Box Hat (Dylan) 6.26
Alternate take (take 1) from *Blonde On Blonde*, Columbia Recording Studios, New York 1 January 1966.
Bob Dylan: vocal, electric guitar, **Michael Bloomfield**: electric guitar, **Paul Griffin**: piano, **Bobby Gregg**: drums, **William E. Lee**: bass, **Al Kooper**: organ
A much slower and meaner version with Dylan sounding stoned and a band who sound like they just blew in from the meanest dive in Southside Chicago. In this version Dylan has his belt wrapped around his head and adds two verses, one about being 'so dirty baby, walking all day in the cold bin' – his hands are dirty and so is his mind – and another about wanting to be her chauffeur, just like Memphis Minnie.

Stuck Inside Of Mobile With The Memphis Blues Again (Dylan) 5.45
Alternate take (take 5) from *Blonde On Blonde*, Columbia Recording Studios, Nashville, 17 February 1966.
Bob Dylan: vocal, guitar, harmonica, **Charlie McCoy**: guitar, **Wayne Moss**: guitar, **Joe South**: guitar, **Al Kooper**: organ, **Hargus 'Pig' Robbins**: piano, **Henry Strzelecki**: bass, **Kenneth Buttrey**: drums
Kooper tells a lovely tale about Dylan not wanting to call the blind pianist here by his nickname 'Pig', so using Al as an intermediary. You can immediately sense the relaxed Nashville vibe yet precise musicianship, and indeed this early run-through is too relaxed for the words it carries that he runs out of, at various points.

Visions Of Johanna (Dylan) 6.38
Alternate take (take 8) from *Blonde On Blonde*, Columbia Recording Studios, New York 30 November 1966.
Bob Dylan: vocal, guitar, harmonica, **Robbie Robertson**: guitar, **Garth Hudson**: organ, **Al Kooper**: organ, **Rick Danko**: bass, **Richard Manuel**: piano, **Levon Helm**: drums
Back to New York for this version with the Hawks plus Kooper. Robbie adds some killer licks, the drumming is martial, the pace upped. As Gorodetsky's notes point out, this is what it might have sounded like if it had been played during the amplified portion of the European tour. But it lacks the beauty of the Nashville version.

Ballad Of A Thin Man (Dylan) 7.46
Live at the ABC Theatre, Edinburgh 20 May 1966.
Bob Dylan: vocals, guitar, harmonica, **Robbie Robertson**: guitar, **Garth Hudson**: organ, **Richard Manuel**: piano, **Rick Danko**: bass, **Mickey Jones**: drums
A stunning slow version from a previously un-accessed show that makes you realize how each performance on this tour is subtly different. Where's the box set Sony? Dylan sings each line like a man knocking nails into folk music's coffin. Hudson is like the phantom of the opera, unhinged at the organ. And Robertson plays all the right notes and no more, plus a rhythm section inventing heavy metal.

Like A Rolling Stone (Dylan) 8.12
Live at the Free Trade Hall, Manchester 17 May 1966, previously released on *The Bootleg Series Volume 4: Live 1966*.
Bob Dylan: vocal, guitar, harmonica, **Robbie Robertson**: guitar, **Rick Danko**: bass, **Richard Manuel**: piano, **Garth Hudson**: organ, **Mickey Jones**: drums
The point that four hours of stunning documentary have moved towards. It's a long way from 'You've Got Troubles', but this slender young man sure has.

DVD Release: Paramount PHE 8823 (UK 111184) 2-DVD

BOB DYLAN LIVE AT THE GASLIGHT 1962

US Release: 30 August 2005

Producer: Jeff Rosen and Steve Berkovitz, mastered by Mark Wilder.

Columbia Legacy A96016
'360' Stereo Sound digipack
Running Time: 46.31

Available only from US outlets of Starbucks, licensed to the company for an initial 18 months before general release by Sony. Contains 12-page booklet with sleeve notes by Sean Wilentz giving details about Greenwich Village in the early 60s.

A Hard Rain's A-Gonna Fall; Rocks and Gravel; Don't Think Twice, It's All Right; The Cuckoo; Moonshiner; Handsome Molly; Cocaine; John Brown; Barbara Allen; West Texas
Tracks 1-3 written by Dylan, 4-10 traditional, adapted and arranged by Dylan

We are back almost where we started, with Dylan scuffling around the Greenwich Village coffeehouse scene. It is a world he wrote about memorably in his sleeve notes to the Peter Paul and Mary LP *In The Wind*, in an artfully syntax-free style, which would given Lynne Truss nightmares.

Sean Wilenz has again annotated this package with his usual care. The Gaslight opened in the 50s in the basement of 116 MacDougal Street as a poets café where visiting Beat poets would read from their latest collections. By 1961 it had become the most prestigious of venues catering for the new folk and jazz crowd. The CD digipack includes a photo of the outside of the Gaslight at around this time. Directly across the road was the Café Wha where Dylan played his first NY shows in the winter of 1961. Musicians were paid properly, not just reliant on the begging bowl of a passed-round basket.

The Gaslight was a place that Bob 'wanted to play, needed to play'. It was intimate, holding a hundred people at most. If you listen carefully to the CD, you can hear real audio verite, as denizens of this subterranean hole cough and sing along, and cars honk from the street above. It was Dickensian, Tiffany lamps provided illumination, leaky pipes dripped water onto what

Bob Dylan
Live at The Gaslight
1962

passed for a stage, the sound system was rudimentary, and there was no alcohol, except what you could smuggle in from elsewhere. Police raids were not uncommon.

Terri Van Ronk, Dylan's manager at the time, had taped a rougher and readier Dylan here a year before, as a calling card for out-of-town booking agents who took one listen and passed up their greatest ever stroke of luck. The tape accessed here is probably spliced from two separate sets. Some songs stop abruptly where the tape recorder was turned off. As Wilenz observes, this disc captures a young ragamuffin making giant creative strides 'in a dank, smoke-filled, hole-in-the-ground coffee-house, in the heart of America's last authentic bohemia'. The very antithesis of Starbucks.

The following April he finished recording *Freewheelin'*, including some of the new compositions captured here. He would never look back.

A Hard Rain's A-Gonna Fall (Dylan) 6.42
Straight into a bona-fide classic. It sounds small and intimate, with the background clatterings making it all the more urgent. The audience are already familiar with this, hence the way some join in the chorus. He performed this at Carnegie Hall, three weeks before the Cuban Missile Crisis that supposedly had inspired it, just as *Love and Theft* prefigures 9-11. It breaks off at the end as if someone just turned off all the lights.

Rocks and Gravel (Dylan) 4.59
A tough reworking of this folk standard written by Brownie McGhee and Leroy Carr with driving guitar and long, drawn-out moans from Dylan. The line 'don't my girl look fine when she's coming after me' will find its perfect setting on *Highway 61 Revisited*.

Don't Think Twice, It's All Right (Dylan) 3.11
He omits or hums some of the lyrics, as the song is not yet quite finished. Like a preliminary pencil sketch for a famous painting. The guitar is slightly out of tune.

The Cuckoo (Trad, arr Dylan) 2.21
In the weird way that record chronologies work, this Appalachian favourite has already been referred to on the 2001 song 'High Water (for Charley Patton)'. Dylan becomes the most ornery hillbilly imaginable, at least in his own mind.

Moonshiner (Trad, arr Dylan) 4.07
Just imagine being down in the folk cellar and hearing something this atmospheric. Intensity is what set Dylan apart from his competitors right from the start. It sure would have you made you crave a whisky in a teetotal club.

Handsome Molly (Trad, arr Dylan) 2.46
Recorded earlier by Bob's heroes, the Stanley Brothers. Somehow this ancient song has crossed the Atlantic, lodged for a century or two in the hills of Virginia, and is now being brought back to life in the heart of the city by the descendent of Russian émigrés who probably learnt it off a record. And it is as authentic as hell.

Cocaine (Trad, arr Dylan) 2.58
Most of the folk crew would choose to specialize in one particular aspect of folk music. Dylan is promiscuous, from ballads to blues to old time to ragtime, and he somehow nails each one, adapting a host of personae. He becomes the song he inhabits, like a spirit, and funny too.

John Brown (Trad, arr Dylan) 5.55
Despite the attribution, this is surely Dylan's own composition, he certainly copyrighted it in 1963 and it has his unique brand of biting sarcasm. Just about every one of Bob's own highly original compositions has a traditional root somewhere along the line.

Barbara Allen (Trad, arr Dylan) 7.52
The traditional English ballad transplanted to the United States. Dylan sets up a mood and dives deep. As he said later, 'all those songs about roses growing out of people's brains and lovers who are really geese and swans that turn into angels – they're not going to die'.

West Texas (Trad, arr Dylan) 5.38
Another tough blues that just needs Bloomfield and the crew and you'd have folk rock a few years before schedule. It cuts dead, just like that.

MORE DYLAN

DYLAN'S CONTRIBUTIONS TO OTHER ALBUMS

The albums listed below are restricted to those with Dylan as a named artist on at least one track – albeit sometimes under the pseudonyms Blind Boy Grunt, Lucky Wilbury and the like – and not those where he acted as a backing musician. That would be an even more substantial list, taking in everyone from Harry Belafonte to Kurtis Blow, U2 to Bette Midler, Mike Seeger to Allen Ginsberg.

BROADSIDE BALLADS VOLUME 1
US Release: 1963 Broadside BR 301
Contains three tracks by Dylan, aka Blind Boy Grunt: 'Only A Hobo', 'Talkin' Devil' and 'John Brown', plus Happy Traum's version of Dylan's song 'Let Me Die In My Footsteps'.

NEWPORT BROADSIDE
US Release: 1964 Vanguard VRS 9144/VSD 79148 (mono/stereo)   **UK Release:** 1964 Fontana TFL 6038
Contains two duets recorded at the 1963 Newport Folk Festival, 'Playboys and Playgirls' with Pete Seeger and 'With God On Our Side' with Joan Baez.

EVENING CONCERTS AT NEWPORT VOLUME 1
US Release: 1964 Vanguard VRS 9148/VSD 79148 (mono/stereo)   **UK Release:** 1965 Fontana TFL 6041

NEWPORT FOLK FESTIVAL EVENING CONCERT VOL 1
UK Release: 1965 Fontana TFL 6041
Both these Newport collections contain an ensemble performance, with Dylan on vocals, of his anthem 'Blowin' In The Wind'.

WE SHALL OVERCOME: DOCUMENTARY OF THE MARCH ON WASHINGTON
US Release: 1964 Folkways FH5592
Contains 'Only A Pawn In Their Game' broken by extracts from speeches live at the March on Washington, August 1963.

A TRIBUTE TO WOODY GUTHRIE PART ONE
US Release: 1971 Columbia KC 31171   **UK Release** 1972 CBS 64861
US 2-CD set: WB9-26036-2
Bob Dylan and the Band perform 'I Ain't Got No Home' (Woody Guthrie), 'Dear Mrs Roosevelt' (adapted by Woody Guthrie) and 'The Grand Coulee Dam' (Woody Guthrie) taped live at Carnegie Hall, New York 20 January 1968. Dylan provides backing vocals on Judy Collins' version of 'This Land Is Your Land'.

THE CONCERT FOR BANGLA DESH
US Release: 1971 Apple STCX 3385   **UK Release** 1971 Apple STCX 3385
2-CD Box Set: Epic 82876729862
Produced by George Harrison and Phil Spector. The concert took place at Madison Square Garden, New York, 1 August 1971. The proceeds went to the refugees who had crowded into Indian camps after Pakistan's leader General Khan had exercized savage repression on those who had voted for an independent democratic state. Dylan played a six-song set, of which five appeared on side 5 of the original vinyl box set, issued on The Beatles' own record label, backed by an all-star crew of George Harrison, Leon Russell and Ringo Starr. The recent CD box set adds 'Love Minus Zero/No Limit' (Dylan) as a bonus track at the end.

A Hard Rain's A-Gonna Fall (Dylan) 5.44
Bob Dylan: vocal, harmonica, acoustic guitar, **George Harrison:** electric guitar, **Leon Russell:** bass, **Ringo Starr:** tambourine
A good-natured run through with Dylan back to his old voice. Sprightly.

It Takes A Lot To Laugh, It Takes A Train To Cry (Dylan) 3.07
Bob Dylan: vocal, harmonica, acoustic guitar, **George Harrison:** electric guitar, **Leon Russell:** bass, **Ringo Starr:** tambourine
More Dylan karaoke with some nice electric slide from George. Disposable.

Blowin' In The Wind (Dylan) 4.07
Bob Dylan: vocal, harmonica, acoustic guitar, **George Harrison:** electric guitar, **Leon Russell:** bass, **Ringo Starr:** tambourine
Dylan gets a bit more impassioned here and brings his *Nashville Skyline* voice out of the locker. Ringo bangs his tambourine (although he is unlikely to be taking anyone through the smoke rings of his mind), Leon plays basic bass and George some nice country licks. Lively.

Mr Tambourine Man (Dylan) 4.45
Bob Dylan: vocal, harmonica, acoustic guitar, **George Harrison:** electric guitar, **Leon Russell:** bass, **Ringo Starr:** tambourine
More of the same at the same jovial tempo with Bob singing with a smile in his voice and almost cracking up. Undemanding.

Just Like A Woman (Dylan) 4.48
Bob Dylan: vocal, harmonica, acoustic guitar, **George Harrison**: electric guitar, vocals, **Leon Russell:** bass, vocals, **Ringo Starr:** tambourine
Some nice guitar at the start, then they slow things down in an amateurish kind of way, and Bob delivers his best vocal of the night with George's reedy harmonies. Heartfelt.

Love Minus Zero/No Limit (Dylan) 4.20
Bob Dylan: vocal, harmonica, acoustic guitar, **George Harrison**: electric guitar,
Leon Russell: bass, **Ringo Starr**: tambourine
Starts off like 'If Not For You', then switches song. Minimal tambourine, simple bass, nice guitar, and Dylan caresses the words. Appealing.

BROADSIDE REUNION
US Release: 1972 Folkways FR 5315
Contains four tracks recorded by Dylan for *Broadside* magazine in 1962 and 1963: 'I'd Hate To Be You On That Dreadful Day', 'The Ballad Of Emmett Till', 'The Ballad of Donald White' and 'Train A-Travelling'. 'Ballad of Donald White' and 'John Brown' were later included on *The Best Of Broadside* CD (Folkways August 2000).

THE BAND: THE LAST WALTZ
UK Release: 1978 3-LP set and booklet WB K 66076
4-CD Box Set: 2002 Rhino 8122-78278-2
The concert took place on 26 November 1976, Dylan's first concert appearance since the second leg of the *Rolling Thunder Revue*. He fronts the Band for five songs all on Record 3, Side 1. The augmented 4-CD box reissue adds 'Hazel' in its rightful place, as the second song in Dylan's set captured on CD 3. Robertson is quoted in the augmented booklet about this choice of song – 'Bob would do things like that. He would do something that seemed to make a lot of sense then throw in something that didn't seem to make any'.

Baby Let Me Follow You Down (Rev Gary Davis) 2.56
Bob Dylan: vocal, guitar, **Robbie Robertson:** guitar, **Garth Hudson:** organ,
Richard Manuel: piano, **Rick Danko:** bass, **Levon Helm:** drums
'We'd like to bring on one more very good friend of ours'. They sound like the old friends they are, recollected in tranquillity. Hudson and Robbie do their musical party tricks, but it is a long way from 1966. This is essentially good-natured with good thumping drums from Helm. Dylan almost whoops for joy, even promising to buy a wedding gown.

Hazel (Dylan) 3.41
Bob Dylan: vocal, guitar, **Robbie Robertson:** guitar, **Garth Hudson:** organ,
Richard Manuel: piano, **Rick Danko:** bass, **Levon Helm:** drums
The Band slow things down and up the emotional temperature for a lesser-known *Planet*

Waves song. Dylan sings deep, yelping out the words, and Robbie takes an unusually long solo for him. Not a note is wasted.

I Don't Believe You (She Acts Like We Never Have Met) (Dylan) 3.29
Bob Dylan: vocal, guitar, **Robbie Robertson:** guitar, **Garth Hudson:** organ, **Richard Manuel:** piano, **Rick Danko:** bass, **Levon Helm:** drums
Another key song revolutionized on the 1966 tour, the opening riff now turned mellow and Dylan quizzical rather than splenetic. Robbie takes things higher on the break and Garth sounds otherworldly.

Forever Young (Dylan) 5.51
Bob Dylan: vocal, guitar, **Robbie Robertson:** guitar, **Garth Hudson:** organ, **Richard Manuel:** piano, **Rick Danko:** bass, **Levon Helm:** drums
The key song from *Planet Waves*, this passionate version probably eclipses even the original. The Band still fit Dylan's voice like a glove and Hudson plays with almost supernatural powers around him. Remember them this way.

Baby Let Me Follow You Down (Reprise) (Rev Gary Davis) 2.59
Bob Dylan: vocal, guitar, **Robbie Robertson:** guitar, **Garth Hudson:** organ, **Richard Manuel:** piano, **Rick Danko:** bass, **Levon Helm:** drums
A reprise for no good reason, slightly longer than the prequel but really just adding more of the same. How could such a wonderful group ever split up – it did none of them any good in the long run.

I Shall Be Released (Dylan) 4.50
Bob Dylan: vocal, guitar, **Robbie Robertson:** guitar, **Garth Hudson:** organ, **Richard Manuel:** piano, vocal, **Rick Danko:** bass, **Levon Helm:** drums, **Ron Wood:** guitar, **Ringo Starr:** drums, **Paul Butterfield**, **Bobby Charles**, **Eric Clapton**, **Neil Diamond**, **Ronnie Hawkins**, **Dr John**, **Joni Mitchell**, **Van Morrison**, **Neil Young:** backing vocals

The usual superstar jam nonsense. However, this transcends the template because of the greatness of the song and of Manuel's vocal, a fragile and tenuous thing (like Richard himself). Dylan sings with grace and fire too and the billion pound chorus earn their spurs, like a celestial choir. Maybe this went through Manuel's mind after one backwater gig too many. One certainly hopes so.

FIONA, BOB DYLAN & RUPERT EVERETT: HEARTS OF FIRE ORIGINAL SOUNDTRACK
US Release: 20 October 1987 Columbia C 40870   **UK Release:** CBS 460 001-1
CD Release: CK40870

The Usual (John Hiatt) 1.32
Just Dylan and acoustic guitar.

Night After Night (Dylan) 3.38

Had A Dream About You, Baby
Remixed for *Down In The Groove* with a new backing track and two overdubbed vocal lines. The album also features five tracks sung by 'Fiona' and two sung by Rupert Everett.

VARIOUS ARTISTS: FOLKWAYS, A VISION SHARED TRIBUTE TO WOODY GUTHRIE & LEADBELLY
US Release: 1988 Columbia CK 44034
Dylan sings 'Pretty Boy Floyd' (Guthrie).

THE TRAVELLING WILBURYS: VOL ONE
UK Release: 1988 Warners Wilbury Record Co 925 796-1 WX224
Produced by Otis and Nelson Wilbury (Jeff Lynne and George Harrison).

Side One: Handle With Care; Dirty World; Rattled; Last Night; Not Alone Any More.

Side Two: Congratulations; Heading For The Light; Margarita; Tweeter And The Monkey Man; End Of The Line.

All songs credited jointly to the Travelling Wilburys.
Bob Dylan 'Lucky Wilbury': acoustic guitar, lead and backing vocals, **George Harrison 'Nelson Wilbury'**: guitars, lead and backing vocals, **Jeff Lynne 'Otis Wilbury'**: keyboards, guitar, lead and backing vocals, **Roy Orbison 'Left Wilbury'**: acoustic guitar, lead and backing vocals, **Tom Petty 'Charlie T Wilbury'**: acoustic guitar, lead and backing vocals

Dylan had shipped over the equipment from Rundown to his garage in Malibu, so it was all in place when his mates came over for some fun and resurrected something of the anarchic spirit of *The Basement Tapes*. The first album was laid down between 3 April and 16 May 1988, as a collaborative project. Dylan is presumed to sing lead on three of the songs: 'Dirty Mind', pieced together in Dave Stewart's LA kitchen with lyrics taken at random from glossy magazines, 'Congratulations' – 'righteously bitter' – and 'Tweeter And The Monkey Man', supposedly a satire on Bruce Springsteen. Bob was later a little dismissive of the project: 'Co-operation is great on something like that because you never get stuck. It was a pretty rushed affair. A lot of stuff was scraped up from jam tapes'.

This gave Dylan his first double platinum album and remained on the US album charts for almost a year. Photographs of the famous five appear on the front cover, all in dark glasses, but clearly recognisable. The inner album sleeve contains a spoof biography of the band. 'The songs gathered here represent the popular laments, the epic and heroic tales which characterize the apotheosis of the elusive Wilbury sound'.

VARIOUS ARTISTS: FLASHBACK ORIGINAL SOUNDTRACK
US Release: 1990 WTG NK 46042
Dylan sings 'People Get Ready' (Curtis Mayfield).

THE TRAVELLING WILBURYS: VOL THREE
UK Release: October 1990 Wilbury Records/WB 7599-26324-1
Produced by Spike and Clayton Wilbury (George Harrison and Jeff Lynne).

Side One: She's My Baby; Inside Out; If You Belonged To Me; The Devil's Been Busy; 7 Deadly Sins; Poor House.

Side Two: Where Were You Last Night; Cool Dry Place; New Blue Moon; You Took My Breath Away; Wilbury Twist.

All songs credited to the Travelling Wilburys.
Bob Dylan 'Boo Wilbury': acoustic guitar, harmonica, lead and backing vocals, **George Harrison 'Spike Wilbury'**: acoustic and electric guitars, mandolin, sitar, lead and backing vocal, **Jeff Lynne 'Clayton Wilbury'**: acoustic guitar, bass, keyboards, lead and backing vocals, **Tom Petty 'Muddy Wilbury'**: acoustic guitar, lead and backing vocals

This was recorded in April 1990. Producer Jeff Lynne dropped Dylan's 'Like A Ship' from the running order, covered over some of his vocals and even overlaid some of his harmonica breaks. Creatively, lightning didn't strike twice, although this remains a thoroughly entertaining listen. As Dylan said, 'there's no telling what kind of record we would have made with Roy. Everybody missed him, but it wasn't like anyone sat and talked about it. The songs are more developed. If people liked the first one, they'll love this one'.

New pseudonyms but this is the same line-up as Volume One apart from Roy Orbison, who had died the previous December. There was no Volume Two. The four pose on the front cover, three again in rock-star dark glasses, Dylan squinting direct at the camera in a white skullcap. The inner sleeve contains a spoof academic dispute about the origin of the band's name. These 'itinerant, mundivagrant peripatetic nomads' have already recorded one album for the 'hedonistic gratification of the hoi polloi'. Now here's another one.' The Wilbury Record Company is 'a subdivision of the Trans-Wilbury Corporation of Mongolia' we are informed, with a warning that 'pirated records damage your equipment'. The sleeve also gives instructions as to how to dance the 'Wilbury Twist' with photographs.

THE TRAVELLING WILBURYS: SHE'S MY BABY/NEW BLUE MOON (INSTRUMENTAL VERSION)/ RUNAWAY
1990 Warner Brothers 12-inch single W 9523 (T)
Composition of 'Runaway' credited to Del Shannon/Max D Cook, other two tracks to the Travelling Wilburys.

VARIOUS ARTISTS: FOR OUR CHILDREN
US Release: 1991 Disney 60616-2
Dylan sings 'This Old Man' (Trad) on this charity album to benefit children with AIDS.

WILLIE NELSON: ACROSS THE BORDERLAND
US Release: March 1993 Columbia CK 527TL
Dylan and Willie duet on 'Heartland' (Dylan-Nelson).

JOAN BAEZ: RARE, LIVE AND CLASSIC
US Release: 31 August 1993 Vanguard VCD3 R3-7
Dylan and Baez duet on 'Troubled And I Don't Know Why', Forest Hills, NY 17 August 63, and 'Blowin' In The Wind', Fort Collins 23 May 76, wrongly attributed to 16 May 76.

NATURAL BORN KILLERS ORIGINAL SOUNDTRACK
US Release: December 1994 Uni 92460
Dylan sings 'You Belong To Me' (Pee Wee King/Red Stewart/Chilton Price).

VARIOUS ARTISTS: WOODSTOCK 94
US Release: 1994 A&M
Dylan sings 'Highway 61 Revisited'.

VARIOUS ARTISTS: TIL THE NIGHT IS GONE – A TRIBUTE TO DOC POMUS
US Release: April 1995 Rhino 71878
Dylan sings 'Boogie Woogie Country Girl' (Pomus/Reginald Amby).

FEELING MINNESOTA ORIGINAL SOUNDTRACK
US Release: September 1996 Atlantic 82865-2
Dylan sings 'Ring Of Fire' (June Carter/Kilgore).

VARIOUS ARTISTS: THE CONCERT FOR THE ROCK AND ROLL HALL OF FAME
US Release: 1996 Columbia
Dylan sings 'All Along The Watchtower'.

VARIOUS ARTISTS: JERRY MCGUIRE ORIGINAL SOUNDTRACK
US Release: December 1996 Epic EXC 67910
'Shelter From The Storm' (alt version, extra verse).

VARIOUS ARTISTS: THE SONGS OF JIMMIE RODGERS – A TRIBUTE
US Release: September 1997 Egyptian/Columbia CK 67676
Dylan covers 'Blue Eyed Jane' (Rodgers/Lulu Belle White). He put the whole thing together as the inaugural – and so far only – release on his new record label

JOAN BAEZ: LIVE AT NEWPORT
US Release: 1997 Vanguard 77013-2
Bob and Joan duet on 'It Ain't Me, Babe' at Newport, 24 July 64.

VARIOUS ARTISTS: THE 60s ORIGINAL NBC MOTION PICTURE SOUNDTRACK
US Release: January 1999 Mercury 314528743-2
Dylan and Joan Osborne duet on 'Chimes Of Freedom'.

VARIOUS ARTISTS: WONDER BOYS MUSIC FROM THE MOTION PICTURE
US Release: 15 February 2000 Columbia CK 63849
Dylan sings 'Things Have Changed'.

VARIOUS ARTISTS: STOLEN ROSES, SONGS OF THE GRATEFUL DEAD
US Release: 8 August 2000 Arista GDCD 4073
Dylan covers 'Friend Of The Devil' (Robert Hunter/Jerry Garcia).

VARIOUS ARTISTS: SELECTIONS FROM THE BEST OF BROADSIDE 1962-1988
US Release: 22 August 2000 Smithsonian Folkways SFNCD40
Dylan sings 'The Ballad Of Donald White'.

VARIOUS ARTISTS: THE SOPRANOS – PEPPERS AND EGGS
US Release: 8 May 2001 Columbia C2K 85453 2-CD set
TV soundtrack album, includes Dylan's cover version of the Dean Martin song 'Return To Me' (Diminni/Lombardo).

VARIOUS ARTISTS: TIMELESS – HANK WILLIAMS TRIBUTE
US Release: September 2001 Lost Highway 170 239-2
Dylan covers 'I Can't Get You Off My Mind' (Hank Williams).

VARIOUS ARTISTS: GOOD ROCKIN' TONIGHT – THE LEGACY OF SUN RECORDS
US Release: 30 October 2001 Sire 31165-2
Dylan covers 'Red Cadillac And A Black Moustache' (Lillian May/Willie Bea Thompson).

VARIOUS ARTISTS: THERE IS NO EYE – MUSIC FOR PHOTOGRAPHS
US Release: November 2001 Smithsonian Folkways 40091
Dylan sings 'Roll On John', a previously unreleased 1962 recording taken from Cynthia Gooding's show *Folksingers' Choice*.

GRATEFUL DEAD: POSTCARDS OF THE HANGING – GRATEFUL DEAD PERFORM THE SONGS OF BOB DYLAN
US Release: 19 March 2002 Arista 4069/7822-14069-2
Bob Dylan and the Dead sing 'Man of Peace'.

VARIOUS ARTISTS: MUSIC FROM THE MOTION PICTURE DIVINE SECRETS OF THE YA YA SISTERHOOD
US Release: 28 May 2002 Columbia SK 96534
Dylan sings 'Waitin' For You'.

VARIOUS ARTISTS: KINDRED SPIRITS – A TRIBUTE TO THE SONGS OF JOHNNY CASH
US Release: 24 September 2002 Lucky Dog/Columbia CK 83610
Dylan covers 'Train Of Love' (Cash).

VARIOUS ARTISTS: GOTTA SERVE SOMEBODY – THE GOSPEL SONGS OF BOB DYLAN
US Release: 24 March 2003   **UK release**: COL 511126 2
Columbia Legacy CK 89025
Bob and Mavis Staples duet on 'Gonna Change My Way Of Thinking'.

VARIOUS ARTISTS: GODS AND GENERALS ORIGINAL SOUNDTRACK
US Release: 24 March 2003 Sony CK 89015
Dylan sings 'Cross The Green Mountain'.

VARIOUS ARTISTS: ENJOY EVERY SANDWICH – THE SONGS OF WARREN ZEVON
US Release: 19 October 2004 Arteris
Dylan sings 'Mutineer' (Zevon).

VARIOUS ARTISTS: BONNARROO FESTIVAL 2004
US Release: 5 May 2005 Sanctuary 0607684736-2
Dylan sings 'Down Along The Cove'.

VARIOUS ARTISTS: MUSIC FROM THE MOTION PICTURE 'NORTH COUNTRY'
US Release: 11 October 2005 Sony CK 97777
Dylan sings 'Tell Ol' Bill'.

THE BAND: A MUSICAL HISTORY
UK Release 2005: Capitol 7 24357 18790 9 5-CD with DVD Box Set
CD 1: Tell Me Mama/Just Like Tom Thumb's Blues (Odeon, Liverpool 14 May 1966); Odds and Ends (*Basement Tapes*).
CD 2: Don't Ya Tell Henry (*Basement Tapes*); I Ain't Got No Home (Carnegie Hall, 20 January 1968).
CD 3: Rainy Day Women #12 & 35 (Forum, Inglewood 13 February 1974); Highway 61 Revisited (Madison Square Gardens 31 January 1974). These tracks have Dylan on lead vocals.

SELECTED DYLAN BOOTLEGS

There are four generations of Dylan bootlegs. First came vinyl productions by the likes of Trade Mark of Quality, now highly prized by collectors, that often cut across different session dates, and whose packaging ranged from stark and uninformative, to the stunning and highly amusing colour illustrations by William Stout that deserve a book in their own right.

Secondly, signposted by the likes of 'Paul Cable', were a generation of tape swappers who gathered together individual recording sessions and complete tour recordings – this is a far more informed and somewhat less legally questionable pursuit.

Thirdly, that same neo-academic approach led to a generation of factory-mastered CDs by the likes of The Genuine Series or Hollow Horn, in small print runs and put together with great care and attention. These often put Dylan's own commercial attempts to revisit his back catalogue in the shade with near-definitive box sets of key periods, leading, for example, to a huge revaluation of the likes of the *Rolling Thunder Review* or the evangelical concerts of 1979-80. Only a large box set could do justice to the complete *Basement Tapes*, or the huge variety of cover versions essayed in the Never Ending Tour. The same impulse resulted in some extraordinary DVD releases that were put in the shade by Martin Scorsese's official chronicle of Dylan's progress from Greenwich Village to the 1966 apocalypse.

Most recently the rise of cheap CD recorders, mini-disc technology and the availability of internet downloads, including Dylan's own official website, have led to a near uncontrollable influx of products and the constant repackaging of classic recordings can be a trap for the unwary. While I make no attempt to justify the distribution of music by those who benefit illegally from it, ironically, all this has led to properly produced bootlegs being largely driven off the market where they now enjoy a luxury status that is often reflected in their price. These versions are far removed from those first roughly stamped and muddled vinyl try-outs that now attract their own hard-core collectors and are expensive items in their own right.

Isis, via *Henry Porter's Wreckin' Lot*, provides an invaluable chronicle of commercial CD bootlegs and the huge CD-R trading sub-world, and of the many lost sessions and concerts that leak onto the market. It is like an ocean of song from which official releases are buckets dipped into the flow. Knowledge of this material helps put Dylan's commercially released albums into context. What follows is a highly partial list restricted to those key recording sessions and concerts that provide a shadow history of Dylan's official album discography.

Gaslight Café, New York 6th September 1961 (Historical Archives Vol 1)
includes the traditional ballad 'Pretty Polly' and an early Dylan song, the grimly comic 'Talkin' Bear Mountain Picnic Massacre Blues'.

Early Dylan
Includes the Carnegie Concert Hall, November 1961, with lots of tuning up and surrealistic chat between recreations of vintage Americana, including Guthrie's sombre '1913 Massacre' from which he later appropriated the tune for 'Song to Woody'. This is preceded by a radio WNYC interview plugging the show, during which Dylan claims he was raised in New Mexico, 'I got a lot of cowboy songs there, Indian songs, carnival songs, vaudeville kind of stuff'.

Bob Dylan – The Bootleg (Wanted Man 022)
Combines the mono mix of Dylan's debut album, taped in November 1961, with seven songs from the Leeds Music demos, recorded in January 1962. *Early 60s Revisited* (Trade Mark Of Quality 71083) adds a radio broadcast from Riverside Church, July 1961, including a duet by Dylan and Rambling Jack Elliott on 'Acne (Doo Wah)'.

Second Gaslight Tape (Wild Wolf) Live at the Gaslight Club, 116 McDougal Street, 10-62
17 songs, only ten of which made it to the official album recently licensed to Starbucks.

A Hard Rain's A Gonna Fall; Don't Think Twice It's Alright; Black Cross; No More Auction Block; Rocks and Gravel; Barbara Allen; Moonshine Blues; Motherless Children; Handsome Molly; John Brown; Ballad of Hollis Brown; Kind Hearted Woman Blues; See That My Grave Is Kept Clean; Ain't No More Cane; Cocaine; The Cuckoo Is A Pretty Bird; West Texas.

Broadside (Gunsmoke GSRII) Broadside Sessions November 1962-March 1963
14 songs including those which later appeared officially on *Broadside Reunion* (1972) and *Broadside Ballads* (1963), plus a complete take of 'Only A Pawn In Their Game', recorded at the March on Washington, 28 August 1963. Fragments of this appear on *We Shall Overcome* (1964).

Complete Concert Town Hall, New York 12 April 1963
Includes versions of 'I'll Keep It With Mine' and 'Masters of War'.

Bob Dylan in Concert (Wild Wolf 6401)
Repro of officially scheduled album for Christmas 1963 that was withdrawn at the last moment. It combines highlights from two concerts: New York Town Hall, 12 April 1963, and Carnegie Hall, New York, 26 October 1963.

Last Thoughts on Woody Guthrie; Lay Down Your Weary Tune; Dusty Old Fairgrounds; John Brown; When The Ship Comes In; Who Killed Davy Moore?; Percy's Song; Bob Dylan's New Orleans Rag; Seven Curses.

The Lonesome Sparrow Sings (Black Nite Crash BNC-003)
Outtakes from *Bringing It All Back Home*, *Highway 61* and *Blonde On Blonde*.

1965 Revisited (Great Dane 9419) 14-CD box set
With a booklet, this is an astonishing chronicle of a tangled year, that includes album outtakes, concerts, TV appearances (including the BBC special filmed on 1 June), press conference, the

Newport Folk Festival and subsequent concerts with the Hawks up to Berkeley Community Theatre on 4 December.

Highway 61 Revisited Again
This CD contains tracks taken from an acetate of rough mixes, of which the earlier take of 'Desolation Row' with the line about Casanova being spoon fed 'the boiled guts of birds', 'Positively 4th Street' and the first take of 'Please Can You Crawl Out Your Window' were dropped from the album. The running order is interesting too.

Like A Rolling Stone; Ballad Of A Thin Man; Just Like Tom Thumb's Blues; Highway 61 Revisited; Positively Fourth Street; It Takes A Lot To Laugh; Tombstone Blues; Can You Please Crawl Out Your Window; Desolation Row; Queen Jane Approximately; From A Buick Six.

Highway 61 Revisited/Blonde On Blonde. The Mono Mixes (Gold Standard BN-339/HM 313)
2 CDs. In typical bootleg style each disk is mislabelled as the other but this further indicates the substantial differences between mono and stereo mixes of these two crucial albums

Guitars Kissing And The Contemporary Fix
A 2-CD release that predated the official release of the epochal concert at Manchester Free Trade Hall on 17 May 1966 and has a slightly different mix and sound. This is a pirate copy of the version prepared for commercial release in the mid 1990s and then cancelled. As Columbia puts it, this earlier version 'filtered out most of the audience and hall sound. This added a closeness and clarity to the vocals but took away from the manic edginess of the room feel; it was abandoned in favour of the rawer sound heard here'.

Record Collector reckons 'the change is dramatic; on the original remastering the audience were off in the distance, this time you're in the front row of the stalls surrounded by the tense buzz of Dylan fans preparing for a revolution'. One other noticeable difference is that the acoustic disc runs faster on the official version than on *Guitars Kissing*, 'by about two per cent. This slightly alters the key of the songs and chops five or six seconds apiece out of their running time'.

Live 1966 (Scorpion)
A stunning 8-CD box set with deluxe packaging and the result of sourcing the best surviving tapes of every professionally recorded stage performance in that tumultuous year. It includes a newly discovered complete concert from Sydney, 13 April 1966, plus two info-packed booklets, poster and postcards. Each disc is given the cheeky label GBS.

In 1966 There Was (Vigotone)
26 CD-Rs in a cardboard box. For real completists, a torrent of audience tapes, recording sessions, press conferences, and the soundtrack of *Eat The Document*, all in roughly chronological order. A desert island choice.

A Tree With Roots (White Bear January 04)
4-CD set of all the *Basement Tapes* material, 1967, Big Pink, West Saugerties, Woodstock, with the Band. The best version yet available, it is a remastered version of *The Genuine Bootleg Tapes Vols 1-5* (BD 2002-6) of which Volume Three was pressed in mono by mistake.

This is the rock from which Dylan's new musical style, post Judas, is being hewn, literally as we listen. Based on five reel-to-reel tapes and now in the chronological order in which these scraps and diamonds were laid down, first in the Red Room at Dylan's own house in June 1967, and then at Big Pink for the rest of that year. It presents a grab bag of Americana, both traditional and sometimes tongue in cheek, of songs by everyone from the Carter Family to Hank Williams, Johnny Cash and Ian and Sylvia. There are all kinds of spoken asides, parodies of rock'n'roll clichés and improvisations. The first few discs can be hard work for the listener at times, being music made principally for the enjoyment of its makers and overheard here as if through a keyhole. But the version of 'Young But Daily Growing' can freeze the blood. There are many such moments.

The Band fit their lead singer like a glove, following his every mood. Garth Hudson and Robbie Robertson embroider the songs in a subtle and laid back way, Danko hitting the low notes with unerring accuracy and Manuel bringing his lonesome voice to the party. Levon Helm is noticeable by his absence until the final session. Dylan's own new songs progress from rough ideas to a new style, combining the surrealism of old with in-jokes and a strong dose of homeliness as befits a man now planning to settle down and raise a family out in the country. There are glances back to 'See That My Grave Is Kept Clean' from the debut album, some blues and soul classics and even a parody of the hit single 'Ode To Billy Joe'.

CD 1
Lock Your Door; Baby, Won't You Be My Baby; Try Me Little Girl; Young But Daily Growin' (Trad); Bonnie Ship The Diamond (Trad); The Hills Of Mexico (Trad); Down On Me (Trad); I Can't Make It Alone; Don't You Try Me Now; One For The Road; I'm Alright; One Single River (Ian Tyson/Sylvia Fricker); People Get Ready (Curtis Mayfield); I Don't Hurt Anymore (Don Robertson/Jack Rollins); (Be Careful Of) The Stones That You Throw; One Man's Loss (Bonnie Dodd); Baby Ain't That Fine (Dallas Frazier); Rock, Salt And Nails (Bruce Phillips); A Fool Such As I (Bill Trader); Silouette (Frank C Slay Jr/Bob Crewe); Bring It On Home; King Of France; Nine Hundred Miles (Trad); Goin' Down The Road (Trad); Spanish Is The Loving Tongue (Charles Badger Clark/J Williams); Po' Lazarus (Trad)

CD 2
On A Rainy Afternoon; I Can't Come In With A Broken Heart; Come All Ye Fair And Tender Ladies (Trad); Under Control; Ol' Roison The Beau (Trad); I'm Guilty Of Loving You; Johnny Todd (Trad); Cool Water (Bob Nolan); Banks Of The Royal Canal (Brendan Behan); Belchezaar (Johnny Cash); I Forgot To Remember To Forget Her (Stanley Kesler/Charlie Feathers); You Win Again (Hank Williams); Still In Town, Still Around (Johnny Cash); Waltzin' With Sin (Hayes/Burns); Big River (Johnny Cash) – take 1; Big River (Johnny Cash) – take 2, Folsom Prison Blues (Johnny Cash); Bells Of Rhymney (Idris Davies/Pete Seeger); I'm A Fool For You – false start and take; Next Time On The Highway; Tupelo (John Lee Hooker); You Gotta Quit Kickin' My Dog Aroun'

(Webb M Oungst/Cy Perkins); See You Later, Allen Ginsberg (Robert Guidry); Tiny Montgomery; The Spanish Song – take 1; The Spanish Song – take 2; I'm Your Teenage Prayer

CD 3
Four Strong Winds (Ian Tyson); The French Girl (Ian Tyson) – take 1; The French Girl (Ian Tyson) – take 2; Joshua Gone Barbados (Eric Von Schmidt); I'm In The Mood For Love (John Lee Hooker); All-American Boy (Bobby Bare/Orville Lunsford); Sign On The Cross; Santa Fe; Silent Weekend; Don't Tell Henry; Bourbon Street; Million Dollar Bash – take 1; Yea! Heavy And A Bottle Of Bread – take 1; Million Dollar Bash – take 2; Yea! Heavy And A Bottle Of Bread – take 2; I'm Not There (1956); Please Mrs Henry; Crash On The Levee (Down In The Flood) – take 1; Crash On The Levee (Down In The Flood) – take 2; Lo And Behold – take 1; Lo And Behold – take 2; You Ain't Going Nowhere – take 1; Too Much Of Nothing – take 1; This Wheel's On Fire; You Ain't Going Nowhere – take 2; I Shall Be Released.

CD 4
Too Much Of Nothing – take 2; Tears Of Rage – take 1; Tears Of Rage – take 2; Tears Of Rage – take 3; Quinn The Eskimo (The Mighty Quinn) – take 1; Quinn The Eskimo (The Mighty Quinn) – take 2; Open The Door Homer – take 1; Open The Door Homer – take 2; Open The Door Homer – take 3; Nothing Was Delivered – take 1; Nothing Was Delivered – take 2; Goin' To Acapulco; Gonna Get You Now; Wildwood Flower (A.P. Carter); See That My Grave Is Kept Clean (Trad arr Jefferson); Comin' Round The Mountain (Trad); Instrumental Jam; Flight Of The Bumble Bee; Confidential To Me (Dorinda Morgan); Odds And Ends – take 1; Nothing Was Delivered – take 3; Odds And Ends – take 2; Get Your Rocks Off; Clothesline Saga (Answer To Ode); Apple Sucking Tree – take 1; Apple Sucking Tree – take 2; All You Have To Do Is Dream – take 1; All You Have To Do Is Dream – take 2.

All songs presumed to be written by Bob Dylan, unless otherwise stated.

The Original Dwarf Music Acetate
Circulated in mono, this was a 10-track publisher's demo, copyrighted in October 1967:

Million Dollar Bash – take 2; Yeah, Heavy And A Bottle Of Bread – take 2; Please Mrs Henry; Crash On The Levee (Down In The Flood) – take 2; Lo And Behold; Tiny Montgomery; This Wheel's On Fire; You Ain't Going Nowhere – take 2; I Shall Be Released; Too Much Of Nothin' – take 2.
This was followed by a 5-track publisher's demo, again in mono, copyrighted in January 1968.

Tears Of Rage – take 3; Quinn The Eskimo – take 2; Open The Door Homer – take 3; Nothing Was Delivered – take 1; Get Your Rocks Off.

13 of these songs were much bootlegged on vinyl in the early 1970s. Once again the original stereo mixes were folded into mono from their original panned stereo and the tracks were in a different order, missing out 'Too Much Of Nothing' and 'Get Your Rocks Off'.

The most notable of these albums was *Little White Wonder*, released without footnotes or explanations. The most legendary and now collectable was the reissue by Rover Records of Holland that had cartoon artwork by 'Peter Pontiac' illustrating each song. That album credits 'Tears of Rage' to Dylan and Manuel and 'This Wheel's On Fire' to Dylan and Danko.

In his review for *Rolling Stone*, where he said 'Dylan's Basement Tapes should be released', Jann Wenner comments 'even though he used one of the finest rock'n'roll bands ever assembled on the *Highway 61* album, here he works with his own band, for the first time. Dylan brings that instinctual feel for rock'n'roll to his voice for the first time. If this were ever to be released, it would be a classic'. Surely a proper revaluation of the *Basement Tapes* material in original stereo and without later interpolations from the Band without Dylan, should be attempted by Sony Legacy.

The Dylan Cash Sessions (Spank SP 106)
Studio outtakes from *Nashville Skyline*, including 5 tracks from the quadraphonic mix.

Isle of Wight (Wanted Man 39)
Complete audience recording of Dylan's concert with the Band, Woodside Bay, 31 August 1969, some of which later surfaced on *Self Portrait*.

She Belongs To Me; I Threw It All Away; Maggie's Farm; Wild Mountain Thyme (Traditional); It Ain't Me Babe; To Ramona; Mr Tambourine Man; I Dreamed I Saw St Augustine; Lay Lady Lay; Highway 61; One Too Many Mornings; I Pity The Poor Immigrant; Like A Rolling Stone; I'll Be Your Baby Tonight; Quinn The Eskimo; Minstrel Boy; Rainy Day Women.

Possum Belly Overalls (Gold Standard NASH 105)
Outtakes from *New Morning* and *Self Portrait*, including the amusing if abortive recording session with George Harrison.

Pecos Blues (Spark SP 107)
Outtakes from *Pat Garrett & Billy The Kid*.

Blood On The Tracks: New York Sessions (A&R S-19322)
A straight copy of the original acetate of the album as laid down in New York in September 1974 before half of it was re-recorded up in Minneapolis.

Blood On The Tapes (Columbus Col 2-1070)
Supposedly licensed from Sono records. Eleven studio takes from three New York sessions in chronological order.

Cambridge 1975 (Screamer 04021-023)
3-CD set from Harvard Square Theatre, 20 November 1975 that chronicles the whole show, interspersing Dylan's vocals spots with sets by backing musicians Guam, Joni Mitchell, Ramblin' Jack Elliott, Roger McGuinn and Joan Baez, who also duets with Dylan on five songs. Everyone gets together at the end to sing Woody Guthrie's anthem 'This Land is Your Land'. It puts the official *Bootleg Series* recording in context.

Friends and Other Strangers (Moontunes 016)
Recordings from the Last Waltz, Winterland 26 November 76, these are taken from the rough-mix master, unedited, unabridged and undubbed. It includes the complete set by Dylan and the Band.

Rock Solid (Junkyard Angel 004)
Unreleased live album recorded at the Massey Hall, Toronto, 19 April 1980 that culminates in a spinetingling 'In The Garden'. A concert the following night was covered in full on two double CDs, *The Born Again Music* (Flashback 02.93.0204) and *Gospeller* (Super Sonic 200030/31).

Between Shot and Saved (Dandelion DL 105)
Recorded at United Western Studios and Rundown Studios, March to April 1981, including some bonus tracks 'stolen from Scorpio Records' in a dog-eat-dog move.

A Friend To The Martyr: Outfidels (Silver Rarities SIRA 44)
Infidels outtakes, The Power Station, New York April-May 1983. See also *Rough Cuts: The Infidels Studio Sessions* (Red Devil100 1-1/2). 2 CDs, over two hours of outtakes, including alternate second takes.

Clean Cuts (Henry Porter's 115th Dream) (Sick Cat GRA8 003)
Empire Burlesque sessions, recorded July 1984–March 1985, this plays too fast but was updated by *Tempest Storm: Empire Burlesque Outtakes* (Theramin, Golden Archive 14). Both feature the original 'New Danville Girl', a career highlight, before Arthur Baker covered everything in heavy bass and synth drums.

Important Words (Wanted Man 014)
Outtakes from *Empire Burlesque* and *Down In The Groove*.

The Never Ending Tour (Deep MIK 012/3)
Hearts of Fire outtakes, recorded August 1986 with Eric Clapton at the Townhouse Studios, London. There are three takes of 'The Usual', seven of 'Had A Dream About You Baby', three of 'Old 5 And Dimers', and single takes of 'Some Kind Of Way' and 'To Fall In Love With You'.

Volume Two (Beta CDWA 431)
Outtakes from *Travelling Wilburys Volume One*, recorded in Dylan's garage, Spring 1988.

The Deeds Of Mercy (Razor's Edge RA2)
Oh Mercy outtakes, recorded March 1989.

Volume Four (In The Groove AWCD 21)
Travelling Wilburys Volume Three outtakes, recorded April 1990, a different selection from that on *Volume Four and a Half* (Adam VIII CD 49-021).

Kaatskill Serenade and Three More Songs (Ashes and Sand AAS-16)
Four songs recorded in the summer of 1992 at Acme Studios, Chicago with the David Bromberg band, from an abandoned album project. All four are cover versions including a haunting version of Bromberg's own 'Catskill Serenade', Jimmie Rodgers' 'Miss The Mississippi and You', bluesman Jimmy Rogers' 'Sloppy Drunk', plus the traditional 'Polly Vaughan' on which Dylan's rendition is as supernatural as the song itself. The same year saw Dylan revisit his traditional roots for a whole album on *Good As I Been To You*, but nothing cuts quite as deep as this.

Great Music Experience, Nara City, Todaji Temple, Japan, 20-22 May 1994
The third of these concerts was broadcast on TV. 'A Hard Rain's A Gonna Fall' (with full orchestra) was officially released on a CD single and also on the bootleg *Hard To Find*, plus 'I Shall Be Released' and 'Ring Them Bells', on *Harder to Find (Lost Recordings 1986-96)*. Dylan sang just these three songs each night.

Completely Unplugged (Moontunes MOON 006/007)
MTV Studios, New York.

17 November 1994: Tombstone Blues; I Want You (1); Don't Think Twice; Desolation Row (1); Hazel; Everything Is Broken; The Times They Are A-Changin'; Love Minus Zero/No Limit; Dignity (1); With God On Our Side.
18 November 1994: Absolutely Sweet Marie; Shooting Star; All Along The Watchtower; My Back Pages; Rainy Day Women; John Brown; Times They Are A-Changin'; Dignity (2), Knockin' On Heaven's Door; Like A Rolling Stone; Tonight I'll Be Staying Here With You; Desolation Row (2); I Want You (2).

HOLLOW HORN REFERENCE RECORDINGS

Complete album outtakes on eight double CDs.

Vol 1: Walk Like A Duck; Smell Like A Skunk: Bob Dylan; The Freewheelin Bob Dylan'; The Times They Are A-Changin'; Another Side Of Bob.

Vol 2: Now Your Mouth Cries Wolf; Bringing It All Back Home; Highway 61 Revisited; Blonde On Blonde.

Vol 3: A Fish That Walks; Nashville Skyline; Self Portrait (studio session with Happy Traum); New Morning.

Vol 4: Blood On Your Saddle; Pat Garrett and Billy The Kid; Blood On The Tracks.

Vol 5: Where The Monkey Dances; Planet Waves; Desire; Street Legal; Slow Train Coming; Shot Of Love.

Vol 6: One More Layer Of Skin; Infidels; Sweetheart Like You (working session).

Vol 7: A Man With No Alibi; Empire Burlesque; Down In The Groove; Oh Mercy; Under The Red Sky.

Vol 8: Park It Where The Sun Don't Shine: Travelling Wilburys Vol 1, Travelling Wilburys Vol 3, alternate takes November 1961-March 1966, studio sessions June 1992, World Gone Wrong, studio session September 1994.

Besides the outtakes listed in the main album section here, the following tracks appear:

Levy's Recording Studio, London
12th May 1965: 'Bob Dylan Convention Speech'
June 1970, studio unknown: 'Spanish Is The Loving Tongue', 'Tomorrow Is A Long Time'

More Bob Dylan's Greatest Hits/Singles
16 March 1971, Blue Rock Studios, New York: When I Paint My Masterpiece; Watching The River Flow. Both with Leon Russell on piano.
24 September 1971, Columbia Studio B, New York: You Ain't Going Nowhere (x2); Down In The Flood; I Shall Be Released. All with Happy Traum.
4 November, Columbia Studio B: Wallflower; George Jackson.

Studio Session with Bette Midler
Late October, 1975, Secret Sound Studio, New York: Buckets of Rain. Outtake of the version released on Midler's album *Songs For The New Depression*.

Travelling Wilburys Vol 1
April-May 1988, Dylan's Home Recording Studio: When There's A Wilbury There's A Way; Handle With Care; Dirty World; Rattled; Last Night; Congratulations; Heading For The Light; End Of The Line.

Travelling Wilburys Vol 3
April 1990: Fish And Chips; She's My Baby; Inside Out; If You Belonged To Me; Devil's Been Busy; 7 Deadly Sins; Poor House; Where Were You Last Night?; Cool Dry Place; New Blue Moon; You Took My Breath Away; Wilbury Twist; Like A Ship; Maxine; Runaway; Nobody's Child; The Wilburys Are Coming; 7 Deadly Sins 2 (studio playback); Like a Ship (studio playback); Keep On Travelling Folks.

Taken from original tapes before the remix took Dylan/Boo's vocals right down.

David Bromberg Studio Sessions,
June 1992, Acme Recording Studio, Chicago: Miss The Missippi; Polly Vaughan; Kaatskill Serenade; Sloppy Drunk.
Four of the original fifteen tracks of traditional songs and covers prepared for commercial release but finally replaced by the purely acoustic *Good As I Been To You*.

World Gone Wrong
May 1993, Dylan's Home Recording Studio: You Belong To Me.
Given over for the soundtrack of *Natural Born Killers*, this is the original take before actors' voices were dubbed over part of the track.

Tribute To Jimmie Rodgers
May 1994: My Blue Eyed Jane.
Earlier version of this song as released on a tribute album with Emmylou Harris on backing vocals.

Studio Sessions, September 1994
30th September 1994: Any Way You Want Me.
Among tracks laid down for another tribute album, reportedly all with a strong Elvis Presley connection.

THE GENUINE BOOTLEG SERIES (Scorpion 94-14-01/3)
3-CD set plus booklet that reprints Clinton Heylin's splenetic review in *Goldmine* of *The Bootleg Series Vol 1-3*, that he terms a wasted opportunity when it was cut down from four CDs to three. This resurrects the lost tracks and more.

THE GENUINE BOOTLEG SERIES TAKE TWO (Scorpion)
3-CD set, another chronological trawl through the archives, plus a rare 1965 interview from *In Beat* magazine.

THE THIRD ONE NOW (Scorpion GBS3)
3-CD set, yet another chronological series of outtakes and live epiphanies, chosen with the usual care and capped with another revelatory reprinted interview, this time with Paul Zollo – 'there's something about my lyrics that have a gallantry to them. And that might be all they have going for them'.

ACETATES ON THE TRACKS (Howlin Wolf Records)
Various volumes of studio outtakes.

HARD TO FIND/EVEN HARDER TO FIND/HARDEST TO FIND (various labels)
Multi-volume series of live and studio tracks gathered together for the listeners' convenience, including Dylan's contributions to other people's projects.

DISCOGRAPHY

SINGLES, 12-inch SINGLES, CD SINGLES AND EPs

US SINGLES

This list does not include reissues and repackaging of tracks some years after they were first laid down, although some are undoubtedly intriguing. For instance the 1967 combination of 'Like A Rolling Stone'/'Rainy Day Women' or 'Lay, Lady, Lay'/'I Threw It All Away' circa 71.

Mixed Up Confusion/Corrina Corrina (14 December 1962) Columbia 4-42656
Dylan's debut single now very rare. Some authorities date this to March 1962, which would predate his debut album, but this is impossible as the rockabilly-style electric backing was laid down during the Freewheeling sessions, in November 1962. The dates here are those given by Paul Williams, who is as reliable as any human can be. The single was not promoted, disappeared without trace, and a mint copy would now be valued in four figures, whether in dollars or pounds.

Blowin' In The Wind/Don't Think Twice It's Alright (August 1963) Columbia 4-42856

On The Road Again/Bob Dylan's 115th Dream/Gates Of Eden/She Belongs To Me (undated) Columbia 7-9128
Jukebox mini-LP. *Record Collector* describes this extremely rare item as a sampler of the album for jukebox use. The 7-inch sleeve is a scaled-down version of the album cover, and notes dryly that '"Gates Of Eden" must have knocked them out in the juke joints'.

Subterranean Homesick Blues/She Belongs To Me (March 1965) Columbia 4-43242
Record Collector dates this to April and lists an extremely rare picture-sleeve promo version.

Like A Rolling Stone/Gates Of Eden (20 July 1965) Columbia 4-43346
One of the few 45 rpm singles to inspire a whole book. This pocket-sized edition, by rock'n'roll professor Greil Marcus is called *Like A Rolling Stone, Bob Dylan At The Crossroads* (2005).

Positively 4th Street/From A Buick 6 (7 September 1965) Columbia 4-43389
A mis-pressed version briefly available in California featured the first take of 'Can You Please Crawl Out Your Window' in lieu of the title track.

Can You Please Crawl Out Your Window/Highway 61 Revisited (30 November 1965) Columbia 4-43477

One Of Us Must Know/Queen Jane Approximately (February 1966) Columbia 4-43541

Rainy Day Women #12 & 35/Pledging My Time (April 1966) Columbia 4-43592

I Want You/Just Like Tom Thumb's Blues (June 1966) Columbia 4-43683
In picture sleeve.

Just Like A Woman/Obviously 5 Believers (August 1966) Columbia 4-43792

Leopard-Skin Pill-Box Hat/Most Likely You Go Your Way And I'll Go Mine (March 1967) Columbia 4-44069

I Threw It All Away/Drifter's Escape (April 1969) Columbia 4-44826

Lay, Lady, Lay/Peggy Day (July 1969) Columbia 4-44826

Tonight I'll Be Staying Here With You/Country Pie (October 1969) Columbia 4-45004

Wigwam/Copper Kettle (June 1970) Columbia 4-45409

Watching The River Flow/Spanish Is The Loving Tongue (3 June 1971) Columbia 4-45409

George Jackson (acoustic version)/**George Jackson** (big band version) **(November 1971) Columbia 4-45516**
Paul Williams makes the big band version the A side.

Knockin' On Heaven's Door/Turkey Chase (August 1973) Columbia 4-45913

A Fool Such As I/Lily Of The West (November 1973) Columbia 4-45982

On A Night Like This/You Angel You (February 1974) Asylum 11033

Something There Is About You/Tough Mama (March 1974) Asylum 11035

Most Likely You Go Your Way/Stage Fright (The Band only) (July 1974) Asylum 11043

All Along The Watchtower/It Ain't Me Babe (November 1974) Asylum E-45212
Williams does not list this item – note different catalogue prefix.

Tangled Up In Blue/If You See Her Say Hello (February 1975) Columbia 3-10106

Million Dollar Bash/Tears Of Rage (July 1975) Columbia 3-10217

Hurricane (Part 1)/ **Hurricane** (Part 2) **(November 1975) Columbia 3-10245**

Mozambique/Oh Sister (February 1976) Columbia 3-10298

Rita Mae/Stuck Inside Of Mobile (30 November 1976) Columbia 3-10454

Baby Stop Crying/New Pony (31 July 1978) Columbia 3-10805

Changing Of The Guard/Senor (September 1978) Columbia 3-10805

Gotta Serve Somebody/Trouble In Mind (August 1979) Columbia 3-11072

**When You Gonna Wake Up/Man Gave Names To All The Animals (November 1979)
Columbia 3-11168**

Slow Train/Do Right To Me Baby (February 1980) Columbia 1-11235

Solid Rock/Covenant Woman (2 June 1980) Columbia 1-11318

Saved/Are You Ready (August 1980) Columbia 1-11370

**Heart of Mine/The Groom's Still Waiting At The Altar (11 September 1981)
Columbia 18-02510**

Sweetheart Like You/Union Sundown (November 1983) Columbia 38-04301

Jokerman/Isis (20 February 1984) Columbia 38-04425

**Tight Connection To My Heart/We Better Talk This Over (September 1985)
Columbia 38-04933**

**Emotionally Yours/When The Night Comes Falling From The Sky (April 1986)
Columbia 38-05697**

Band Of The Hand (non-Dylan track) **(June 1988) MCA-52811**

Silvio/Driftin' Too Far From Shore (October 1989) Columbia 38-07970

Everything Is Broken/Dead Man, Dead Man (April 1990) cassette single only

UK SINGLES

The Times They Are A-Changin'/Honey Just Allow Me One More Chance (March 1965) CBS 201751
Some early copies are rumoured to have 'She Belongs To Me' on the B side.

Subterranean Homesick Blues/She Belongs To Me (April 1965) CBS 201753

With God On Our Side (with Joan Baez) **(April 1965) Fontana TFE181009**

Ye Playboys and Playgirls (with Pete Seeger) **(April 1985) Fontana TFE18011**

Don't Think Twice, It's Alright/Blowin' In The Wind/Corrina, Corrina/ When The Ship Comes In (1965) CBS EP 5051
Picture sleeve of Dylan with acoustic guitar, as if painted by Seurat. The sleeve notes 'Dylan is a deeply committed young man who conveys his concern for the world around him through unique and poetic imagery that makes explicit the human condition....'

Maggie's Farm/On The Road Again (June 1965) CBS 201781

Like A Rolling Stone/Gates Of Eden (August 1965) CBS 201811

Positively 4th Street/From A Buick Six (October 1965) CBS 201824

Can You Please Crawl Out Your Window?/Highway 61 Revisited (January 1966) CBS 201900

One Of Us Must Know (Sooner Or Later)/Queen Jane Approximately (April 1966) CBS 202053

One Too Many Mornings/Spanish Harlem Incident/Oxford Town/It Ain't Me Babe/She Belongs To Me (April 1966) CBS EP 6070
Picture sleeve with a black and green drawing of Dylan in a spiky style.

Rainy Day Women #12 & 35/Pledging My Time (May 1966) CBS 202307

I Want You/Just Like Tom Thumb's Blues (July 1966) CBS 202258
The B side was recorded live in concert in Liverpool in 1966.

Mr Tambourine Man/Subterranean Homesick Blues/It's All Over Now Baby Blue (October 1966) CBS EP 6078
Picture sleeve shows Dylan sitting cross legged, framed in an art nouveau design.

Leopard-Skin Pill-Box Hat/Most Likely You Go Your Way And I'll Go Mine (September 1966) CBS 2700
Some copies appear in a monochrome picture sleeve that has Dylan's face half hidden beneath dark glasses.

No singles were issued during the 32 months of Dylan's retreat to Woodstock, although 'Mixed Up Confusion' was given a UK catalogue number, CBS202476 and a projected release date of late 1966. There is no lead single from *John Wesley Harding*.

I Threw It All Away/The Drifter's Escape (May 1969) CBS 4219
Dylan's first UK single to be released in stereo.

Lay Lady Lay/Peggy Day (August 1969) CBS 4434

Tonight I'll Be Staying Here With You/Country Pie (November 1969) CBS 4611

Wigwam/Copper Kettle (The Pale Mountain) (June 1970) CBS 5122

If Not For You/New Morning (February 1971) CBS 7092

Watching The River Flow/Spanish Is The Living Tongue (June 1971) CBS 7329
Flip-side is a different and greatly superior rendition to that on *Self Portrait*.

George Jackson (acoustic version)/**George Jackson** (big band version) **(December 1971) CBS 7688**
One of the few Dylan songs that he has never performed in concert, at least at the time of writing.

Just Like A Woman/I Want You (April 1973) CBS 1158

Knockin' On Heaven's Door/Turkey Chase (September 1973) CBS 1762

A Fool Such As I/Lily Of The West (January 1974) CBS 2006

On A Night Like This/Forever Young (February 1974) Island WIP 6168

Tangled Up in Blue/If You See Her Say Hello (February 1975) CBS 3160

Million Dollar Bash/Tears Of Rage (October 1975) CBS 3665

Hurricane (Part One)/**Hurricane** (full version, 33 rpm) **(January 1976) CBS 3878**
Early copies in picture sleeves show Carter in boxing gloves.

Lay, Lady, Lay/I Threw It All Away (February 1976) CBS 3995 PS

Mozambique/Oh Sister (March 1976) CBS 4113

Rita May/Stuck Inside Of Mobile With The Memphis Blues Again (live) **(January 1977) SCBS 48659**
Early copies were in picture sleeves. The record label mislabels 'Stuck Inside Of Mobile' as the A side.

Baby Stop Crying/New Pony (July 1978) CBS 6499/12-6499
12-inch version in a picture sleeve.

Is Your Love In Vain/We Better Talk This Over (October 1978) CBS 6718/12-6718
12-inch version. The picture sleeve shows three Dylans in a row.

Changing Of The Guards/Senor (December 1978) CBS 6935

Forever Young (live)**/All Along The Watchtower** (live)**/I Want You** (live) **(June 1979) CBS 7473**
All three tracks were recorded live at Budokan.

Precious Angel/Trouble In Mind (August 1979) CBS 7828

Man Gave Names To All The Animals/When He Returns (October 1979) CBS 7970

Gotta Serve Somebody/Gonna Change My Way Of Thinking (January 1980) CBS 8134

Saved/Are You Ready (June 1980) CBS 8743

Heart Of Mine/Let It Be Me (July 1981) CBS A 1406
US issue has a different and far superior B side, 'The Groom's Still Waiting At The Altar'.

Lenny Bruce/Dead Man, Dead Man (September 1981) CBS A 1640
Picture sleeve of a pensive Dylan.

Union Sundown/Angels Flying Too Close To The Ground (October 1983) CBS 3916
B side written by Willie Nelson but misattributed to Dylan. The picture sleeve shows a bearded Dylan in shades.

Jokerman/Licence To Kill (June 1984) CBS A 4055 Picture sleeve.

Highway 61 Revisited (live)/**It Ain't Me Babe** (live) **(January 1985) CBS A 5020**
Picture sleeve. Also issued in gatefold sleeve **CBS GA 5020**

Tight Connection To My Heart/We Better Talk This Over (June 1985) CBS A 6303
Picture sleeve.

When The Night Comes Falling (edit)/**Dark Eyes (August 1985) CBS A 6469**
Available in two different mixes of the A side. The picture sleeve is a variant of the *Empire Burlesque* sleeve.

When The Night Comes Falling (full length version)/ **Dark Eyes (August 1985) CBS TA 6469**
12-inch single.

Band Of The Hand (with the Heartbreakers)/
Theme From Joe's Death (non-Dylan track) **(August 1986) MCA 1078**
Picture sleeve.

Band Of The Hand (with the Heartbreakers)/**Theme From Joe's Death** (non-Dylan track) **(August 1986) MCAT 1076**
12-inch single in a picture sleeve.

The Usual/Got My Mind Made Up (October 1987) CBS 651 148 -7
Picture sleeve.

The Usual/Got My Mind Made Up/They Killed Him (October 1987) CBS 651 148-6
12-inch single in a picture sleeve. The final track is listed as 'They Killed Him' on the sleeve and on the label but plays 'Precious Memories' or 'Drifting Too Far From The Shore'.

Silvio/When Did You Leave Heaven (July 1988) CBS 651 406-7
Picture sleeve with a script but no photo.

Silvio/When Did You Leave Heaven/Driftin' Too Far From The Shore 12-inch **(July 1988) CBS 651 406**

Everything Is Broken/Death Is Not The End (October 1989) CBS 655 358-7

Everything Is Broken/Dead Man, Dead Man (live)/**I Want You** (live) 12-inch with free print **(October 1989) CBS 655 358 6 PS, CBS 655 358-8**

Everything Is Broken/Where The Teardrops Fall/Dead Man Dead Man/Ugliest Girl In The World CD single **(October 1989) CBS 655 358**
The picture sleeve is a close-up of the album sleeve.

Political World/Ring Them Bells (January 1990) CBS 655 643-7

Political World/Ring Them Bells/Silvio/All Along The Watchtower (live)
12-inch **(January 1990) CBS 655 643-6**

Political World/Ring Them Bells/Silvio/All Along The Watchtower
(live, from *Live and Dead*) CD single **(January 1990) CBS 655 643-2**

Political World/Caribbean Wind/You're A Big Girl Now/It's All Over Now, Baby Blue
CD single **(February 1990) CBS 655 643-2**

It's Unbelievable/10,000 Men (September 1990) CBS 656 304-7
The picture sleeve shows Dylan crouched on the ground.

It's Unbelievable/10,000 Men/In The Summertime/Jokerman
CD single **(September 1990) CBS 656304-2**

Political World/Caribbean Wind/You're A Big Girl Now/It's All Over Now, Baby Blue
CD **(February 1991) CBS 655 643-5**

Series of Dreams/Seven Curses (1991) CBS 656 707-7 PS

Series of Dreams/Seven Curses/Tangled Up In Blue/Like A Rolling Stone
CD **(1991) CBS 656 707-5**

Dignity 5.09 (unplugged Edit)/**Dignity** (unplugged full-Length version/**John Brown**
(unplugged)/**It Ain't Me Babe** 5.19 (from *Renaldo and Clara* soundtrack,1995)
Columbia CD single, **662 076-5**
The cover picture shows Dylan in polka-dot shirt.

Dignity (unplugged version)/**Dignity** (full-length studio version)/**A Hard Rain's A-Gonna Fall** 1995, CD single **Columbia 662 076-2**
Recorded live at the Great Music Experience with the Tokyo New Philharmonic Orchestra, conducted by Michael Kamen. The cover picture is a slight variant of that on the CD above. Five of these tracks, lacking the studio version of 'Dignity', appear on the US CD single *Dignity*, **Columbia 661400 2**. There is also a UK promo-only one-track CD single of 'Dignity', **xpcd 580, dated 1994**.

Love Sick (Live 'Grammy' version, live **25 February 1998**)/**Cold Irons Bound** (field recording **December 1997**)/ **Cocaine Blues** (field recording **December 1997**)/**Born in Time** (field recording' **August 1997**) **Columbia** CD single **1998 Col 665 997-2**
Picture sleeve shows a close up of Dylan in a dark jacket.

Love Sick (original version)/**Can't Wait** (field recording **December 1997**)/**Roving Gambler** (field recording **December 1997**)/**Blind Willie McTell** '(field recording' **February 1998**) **Columbia** CD single **1998 Col 665 997-5**

The picture sleeve is a longer-focus shot of above.

Things Have Changed (radio edit)/**To Make You Feel My Love** (live version)/**Hurricane/ Things Have Changed** (video) **2000 Columbia 669 379**
CD single. The picture sleeve shows Dylan in a cowboy hat.

ALBUMS

US release dates are given, with UK release dates in parenthesis except where albums were released in the same month.

Bob Dylan
Side One: You're No Good; Talkin' New York; In My Time Of Dyin'; Man Of Constant Sorrow; Fixin' To Die Blues; Pretty Peggy-O; Highway 51 Blues.

Side Two: Gospel Plow, Baby Let Me Follow You Down, House Of The Rising Sun, Freight Train Blues, Song to Woody, See That My Grave Is Kept Clean.
19 March 1962 (July 1962)

The Freewheelin' Bob Dylan
Side One: Blowin' In The Wind; Girl From The North Country; Masters Of War; Down The Highway; Bob Dylan's Blues; A Hard Rain's A-Gonna Fall.

Side Two: Don't Think Twice, It's All Right; Bob Dylan's Dream, Oxford Town, Talkin' World War III Blues, Corrina, Corrina, Honey, Just Allow Me One More Chance, I Shall Be Free.
May 1963 (November 1963)

The Times They Are Are A-Changin'
Side One: The Times They Are A-Changin'; Ballad Of Hollis Brown; With God On Our Side; One Too Many Mornings; North Country Blues.

Side Two: Only A Pawn In Their Game, Boots of Spanish Leather, When The Ship Comes In, The Lonesome Death Of Hattie Carroll, Restless Farewell.
13 January 1964 (May 1964)

Another Side of Bob Dylan
Side One: All I Really Want To Do; Black Crow Blues; Spanish Harlem Incident; Chimes Of Freedom.

Side Two: Motorpsycho Nitemare, My Back Pages, I Don't Believe You, Ballad in Plain D, It Ain't Me Babe.
8 August 1964 (November 1964)

Bringing It All Back Home
Side One: Subterranean Homesick Blues; She Belongs To Me; Maggie's Farm; Love Minus Zero/No Limit; Outlaw Blues; On The Road Again; Bob Dylan's 115th Dream.

Side Two: Mr Tambourine Man; Gates Of Eden, It's Alright Ma (I'm Only Bleeding), It's All Over Now, Baby Blue.
22 March 1965 (May 1965)

Highway 61 Revisited
Side One: Like A Rolling Stone; Tombstone Blues; It Takes A Lot To Laugh, It Takes A Train To Cry; From A Buick 6; Ballad Of A Thin Man.

Side Two: Queen Jane Approximately, Highway 61 Revisited, Just Like Tom Thumb's Blues, Desolation Row.
30 August 1965 (September 1965)

Blonde On Blonde
Side One: Rainy Day Women #12 & 35; Pledging My Time; Visions of Johanna; One Of Us Must Know.

Side Two: I Want You, Memphis Blues Again; Leopard-Skin Pill-Box Hat; Just Like A Woman.

Side Three: Most Likely You Go Your Way And I'll Go Mine; Temporary Like Achilles; Absolutely Sweet Marie; 4th Time Around; Obviously 5 Believers.

Side Four: Sad Eyed Lady Of The Lowlands.
May 1966 (August 1966)

Bob Dylan's Greatest Hits
Side One: Blowin' In The Wind; It Ain't Me Babe; The Times They Are A Changin'; Mr Tambourine Man; She Belongs To Me; It's All Over Now; Baby Blue.

Side Two: Subterranean Homesick Blues; One Of Us Must Know; Like A Rolling Stone; Just Like A Woman; Rainy Day Women Nos 12 & 35; I Want You.
(17 March 1967)

John Wesley Harding
Side One: John Wesley Harding; As I Went Out One Morning; I Dreamed I Saw St Augustine; All Along The Watchtower; The Ballad of Frankie Lee and Judas Priest; Drifter's Escape.

Side Two: Dear Landlord; I Am A Lonesome Hobo; I Pity The Poor Immigrant; The Wicked Messenger; Down Along The Cove; I'll Be Your Baby Tonight.
January 1968 (23 February 1968)

Nashville Skyline
Side One: Girl From The North Country (with Johnny Cash); Nashville Skyline Rag; To Be Alone With You; I Threw It All Away; Peggy Day.

Side Two: Lay Lady Lay; One More Night; Tell Me That It Isn't True; Country Pie; Tonight I'll Be Staying Here With You.
9 April 1969

Self Portrait
Side One: All The Tired Horses; Alberta #1; I Forgot More Than You'll Ever Know; Days of 49; Early Morning Rain; In Search Of Little Sadie.
Side Three: Copper Kettle; Gotta Travel On; Blue Moon; The Boxer; The Mighty Quinn (Quinn The Eskimo); Take Me As I Am.

Side Two: Let It Be Me; Little Sadie; Woogie Boogie; Belle Isle; Living The Blues; Like A Rolling Stone.

Side Four: Take A Message To Mary; It Hurts Me Too; Minstrel Boy; She Belongs To Me; Wigwam; Alberta #2.
8 June 1970

New Morning
Side One: If Not For You; Day Of The Locusts; Time Passes Slowly; Went To See The Gypsy; Winterlude.

Side Two: New Morning; Sign On The Window; One More Weekend; The Man In Me; Three Angels; Father Of Night.
21 October 1970

More Bob Dylan's Greatest Hits
Side One: Watching The River Flow; Don't Think Twice, It's All Right ; Lay, Lady, Lay; Stuck Inside of Mobile With The Memphis Blues Again.
Side Two: I'll Be Your Baby Tonight; All I Really Want To Do; My Back Pages; Maggie's Farm; Tonight I'll Be Staying Here With You.

Side Three: She Belongs To Me; All Along The Watchtower; The Mighty Quinn (Quinn The Eskimo); Just Like Tom Thumb's Blues; A Hard Rain's A-Gonna Fall.
Side Four: If Not For You; It's All Over Now, Baby Blue; Tomorrow Is A Long Time; When I Paint My Masterpiece; I Shall Be Released; You Ain't Going Nowhere; Down in the Flood.
17 November 1971 (December 1971)

More Greatest Hits
Side One: I Want You; One Of Us Must Know; It Takes A Lot To Laugh, It Takes A Train To Cry; Just Like Tom Thumb's Blues; Masters Of War; Chimes Of Freedom.

Side Two: Just Like A Woman; Obviously 5 Believers; Rainy Day Women #12 & 35; Gates Of Eden; Leopard-Skin Pill-Box Hat; Absolutely Sweet Marie.
(December 1971)

Pat Garrett And Billy The Kid
Side One: Main Title Theme (Billy); Cantina Theme (Workin' For The Law); Billy 1; Bunkhouse Theme; River Theme.

Side Two: Turkey Chase; Knockin' On Heaven's Door; Final Theme; Billy 4; Billy 7.
13 July 1973 (November 1973)

Dylan
Side One: Lily Of The West; Can't Help Falling In Love; Sarah Jane; The Ballad Of Ira Hayes.

Side Two: Mr Bojangles; Mary Ann; Big Yellow Taxi; A Fool Such As I; Spanish Is The Loving Tongue.
16 November 1973

Planet Waves
Side One: On A Night Like This; Going, Going, Gone; Tough Mama; Hazel; Something There Is About You; Forever Young.

Side Two: Forever Young; Dirge; You Angel You; Never Say Goodbye; Wedding Song.
17 January 1974

Before The Flood
Side One: Most Likely You Go Your Way (And I'll Go Mine); Lay, Lady, Lay; Rainy Day Women #12 & 35; Knockin' On Heaven's Door; It Ain't Me Babe; Ballad Of A Thin Man.

Side Two: Up On Cripple Creek; I Shall Be Released; Endless Highway; The Night They Drove Old Dixie Down; Stage Fright.

Side Three: Don't Think Twice, It's Alright; Just Like A Woman; It's Alright Ma (I'm Only Bleeding); The Shape I'm In; When You Awake; The Weight.

Side Four: All Along The Watchtower; Highway 61 Revisited; Like A Rolling Stone; Blowin' In The Wind.
20 June 1974

Blood On The Tracks
Side One: Tangled Up In Blue; Simple Twist Of Fate; You're A Big Girl Now; Idiot Wind; You're Gonna Make Me Lonesome When You Go

Side Two: Meet Me In The Morning; Lily, Rosemary And The Jack Of Hearts; If You See Her, Say Hello; Shelter From The Storm; Buckets Of Rain.
17 January 1975

The Basement Tapes
Side One: Odds And Ends; Orange Juice Blues (Blues For Breakfast); Million Dollar Bash; Yazoo Street Scandal; Going To Acapulco; Katie's Been Gone
Side Two: Lo And Behold!; Bessie Smith; Clothes Line Saga; Apple Sucking Tree; Please Mrs Henry; Tears Of Rage.
Side Three: Too Much Of Nothing; Yea! Heavy And A Bottle Of Bread; Ain't No More Cane; Crash On The Levee (Down In The Flood); Ruben Remus; Tiny Montgomery
Side Four: You Ain't Goin' Nowhere; Don't Ya Tell Henry; Nothing Was Delivered; Open The Door, Homer; Long Distance Operator; This Wheel's On Fire.
1 July 1975

Desire
Side One: Hurricane; Isis; Mozambique; One More Cup Of Coffee; Oh, Sister.
Side Two: Joey; Romance In Durango; Black Diamond Bay; Sara.
16 January 1976

Hard Rain
Side One: Maggie's Farm; One Too Many Mornings; Stuck Inside Of Mobile With The Memphis Blues Again; Oh, Sister; Lay, Lady, Lay
Side Two: Shelter From The Storm; You're A Big Girl Now; I Threw It All Away; Idiot Wind.
September 1976

Street Legal
Side One: Changing Of The Guard; New Pony; No Time To Think; Baby Stop Crying
Side Two: Is Your Love In Vain; Senor (Tales Of Yankee Power); True Love Tends To Forget; We Better Talk This Over; Where Are You Tonight? (Journey Through Dark Heat).
15 June 1978

At Budokan
Side One: Mr Tambourine Man; Shelter From The Storm; Love Minus Zero/No Limit; Ballad Of A Thin Man; Don't Think Twice, It's All Right.
Side Three: Blowin' In The Wind; Just Like A Woman; Oh Sister; Simple Twist Of Fate; All Along The Watchtower; I Want You.
Side Two: Maggie's Farm; One More Cup Of Coffee (Valley Below); Like A Rolling Stone; I Shall Be Released; Is Your Love In Vain?; Going, Going, Gone.
Side Four: All I Really Want To Do; Knockin' On Heaven's Door; It's Alright Ma (I'm Only Bleeding); Forever Young; The Times They Are A-Changin'. **April 1979**

Slow Train Coming
Side One: Gotta Serve Somebody; Precious Angel; I Believe In You; Slow Train
Side Two: Gonna Change My Way Of Thinking; Do Right To Me Baby (Do Unto Others); When You Gonna Wake Up; Man Gave Names To All The Animals; When He Returns. **18 August 1979**

Saved
Side One: A Satisfied Mind; Saved: Covenant Woman; What Can I Do For You?; Solid Rock
Side Two: Pressing On; In The Garden; Saving Grace; Are You Ready? **20 June 1980**

Shot Of Love
Side One: Shot Of Love; Heart Of Mine; Property Of Jesus; Lenny Bruce; Watered-Down Love
Side Two: Dead Man, Dead Man; In The Summertime; Trouble; Every Grain Of Sand. **12 August 1981**

Infidels
Side One: Jokerman; Sweetheart Like You; Neighbourhood Bully; License To Kill

Side Two: Man Of Peace; Union Sundown; I And I; Don't Fall Apart On Me Tonight.
1 November 1983

Real Live
Side One: Highway 61 Revisited; Maggie's Farm; I And I; License To Kill; It Ain't Me, Babe

Side Two: Tangled Up In Blue; Masters Of War; Ballad Of A Thin Man; Girl From The North Country; Tombstone Blues.
29 November 1984

Empire Burlesque
Side One: Tight Connection To My Heart (Has Anybody Seen My Love?); Seeing The Real You At Last; I'll Remember You; Clean Cut Kid; Never Gonna Be The Same Again

Side Two: Trust Yourself; Emotionally Yours; When The Night Comes Falling From The Sky; Something's Burning, Baby; Dark Eyes.
8 June 1985

Biograph
CD 1: Lay, Lady, Lay; Baby, Let Me Follow You Down; If Not For You; I'll Be Your Baby Tonight; I'll Keep It With Mine; The Times They Are A-Changin'; Blowin' In The Wind; Masters Of War; Lonesome Death of Hattie Carroll; Percy's Song; Mixed-Up Confusion; Tombstone Blues; The Groom's Still Waiting At The Altar; Most Likely You Go Your Way; Like A Rolling Stone; Lay Down Your Weary Tune; Subterranean Homesick Blues; I Don't Believe You.

CD 2: Visions Of Johanna; Every Grain Of Sand; Quinn The Eskimo; Mr Tambourine Man; Dear Landlord; It Ain't Me Babe; You Angel You; Million Dollar Bash; To Ramona; You're A Big Girl Now; Abandoned Love; Tangled Up In Blue; It's All Over Now Baby Blue; Can You Please Crawl Out Your Window; Positively 4th Street; Isis; Jet Pilot.

CD 3: Caribbean Wind; Up To Me; Baby, I'm In The Mood For You; I Wanna Be Your Lover; I Want You; Heart Of Mine; On A Night Like This; Just Like A Woman; Romance In Durango; Senor (Tales Of Yankee Power) ; Gotta Serve Somebody; I Believe In You; Time Passes Slowly; I Shall Be Released; Knockin' On Heaven's Door; All Along The Watchtower; Solid Rock; Forever Young.
28 October 1985

Knocked Out Loaded
Side One: You Wanna Ramble; They Killed Him; Drifting Too Far From The Shore; Precious Memories; Maybe Someday.

Side Two: Brownsville Girl; Got My Mind Made Up; Under Your Spell.
8 August 1986

Down In The Groove
Side One: Let's Stick Together; When Did You Leave Heaven?; Sally Sue Brown; Death Is Not The End; Had A Dream About You, Baby.

Side Two: Ugliest Girl In The World; Silvio; Ninety Miles An Hour (Down A Dead End Street); Shenandoah; Rank Strangers To Me.
31 May 1988

Dylan And The Dead
Side One: Slow Train; I Want You; Gotta Serve Somebody; Queen Jane Approximately.

Side Two: Joey; All Along The Watchtower; Knockin' On Heaven's Door.
6 February 1989

Oh Mercy
Side One: Political World; Where Teardrops Fall; Everything Is Broken; Ring Them Bells; Man In The Long Black Coat.

Side Two: Most Of The Time; What Good Am I?; Disease Of Conceit; What Was It You Wanted; Shooting Star.
22 September 1989

Under The Red Sky
Side One: Wiggle Wiggle; Under The Red Sky; Unbelievable; Born In Time; TV Talkin' Song.

Side Two: 10,000 Men; 2 x 2; God Knows; Handy Dandy; Cat's In The Well.
11 September 1990

The Bootleg Series Vols 1-3
CD 1: Hard Times In New York Town; He Was A Friend Of Mine; Man On The Street; No More Auction Block; House Carpenter; Talking Bear Mountain Picnic Massacre Blues; Let Me Die In My Footsteps; Rambling Gambling Willie; Talkin' Hava Negeilah Blues; Quit Your Low Down Ways; Worried Blues; Kingsport Town; Walkin' Down The Line; Walls Of Red Wing; Paths of Victory; Talkin' John Birch Paranoid Blues; Who Killed Davey Moore?; Only A Hobo; Moonshiner; When The Ship Comes In; The Times They Are A' Changin'; Last Thoughts on Woody Guthrie.

CD 2: Seven Curses; Eternal Circle; Suze (The Cough Song); Mama, You Been On My Mind; Farewell Angelina; Subterranean Homesick Blues; If You Gotta Go, Go Now (Or Else You Got To Stay All Night); Sitting On A Barbed Wire Fence; Like A Rolling Stone; It Takes A Lot To Laugh, It Takes A Train To Cry; I'll Keep It With Mine; She's Your Lover Now; I Shall Be Released; Santa-Fe; If Not For You; Wallflower; Nobody 'Cept You; Tangled Up In Blue; Call Letter Blues; Idiot Wind.

CD 3: If You See Her, Say Hello; Golden Loom; Catfish; Seven Days; Ye Shall Be Changed; Every Grain Of Sand; You Changed My Life; Need A Woman; Angelina; Someone's Got A Hold Of My Heart; Tell Me; Lord Protect My Child; Foot Of Pride; Blind Willie McTell; When The Night Comes Falling From The Sky; Series Of Dreams.
26 March 1991

Good As I Been To You
Side One: Frankie & Albert; Jim Jones; Blackjack Davey; Canadee-I-O; Sittin' On Top Of The World; Little Maggie; Hard Times.

Side Two: Step It Up And Go: Tomorrow Night; Arthur McBride; You're Gonna Quit Me; Diamond Joe; Froggie Went A Courtin'.
3 November 1992

30th Anniversary Concert Celebration
It's Alright Ma (I'm Only Bleeding); Girl Of The North Country.
24 August 1993

World Gone Wrong
Side One: World Gone Wrong; Love Henry; Ragged & Dirty; Blood In My Eyes; Broke Down Engine

Side Two: Delia; Stack A Lee; Two Soldiers; Jack-A-Roe; Lone Pilgrim.
26 October 1993 (December 1993)

Bob Dylan's Greatest Hits Vol 3
Tangled Up In Blue; Changing Of The Guards; The Groom's Still Waiting At The Altar; Hurricane; Forever Young; Jokerman; Dignity; Silvio; Ring Them Bells; Gotta Serve Somebody; Series of Dreams; Brownsville Girl; Under The Red Sky; Knockin' On Heaven's Door.
15 November 1994

MTV Unplugged
Tombstone Blues; Shooting Star; All Along The Watchtower; The Times They Are A'Changin'; John Brown; Desolation Row; Rainy Day Women #12 & 35; Love Minus Zero/No Limit; Dignity; Knockin' On Heaven's Door; Like A Rolling Stone; With God On Our Side .
25 April 1995

Time Out Of Mind
Love Sick; Dirt Road Blues; Standing In The Doorway; Million Miles; Tryin' To Get To Heaven; 'Til I Fell In Love With You; Not Dark Yet; Cold Irons Bound; Make You Feel My Love; Can't Wait; Highlands.
30 September 1997

The Best Of Bob Dylan
Blowin' In The Wind; The Times They Are A-Changin'; Don't Think Twice It's Alright; Mr Tambourine Man; Like a Rolling Stone; Just Like A Woman; All Along The Watchtower; Lay, Lady, Lay; I Shall Be Released; If Not For You; Knockin' On Heaven's Door; Forever Young; Tangled Up In Blue; Oh Sister; Gotta Serve Somebody; Jokerman; Everything Is Broken; Shelter From The Storm.
(6 August 1997)

Bob Dylan Live 1966: The 'Royal Albert Hall' Concert
CD 1: She Belongs To Me; Fourth Time Around; Visions Of Johanna; It's All Over Now, Baby Blue; Desolation Row; Just Like A Woman; Mr Tambourine Man.

CD 2: Tell Me, Mama; I Don't Believe You (She Acts Like We Never Have Met); Baby, Let Me Follow You Down; Just Like Tom Thumb's Blues; Leopard-Skin Pill-Box Hat; One Too Many Mornings; Ballad Of A Thin Man; Like A Rolling Stone.
13 October 1998

The Best Of Bob Dylan Vol 2
Things Have Changed; A Hard Rain's A-Gonna Fall; It Ain't Me Babe; Subterranean Homesick Blues; Positively 4th Street; Highway 61 Revisited; Rainy Day Women #12 And 35; I Want You; I'll Be Your Baby Tonight; Quinn The Eskimo (The Mighty Quinn); Simple Twist Of Fate; Hurricane; Changing Of The Guards; License To Kill; Silvio; Dignity; Not Dark Yet.
8 May 2000

The Essential Bob Dylan
CD 1: Blowin' In The Wind; Don't Think Twice, It's Alright; The Times They Are A-Changin'; It Ain't Me Babe; Maggie's Farm; It's All Over Now Baby Blue; Mr Tambourine Man; Subterranean Homesick Blues; Like A Rolling Stone; Positively 4th Street; Can You Please Crawl Out Your Window?; I Want You; Just Like A Woman; Rainy Day Women #12 & 35; All Along The Watchtower; Quinn The Eskimo (The Mighty Quinn); I'll Be Your Baby Tonight; Lay, Lady, Lay; If Not For You; I Shall Be Released; You Ain't Going Nowhere; Knockin' On Heaven's Door.

CD 2: Forever Young; Tangled Up In Blue; Shelter From The Storm; Hurricane; Changing Of The Guards; Gotta Serve Somebody; Blind Willie McTell; Jokerman; Tight Connection To My Heart (Has Anybody Seen My Love); Silvio; Everything Is Broken; Dignity; Not Dark Yet; Things Have Changed.
31 October 2000 (21 May 2001)

"Love And Theft"
Tweedle Dee and Tweedle Dum; Mississippi; Summer Days; Bye And Bye; Lonesome Day Blues; Floater (Too Much To Ask); High Water (For Charley Patton); Moonlight; Honest With Me; Po' Boy; Cry A While; Sugar Baby.
11 September 2001

Bob Dylan Live 1975: The Bootleg Series Vol 5, The Rolling Thunder Review
CD 1: Tonight I'll Be Staying Here With You; It Ain't Me Babe; A Hard Rain's A-Gonna Fall; The Lonesome Death of Hattie Carroll; Romance in Durango; Isis; Mr Tambourine Man; Simple Twist Of Fate; Blowin' In The Wind; Mama, You Been On My Mind; I Shall Be Released.

CD 2: It's All Over Now, Baby Blue; Love Minus Zero/No Limit; Tangled Up In Blue; The Water Is Wide; It Takes A Lot To Laugh, It Takes A Train To Cry; Oh, Sister; Hurricane; One More Cup Of Coffee (Valley Below); Sara; Just Like A Woman; Knockin' On Heaven's Door.
26 November 2002

Masked And Anonymous
Down In The Flood; Diamond Joe; Dixie; Cold Irons Bound. **21 July 2003**

Bob Dylan Live 1964: Concert at Philharmonic Hall, Bootleg Series Vol 6
CD 1: The Times They Are A Changin'; Spanish Harlem Incident; Talkin' John Birch Paranoid Blues; To Ramona; Who Killed Davey Moore?; Gates Of Eden; If You Gotta Go, Go Now (Or Else You Got To Stay All Night); It's Alright Ma, I'm Only Bleeding; I Don't Believe You (She Acts Like We Never Have Met); Mr Tambourine Man; A Hard Rain's A-Gonna Fall.

CD 2: Talkin' World War III Blues; Don't Think Twice, It's All Right; The Lonesome Death Of Hattie Carroll; Mama, You Been On My Mind; Silver Dagger; With God On Our Side; It Ain't Me, Babe; All I Really Want To Do.
30 March 2004

No Direction Home; The Soundtrack. Bootleg Series Vol 7
CD 1: When I Got Troubles; Rambler, Gambler; This Land Is Your Land; Song To Woody; Dink's Song; I Was Young When I Left Home; Sally Gal; Don't Think Twice, It's All Right; Man Of Constant Sorrow; Blowin' In The Wind; Masters Of War; A Hard Rain's A-Gonna Fall; When The Ship Comes In; Mr Tambourine Man; Chimes Of Freedom; It's All Over Now, Baby Blue.

CD 2: She Belongs To Me; Maggie's Farm; It Takes A Lot To Laugh, It Takes A Train To Cry; Tombstone Blues; Just Like Tom Thumb's Blues; Desolation Row; Highway 61 Revisited; Leopard-Skin Pill-Box Hat; Stuck Inside Of Mobile With The Memphis Blues Again; Visions Of Johanna; Ballad Of A Thin Man; Like A Rolling Stone. **30 August 2005**

Bob Dylan Live At The Gaslight 1962
A Hard Rain's A-Gonna Fall; Rocks and Gravel; Don't Think Twice, It's All Right; The Cuckoo; Moonshiner; Handsome Molly; Cocaine; John Brown; Barbara Allen; West Texas.
30 August 2005 (US only)

OTHER IMPORTANT RELEASES

There is a huge grey area between official items openly for sale and the bootleg market hidden away under the counter. This comprises obscure foreign rarities and promotional items available for sale only to a limited clientele. All these are highly prized by the hardcore collector, sated with discs that an everyday fan can buy easily. They provide a sense of one-upmanship and although they tend to feature unusual packaging, they rarely feature material not otherwise commercially available. The key items listed below are the most important exceptions.

12-inch Single Promo

Four Songs From Renaldo and Clara: A Film By Bob Dylan
US promo 12-inch EP January 78, Columbia AS 422 XSM 164036
Plain white cover with pasted-down title and list of songs, stamped 'Demonstration, Not For Sale'.

Side One:
People Get Ready (Curtis Mayfield) (Rolling Thunder NY Rehearsals); Never Let Me Go (Dylan) (live, Cambridge, Massachusetts 20 November 1975).

Side Two:
Isis (Dylan) (live, Montreal 4 December 1975), It Ain't Me Babe (Dylan) (live, Montreal 4 December 1975).

CD Promos

Live '96: 1997, Columbia CSK 3818
My Back Pages; Tombstone Blues; Ballad Of A Thin Man; Boots Of Spanish Leather.
(live Atlanta 3-4 August 1996)

Things Have Changed: Live and Unreleased (2000) CSK 16720. Two CD promos that feature between them the title song live at Portsmouth 25 September 2000 and six others: 'Highlands' and 'Blowin' In The Wind' (Santa Cruz 16 March 2000), 'Blind Willie McTell' (Jones Beach 17 August 1997), 'To Make You Feel My Love' (Pauley Pavilion 21 May 1998) and 'Roving Gambler' and 'Can't Wait' (El Ray Theatre, Los Angeles 17 and 20 December 1997).

Live and Rare 2: Million Miles
Live Binghamton NY 19 February 1999.
Blowin' In The Wind (location and date unknown); Blind Willie McTell (recorded live Wantaugh, NY 19 February 1998) (2002) Columbia promo, Sampcd 11408, UK CD sampler. The picture sleeve is the same as is used on *"Love And Theft"*.

Live at Carnegie Hall 26.10.1963
US Issue: 15 November 2005 Columbia Legacy CSK 17254.
Available with certain purchases from bobdylan.com and US branches of Borders, stunning quality show with loud audience participation and a young and bouncy Bob up for whatever they can throw at him. Close your eyes and you're right there.
The Times They Are A-Changin; Ballad of Hollis Brown; Boots Of Spanish Leather; He introduces this thus: 'all it is is a "when you can't get what you want you've gotta settle for less" kind of song'; Lay Down Your Weary Tune; North Country Blues; With God On Our Side.

Bob Dylan Live 1961-2000
Japanese CD Issue 28 February 2001 SRCS2438
Widely imported into the UK but not given a UK or US release, put together by Sony Japan to

tie in with some tour dates there. The archive photographs where credited are in Japanese but are startling. The front shot is a monochrome image of Dylan lost in song and the back is the original photograph around which the cancelled *In Concert* sleeve was based. Inside it gets even more intriguing, with Dylan and Tom Wilson on an empty stage, presumably prior to a live recording. Crouched down in his Huckleberry Finn hat, Dylan has his set list taped to his guitar.

Somebody Touched Me (Trad arr Dylan) 2.42
Portsmouth 2000.
Dylan has taken to starting his gigs with an old-timey spiritual of impeccable vintage, many from the Stanley Brothers repertoire. He even looks like a hellfire preacher these days, and sings this with an intensity denied some of his own back catalogue. I am one of the people cheering in the background, so immortality at last.

Wade In The Water (Trad arr Dylan) 3.01
Minneapolis 1961.
Dylan already sounds fierce and old as a young man, with stomping boot heel and driving gutbucket guitar.

Handsome Molly (Trad arr Dylan) 2.49
Gaslight 1962.

To Ramona (Dylan) 4.30
Sheffield 1965.
This is a *Don't Look Back* outtake. Taken at a fast lick, but sung with feeling to a slight echo in the hall.

I Don't Believe You (Dylan) 6.00
Free Trade Hall, Manchester 1966.

Grand Coulee Dam (Woody Guthrie) 2.57
From *A Tribute to Woody Guthrie.* Ramshackle and hugely exciting. Dylan might have taken to the hills but he can still sing like a coyote – no country burr here! This is the Basement crew briefly surfacing in public with some rough manly harmonies and bar-room boogie.

Knockin' On Heaven's Door (Dylan) 3.50
From *Before The Flood.*

It Ain't Me, Babe (Dylan) 5.16
From *Renaldo and Clara.*

Shelter From The Storm (Dylan) 5.26
From *Hard Rain.*

Dead Man, Dead Man (Dylan) 3.57
New Orleans, 1981
A real treat, a gospel holy roller with a catchy chorus and iron in its soul. The band really drive him with pounding electric piano and wailing women. If this is heaven, book me a ticket.

Slow Train (Dylan) 4.59
From *Dylan and the Dead.*

Dignity (Dylan) 6.35
From *MTV Unplugged.*

Cold Irons Bound (Dylan) 6.50
Los Angeles 1997
Not the *Masked and Anonymous* version, this is slower and more desperate. The sound is blurry.

Born In Time (Dylan) 5.21
New Jersey 1998
A weird one this, with Dylan sounding as if he is free-associating. He half sings, half talks this and the band play their socks off, as if deliberately ignoring their eccentric lead singer.

Country Pie (Dylan) 2.48
Portsmouth 2000
This was one of the great surprises of that year's tour. Bob has great fun with it, climbing all over the lyric with some clean country picking behind him.

Things Have Changed (Dylan) 5.53
Portsmouth 2000
Dylan dramatizes this when he says he saw something move, you instinctively look over your shoulder. But it somehow lacks focus. 'Times are strange' and they always will be so long as Dylan draws breath. Long may he run.

THE WRITTEN WORD

BOOKS AND WRITINGS BY BOB DYLAN

Sleeve note to *Joan Baez In Concert Part 2* (Vanguard, TFL 6035) 1963.
'In my youngest years, I used t'kneel…'

Sleeve note to *Peter Paul and Mary In The Wind* (Warner Bros WM 8142) 1963.
'Snow was piled up the stairs an onto the street…'

Tarantula (McKibbon and Kee, 1971). A collection of prose fictions written in 1966 and first published in bootleg typescripts.
   Dylan: 'I wrote the book because there's a lot of stuff in there I can't possibly sing – all the collages. The majority of the audience – I don't care where they're from, how hip they are – I think it would just get totally lost. Something that had no rhyme, all cut up, no nothing, except something happening – which is words. The book don't begin or end'. Los Angeles, September 1965

Writings and Drawings (Jonathan Cape, 1973), revised edition 1987, includes line drawings, sleeve notes, poems, songs not then officially released etc.

Chronicles, Volume One (Simon and Schuster, 2004). Five extracts of an autobiography from early days in New York to 1987 and the recording of *Oh Mercy*.

Lyrics 1962-2001 (Simon and Schuster, 2004). Extraneous poems, drawings and the like are excised here in favour of some working manuscripts and an ever-growing list of songs, both officially released and not. This has helped fuel collectors' interest in Dylan's hinterland.

The Bob Dylan Scrapbook 1956-1966 (Simon and Schuster, 2005). Contains facsimiles of handwritten lyrics, concert posters, programmes, tickets and a CD of Dylan interviews. Text by Robert Santelli.

WEBSITES AND FANZINES

Dylan's official website is www.bobdylan.com. It includes news and information and sometimes downloads of rare material. Its best unofficial counterpart is Olof Bjorner's extraordinary labour of love of all things Dylan, www.bjorner.com/bob.htm. But even this pales next to www.searchingforagem.com, which has thousands of brightly illustrated pages going in minute detail into all of Dylan's official releases, and scans sent by fans worldwide. It is particularly good on rarities and promos. But enter Bob Dylan into any reputable search engine and a whole world of private fanaticism will open up before you.

Isis, under the expert stewardship of Derek Barker, is now generally considered to be the leading Dylan fanzine, despite the excellence of the more scholarly *Judas*. It is a magazine that continues the late John Bauldie's mixture of wry fanaticism in all things Bob. Its bi-monthly issues include Ian Woodward's newsletter *The Wicked Messenger*, an excellent review section, and arcane articles on the minutiae of Dylanology. The best of these are now collected in two anthologies. *Isis* is also linked to *My Back Pages*, who sell a wide range of Dylan-centred publications. Both can be located at www. bobdylanisis.com. *Isis*'s terrestrial address is c/o PO Box 1182, Bedworth, Warwickshire CV12 0ZA.

For a fascinating survey of variant 45 rpm picture sleeves and track listings arising from non-English speaking territories, see Peter Doggett's article 'Dylan's World View' in *Record Collector* 250 (June 2000).

INDEX

Bold entries indicate album titles.

2x2 249, 254, 435
7 Deadly Sins 386, 406
7 Deadly Sins (2) 406
30th Anniversary Celebration 284-287, 437
1965 Revisited 395-396
10,000 Men 249, 253-254, 423, 435
Abandoned Love 146, 208, 215, 434
Absolutely Sweet Marie 53, 58, 284, 404, 427, 429
Acne (Doo Wah) 394
Ain't No More Cane 130, 136, 394, 431
Alberta #1 76, 79, 428
Alberta #2 76, 83, 428
All Along The Watchtower 65, 68, 89, 92, 111, 116, 159, 164, 208, 219, 233, 238, 284, 296, 298, 313, 327, 328, 388, 404, 413, 420, 423, 428, 429, 430, 432, 434, 435, 437, 438, 439
All Dangerous To Me 187
All I Really Want To Do 35, 37, 89, 92, 159, 165, 350, 355, 361, 427, 429, 432, 440
All The Tired Horses 76, 79, 428
All The Way Down 187
All You Have To Do Is Dream 88, 399
All-American Boy 399
Almost Persuaded 187
And He's Killed Me Too 100
Angelina 187, 256, 273
Angels Flying Too Close To The Ground 193, 421
Another Side of Bob Dylan 34-39, 405, 427
Any Way You Want Me 407
Apple Sucking Tree 130, 135, 399, 431
Are You Ready? 174, 179, 414, 420, 432

Arthur McBride 277, 282, 436
As I Went Out One Morning 65, 67, 428
At Budokan 159-166, 432

Baby Ain't That Fine 398
Baby I'm In The Mood For You 27, 208, 217, 434
Baby Let Me Follow You Down 15, 18, 208, 210, 315, 322, 382, 383, 426, 434, 438
Baby Please Don't Go 27
Baby Stop Crying 152, 156, 413, 419, 431
Ballad In Plain D 35, 39, 427
Ballad of A Thin Man 47, 51, 111, 115, 159, 162, 194, 198, 315, 323, 362, 371, 396, 427, 430, 432, 433, 438, 440, 442
Ballad of Donald White, The 382, 389
Ballad of Emmett Till, The 382
Ballad of Frankie Lee And Judas Priest, The 65, 68, 428
Ballad of Hollis Brown 27, 28, 31, 394, 426, 442
Ballad of Ira Hayes, The 101, 102, 430
Band, The: A Musical History 392
Band, The: The Last Waltz 382
Band of The Hand 415, 421, 422
Banks of The Royal Canal 398
Barbara Allen 372, 375, 394, 440
Basement Tapes, The 130-138, 431
(Be Careful of) The Stones That You Throw 398
Before The Flood 111-116, 430
Belchezaar 398
Belle Isle 76, 81, 428
Bells of Rhymney 398
Bessie Smith 130, 135, 431
Best of Bob Dylan, The 312-314, 438
Best of Bob Dylan Vol 2, The 324-326, 438
Between Shot And Saved 402
Big River 75, 398
Big Yellow Taxi 101, 104, 430
Billy 100
Billy (1) 95, 96, 100, 429

Billy (4) 95, 99, 100, 429
Billy (7) 95, 99, 100, 429
Billy Surrenders 100
Biograph 208-219, 434
Black Cross 394
Black Crow Blues 35, 37, 427
Black Diamond Bay 139, 145-146, 431
Blackjack Davey 277, 281, 436
Blind Willie McTell 193, 256, 275, 327, 330, 425, 439, 442
Blonde On Blonde 53-59, 395, 405, 427
Blood In My Eyes 288, 291, 437
Blood On The Tapes 401
Blood On The Tracks 117-129, 405, 430
Blood On The Tracks: New York Sessions 401
Blood On Your Saddle 405
Blowin' In The Wind 20, 23, 60, 62, 111, 116, 159, 164, 208, 211, 284, 313, 326, 327, 328, 340, 346, 362, 366, 379, 380, 387, 410, 416, 426, 428, 430, 432, 434, 438, 439, 440, 442
Blue Moon 76, 81, 428
Blue Yodel #1 75
Blue Yodel #6 75
Bob Dylan 14-19, 405, 426
Bob Dylan - The Bootleg 394
Bob Dylan Convention Speech 405
Bob Dylan In Concert 395
Bob Dylan Live 1961-2000 442
Bob Dylan Live 1964: The Bootleg Series Vol 6, Concert At Philharmonic Hall 354-361, 440
Bob Dylan Live 1966: The Bootleg Series Vol 4, The 'Royal Albert Hall' Concert 315-323, 438
Bob Dylan Live 1975: The Bootleg Series Vol 5, The Rolling Thunder Review 340-349, 439
Bob Dylan Live At The Gaslight 1962 372-375, 440
Bob Dylan's 115th Dream 40, 44, 410, 427
Bob Dylan's Blues 20, 24, 426
Bob Dylan's Dream 20, 25, 426
Bob Dylan's Greatest Hits (US version) 62-63

Bob Dylan's Greatest Hits Vol 3 293-295, 437
Bob Dylan's New Orleans Rag 33, 395
Bonnie Ship The Diamond 398
Boogie Woogie Country Girl 388
Bootleg Series Vols 1-3, The 256-276, 436
Boots of Spanish Leather 28, 32, 426, 442
Born In Time 248, 249, 253, 424, 435, 445
Borrowed Time 187
Bourbon Street 399
Boxer, The 76, 82, 428
Bring It On Home 398
Bringing It All Back Home 40-46, 395, 405, 427
Broadside Ballads Vol 1 378
Broadside Reunion 382
Broadside Sessions November 1962-March 1963 395
Broke Down Engine 288, 291, 437
Brownsville Girl 220, 224-225, 294, 434, 437
Buckets of Rain 117, 129, 406, 430
Bunkhouse Theme 95, 98, 100, 429
Bye And Bye 331, 336, 439

California 46
Call Letter Blues 129, 256, 270, 436
Cambridge 1975 402
Can You Please Crawl Out Your Window 52, 59, 208, 216, 327, 328, 396, 411, 417, 434, 439
Canadee-I-O 277, 281, 436
Can't Help Falling In Love 101, 102, 430
Can't Wait 303, 310, 425, 437, 442
Cantina Theme (Workin' For The Law) 95, 96, 100, 429
Careless Love 75
Caribbean Wind 187, 208, 217, 423, 434
Catfish 146, 256, 271
Cat's In The Well 249, 255, 435
Changing of the Guards 152, 156, 294, 324, 326, 327, 330, 413, 420, 431, 437, 438, 439
Child To Me 187

Chimes of Freedom 35, 37, 362, 367, 389, 427, 429, 440
City of Gold 350
Clean Cut Kid 193, 199, 204, 207, 433
Clean Cuts (Henry Porter's 115th Dream) 403
Clothesline Saga (Answer To Ode) 130, 135, 399, 431
Cocaine 372, 375, 394, 440
Cocaine Blues 424
Cold Irons Bound 303, 309, 424, 437, 445
Cold Irons Bound (Masked And Anonymous version) 350, 353, 440
Cold Turkey 100
Come All Ye Fair And Tender Ladies 398
Comin' Round The Mountain 399
Coming From The Heart 158
Complete Concert Town Hall, New York 12 April 1963 395
Completely Unplugged 404
Concert For Bangla Desh, The 379-381
Confidential To Me 399
Congratulations 385, 406
Connection Cowboy 19
Cool Dry Place 386, 406
Cool Water 398
Copper Kettle (The Pale Moonlight) 76, 81, 412, 418, 428
Corrina, Corrina 20, 26, 27, 410, 416, 426
Country Pie 70, 75, 412, 418, 428, 445
Covenant Woman 174, 178, 414, 432
Crash On The Levee (Down In The Flood) 130, 136, 399, 400, 431
Cross The Green Mountain 391
Crosswind Jubilee 110
Cry A While 331, 338, 439
Cuckoo, The 372, 374, 440
Cuckoo Is A Pretty Bird, The 394
Cupid 88

Da Doo Ron Ron 88
Dark Eyes 199, 206, 421, 433

Dark Groove 193
David Bromberg Studio Sessions 407
Day Of The Locusts 84, 86, 429
Days of 49 76, 80, 428
Dead Man, Dead Man 180, 185, 415, 420, 422, 423, 432, 444
Dear Landlord 65, 68, 208, 215, 428, 434
Dear Mrs Roosevelt 379
Death Is Not The End 193, 227, 230, 422, 435
Death of Emmett Till, The 27
Deeds of Mercy, The 403
Delia 288, 291, 437
Denise 39
Desire 139-146, 405
Desolation Row 47, 51-52, 296, 299, 301, 315, 320, 362, 369, 396, 404, 427, 437, 438, 440
Devil's Been Busy, The 386, 406
Diamond Joe 277, 282, 350, 352, 436, 440
Dignity 248, 294, 296, 300, 324, 326, 327, 330, 404, 424, 437, 438, 439, 445
Dink's Song 362, 365, 440
Dirge 105, 110, 430
Dirt Road Blues 303, 307, 437
Dirty World 385, 406
Disease of Conceit 239, 247, 248, 435
Dixie 350, 352-353, 440
Do Right To Me Baby (Do Unto Others) 167, 172, 414, 432
Don't Fall Apart On Me Tonight 188, 193, 433
Don't Fly Unless It's Safe 193
Don't Take Yourself Away 187
Don't Think Twice, It's All Right 20, 25, 88, 89, 91, 111, 115, 159, 162, 284, 313, 327, 328, 355, 360, 362, 366, 372, 374, 394, 404, 410, 416, 426, 429, 430, 432, 438, 439, 440
Don't Ya Tell Henry 130, 137, 392, 399, 431
Don't You Try Me Now 398
Down Along The Cove 65, 69, 392, 428
Down In The Flood 89, 94, 406, 429

Down In The Flood (new version) 350, 352, 440
Down In The Groove 227-232, 403, 405, 435
Down On Me 398
Down The Highway 20, 24, 426
Drifter's Escape 65, 68, 412, 418, 428
Drifting Too Far From The Shore 207, 220, 223, 415, 422, 434
Dusty Old Fairgrounds 395
Dylan 101-104, 430
Dylan And The Dead 233-238, 435
Dylan Cash Sessions, The 400

Early Dylan 394
Early Mornin' Rain 76, 80, 428
East Laredo Blues 33
Emotionally Yours 199, 205, 284, 414, 433
Empire Burlesque 199-207, 403, 405, 433
End of The Line 385, 406
Endless Highway 111, 430
Essential Bob Dylan, The 327-330, 439
Eternal Circle 33, 256, 266, 436
Evening Concerts At Newport Vol 1 378
Every Grain of Sand 180, 186-187, 208, 214, 256, 272, 432, 434
Everything Is Broken 239, 244, 248, 313, 314, 327, 330, 404, 415, 422, 423, 435, 438, 439

Farewell 33
Farewell, Angelina 46, 256, 266, 436
Father of Night 84, 88, 429
Feeling Minnesota - Original Soundtrack 388
Final Theme 95, 99, 100, 429
Final Theme (3) 100
Fiona, Bob Dylan & Rupert Everett: Hearts of Fire Original Soundtrack 384
Fish And Chips 406
Fish That Walks 405
Fishing Blues 88

Fixin' To Die 15, 17, 426
Flight of The Bumble Bee 399
Floater (Too Much To Ask) 331, 336, 439
Folsom Prison Blues 83, 398
Fool Such As I, 6, 101, 104, 398, 412, 419, 430
Foot of Pride 193, 256, 275, 284
Forever Young 105, 109, 110, 159, 165, 208, 219, 294, 313, 314, 327, 330, 383, 419, 420, 430, 432, 434, 437, 438, 439
Four Strong Winds 399
Fourth Time Around 53, 58, 315, 319, 427, 438
Frankie & Albert 277, 280, 436
Freedom For The Station 207
Freewheelin' Bob Dylan, The 20-27, 405, 426
Freight Train Blues 15, 19, 426
French Girl, The 399
Friend of The Devil 389
Friend To The Martyr, A 402
Friends And Other Strangers 402
Froggie Went A Courtin' 277, 283, 436
From A Buick 6 47, 50, 52, 396, 411, 416, 427

Gaslight Café, New York 6th September 1961 394
Gates of Eden 40, 45, 88, 355, 358, 410, 411, 416, 427, 429, 440
Genuine Bootleg Series, The 407
Genuine Bootleg Series Take Two, The 408
George Jackson 406, 412, 418
Get Your Rocks Off 399, 400
(Ghost) Riders In The Sky 88
Girl From The North Country 20, 23, 194, 198, 284, 287, 426, 433, 437
Girl From The North Country (with Johnny Cash) 70, 73, 75, 428
Girl From The Red River Shore 311
Go 'Way Little Boy 207
God Knows 248, 249, 254, 435
Goin' Down The Road 398

453

Going (Down) To New Orleans 27
Going, Going, Gone 105, 108, 159, 163, 430, 432
Going To Acapulco 130, 134, 399, 431
Golden Loom 146, 256, 271
Gonna Change My Way of Thinking 167, 172, 391, 420, 432
Gonna Get You Now 399
Gonna See Her 187
Good As I Been To You 277, 404, 407, 436
(Good Old) Mountain Dew 75
Goodbye Holly 100
Gospel Plow 15, 18, 426
Got Love If You Want It 232
Got My Mind Made Up 220, 226, 422, 434
Gotta Serve Somebody 167, 170, 208, 219, 233, 237, 294, 313, 314, 327, 330, 350, 413, 420, 432, 434, 435, 437, 438, 439
Gotta Travel On 76, 81, 428
Grand Coulee Dam, The 379, 444
Grateful Dead: Postcards of The Hanging -Grateful Dead Perform The Songs of Bob Dylan 390
Great Music Experience, Nara City, Todaji Temple, Japan, 20-22 May 1994 404
Greatest Hits (UK version) 60-61, 428
Groom's Still Waiting At The Altar, The 180, 185, 208, 212, 294, 414, 420, 434, 437
Guess Things Just Happen That Way 75
Guitars Kissing And The Contemporary Fix 396-397

Had A Dream About You, Baby 227, 231, 384, 403, 435
Handle With Care 385, 406
Handsome Molly 372, 375, 394, 440, 443
Handy Dandy 249, 255, 435
Hard Rain 147-151, 431
Hard Rain's A-Gonna Fall, A 20, 24, 89, 93, 324, 340, 345, 355, 360, 362, 366, 372, 374, 380, 394, 404, 424, 426, 429, 438, 439, 440

Hard Times 277, 281, 436
Hard Times In New York Town 256, 259, 436
Hard To Find/Even Harder To Find/Hardest To Find 408
Hazel 105, 108, 382-383, 404, 430
He Was A Friend Of Mine 19, 256, 260, 436
Heading For The Light 385, 406
Heart of Mine 180, 184, 187, 208, 218, 414, 420, 432, 434
Heartland 387
Hero Blues 27, 33
High Away (Ah Ah Ah) 187
High Water (For Charley Patton) 331, 336-337, 439
Highlands 303, 310-311, 326, 437, 442
Highway 51 15, 18, 426
Highway 61 Revisited 47-52, 395, 405
Highway 61 Revisited 47, 51, 111, 116, 194, 196, 284, 324, 326, 362, 370, 388, 392, 396, 401, 411, 417, 421, 427, 430, 433, 438, 440
Highway 61 Revisited/Blonde On Blonde. The Mono Mixes 396
Highway 61 Revisited Again 396
Hills of Mexico, The 398
Hollow Horn Reference Recordings 405
Honest With Me 331, 337, 439
Honey, Just Allow Me One More Chance 20, 26, 416, 426
Honey Wait 207
House Carpenter 19, 256, 260, 436
House of The Risin' Sun 15, 18, 110, 426
Hurricane 139, 143, 146, 294, 324, 326, 327, 330, 340, 348, 413, 419, 425, 431, 437, 438, 439

I Ain't Got No Home 379, 392
I Am A Lonesome Hobo 65, 68-69, 428
I And I 188, 193, 197, 433
I Believe In You 167, 171, 208, 219, 432, 434
I Can't Come In With A Broken Heart 398
I Can't Get You Off My Mind 390
I Can't Make It Alone 398

I Don't Believe You (She Acts Like We Never Have Met) 35, 38-39, 88, 208, 213-214, 259, 315, 321, 355, 383, 427, 434, 438, 440, 444
I Don't Hurt Anymore 398
I Dreamed I Saw St Augustine 65, 67, 401, 428
I Forgot More Than You'll Ever Know 76, 80, 428
I Forgot To Remember To Forget Her 398
(I Heard That) Lonesome Whistle 27
I Pity The Poor Immigrant 65, 69, 401, 428
I Shall Be Free 20, 26, 27, 426
I Shall Be Free #10 35, 38, 39
I Shall Be Released 89, 94, 111, 138, 159, 163, 208, 219, 256, 269, 284, 313, 327, 328, 340, 347, 383-384, 399, 400, 404, 406, 429, 430, 432, 434, 436, 438, 439
I Still Miss Someone 75
I Threw It All Away 70, 73, 88, 147, 150, 401, 412, 418, 419, 428, 431
I Walk The Line 75
I Wanna Be Your Lover 59, 208, 218, 434
I Want To 187
I Want You 53, 57, 60, 62, 159, 164, 208, 218, 233, 237, 324, 326, 327, 328, 404, 417, 418, 420, 422, 427, 428, 429, 432, 434, 435, 438, 439
I Was Young When I Left Home 339, 362, 365, 440
I'd Hate To Be You On That Dreadful Day 382
Idiot Wind 117, 125-126, 129, 147, 151, 256, 270-271, 430, 431, 436
Idiot Wind (2) 129
If Dogs Run Free 84, 87
If Not For You 84, 86, 88, 89, 93, 208, 211, 256, 269, 313, 327, 328, 329, 418, 429, 434, 436, 438, 439
If You Belonged To Me 386, 406
If You Gotta Go, Go Now (Or Else You Gotta Stay All Night) 46, 256, 267, 355, 358-359, 436, 440
If You See Her, Say Hello 117, 128, 129, 256, 271, 350, 413, 419, 430
If You See Her Say Hello (2) 129
I'll Be Your Baby Tonight 65, 69, 89, 92, 208, 211, 284, 324, 326, 327, 328, 401, 428, 429, 434, 438, 439
I'll Keep It With Mine 46, 59, 208, 211, 256, 268, 395, 434, 436
I'll Remember You 199, 204, 433
I'm A Fool For You 398
I'm Alright 398
I'm Guilty of Loving You 398
I'm In The Mood For Love 399
I'm Not There 399
I'm Your Teenage Prayer 399
Important Words 232
Important Words 403
In 1966 There Was 397
In My Time of Dyin' 15, 17, 426
In Search of Little Sadie 76, 80, 428
In The Garden 174, 179, 402, 432
In The Summertime 180, 186, 207, 423, 432
Infidels 188-193, 405, 433
Inside Out 386, 406
Instrumental Calypso 187
Instrumental Jam 399
Is It Worth It? 187
Is Your Love In Vain? 152, 157, 159, 163, 420, 431, 432
Isis 139, 143-144, 208, 216, 340, 345-346, 349, 414, 431, 434, 439, 441
Isle of Wight 401
It Ain't Me Babe 35, 39, 60, 62, 111, 115, 194, 197, 208, 215, 284, 324, 327, 328, 340, 344, 355, 361, 389, 401, 413, 417, 421, 424, 427, 428, 430, 433, 434, 438, 439, 440, 441, 444
It Hurts Me Too 76, 82, 428
It Takes A Lot To Laugh, It Takes A Train To Cry 47, 50, 256, 268, 340, 348, 362, 368, 380, 396, 427, 429, 436, 439, 440
It's All Over Now, Baby Blue 40, 45, 46, 60, 89, 93, 208, 216, 315, 320, 327, 328, 340, 347, 350, 362, 367, 417, 423, 427, 428, 429, 434, 438, 439, 440
It's Alright, Ma (I'm Only Bleeding) 40, 45, 111, 115, 159, 165, 284, 287, 355, 359, 427, 430, 432, 437, 440

455

Jack-A-Roe 288, 292, 437
Jet Pilot 59, 208, 213, 434
Jim Jones 277, 280, 436
Joan Baez: Live At Newport 389
Joan Baez: Rare, Live And Classic 387
Joey 139, 145, 233, 238, 431, 435
John Brown 296, 299, 301, 372, 375, 378, 382, 394, 395, 404, 424, 437, 440
John Wesley Harding 64-69, 428
John Wesley Harding 65, 67, 428
Johnny Todd 398
Jokerman 188, 191, 193, 294, 313, 314, 327, 330, 414, 421, 423, 433, 437, 438, 439
Joshua Gone Barbados 399
Julius And Ethel 193
(Just) A Closer Walk With Thee 75
Just Allow Me One More Chance 88
Just Like A Woman 53, 57-58, 60, 62, 111, 115, 159, 164, 208, 218, 284, 313, 315, 320, 327, 328, 340, 349, 380, 411, 418, 427, 429, 430, 432, 434, 438, 439
Just Like Tom Thumb's Blues 47, 51, 88, 89, 93, 284, 315, 322, 362, 369, 392, 396, 417, 427, 429, 438, 440
Just When I Needed You Most 232

Kaatskill Serenade 404, 407
Kaatskill Serenade And Three More Songs 404
Katie's Been Gone 130, 134, 431
Keep On Travelling Folks 406
Kind Hearted Woman Blues 394
King of France 398
Kingsport Town 27, 256, 262, 436
Knocked Out Loaded 220-226, 434
Knockin' On Heaven's Door 95, 98-99, 100, 111, 114, 159, 165, 208, 219, 233, 238, 284, 287, 294, 296, 300, 313, 314, 327, 328, 340, 349, 404, 412, 418, 429, 430, 432, 434, 435, 437, 438, 439, 444
Knockin' On Heaven's Door (2) 100
Knockin' On Heaven's Door (3) 100

Knockin' On Heaven's Door (instrumental) 100
Las Vegas Blues 88
Last Night 385, 406
Last Thoughts On Woody Guthrie 256, 265, 395, 436
Lay Down Your Weary Tune 33, 208, 213, 395, 434, 442
Lay, Lady, Lay 70, 74, 89, 91, 111, 114, 147, 150, 208, 210, 313, 327, 328, 401, 412, 418, 419, 428, 429, 430, 431, 434, 438, 439
Lenny Bruce 180, 184, 420, 432
Leopard-Skin Pill-Box Hat 53, 57, 284, 315, 322, 362, 370, 411, 417, 427, 429, 438, 440
Let It Be Me 76, 80, 187, 420, 428
Let Me Die In My Footsteps 27, 256, 261, 378
Let Me See 187
Let's Stick Together 227, 230, 232, 435
License To Kill 188, 192, 193, 194, 197, 284, 324, 326, 421, 433, 438
Like A Rolling Stone 47, 50, 52, 60, 62, 76, 81, 111, 116, 159, 163, 208, 212, 256, 267, 284, 296, 300, 313, 315, 323, 327, 328, 350, 362, 371, 396, 401, 404, 411, 416, 424, 427, 428, 430, 432, 434, 436-440
Like A Ship 406
Lily, Rosemary And The Jack of Hearts 117, 127-128, 129, 430
Lily of the West 101, 102, 412, 419, 430
Little Maggie 277, 281, 436
Little Sadie 76, 80, 428
Live 1966 397
Live '96 442
Live And Rare 2: Million Miles 442
Live At Carnegie Hall 26.10.1963 442
Living The Blues 76, 81, 428
Lo And Behold 130, 135, 399, 400, 431
Lock Your Door 398
Lone Pilgrim 288, 292, 437
Lonesome Day Blues 331, 336, 439
Lonesome Death of Hattie Carroll, The 28, 32-33, 208, 211, 340, 345, 355, 360, 426, 434, 439, 440

Lonesome Sparrow Sings, The 395
Long Distance Operator 130, 138, 431
Lord Protect My Child 193, 256, 274
"Love And Theft" 331-339, 439
Love Henry 288, 290, 437
Love Minus Zero/No Limit 40, 43, 46, 159, 162, 296, 300, 301, 340, 347, 350, 379, 381, 404, 427, 432, 437, 439
Love Sick 303, 306-307, 424, 425, 437

Maggie's Farm 40, 43, 89, 92, 147, 150, 159, 163, 194, 197, 327, 328, 362, 368, 401, 416, 427, 429, 431, 432, 433, 439, 440
Magic 187
Main Theme (Billy) 100
Main Title Theme (Billy) 95, 96, 429
Make You Feel My Love 303, 309-310, 437
Mama, You Been On My Mind 39, 88, 256, 266, 340, 346, 355, 360-361, 436, 439, 440
Man Gave Names To All The Animals 167, 173, 414, 420, 432
Man In Me, The 84, 88, 429
Man In The Long Black Coat 239, 245, 435
Man of Constant Sorrow 15, 17, 362, 366, 426, 440
Man of Peace 188, 192, 193, 390, 433
Man On The Street 19, 256, 260, 436
Man With No Alibi, A 405
Margarita 385
Mary Ann 101, 104, 430
Masked And Anonymous 350-353, 440
Masters of War 20, 23, 194, 198, 208, 211, 284, 362, 366, 395, 426, 429, 433, 434, 440
Matchbox 75, 88
Maxine 406
Maybe Someday 220, 224, 434
Medicine Sunday 59
Meet Me In The Morning 117, 127, 430
Memphis Blues Again 53, 57, 427

Milkcow's Calf Blues 27
Million Dollar Bash 130, 134, 208, 215, 399, 400, 413, 419, 431, 434
Million Miles 303, 308, 437
Minstrel Boy 76, 83, 401, 428
Miss The Mississippi And You 404, 407
Mississippi 311, 331, 335, 439
Mixed-Up Confusion 27, 208, 212, 410, 434
Moonlight 331, 337, 350, 439
Moonshine Blues 394
Moonshiner 33, 256, 264, 372, 375, 436, 440
More Bob Dylan's Greatest Hits 89-94, 429
More Bob Dylan's Greatest Hits/Singles 406
More Greatest Hits 429
More To This 187
Most Likely You Go Your Way (And I'll Go Mine) 53, 58, 111, 114, 208, 212, 411, 413, 417, 427, 430, 434
Most of The Time 239, 246, 248, 350, 435
Most of The Time (2) 248
Motherless Children 394
Motorpsycho Nitemare 35, 38, 427
Mozambique 139, 144, 413, 419, 431
Mr Bojangles 101, 104, 430
Mr Tambourine Man 39, 40, 44, 60, 62, 159, 162, 208, 214, 284, 313, 315, 320, 327, 328, 340, 346, 355, 359, 362, 367, 380, 401, 417, 427, 428, 432, 434, 438, 439, 440
MTV Unplugged 296-301, 437
Mutineer 391
My Back Pages 35, 38, 89, 92, 284, 287, 350, 404, 427, 429, 442
My Blue Eyed Jane 389, 407
My Oriental Home 187
Mystery Train 187
Nashville Skyline 70-75, 400, 405, 428
Nashville Skyline Rag 70, 73, 428
Natural Born Killers - Original Soundtrack 388, 407
Need A Woman 187, 256, 273

Neighbourhood Bully 188, 192, 433
Never Ending Tour, The 403
Never Gonna Be The Same Again 199, 204-205, 433
Never Let Me Go 441
Never Say Goodbye 105, 110, 430
New Blue Moon 386, 406
New Danville Girl 207, 403
New Morning 84-88, 401, 405, 429
New Morning 84, 87, 418, 429
New Pony 152, 156, 413, 419, 431
Newport Broadside 378
Newport Folk Festival Evening Concert Vol 1 379
Next Time On The Highway 398
Night After Night 384
Night They Drove Old Dixie Down, The 111, 430
Nine Hundred Miles 398
Ninety Miles An Hour (Down A Dead End Street) 227, 231, 435
No Direction Home: The Soundtrack. Bootleg Series Vol 7 362-371, 440
No More Auction Block 256, 260, 394, 436
No Time To Think 152, 156, 431
No Turning Back 311
Nobody 'Cept You 110, 256, 270, 436
Nobody's Child 406
North Country Blues 28, 31, 426, 442
Not Alone Any More 385
Not Dark Yet 303, 309, 324, 326, 327, 330, 437, 438, 439
Nothing Was Delivered 130, 137, 399, 400, 431
Now Your Mouth Cries Wolf 405
Number One 59

Obviously 5 Believers 53, 58, 411, 427, 429
Odds And Ends 130, 134, 392, 399, 431
Oh Mercy 239-248, 403, 405, 435
Oh Sister 139, 144, 147, 150, 159, 164, 313, 314, 340, 348, 413, 419, 431, 432, 438, 439
Oh Susannah 193

Ol' Roison The Beau 398
Old 5 And Dimers 403
On A Night Like This 105, 108, 208, 218, 350, 412, 419, 430, 434
On A Rainy Afternoon 398
On The Road Again 40, 44, 410, 416, 427
One For The Road 398
One Man's Loss 398
One More Cup of Coffee (Valley Below) 139, 144, 159, 163, 340, 348, 350, 431, 432, 439
One More Layer of Skin 405
One More Night 70, 74, 428
One More Weekend 84, 87, 429
One of Us Must Know (Sooner Or Later) 53, 56, 60, 411, 417, 427, 428, 429
One Single River 398
One Too Many Mornings 28, 31, 75, 88, 147, 150, 315, 322-323, 401, 417, 426, 431, 438
Only A Hobo 33, 256, 264, 378, 436
Only A Pawn In Their Game 28, 32, 379, 395, 426
Open The Door, Homer 130, 137, 399, 400, 431
Orange Juice Blues (Blues For Breakfast) 130, 134, 431
Original Dwarf Music Acetate, The 400
Outlaw Blues 40, 44, 427
Oxford Town 20, 25, 417, 426

Park It Where The Sun Don't Shine 405
Pat Garrett And Billy The Kid: Original Soundtrack Recording 95-100, 401, 405, 429
Paths of Victory 33, 256, 263, 436
Pecos Blues 100
Pecos Blues 401
Peggy Day 70, 73, 412, 418, 428
People Get Ready 283, 386, 398, 441
Percy's Song 33, 208, 212, 395, 434
Phantom Engineer 52
Planet Waves 105-110, 405, 430
Playboys and Playgirls 378, 416

458

Please Mrs Henry 130, 135, 399, 400, 431
Pledging My Time 53, 56, 411, 417, 427
Po' Boy 331, 337-338, 439
Po' Lazarus 398
Political World 239, 243, 248, 423, 435
Polly Vaughan 404, 407
Poor House 386, 406
Positively 4th Street 52, 62, 92, 208, 216, 324, 326, 327, 328, 396, 411, 416, 434, 438, 439
Possum Belly Overalls 401
Precious Angel 167, 170, 420, 432
Precious Memories 220, 224, 422, 434
Pressing On 174, 179, 432
Pretty Boy Floyd 283, 384
Pretty Peggy-O 15, 17, 426
Pretty Polly 394
Property of Jesus 180, 184, 432

Queen Jane Approximately 47, 51, 233, 237, 396, 411, 417, 427, 435
Quinn The Eskimo (The Mighty Quinn) 76, 82, 89, 93, 138, 208, 214, 324, 327, 328, 399, 400, 401, 428, 429, 434, 438, 439
Quit Your Low Down Ways 27, 256, 262, 436

Ragged & Dirty 288, 290, 437
Rainy Day Women #12 & 35 53, 56, 60, 62, 88, 111, 114, 284, 296, 299, 324, 326, 327, 328, 392, 401, 404, 411, 417, 427-430, 437, 438, 439
Rambler, Gambler 362, 364, 440
Ramblin' Gamblin' Willie 27, 256, 261, 436
Rank Strangers To Me 227, 232, 435
Rattled 385, 406
Real Live 194-198, 433
Red Cadillac And A Black Moustache 390
'Renaldo and Clara': A Film By Bob Dylan 441
Restless Farewell 28, 33, 426
Return To Me 390

Ride Billy Ride 100
Ring of Fire 75, 83, 388
Ring Them Bells 239, 245, 248, 294, 404, 423, 435, 437
Rita Mae 146, 413, 419
Rita Mae (2) 146
River Theme 95, 98, 100, 429
Rock Me Mama 100
Rock, Salt And Nails 398
Rock Solid 402
Rockin' Boat 187
Rocks And Gravel 27, 372, 374, 394, 440
Roll On John 390
Romance In Durango 139, 145, 208, 218, 340, 345, 431, 434, 439
Roving Gambler 425, 442
Ruben Remus 130, 137, 431
Runaway 406

Sad Eyed Lady of The Lowlands 53, 59, 427
Sally Gal 27, 362, 365, 440
Sally Sue Brown 227, 230, 435
Santa Fe 256, 269, 399, 436
Sara 139, 146, 340, 348-349, 431, 439
Sarah Jane 101, 102, 430
Satisfied Mind, A 174, 177, 432
Saved 174-179, 432
Saved 174, 177, 414, 420, 432
Saving Grace 174, 179, 432
Second Gaslight Tape: Live At The Gaslight Club 394
See That My Grave Is Kept Clean 15, 19, 394, 399, 426
See You Later, Allen Ginsberg 399
Seeing The Real You At Last 199, 203, 207, 433
Self Portrait 76-83, 401, 405, 428
Senor (Tales of Yankee Power) 152, 157, 208, 218, 350, 413, 420, 431, 434
Series of Dreams 248, 256, 276, 294, 424, 437
Seven Curses 33, 256, 265, 395, 424, 436

Seven Days 256, 272, 284
Shape I'm In, The 111, 430
She Belongs To Me 40, 43, 46, 60, 76, 83, 89, 92, 315, 319, 362, 368, 401, 410, 416, 417, 427, 428, 429, 438, 440
Shelter From The Storm 117, 128, 129, 147, 151, 159, 162, 313, 314, 327, 330, 430, 431, 432, 438, 439, 444
Shelter From The Storm (alternate version) 388
Shenandoah 227, 231, 435
She's My Baby 386, 406
She's Your Lover Now 59, 256, 268, 436
Shooting Star 239, 248, 296, 298, 404, 435, 437
Shot of Love 180-187, 405, 432
Shot of Love 180, 183, 187, 432
Sign On The Cross 399
Sign On The Window 84, 87, 429
Silent Weekend 399
Silhouette 398
Silver Dagger 355, 361, 440
Silvio 227, 231, 294, 324, 326, 327, 330, 415, 422, 423, 435, 437, 439
Simple Twist of Fate 117, 125, 159, 164, 324, 326, 340, 346, 430, 432, 438, 439
Sittin' On Top Of The World 277, 281, 436
Sitting On A Barbed Wire Fence 52, 256, 267, 436
Sloppy Drunk 404, 407
Slow Train 167, 171, 233, 237, 414, 432, 435, 445
Slow Train Coming 167-173, 405, 432
Solid Rock 174, 178, 208, 219, 414, 432, 434
Some Kind of Way 403
Somebody Touched Me 443
Someone's Got A Hold Of My Heart 193, 256, 274
Something There Is About You 105, 109, 412, 430
Something's Burning, Baby 199, 206, 207, 433
Song To Woody 15, 19, 88, 362, 365, 394, 426, 440
Spanish Harlem Incident 35, 37, 355, 357, 417, 427, 440
Spanish Is The Loving Tongue 101, 104, 398, 405, 412, 418, 430

Spanish Song, The 399
Stack A Lee 288, 291, 437
Stage Fright 111, 413, 430
Standing In The Doorway 303, 307-308, 437
Step It Up And Go 277, 282, 436
Still Around 398
Still In Town 398
Stop Now 158
Straight A's In Love 207
Straw Hat 187
Street Legal 152-158, 405, 431
Stuck Inside of Mobile With The Memphis Blues Again 89, 91, 147, 150, 350, 362, 370, 413, 419, 429, 431, 440
Studio Session With Bette Midler 406
Subterranean Homesick Blues 40, 43, 46, 60, 62, 208, 213, 256, 267, 324, 326, 327, 328, 410, 416, 417, 427, 428, 434, 436, 438, 439
Sugar Baby 331, 338-339, 439
Summer Days 331, 336, 439
Suze (The Cough Song) 33, 256, 266, 436
Sweet Amarillo 100
Sweetheart Like You 188, 191, 193, 414, 433
Sweetheart Like You (working session) 405

Take A Message To Mary 76, 82, 428
Take Me As I Am (Or Let Me Go) 76, 82, 428
Talkin' Bear Mountain Picnic Massacre Blues 27, 256, 261, 394, 436
Talkin' Devil 378
Talkin' Hava Negeilah Blues 27, 256, 262, 436
Talkin' John Birch Paranoid Blues 27, 256, 263, 355, 357, 436, 440
Talkin' New York 15, 17, 426
Talkin' World War III Blues 20, 25, 355, 360, 426, 440
Tangled Up In Blue 117, 124, 129, 194, 197-198, 208, 216, 256, 270, 294, 313, 314, 327, 330, 340, 347, 349, 350, 413, 419, 424, 430, 433, 434, 436-439
Tangled Up In Blue (2) 129

Tears of Rage 130, 136, 399, 400, 413, 419, 431
Tell Me 193, 256, 274
Tell Me, Mama 315, 321, 392, 438
Tell Me That It Isn't True 70, 74, 428
Tell Ol' Bill 392
Temporary Like Achilles 53, 58, 427
That's Alright Mama 27, 33, 75
Theme From Joe's Death 421, 422
They Killed Him 220, 223, 422, 434
Things Have Changed 324, 327, 330, 389, 425, 438, 439, 442, 445
Things Have Changed: Live And Unreleased 442
Third One Now, The 408
This Land Is Your Land 362, 365, 402, 440
This Land Is Your Land (Judy Collins' version) 379
This Old Man 387
This Was My Love 193
This Wheel's On Fire 130, 138, 399, 400, 431
Three Angels 84, 88, 429
Tight Connection To My Heart (Has Anybody Seen My Love?) 199, 203, 327, 330, 414, 421, 433, 439
'Til I Fell In Love With You 303, 308-309, 437
Time Out of Mind 302-311, 437
Time Passes Slowly 84, 86, 208, 219, 429, 434
Times They Are A-Changin', The 28-33, 405, 426
Times They Are A-Changin', The 28, 30, 33, 60, 62, 159, 165, 208, 211, 256, 265, 284, 296, 299, 313, 327, 328, 355, 357, 404, 416, 426, 428, 432, 434, 436-440, 442
Times They Are A-Changin', The (alternate version) 339
Tiny Montgomery 130, 137, 399, 400, 431
To Be Alone With You 70, 73, 428
To Fall In Love With You 403
To Make You Feel My Love 425, 442
To Ramona 35, 38, 208, 215, 355, 357, 401, 434, 440, 444
Tom Turkey 100
Tombstone Blues 47, 50, 194, 198, 208, 212, 296, 298, 301, 362, 369, 396, 404, 427, 433, 434, 437, 440, 442

Tomorrow Is A Long Time 89, 93, 405, 429
Tomorrow Night 277, 282, 436
Tonight I'll Be Staying Here With You 70, 75, 89, 92, 340, 344, 404, 412, 418, 428, 429, 439
Too Much of Nothing 130, 136, 399, 400, 431
Tough Mama 105, 108, 412, 430
Train A-Travelling 382
Train of Love 391
Travelling Wilburys, The: She's My Baby/New Blue Moon (instrumental version)/Runaway 387
Travelling Wilburys, The: Vol One 385, 403, 405, 406
Travelling Wilburys, The: Vol Three 386-387, 403, 405, 406
Tree With Roots, A 397-399
Tribute To Jimmie Rodgers 407
Tribute To Woody Guthrie Part One, A 379
Trouble 180, 186, 432
Trouble In Mind 173, 413, 420
Troubled And I Don't Know Why 387
True Love Tends To Forget 152, 157, 431
Trust Yourself 199, 205, 433
Try Me Little Girl 398
Tryin' To Get To Heaven 303, 308, 437
Tune 187
Tupelo 398
Turkey 100
Turkey Chase 95, 98, 100, 412, 418, 429
Turkey Trot 100
TV Talkin' Song 249, 253, 255, 435
Tweedle Dee & Tweedle Dum 331, 335, 439
Tweeter And The Monkey Man 385
Twist And Shout 232
Two Soldiers 288, 292, 437

Ugliest Girl In The World 227, 231, 423, 435
Unbelievable 249, 252, 423, 435
Under Control 398
Under The Red Sky 249-255, 405, 435

Under The Red Sky 249, 252, 294, 435, 437
Under Your Spell 220, 226, 434
Union Sundown 188, 193, 414, 421, 433
Union Sundown (2) 193
Up On Cripple Creek 111, 430
Up To Me 129, 208, 217, 434
Usual, The 384, 403, 422

Various Artists: Bonnaroo Festival 2004 392
Various Artists: Enjoy Every Sandwich - The Songs of Warren Zevon 391
Various Artists: Flashback - Original Soundtrack 386
Various Artists: Folkways, A Vision Shared - Tribute To Woody Guthrie & Leadbelly 384
Various Artists: For Our Children 387
Various Artists: Gods And Generals - Original Soundtrack 391
Various Artists: Good Rockin' Tonight - The Legacy of Sun Records 390
Various Artists: Gotta Serve Somebody - The Gospel Songs of Bob Dylan 391
Various Artists: Jerry McGuire - Original Soundtrack 388
Various Artists: Kindred Spirits - A Tribute To The Songs of Johnny Cash 391
Various Artists: Music From The Motion Picture Divine Secrets of The Ya Ya Sisterhood 391
Various Artists: Music From The Motion Picture 'North Country' 392
Various Artists: Selections From The Best of Broadside 1962-1988 389
Various Artists: Stolen Roses, Songs of The Grateful Dead 389
Various Artists: The 60s - Original NBC Motion Picture Soundtrack 389
Various Artists: The Concert For The Rock And Roll Hall of Fame 388
Various Artists: The Songs of Jimmie Rodgers - A Tribute 389
Various Artists: The Sopranos - Peppers And Eggs 390
Various Artists: There Is No Eye - Music For Photographs 390
Various Artists: Til The Night Is Gone - A Tribute To Doc Pomus 388
Various Artists: Timeless - Hank Williams Tribute 390
Various Artists: Wonder Boys - Music From The Motion Picture 389
Various Artists: Woodstock 94 388
Very Thought of You, The 207
Visions of Johanna 53, 56, 59, 208, 214, 315, 319, 362, 371, 427, 434, 438, 440
Volume Four 403
Volume Two 403

Wade In The Water 443
Wait And See 187
Waitin' For You 391
Waiting To Get Beat 207
Walk Like A Duck, Smell Like A Skunk 405
Walkin' Down The Line 256, 263, 436
Walking On Eggs 187
Wallflower 256, 269, 406, 436
Walls of Red Wing 27, 256, 263, 436
Waltzin' With Sin 398
Watching The River Flow 89, 91, 406, 412, 418, 429
Water Is Wide, The 340, 347, 439
Watered-Down Love 180, 185, 187, 432
We Better Talk This Over 152, 157, 414, 420, 421, 431
We Shall Overcome: Documentary of The March On Washington 379
Wedding Song 105, 110, 430
Weight, The 111, 430
Well Water 187

Went To See The Gypsy 83, 84, 87, 429
West Texas 372, 375, 394, 440
What Can I Do For You? 174, 178, 432
What Good Am I? 239, 246, 248, 435
What Was It You Wanted 239, 247, 248, 284, 435
Whatcha Gonna Do? 27
When Did You Leave Heaven? 227, 230, 232, 422, 435
When He Returns 167, 173, 420, 432
When I Got Troubles 362, 364, 440
When I Paint My Masterpiece 89, 94, 284, 406, 429
When The Night Comes Falling From The Sky 199, 205-206, 207, 256, 276, 414, 421, 433
When The Ship Comes In 28, 32, 256, 264, 284, 362, 367, 395, 416, 426, 436, 440
When There's A Wilbury There's A Way 406
When You Awake 111, 430
When You Gonna Wake Up 167, 172, 414, 432
Where Are You Tonight (Journey Through Dark Heat) 152, 158, 431
Where Teardrops Fall 239, 244, 423, 435
Where The Monkey Dances 405
Where Were You Last Night? 386, 406
Who Killed Davey Moore? 256, 264, 355, 358, 395, 436, 440
Who Loves You More 207
Wichita (Going To Louisiana) 27
Wicked Messenger, The 65, 69, 428
Wiggle Wiggle 249, 252, 435
Wigwam 76, 83, 412, 418, 428
Wilbury Twist 386, 406
Wilburys Are Coming, The 406
Wild Mountain Thyme 401
Wild Track 100
Wildwood Flower 399
Willie And The Hand Jive 232
Willie Nelson: Across The Borderland 387
Wind Blowing On The Water 187
Winterlude 84, 87, 429

With God On Our Side 28, 31, 296, 301, 355, 361, 404, 426, 437, 440, 442
With God On Our Side (with Joan Baez) 378, 416
Won't You Be My Baby 398
Woogie Boogie 76, 80, 428
Working On A Guru 88
World Gone Wrong 288-292, 405, 407, 437
World Gone Wrong 288, 290, 437
Worried Blues 27, 256, 262, 436

Yazoo Street Scandal 130, 134, 431
Ye Shall Be Changed 173, 256, 272
Yea! Heavy And A Bottle of Bread 130, 136, 399, 400, 431
Yes Sir No Sir 187
Yesterday 88
Yonder Comes Sin 187
You Ain't Goin' Nowhere 89, 94, 130, 137, 284, 327, 328, 399, 400, 406, 429, 431, 439
You Angel You 105, 110, 208, 215, 412, 430, 434
You Are My Sunshine 75
You Belong To Me 292, 388, 407
You Changed My Life 187, 256, 273
You Don't Have To Do That 46
You Gotta Quit Kickin' My Dog Aroun' 398-399
You Took My Breath Away 386, 406
You Wanna Ramble 220, 223, 434
You Win Again 398
Young But Daily Growin' 398
Your True Love 88
You're A Big Girl Now 117, 125, 129, 147, 150, 208, 215, 423, 430, 431, 434
You're Gonna Make Me Lonesome When You Go 117, 127, 430
You're Gonna Quit Me 277, 282, 436
You're No Good 15, 16, 426

463

Acknowledgments

Thanks in particular to Joanne Wilson, my editor, who knows exactly when to apply the stick and when the carrot, to Mike Evans – who played with Adrian Henri's Liverpool Scene on the same stage as Dylan at the 1969 IOW festival – for turning my rambles into good sense, to the lovely Vickie for sorting out the rights, to Terry Kelsey for scanning in (and cleaning up) my original vinyl albums, and to Iain MacGregor for remembering me from the Sanctuary days.

Special thanks to Geoff Wall – archivist supreme – and to John Delaney, who was an immense help over some of the more arcane aspects of Dylanology, on which he is so knowledgable. To Henry Porter and all at *Isis*, my favourite bedtime reading. To Clinton Heylin, who told me where I was going wrong (with great pleasure), and more importantly showed me where to go right. To Billy Childish, who plays his gigs with some of the devil-may-care attitude of vintage Bob, and is – dare one say it – a far better painter.

To Katarzyna Coleman, an amazing painter, who recreates ghost landscapes and industrial spirit trails in her Lowestoft studio, in the spirit (and often to the soundtrack of) *Time Out Of Mind*.

To Julian Bell, to Jo Elvery, who got me writing again, and to dear Ellie. To Ashley Hutchings, Britain's most creative Dylan fan. To Jeff Lewis, Roger Careless and the couple from Brighton for getting me rare items, to Stephen Lee, Brian Puttock, the Vaguely Sunny boys and all the other Island bobcats. I'll never forget that terror drive the morning after the hurricane to see a bemused Dylan at Wembley. To Catherine Cameron-Martin who accompanied me to the Bournemouth gig when Bob came back from the dead. To Iain Sinclair – another bloody chronicle!

To John Giddings, Lindsay and the Solo team, for their amazing task of recreating the IOW Festivals, in a new context. And to all the patient staff and volunteers at Dimbola, where a life-sized statue of Hendrix is about to go up, and where – who knows – a bronze of Dylan might join him some day.

And maybe the real thing might even eventually visit Farringford, as falsely promised back in 1969. I will be more than delighted to act as tour guide.

CREDITS
Album artwork, copyright Sony/ Columbia/ CBS apart from *Planet Waves*: Island/ Asylum/ Columbia

Every effort has been made to contact the copyright holders, however please contact the publishers if any omissions have inadvertently been made.